Red Hot

Resumes

Robert Meier

To my children, Arielle, Colten, Calais & Trinity - gifts from God.

To protect the confidentiality of the people featured in this book, names, addresses, company names, and other contact information have been changed.

LightSpeed Press
www.jobclinic.org
5240 Silver Charm Terrace
Wesley Chapel, FL 33544
813-746-5844

Cover design by Marisa Hunt

Library of Congress Cataloging-in-Publication Data on file with the publisher.
ISBN: 9780974448312

Printed in the United States
First printing 2009

TABLE OF CONTENTS

TABLE OF CONTENTS

TABLE OF CONTENTS

TABLE OF CONTENTS

TABLE OF CONTENTS

BOOK FACTS

112 resumes

34 career categories

100+ industries covered

443 job titles

1800+ years of work history evaluated

Start Here

As a career coach and resume writer for the past 19 years, what guides my compositional style is an unwavering confidence that each of my clients is absolutely unique, that they have been gifted with rare attributes and that they add value to their companies. I just dig for their career jewels, meaning, I uncover the accomplishments in their careers that prove my opinion is accurate. I then craft the resume as a setting to display the sparkle in their career. I think of it like how an engagement ring holds the diamond. The end result of my resume compositions is that the talent buyer wants to purchase the jewel that my client's career represents.

The point is, you are a one-of-a-kind individual, your thumbprint proves that, and you have unique career characteristics that make you valuable to an employer. Your resume needs to be crafted in a manner that reveals the facets of your career so that the hiring manager can pick you from the baubles that your job-seeking competition represents.

Your resume is your number one selling tool, let's make it sing a glorious song of praise to your career.

Robert Wm. Meier
Career & Executive Coach

Introduction

What if there was only one rather simple thing you needed to do to earn a million dollars, would you do it? Or, what if I said that locked inside you, like raw diamonds in a mine, is a stored value that could elevate your standard of living, quality of life and happiness? Would you grab the proverbial "pick" and go digging?

Every serious exploration requires a guide and the exploration of your personal worth to the employment market is no different. That's why I wrote *Red Hot Resumes* to be a guide, or map as it were, to show you how to uncover your gifts and professional attributes in order to present them to a potential employer in a manner that overcomes the hurdles that must be jumped to win full and rewarding employment.

It's amazing that so many people gladly sacrifice four to six years or more of their life to go to college (as well as take on substantial student loans), will put themselves in debt for up to six years to buy a car or add new credit card debt to go on a vacation each year, but give only passing attention to the one document, their resume, that has the singular power to make paying off school, car and vacation debt easy. Your ability to sell yourself is directly tied to your ability to write a compelling resume that elevates your career profile above the competition, creates that elusive "wow" effect when read and that proves you are worth much more than your salary.

Don't get me wrong, it is not anyone's fault for writing boring, two-dimensional, bland resumes. How can it be, when nearly every book, resume software program and personal friend has the same "vanilla" looking document. How can a job seeker stand out without appearing strange or eccentric? It's understandably difficult to stand out from the crowd when the crowd is fighting so hard to remain homogenous. Nevertheless, stand out you must and stand out you will! But you must stand out within the context of acceptable business etiquette and there are certain premises that must me be understood to stand out in the proper "light."

GOOD RESUMES COMBINE ART & SCIENCE

First off, you need to think of writing a resume as both an "art" and a "science." The science of a resume refers to structure, meaning that a resume needs to have a certain acceptable format that appeals to the greatest number of readers, such as; name at top, with address, phone and email. You need to have dates, job titles, company names, educational segments, etc. In other words, even an artist has to work within certain scientific restrictions, namely, color combinations, shading characteristics, medium limitations (painting on a canvas as opposed to sculpting marble, for example), but what they do within these scientific limitations determines beauty. Art in a resume refers to the prose or the wording, especially as those words paint a picture that compels the reader (i.e., hiring manager, human resource professional or recruiter) to take notice. There are thousands of different artistic avenues that can be taken to paint a beautiful picture of your abilities, or more importantly, your accomplishments. The problem is that the "science" of writing a resume has completely eclipsed the "art" of the resume. What sense does that make? Writing in itself is an art, you are a human being that is not easily defined scientifically, and ask yourself, when you buy an important product like a car, do you only want the scientific explanation of horsepower, torque, towing capacity, speed, etc. or do aesthetic qualities, such as color, design and form attract you? Considering how much Madison Avenue spends to create a compelling image and thereby, open our wallets, the art of selling the car is as important as the science of selling the car.

Introduction

When writing your resume, the key is to maintain balance between art and science. In other words, don't focus on format to the exclusion of quality and originality. *Red Hot Resumes* is a book of over 100 model examples from which to draw inspiration and that should act as templates from which you can compare with your artistic effort.

You may have already guessed that this resume book is not your father's resume book, in other words, it is not supposed to be some dry, didactic treatise on functional rules (i.e., proper fonts, typographical point size, page count and key words) but rather a dialog between me, a professional resume writer, who will act as your guide and you, the reader who longs to write a dynamically compelling story within the context of the resume style.

The art of the resume is illustrated in the first section titled, "The Ten Commandments of a Red Hot Resume" where the artistic rules that paint the perfect resume are defined. Since visual art, especially paintings, have several factors that affect the way we perceive the image, it's worth noting that an artist strives to balance a number of disparate issues concurrently such as; how certain colors harmonize, complement or clash together. Likewise, the words, categories and combination of phrases contained in your resume will reveal the image of your professional portrait. Well, this analogy has been stretched to the breaking point. Just remember, you can word-smith a beautiful image that compels decision makers to acquire your talent. One final thought about the painting analogy, you need to realize that you are a one-of-a-kind creation, your thumbprint proves that, and your resume should have individual characteristics that make it unique and different from everyone else's story.

Section One

10 Commandments of a Red Hot Resume

1. **Thou Must Prove Your Value**. Your resume must overcome a skeptic's hurdles and build positive perceptual value to justify the employer's risk.

2. **Thou Must Eliminate Career Problems**. Whatever issues that confront you; choppy career (quick job changes), job gaps, obsolete industry experience, being fired, etc., must be repaired and replaced with results and contributions.

3. **Thou Must Turn Your Resume Into A Script**. Every good story line has three main parts, your resume must have a – beginning, middle and end.

4. **Thou Must Use Numbers To Quantify Your Value**. Numbers are the spice of a great resume, without them the reader has no idea how to measure, benchmark or scale your value.

5. **Thou Must Elevate Your Professional Profile**. The three levels of elevation are: the business unit (also called an office, department or division), the corporate enterprise, and the industry you serve. We must try to reveal contributions made at each of these levels.

6. **Thou Must Have A Cornerstone Accomplishment**. Every building has a cornerstone as reference point, likewise you must have cornerstone results that prove your worth.

7. **Thou Must Be Part Of A Project Team**. Whether you're a manager, executive or line staff, you must demonstrate that you are a team-player who can help the team reach its goals.

8. **Thou Must Define Your Impact On The Bottom Line**. Your contributions to the organization must be quantified monetarily.

9. **Thou Must Prove Your Career Path Is Progressing**. You must show that each step in your career made sense, supports your professional goals and points to the next step, which is the current job opening your are pursuing.

10. **Thou Must Be An Exceptional Performer**. Recruiters are paid to hire the best, you need to prove that your results make you the obvious choice amongst your peers.

Commandment
– 1 –

Thou Must Prove Your Value

Your value to a potential company is either hidden or revealed. If value remains hidden, it is lost. Proving value is related to using your resume to help internal champions in the corporation support you rather than the other candidates for the job opening. A good value-laden resume builds cohesion with the hiring chain. Most people don't realize the importance of the hiring chain and the fact that many links must pull together to get you hired into a new company. A typical hiring chain has at least five links. One link is a headhunter, another link is the human resources manager, another link is the hiring manager who is staffing his or her department, then there is the peer evaluator (a potential team member you may work with if your hired), and finally there's the senior manager that has to approve new head count to the payroll. All these links must pull together and the only way they stay solidly joined is by the impression your resume makes before you ever show up to the interview. Since each link of the chain has to evaluate many other candidates for the position, it's easy for the professionals who are part of the chain to forget details that were revealed in the interview. The resume becomes that black and white reference guide that substantiates your candidacy. Let me put it another way, if I'm the headhunter who is suggesting to a company HR manager that you're the best candidate, then I am your champion and need a document that supports my effort to champion you for the job opening. If you give me a resume that is dull, lifeless and doesn't highlight your impacts, results and contributions, then you are asking me to convince the human resource manager, hiring manager, senior manger, and peer evaluator to dismiss your boring resume and just believe what I tell them even though your resume lacks compelling results and doesn't support my recommendation. In that case, you make my job as your champion much, much harder. Your goal is to create a resume that bonds the links of the hiring chain so that they pull together to bring you into the corporation, where the strength of the bond is created by the value of your results.

Proving value turns you into the needle in the haystack. Your resume must reveal enough value to a potential employer that they want to pay your salary and bet their professional reputation on making you their hiring decision. Not knowing how to compose a compelling, value-centric resume leads to career tragedy. Since 98% of all job candidates are eliminated at the resume screening, if your value on paper isn't strong enough to justify the hire you will be overlooked, eliminated and pushed aside.

PROVING VALUE USING THE MEIER MULTIPLIER

Of course it's during an interview that you land an offer, but the resume leads to the interview. The key to winning job offers is a resume that pre-sells you before you reach the interview. To be pre-sold, you must demonstrate that you are worth many times more than the salary you're requesting. I call this the ***Meier Multiplier***. As example of the Meier Multiplier in action, consider the goal of earning an $80,000 a year salary. In order to justify your salary, you should show that the value you will add, as indicated by contributions you have made in the past to previous employers, is worth $800,000 a year, this is a Ten-Time Meier Multiplier. At the very least you need to show contributions that indicate a Two-Time Meier Multiplier to win employer favor.

Commandment
– 1 –
Continued

If you solve the Meier Multiplier Rule, the hiring decision from the hiring manager's perspective, becomes a "no-brainer." Hiring managers want to hire staff who can deliver multiples of their salary costs. I admit that a Ten-Time Meier Multiplier is a lofty goal that is not always attained, but even if you don't attain the ten-fold proof, you usually get close, and furthermore, if you don't have high goals you tend to achieve mediocrity.

What can be done to help your chances to win an interview?
Write the holy grail of resumes; one that is easy enough to scan in 60 seconds, yet has enough information to prove, not imply, your value. By the way, the quick 1-minute initial resume review is focused on looking for elements of a professional's pedigree; titles, company names, and education. Even complex two or three page resumes can be scanned in 60 seconds if only the pedigree is being reviewed. The fix is not adding white-space by leaving out details, but picking those jewels of your career storyline that will illuminate your professional luster and bait a recruiter's further interest.

A powerful resume proves how your value impacted a company's bottom line, mission or operational goals. The key to avoiding a bland, two- dimensional resume is to avoid emphasizing job functions (i.e., a bullet-list of duties). Most jobs-seekers highlight functional duties, which define them as functionaries, as replaceable as cogs in a machine. What sells a professional is tied to how they contributed to a division, business group, unit, office or enterprise, especially as it relates to making money or preventing the company from spending money inefficiently.

EXAMPLE
Let's say you introduced a new system to share past project quotes, as one of my clients did, that is now accessible to all company employees.

You could write:
Project Created the Knowledge Manager, a searchable database that supplies all past project quotes to simplify the RFQ (request for quote) process.
Result Increased closure rate on pitch-to-assignments from 10% to 22%, which grew revenues by $450,000 - the largest year-to-date increase in company history.

Obviously adding nearly half a million to a company's revenue stream is compelling. To jazz up a resume you must pinpoint the results that prove you add value. Remember, employers hire staff who make a difference to the revenue, profit and cost management goals of the company.

Commandment
– 2 –

Thou must smooth-over career-path problems

Age, choppy career paths, self-employed, women who are returning to the workplace after raising children, job gaps, weak education are all career problems that need to be addressed.

Lets face it, in the real world, when it comes to getting the right job, we are either too young or too old. We don't have the perfect job history, or we don't have the right experience, or we lack current training or knowledge of specific technology applications to justify the hire. Sometimes it is a lack of staff/team management responsibilities, other times it's that we haven't made significant budget decisions. We might have pot-holes or work gaps, legitimate or not. The point is that there are nearly always problems that need to be solved in order to have a powerfully compelling resume. The key to trouble-shooting your career problems is to define your contributions so clearly that people will take the risk of calling you for an interview. Think of it this way, if you were a professional baseball player that lacked speed, you would make up for it with hitting skills. In a like manner, if you lack industry expertise, you need to define the challenges you've met in your career field and the actions that you took to meet these challenges as well as the results you delivered well enough to impress or wow the potential interviewer.

EXAMPLE
A client of mine wanted to work in the rather exclusive world of pharmaceutical sales. What she was up against were candidates with degrees in biology, chemistry or molecular science (her B.A. was in Political Science). In addition, she was competing with medical sales professionals and other experienced pharmaceutical sales representatives. Not only was the competitive arena tremendous, my client didn't have the right work history. She had sold before, but the service she sold was called foil stamping. That is a very small subset of printing (foil can be added to a logo on a business card, for example, to make it standout). The problem she needed to smooth over was the lack of specific industry experience and proper education. When she submitted her resume to Baxter Healthcare and received a call for an interview, she was told the following. "You don't have the right education, the right experience and lack valid industry knowledge, yet we were so intrigued by the challenges, actions and results in your work history that we felt we had to at least give you an interview." What happened? She was as good as her resume and won the job out of 1,200 candidates. She is now a territory sales manager for Baxter's plasma product lines.

There are numerous ways to solve career problems and this book shares at least 112 examples of careers needing fine tuning care to minimize the issues that would have screened them out of the interview process. The fact of the matter is most professionals either have problems that they are aware of and don't know what to do to reduce the perceptual stigma attached to the problem or they don't see their problem and therefore don't attempt to mitigate the negative damage that has been created. If you look closely to the resume examples in this book, you will see that I included 33 "before" resumes (found in chapter 35), meaning resumes that my clients gave me before I began the make-over. If you are struggling to address your career problems, look at what my clients said in their resumes and compare that to what I wrote to see the difference after I removed the warts from their professional profile.

Commandment
– 3 –

Thou Must Turn Your Resume Into A Script

If you write a concise, focused and compelling resume, it becomes your story line used the same way a movie director uses the plot to help an audience stay engaged throughout a movie. In every story line there are three main parts: a beginning, a middle and an end. The director's duty is to make sure the audience understands enough of the beginning so that when the audience is launched into the body of the movie they are not confused. To ensure movie clarity, the director gives enough back-story to explain to the audience where they are in the context of the plot. In like manner, your career contributions need enough historical perspective to make your contributions worthy of a reader's appreciation. Think of yourself as the middle of the corporation's story, what happened before you were hired is the back-story, and the results that were achieved after your involvement, is the end of the story.

EXAMPLE
My client worked for Rockshocks, a manufacturer of bicycle shock-absorbers, something that didn't exist 35 years ago. Rockshocks was the first to market, and being the inventors of the concept, their prices were premium, meaning they charged more because they could. Over time, other bicycle companies came into being and started competing with Rockshocks. The competition eroded Rockshocks' revenues by offering similar product at lower prices. Rockshocks began loosing money as opposed to growing revenues every year, a precursor to the company being acquired or going bankrupt. My client became the national manager of sales with the responsibility to turn around this problem and revive Rockshocks' revenue stream. To reach his objectives, he did a number of things that were innovative, and in the end, grew revenues. Now lets get into the historical story line (the back story). Before my client was hired, Rockshocks had peak revenues of $67 million in 1998. By 2002, those revenues had declined by $7 million to $60 million. My client came into the picture in 2002 and rolled out three new strategies that resulted in adding $5 million to Rockshock's bottom line. When I wrote his resume, I told enough of the back-story to show that Rockshock had lost millions of dollars for four years straight and then a year after his hire, had gained $5 million, a total turnaround of $12 million. In addition, it was the first time in four years that Rockshocks had netted a positive revenue stream. That shows the story line perspective from before my client's involvement, to the middle point where he came in and the resulting end of the story, where positive revenue growth was reestablished.

60-Second Elevator Speech

It is also important to know how to use your resume as a script. In order to understand the script analogy, I need to introduce you to a widely known business concept, the 60-second elevator speech. The elevator speech implies that you should summarize who you are professionally and your value in about a minute. The 60-second reference is how long it takes to go up forty floors in an elevator. To have an elevator speech, you must memorize your resume like an actor commits his script to memory. Now the better the actor knows his or her script the better their performance. After writing a good resume, memorize it and don't be afraid that sticking to it makes you sound redundant. Most interviewees don't like the script concept because they believe the interviewer has read their resume so thoroughly that they will be bored if they recite the resume to closely. This can't be further from the truth. Most interviewers scan resumes to find something they like, they don't memorize resumes.

Commandment
– 3 –
Continued

To illustrate this point, think of watching a performance of "Romeo and Juliet." What would happen if the lead actor, Romeo, decided that the audience was so familiar with the script that he decided to improvise? Do you think the audience would accept the improvisations? The answer is no, obviously not. It would make the audience uncomfortable and the play would end up a big mess. In the same vein, if the recruiter has read your resume and liked you well enough to bring you into an interview and you suddenly ignore the resume as your script and jump to expository dialogue outside of the resume's content, you loose the opportunity to validate the reviewer's initial impression they created after reading the resume in the first place. Don't think that your interviewer has memorized your resume. It is OK to stick to your resume script. You can think of it another way. If you find that you want to talk about something that is not specifically addressed in the resume, but you feel is so compelling that it must be included during the interview, then just add the information into the resume so that both you and the interviewer can stay on the same page.

Commandment
– 4 –

Thou must use numbers to quantify your value

Everyone knows that building a positive impression in today's difficult job market takes really awesome feats of accomplishment. In other words, they realize that it is critical to put up, as major league baseball players are fond of saying, "really big numbers." Its all in the stats they're told, i.e. the bottom line, the ROI, the profit point, etc. The truth is, percentages and quantities do make hiring managers take notice and numbers indicate how your past contributions can help them, but the simple fact remains: don't lie. Hiring managers are so sensitized to embellishments that even if there is a whiff of fiction, the hiring manager's first instinct is to trash the candidate rather than risk their reputation on someone whom they doubt. We can't bulldoze a potential employer with lots and lots of numbers that are unsubstantiated or that don't boldly communicate value.

Of all the possible mistakes a person can make when they write their resume, the most egregious and damaging can be the misuse of numbers. It is so common for job seekers to use untrue, wrong or invalid statistics that most recruiters don't believe the numbers in the resume when they read them in the first place, so it is quite common for them to just dismiss numbers as fallacious. Job seekers need to know that odd statistics raise red flags in the reader's mind and once a red flag is raised, game over. On the other hand, the good use of numbers can emhance your appeal.

It is important to remember that statistical claims without support can sink your chance of winning an interview. I have seen hundreds of bright, successful professionals use statistics in their resume that confused the reader or were so outrageously amazing that the reviewer simply rolled their eyes and dismissed their credentials altogether.

The types of number mistakes I typically see range from the benign accident where the candidate meant something else when they said they grew revenues by 1,000% to the blatant lie, where the candidate says to himself; "my old company has closed down, so really it doesn't matter what I say, they can't confirm the facts." Either way, if you can't validate your numbers clearly, don't use them, or better yet, change them to numbers that you can confirm, that you feel are conservative or that are believable so that you can look in the interviewer's eyes with complete confidence that they are valid. To show you what I mean, lets look at a couple examples.

Example #1 Suzy Q. Here was one of the most impressive sales professionals I had ever met. She started her career as a property leasing consultant for Chicago's prestigious Habitat company. What was interesting were the numbers she used in her role as Business Development Manager (BDM) of Regus Business Centre (the BDM is the re-minted title given to Account Executives).

The thing Suzy was most proud of, as stated on her resume, was:
• Increased price efficiency of current clients from 69% to 90% within a 5 month period.

Commandment
– 4 –

Although increasing anything by 21% in less than half a year is impressive, when I showed her feats to different clients, none understood what she meant by "price efficiency." As I mentioned earlier, if you confuse the resume reviewer with your statistics, its bye-bye Suzy. When I interviewed Suzy to rewrite her resume, I sought hot points that could make her stand out from her competition and latched onto this price efficiency statement. What I learned was her special ability to negotiate profitable shared-office leases. When new clients leased office space from Regus, Suzy had to determine the price per square foot, amenities, the length of contract and possible discount incentives to offer in order to win the customer's signature on the dotted line. This is where Suzy excelled. Whereas her peers at Regus would quickly capitulate on price to win business, she never went below 90% of the list price (the rest of the company averaged less than 70%).

My rewrite noted what she meant by improving price efficiency:
·To maximize profits, I close all deals within 10% of list price (Regus' corporate average is 69% of list), the difference of closing deals at 90% has increased gross profit by $5 million.

The point is, her statistics were valid, but unclear. She thought that she could go to the interview and just explain what price efficiency meant, whereas I thought it was more important to clearly communicate her value in a way that nobody needed extra explanation. You can't be much clearer than noting $5 million in added profit.

Example #2 Joe Brown is your typical young genius. By the age of 28 he was Product Manager for Ameritech DSL (also called high-speed Internet). So obviously, if you are blessed to be on the front-end of launching DSL for one of the largest telecom companies in the world, who cares what you say in your resume, your professional pedigree is established, right? Wrong. Remember the dot.com/telecom melt down of '01? Well Joe was caught in the melt. By the time we met, he had hopped into and out of three additional jobs in four years. His most recent position, which lasted barely over a year, was Director of Marketing for a small, privately held company called Cimco Communications. What Joe was most proud of in this role, as stated in his resume, was increasing brand awareness by over 350% in under 12 months. Great, right? Nearly quadrupled the awareness of the Cimco brand in a year. Only one problem, what does it truly mean to improve brand awareness. It sounds a little suspicious. Quantifying brand awareness is difficult even for major corporations with large marketing departments and extensive brand reach in the consumer market. For a privately held company that no one had ever heard of, saying that you grew brand awareness 350% sounds a little like claiming my apple is 20% more crunchy than your apple, interesting, but hard to prove. Even though brand management, brand extensions, brand awareness and all things brand-centric are important to corporate America, you can't just use numbers tied to hot ideas as key words to magically open the door of opportunity. If, during the interview with a Sr. VP of Marketing, Joe was asked what he did to expand brand awareness and he noted that he had published nine trade journal articles, representing an increase from the company's two previous press mentions, and decide to call that brand awareness, the SVP would laugh him out of his office so fast Joe would need a parachute to slow down before he hit the elevator door. Joe didn't mean to cross his wires between brand awareness and press mentions (which he did quadruple), he just didn't know the right thing to call his success, so he made a classic mistake and misnamed and misrepresented his statistical accomplishment. This is a deadly sin. My rewrite simply stated that one of his key results was increasing press mentions by 450% (by the way, press mentions are an element of brand awareness, not the whole enchilada).

Commandment
– 4 –
Continued

Don't fudge your numbers

Call your accomplishments what they really are, not what you want them to be. If you have someone read your resume, ask them if it is perfectly clear, if it isn't, don't make the excuse that you are speaking to a knowledgeable audience that understands what you meant. It's quite possible to have your resume initially reviewed by an HR Generalist, a kid fresh out of college who then refers the "keeper resumes" to his or her boss. The key is to be clear, use honest numbers and validate your claims with enough substantiating information that the reviewer believes your statements.

Look through the book, every resume I include has a result or an impact. The key to using numbers properly is to estimate the numbers associated with your results ethically and to substantiate your estimations. You need to use numbers that are honest, that you can support and are conservative. If you launched a new product that lasted in the market for 6 months from time of launch to the time you left the company, and in that six month period, generated a million dollars, you wouldn't want to say the product gained two million dollars in the first year, since you are making an unsubstantiated claim (unless you can call someone at your old company and find out the year-long results were $2 million). The key is feeling confident enough that you can look someone in the eye and know that your numbers are legitimate.

How to Use End of Day Numbers
Another trick of using numbers to impress is the end of the day basket sweep, which I define as totaling your entire value to a company over a comprehensive period of time, not just a single year. Think about a sales professional that may have worked at a company for five years. Typically they are measured on annual sales produced and might say they sell $500,000 of widgets every year. An end of the day basket sweep would note that over five years total sales is worth $2,500,000. The same thing with a nurse who is responsible for managing a case load of 100 patients a year, if she were to add up her five years of employment, she supported a total patient case load of 500 patients. The basket sweep creates a wow effect that somebody can hang their hat on. Remember the person that is reviewing you wants to be wowed so that they present you as a "gee whiz" candidate to the rest of the hiring chain.

Commandment
– 5 –

Thou Must Elevate Your Professional Profile

To elevate your profile, the first thing you need to know is that there are three levels to which a professional's work image can be raised. The levels are: business unit, enterprise, and industry. The reason it is important to raise your profile is that most, if not all job-seekers, desire to earn a promotion. In order to justify a career promotion, you need to define how you contribute to your team (department, division or office), the company that hired you (i.e., enterprise) and, if at all possible, the impact you have made, directly or indirectly, on the industry in which you work.

EXAMPLE

To see the three levels in action, consider a cancer-care nurse who I'll call Jackie. Jackie works on an oncology team for a private hospital in Arizona. To elevate her role to the enterprise level she needed to consider how the oncology department contributes to the hospital. What we learn is that her oncology department services 30 patient cases per week, multiplied by 52 weeks per year, the department contribution is serving over 1,500 oncology patients a year. Now the question might be, "what does that mean to hospital ABC monetarily?" If you ask the right questions, you learn that a typical Medicaid or health insurance reimbursement for an oncology patient can range from $10,000 to $150,000. To come up with a gross dollar value, we have to pick a reasonable point that we will use as our base reference, in this case the midpoint is $70,000. A conservative number below the midpoint would be $40,000. By doing the math, meaning we multiple $40,000 times 1,500 patients, the result is that the oncology department contributes $60 million annually. If Jackie is one of five nurses, and she handles an average of 6 cases a week, her contribution at the department level represents 20% of the $60 million (or $12 million) in revenues to ABC hospital. The final level then is the industry. Let's say Jackie worked at a hospital that is nationally recognized as a skin cancer primary care facility. If the industry has only 13 skin-cancer specialty hospitals in the U.S. and hers ranks second, we can put in Jackie's resume the following information:

Jackie's impact described in her resume:

Manage a case load of 300 patients per year, 20% of the department's total volume, for the second largest skin cancer hospital in the U.S. where my client base contributes $12 million annually to the hospital's bottom line.

As review of the three levels

- **At department level:** She handles 20% of the work volume.
- **At the enterprise level:** Her 300 patients generate $12 million in billable revenues.
- **At the industry level:** She is a member of a top oncology team for the second largest skin cancer specialty hospital department in America.

Commandment
– 6 –

Thou Must Have A Cornerstone Accomplishment

The cornerstone accomplishment is based on an architectural premise. In every building, whether it's a home or skyscraper, there is a foundational element known as the cornerstone from which the structure starts. In the context of a resume, a cornerstone accomplishment should accompany each major job that you have held. A career with three major jobs therefore should have three cornerstone accomplishments, one for each position. If you had a job lasting ten years with five different positions, then you should identify a cornerstone accomplishment for each of those positions. The practical application of the cornerstone, in relationship to your resume, is that it anchors your results, meaning it builds a solid platform to sell your impact and value.

Another analogy relates to the jewels in the crown. Basically you want to sprinkle the crown of your career with glorious jewels that highlight significant contributions i.e., efficiencies gained, costs reduced, or revenues improved. To uncover your cornerstone accomplishments, consider efforts that led to man-hours saved, production processes consolidated (i.e., from two steps to one step), or quicker delivery of services, faster closeout times on projects, new business development efforts that impacted revenues or profitability, etc.

EXAMPLE

My client, a marketing manager, launched Chicagotribune.com for the Chicago Tribune Corporation in order to protect the newspaper's advertising revenues from the onslaught of internet competitors. Obviously launching Chicagotribune.com is a cornerstone accomplishment. What I wanted to discover were the expectations at the corporate level. This led me to ask, "Was this an effort to combat advertising revenue decline as online browsers such as Yahoo, MSN became stronger?" What I found may seem obvious now, but it was 1998 when I worked with this client, so everything regarding the Internet was brand new. As a refresher for those who may not be familiar with e-Business strategies of a major newspaper, a few details will shed light on what was going on in the corporate boardroom. To begin, a large portion of the Chicago Tribune's income, millions of dollars a year, is derived from classified advertising sales of things such as cars and job listings. Well edmunds.com came online and ad revenues declined. The help-wanted section now had to compete with hotjobs.com and other job search engines. I wanted to find out what Amy's key challenges were to rollout such an important defensive initiative. I discovered that she had to lead broad cultural change in the organization by shifting the mind-set of editors, marketing and sales professionals from the traditional ways of doing business to where they could compete successfully in the developing online environment. Once I discovered her core focus for the project, I then sought results. In this case, it was positioning the Chicago Tribune to have a robust e-Business platform from which they could continue to compete against encroaching competitors.

Amy's impact, as noted on her resume: Achieved a top 40 ranking for Chicagotribune.com out of 300 million Internet sites. 20% of the standard advertisers began integrating traditional and internet advertising, protecting 20% of the advertising revenues, which represents over $150 million a year.

Commandment
- 7 -

Thou Must Be Part Of A Project Team

In a world that prizes the value of collaboration, you need to show that you have been part of a group or team project and reference the value and impact of the project results.

When I write a resume, I describe projects in many different ways, but essentially the orientation usually has three elements: Project title and brief description of the project, the goals and always a result or multiple results. I may call the three categories by other names, for example I may replace the word project with mandate, key initiative, contribution, challenge, or strategy. I may mix and match, but no matter what, there must always have a result or impact to the project rollout. If an executive's impact was multifaceted, I might break down the project into multiple steps or phases tied to actions for each step and then final results that define the success of the project rollout.

I must also mention that it's very common for me to help clients who have worked on projects that weren't finished before they separated from their company. For example building a new software technology may take years to create and perfect for the market place. Nevertheless, I want to know what happened to the project after my client left, so I ask them to follow up with friends or colleagues that still work at the company so that we have results to claim. Projects illustrate for your resume reviewer an encapsulated segment of how you contributed to the organization during a dynamic need.

There are well over 250 projects in this book to use as reference, look at a few and see how to make a time-delimited assignment (i.e. project) an illustration that shows you are a significant contributor within a team environment.

Commandment
– 8 –

Make recent work history the most relevant experience

Companies operate from the old NFL mantra, "What have you done for me lately", where "lately" means the past 12-24 months. To understand this commandment, you need to visualize your career in the shape of a pyramid where the base is much wider than the peak. With this in mind, it's easy to see that the broad foundational base leads to a narrow peak, likewise, your older jobs act as foundation to your current job, which by default is the pinnacle of your career. The only time this does not hold true is, if by necessity, you had to take a junk job. Treat the junk job with summary attention and focus the lion's share of your resume on the last "real" job you held.

It is not unusual for me to spend a half-page of the resume on a job that only lasted 18 months out of a 15-year work history. That is, if I uncover something compelling, relevant or impressive during that year and a half span. The key philosophy that guides my composition is that most professionals accumulate wisdom over time and what might take five years to accomplish earlier in their careers can now, with the right seasoning, be completed in twelve to eighteen months. I also believe companies feel that a professional is only as good as their most recent accomplishments. Yesterday's news is not as compelling as what is happening right now. It goes without saying that explaining a technology migration that occurred in 1991 is not as important to your next hiring manager as rolling out a new technology system in 2005.

I spend hours crafting the first job on the resume even though it may represent only 10% to 20% of the total work history. Another way to think of it is by comparing your work performance to that of a professional sports team. Quick, who won the World Series 5 years ago? Don't remember, either do I, but last year (2005) the White Sox broke an 80+ year old curse. You are only as good as your last game, so write your resume with a lot of consideration to what your most recent job-role accomplished in results and impact for your company.

Commandment
– 9 –

Thou must prove your career is progressing

If you want to sell your old car at a good value, you wax it and change bald tires. You know how to make a car more attractive, but do you know how to make your career appear fresh and exciting to the hiring managers who buy talent? Only professionals who prove their career is progressing, not flat or declining, are hired. If you don't demonstrate progression you will be overlooked for a job opening. A real problem is when professionals ignore signs of career stagnation until it's too late to do anything about it. A typical excuse is along this line, "I made a lateral job change to put food on the table," ok fine, but you still need to demonstrate that you met expectations that proved valuable to the organization.

Stagnation indicators of a declining career include professionals who swung for the fences on a business venture and struck out (dot-coms were notorious for this), other reasons for a failing career include being downsized, your job being exported overseas, a younger, less costly, colleague winning the promotion. A flat or declining career can also be identified when you've held the same title for five or more years, your salary is flat, you've had many short term positions or, as mentioned above, you've made lateral job changes.

Why do you have to prove that your career is progressing?

A flat or declining career is our worst enemy during an employment search. Companies only want staff with a lot of "gas in the tank." Since hiring managers are paid to be skeptics, in order for you to jump their skeptical hurdles, you need to turn negative perceptions into positive impressions. Since perception is reality for most hiring managers, it is wise to know that the first negative perceptual bias is based on age. Relative to how potential employers perceive our career trajectory, age works against us as we grow older. Although junior professionals typically receive the benefit of the doubt and are assumed to be progressing in their career between 20-35 years old, once we turn 36+, we must prove that we are just hitting our peak, and progressing in each job we hold.

Although seasoned professionals argue that subject matter expertise (i.e. experience) offsets age discrimination, the key is to prove that your wisdom can make a company more profitable, efficient and effective. We can't assume that a 20-year work history is automatically received with appreciation. Think about it. Even a famous film director like Steven Spielberg can't rest solely on historical success. He realizes when his movies don't generate box office sales, studios don't green-light the next $100 million deal. Likewise, it is left to us to prove increased value at every single step of our careers, and you need this proof to be included in your resume. Don't rest on past success. You must prove that your career is progressing each year. What have I done lately needs to be your mantra. A good rule of thumb is to evaluate what you've accomplished in the past 6 months. If it's been a year since you helped save money, earn money or rollout a successful product, service or project, you are probably in career stagnation - it is time for you to shake the dust off.

Commandment
– 9 –
Continued

How do you prove that your career is progressing?
The following example addresses what I did when I found client's career in decline.

Example **Rebuilding a Declining Career.**
Suzy had been a corporate fast tracker who found a position in the marketing department of the prestigious firm, Ernst & Young, after she graduated from college. Four years later she was fired. At that point she became a temporary employee with a staffing firm specializing in creative/marketing staff. Although Suzy was in the prime of her life, 38 years old, her career was on the decline. Worse yet, she saw her temporary position as beneath her and communicated this in her resume and in person during interviews. The first line of her resume read: "Coordinate logistics of National Restaurant Show booth for Alliant Food Service and Illinois Technology Showcase booth for Andersen Consulting."

Suzy clearly illustrates a career in decline. A fast riser gets knocked down. In order to elevate her professional profile, I uncovered and polished her valuable contribution to the clients she served as a temp. When I interviewed Suzy to write her resume, I discovered she was helping two Accenture senior partners (Accenture is the spin-off when Andersen Consulting split its CPA and technology consulting practices). Her role was to support their marketing efforts of the newly formed, Chicago Dot-Com Launch Centre that Accenture wanted to use to grow their consulting presence in the dot com market to a billion dollar business.

For reference, In June 2000 the University of Texas noted that Internet revenues soared to $523 billion. Accenture wanted a piece of this action and expected to generate 60% of new revenues from dot com startups of dot corp spin offs (business segments carved from the Fortune 500). Suzy was instrumental in helping the partners attain visibility and become identified as dot com experts. By properly capturing her value in this venture, Suzy landed a new job within 4 weeks as Associate Marketing Director of KPMG. My key was focusing on the importance of her contribution relative to the value of Accenture's new business unit expecation. What I did was elevate her career to the level of importance of the project she was involved supporting. Suzy needed to reposition her vision from that of a temp to that of a team player on a billion dollar business launch.

Suzy's case-study shows the importance of proving that wherever you work, in whatever capacity, it is up to you to demonstrate that you are not dead-wood. Communicate how you add value, solve problems and positively impact your enterprise or industry. Don't assume that employers believe age brings wisdom that produces profits. Remember, you are only as good as people are made to understand the value of your most recent successes. Ultimately the burden of proof rests on your shoulders to prove that your career is consistently progressing.

•

Commandment
- 10 -

Thou must be more valuable than your peers

This brings us to the good old "apple-to-apple comparison." Most of us don't like to think in a way that makes us feel arrogant or conceited, so we never create a true comparison to our professional peers. In the world of selling your job-skills, buyers want to know that they purchased the best talent. Simple math dictates that 98% of all resumes land in the garbage and if five candidates are interviewed, four will be dismissed. If you can't compare yourself favorably to your peers, it makes the hiring manager work from gut instinct, a tenuous proposition at best. To do a comparison, work from the micro to the macro level of the organizational chart. What I mean is, at the micro level, you belong to a team, office, or department. How does your performance stack up relative to your team members, office mates or department coworkers? Next look at the district, region or area that you are part of and once again identify any areas of accomplishments that stick out better or at the top range of your peer group. Finally, look at the corporate environment; have you helped in any way that you can make a claim that impacted the entire corporation?

Example 1

My client was a department manager at a Talbott's retail store. Before meeting me she had hired another resume writer to help her. I mention my predecessor because they had left out critical details. As I studied her background, I found out that she had worked at three Talbotts, where each store had increasingly larger revenue streams. What I learned was that during her last assignment she had worked at the #1 revenue producing property of 700 Talbotts in the U.S. Her department contributed 28% of the stores sales volume, so she could state as a result in her resume that her department produced over a quarter of the revenues for the number one store in the US. That makes her look like the number one department manager of nearly 3,000 department managers.

Example 2

An Information Technology professional, took over a failed IT project that a consulting firm had been hired to perform. I found out that he replaced five consultants, including the principal of the consulting firm, and was able to get the project implemented properly and with only 2 staff. This makes him look better than the President of a specialized consulting firm.

At other times, I might mention that someone does the work of two or three staff. I might mention that my client is the sole support for dozens of staff. I might mention that a client has achieved the best ever, largest ever or first ever results. This book is rife with examples of professionals standing out from the crowd so read their stories and learn how to define yourself as a diamond amongst baubles.

Section Two

Resume Examples

CHAPTER 1

ADMINISTRATIVE CAREERS

The Administrative Category Has

2 Client Examples

7 Job Titles

22 Years of Work History

CLIENT NAME	JOB TITLES COVERED
1. SHANE JOHNSON	............................Records Clerk Manager
	................................Purchasing Manager
	...............................Mailroom Supervisor
	....Office Assistant
2. RACHEL WILLIAMS*	.....................................Office Manager & Assistant to President
	................................Office Administrator
	..........................Administrative Assistant

* Find the "before resume" in chapter 35

SHANE R. JOHNSON

654 Bently Ave., New York, NY 10005 — 212-803-9268 • sjohns@hotmail.com

OBJECTIVE

To continue a successful career that capitalizes on managing costs, improving operations, attaining objectives and helping a company to meet dynamic challenges in a rapidly changing business environment.

SUMMARY

Proficient at creating and maintaining standards and procedures, working diligently to resolve problems and using organizational skills to maximize the effectiveness of the office and the entire enterprise. Overall, a sincere interest in the quality of my work or the work my team produces, ensures that my company can minimize operating costs, sustain profitability and grow efficiently.

STRENGTHS

- Troubleshooting
- Communications
- Project Management
- Persistence
- Strategic Planning
- Resource Coordination
- Customer Service
- Self Starter
- Team Building
- Responsive
- Accountability
- Dedication

MANAGEMENT EXPERIENCE

10/93 - present **COHEN & GOLDSTEIN, LTD.**

SUPERVISOR ROLES
- Records Clerk Manager
- Purchasing Manager
- Supervisor Mailroom Operations

Overview Lead a team of 5-6 administrative clerks who support a multimillion dollar legal operation that consists of assisting 50 personnel such as:
- 27 attorneys
- 6 paralegals
- 12 secretaries
- 3 accountants/billing clerks

OPERATIONS

Challenge 1 Supporting an operation that has grown by 100% without increasing my support staff.

Response Initiated on job training to prepare each of my employees to be able to handle operations independently.

WORK LOAD

Challenge 2 Set up all standards and operating procedures to meet a constantly changing load of scheduled and unscheduled tasks.

Response Coordinate a flexible task schedule to efficiently allocate 75-100 different jobs a week, varying from messenger service, to legal filings, tax filings, recording documents, etc.

TECHNOLOGY

Challenge 3 Creating a paperless office for the document trail of client interactions.

Response Built an Access database to archive all active/inactive files (20,000 records) tied to an intranet front-end so that attorneys can email new file request (saved 150+ attorney hours a year).

BUDGET

Challenge 4 Budget management and contract negotiations. Primary negotiator and purchasing agent for office equipment and supplies.

Response Determine capital outlay of $207,000 annually across eight categories, ie. temp staff, stationary/printing, document storage, office equipment, couriers, Pitney Bowes supplies, water services.

4/92-10/93 *Office Assistant* **SHUMAN, ABRAMSON, MORAK & WOLK**

Overview Patent research at libraries or via patent services.

EDUCATION

New York University — New York, NY — B.A., ***English***
Graduate Date: 5/02 — Note: Completing degree while working full time as a supervisor.

Columbia University — New York City — Pursued B.S., ***Industrial Engineering***

RACHEL WILLIAMS

7654 Woodline, Hinsdale, IL 60522 • rwilliams@aol.com • • 708/529-5432

OBJECTIVE To continue a successful administrative or office management career.

SUMMARY Administrative professional capable of supporting top executives by creating corporate reports, helping with client relations and by making the office run smoothly. Professional focus centers on creating excellent relationships, indirectly supporting sales efforts and meeting company objectives. Well organized, motivated, creative, capable of providing excellent operational and program development support.

STRENGTHS

• Office Operations	• Support Services	• Reporting	• AP/AR Invoicing
• Bookkeeping	• Organization	• Coordination	• Customer Service

ADMINISTRATIVE & OFFICE MANAGEMENT EXPERIENCE

EXPERIENCE

12/97-2/02 OFFICE MANAGER & ASSISTANT TO PRESIDENT, UBS Oak Brook, IL

Overview......... Sole administrative support for a team of 90 staff: 1 GM, 30 registered representatives and 60 part time insurance agents.

Challenge ***Multi-tasking***: As the sole administrative staff, I handled concurrent roles such as: Office Manager, Secretary, Receptionist, Customer Service Rep. and Bookkeeper.

Challenge ***Leadership***: A business focus was recruiting new sales staff to the branch, it was my duty to provide initial walk-through to familiarize them with our procedures and operational processes.

Challenge ***Training***: As Registered Representatives were promoted to Branch Managers, four of them hand-picked me to provide initial training to their office staff on how to run the administrative aspects of their newly opened offices.

Challenge ***Audit/Edit***: Reviewed completeness on every Insurance and Variable Annuity application that was generated by the office and tracked daily sales activities using MS Excel.

Challenge ***Bookkeeping***: Track office costs and producing invoices for Registered Representatives in Quick Books (average $10,000 per month) for all 100 staff.

Duties

- Order and distribute office supplies
- Departmental Receptionist
- Maintain and setup filing systems
- Designed MS Access database
- Created an inventory control database
- All aspect of Internet use
- Managed records, screened phones and greeted clients

IMPACT This became a Top 10 office 4 years straight out of 3,000 national offices.
IMPACT Won the Top Volume Producer Award from Corporate HQ 4 times.
IMPACT Won the Annual Award for Office Efficiency.

6/96-12/97 OFFICE ADMINISTRATOR -Advance Technology Consultants Oak Brook, IL

Overview......... Started as a temp staff in the billing department until I was promoted to a full-time office administrator.

Challenge ***Operations***: Managed customer relations, wrote quarterly and annual reports for regional managers. processed orders in Excel & Word for sales reps. Collected customer data for billing.

EDUCATION Completing a Technology Certification Program at New Horizons Computer Learning Center
Coursework, Triton College, River Grove, IL

COMPUTER Microsoft, Windows, Excel, Word, Power Point, Front Page, QuickBooks, Outlook.

LANGUAGE Bilingual: Fluent English & Spanish

CHAPTER 2

CONSTRUCTION CAREERS

The Construction Category Has

4 Client Examples

22 Job Titles

93 Years of Work History

NAME	JOB TITLES COVERED
1. TOM NELSON	Sr. Project Superintendent
	Traveling Sr. Project Superintendent
	Sr. Superintendent
2. FRANK ALCOTT	COO Engineering
	Sr. Facility Manager
	Regional Facilities Manager
	Resource Manager
	Modernization Office
	Staff Development Officer
3. SAM ANDERSON	Managing Director
	Senior Vice President
	Equity Vice President
	Vice President
	Sr, Project Manager
	Project Manager
	Development Manager
	Owner Representative
	Project Engineer
	Assistant Supeintendant
4. CHRISTOPHER GELMAN	Building Superintendant
	Carpenter
	Construction Foreman

TOM NELSON

1360 Shorewood Blvd., Madison, WI 53515
608-212-7867 (hm) • 608-325-6721 (cell)

OBJECTIVE To continue a successful career as Senior Superintendent of Hospital Construction in Wisconsin.

SUMMARY Management focus in leading teams, directing subcontractors and making the project profitable and totally acceptable to the client. I create plans to account for all contingencies, execute actions quickly and oversee activities to meet cost objectives and deadlines. Solve problems at a high quality level with the integrity to take ownership until the project is completed.

ACTIONS

Management Develop strategic phasing plans, track progress and control changes to production schedules to minimize or eliminate cost overruns and meet deadline projections.

Coordination Work with clients, designers, tradesmen, contractors and municipal administrators to resolve problems, implement efficiencies and coordinate stages from pre-design to move-in.

Leadership Identify crew potential to create the best possible work teams who can produce at a fast-track pace, yet remain conscientious of the client's business needs and demand for quality.

Negotiations Negotiate subcontractor buyouts and write scope of work to minimize back charges and change orders.

EXPERIENCE

CONSTRUCTION MANAGEMENT	***Total Budgets***	***$250 million***	***Total Footage***	***1.57 m***
• Healthcare Focused •	***Total Projects***	***30 (healthcare)***	***Manpower***	***10-350***

6/99 - Present **BOVIS LEND LEASE**, Chicago, IL
• Sr. Project Superintendent

Overview After leading 3 projects (ie. the $80 million Bayview Hospital, the $21 million Frommert Hospital and the $16.5 million Riverbay Hospital), I was added to the management team that won the Chicago-based $100 million Children's Hospital.

Mandate To win the project, I leveraged a relation I built years earlier with the Director of Real Estate. As Superintendent of the Master Facility Program, I began pre-construction duties such as site mobilization, public relations, securing permits and contractor licenses.

Concurrently led 4 smaller projects and the 1st major phase, a $23 million research laboratory. Rough construction efforts were managed to allow daily clinical operations to function.

Impacts The project is 50% of Bovis's sales volume in Chicago for 2001.
The largest healthcare client in the Midwest Region.

Result Children's Hospital, as stated by the President, justified the staffing budgets for the Chicago office. As it stands, Chicago is now expected to add $50-$80 million in new projects annually - this represents the best opportunity by Bovis to penetrate the 3rd largest market in the US.

10/97 - 6/99 **TURNER CONSTRUCTION**, Chicago, IL
• Traveling Sr. Project Superintendent

Overview Recruited as the ***first*** Traveling Construction Superintendent for Turner Construction. At hire, Turner was in final negotiations to build 10 Wellness Centers in 10 states and needed a manager to setup national purchasing agreements and procedures to standardize assembly, materials and design activities.

Mandate Build a business model based on fast track construction principals to ensure maximum profit and reduce schedules on final delivery of project.

Impact Prepared standardization techniques on assembly/materials/designs to allow Turner to sculpt the project into the site's boundaries with elements of customizing while gaining the price advantages from construction standardization.

Result My construction standardization principals were executed on all Turner's projects (ranging $8-$12 million each) and increased average profitability by 10%.

9/89 - 9/97 **MARSHALL ERDMAN & ASSOCIATES**, Denver, CO
- ***Sr. Superintendent***

Overview Over 10 years, I led 20+ "FAST TRACK" construction projects. The key was to promote Erdman's design/build advantage which was to deliver complete projects 20% faster than the competition. This made us the leader of ambulatory health care facility construction in the US.

Mandate Work profitably at a high degree of quality and customer satisfaction. Act as "The Guy" who represents Marshall Erdman in numerous remote locations and provide the guarantee that all specifications, details and quality of assembly would be strictly followed. This was a full turnkey role, demanding extremely tight deadlines and controlling all P&L objectives on construction projects budgeted between $3-$22 million each.

Impact
#1 Never Missed a Deadline
#2 Never cited for an OSHA violation
#3 Never had a dissatisfied owner
#4 Never had a serious injury

Result Typically completed projects 20% faster than Erdman's construction schedules. Met the budgeted goal to deliver max profit on every project led.

Project Examples

Project		
Dade County Hospital	Challenge	Building on Bedrock 12 inches below grade.
	Action	Blasted in all utilities which allowed the project to be delivered on time/budget. This project won an architectural award.
Riverfront Hospital	Challenge	To orchestrate a 6-phase project before winter conditions set in.
	Action	Completely re-sequenced all project phases which delivered project 4 months ahead of schedule and allowed the client to earn $1.3 million in revenues and save $200K by eliminating the use of temperature enclosures.
Dane County Hospital	Challenge	The surgery and treatment addition was positioned exactly at the hospitals main entrance.
	Actions	Redirected patient flow around construction without disrupting general public attendance.
St. James Pediatric Clinic	Challenge	The facility pulled 700-800 charts daily for 10 pediatricians and saw a child every 6-8 minutes.
	Action	Renovated and remodeled a highly active space without incident as a young patient public was herded around construction areas.
Kaiser Building HMO	Challenge	Infill & remodel project on the top floor of an office tower in Kansas City.
	Action	All material for job had to be hoisted inside the elevator for each phase. All debris had to be transported via public areas without a trace of evidence (noise, dust, vibration were all disguised from the public).
St. Joseph's Clinic	Challenge	Constructing a facility in a low flood plain with 2 feet of mud completely surrounding the site.
	Action	Installed over 4,000 tons of rock and lime stabilization materials to achieve the target date.

EDUCATION Denver Area Technical College, Denver, CO
Four years construction technology including survey, carpentry, millwrighting, precision tooling, optical alignment, welding and drafting.

STUDIES
- Construction Aerosol
- OSHA Standards
- Aerial Lift Training
- Asbestos Awareness
- Mobile Crane Safety
- Rigging Methods
- Fall Protection
- Forklift Safety
- Certified Scaffold

STRENGTHS
- Business Oversight
- Budgeting/Estimating
- Time Management
- Value Engineering
- Fast-track Construction
- Cost Containment
- Strategic Planning
- Managing Subcontractors
- Zero Injury Training

FRANK D. ALCOTT

720 W. Washingotn St., Ithaca, NY 14850 • 607-237-8343 falcott@aol.com

OBJECTIVE Facilities/building manager or construction project manager for a residential or commercial real estate group.

Strengths • Optimizing Scarce Resources • Leading Technical Professionals • Managing & Implementing Change

CONSTRUCTION EXPERIENCE

1997 -1999 **COO Engineering**
Lieutenant Colonel
US Army

Led 1 of only 2 Construction Engineering Divisions in the Army Reserves
My 2 teams, ***Strategic Planning*** and ***Project Execution***, had 80 technical staff i.e. project managers, surveyors, draftsmen, mechanical, civil and construction engineers.

Objective — Prepare my teams to lead a 2,500 person construction labor force that would be assigned during conflicts.

Mandate — Ensure staff could build a city anywhere in the world in 30 days with all necessary facilities to sustain 50,000-100,000 fighting troops.

Challenge 1 — Implement Army's **FIRST** satellite linked Topographical Surveying computer system.

Response — Tuned the system to design/revise construction drawings and estimate resources to build roads and facilities.

Result — Reduced project design time by 66% and project manpower needs by 33%.
Reduced system staff training from 13 weeks to 8 days.

1994-1997 **Sr. Facility Engineer** **Pentagon Consultant** to Army HQ Chief of Staff (3 Star General)
Supervised construction, maintenance, repair and leasing programs for 20 million sq.ft. of facilities — 1,200 mixed use buildings at 4,000 sites. Provided input to annual budget request to Congress.

Challenge 2 — Determine how to reduce costs and eliminate facilities as the Army reduced size by 35%.

Response — Created Army's **FIRST** ***Facilities Reduction Plan*** — an operational and fiscal guide used by 1,200 facility managers to help them execute the plan. Set goals to dispose of surplus facilities and defined criteria to sell excess inventory.

Result — Over a 2-year span, we eliminated 1,500 buildings, 2 million sq.ft. of facilities which reduced operating costs to the government by $70 million a year.

1990-1994 **Regional Facilities Manager** - New York
Managed 12 staff, $4M budget to support 38 centers and 980,000 sq.ft. of facilities.
Liaison to procurement, contractors and supporting engineers.

Challenge 3 — Resolve funding shortages to meet maintenance, repair and construction needs.

Response — Implemented **FIRST** — ***Regional Energy Conservation Plan*** (22% of my fiscal budget was pre-spent on energy costs).

Result — Program reduced energy needs 33% and captured $5 million in state and federal conservation grants which were used to construct new buildings.

Challenge 4 — Create the Army's ***Facility Asset Management*** model.
Which determined
- Equipment, services and facility purchasing requirements
- Space use feasibility
- Cost estimates for new construction or modifications

Response — Implemented **FIRST** – ***Facility Lease Renegotiation Strategy.***

Result — Saved $6.5 million when 250+ leases were terminated or renegotiated.
Program changed government policy and was adopted nationally.

1984-1990 ***Concurrent Titles***

Resource Manager	Focus	Equipment
Modernization Officer	Focus	Integration of New Technology
Staff Development Officer	Focus	Personnel Assignment and Resource Allocation

Conducted manpower studies for a 10,000 person civilian and military organization with divisions in:

• Medical • Combat • Support • Engineering • Military Intelligence
• Administration • Supply • Maintenance • Command & Control

Project — Created **FIRST**— ***Staffing Automation Program*** **-** to eliminate bias when distributing personnel.

Response — Built a computer model that could forecast staffing needs for 5 divisions (100,000-150,000 employees) that would be spread over 25 user groups in 12 Eastern states.

Results — Reduced the time dedicated to staff-forecasting by 12,500 hours a year.
Increased accuracy of staffing needs from a swing of (+/-) 7% to (+/-) 1%.

EDUCATION

• DOD, Logistics Management College, Management of Defense Acquisition Contracts Program
• U.S. Army Command and General Staff College, Fort Leavenworth, KS, Graduate
• Advance Engineering Course, U.S. Army Engineer School, Fort Belvoir, VA, Graduate

Degree

• BS, Engineering Management, Cornell University, Ithaca, NY

References available on request.

SAM P. ANDERSON

713 Briarcliff Ct., Atlanta, GA 30326 • 404-729-7654

SUMMARY

A decisive strategist who positively impacts all aspects of the business. Whether I am a project manager or challenged to create profitable new practices, I drive change and engage staff to work together and accomplish the goals set before us. I'm a resourceful leader with analytical, presentation, and marketing skills, who advises senior staff as well as personally lead initiatives to execute projects and grow the organization within extremely competitive environments.

1989 - Present **JONES LANG LASALLE,** Atlanta, GA

• Managing Director	2001-present	• Vice President	1991-1994
• Senior VP	1996-2001	• Sr. Project Manager	1990-1991
• Equity VP	1994-1996	• Project Manager	1989-1990

Overview As an executive at the world's largest full service real estate provider, and Executive Team Member for 5 years, I've helped shape strategy and provide vision for a division that represents 20% of all revenues in the Americas. My division, is the most profitable and fastest growing of 8 company divisions, averaging 25% growth a year for 5 years straight - notable when our industry is negative to flat during the last 2 years.

Snap-shot Since '98, I've lead 13 managers (2 SVPs, 9 VPs and 2 Project Managers) and completed 125 projects - 17 million SF, an aggregate of $4.5 billion in total project costs.

Value My projects delivered $114MM in Jones Lang LaSalle revenues at an average profit of 25%.

Impact #1 GROW REVENUES – Of 4 speciality practices, I made my group the largest single producer of revenues and profit.
Pattern – In '98, we generated $12MM. By '03, we contributed $30MM.

Impact #2 PENETRATE NEW MARKETS – Repositioned division from near complete reliance on office construction ('98 almost 85% of all revenues) to where we pursued a broader market strategy.
Pattern – Now 70% of our revenues originate from new segments such as residential, hotels, higher education, health care, retail and industrial as stand-alone specialities. I also strive to make Jones Lang LaSalle the accepted market leader in each segment, which has grown project profitability 5-10% across the board.

Impact #3 DRIVE BEST PRACTICES – Created standards as part of Jones Lang LaSalle's branding strategy to be the "Best In Class" provider of high-quality and project execution efficiency.

Created
1. Standard Anticipated cost reporting systems
2. Standard Contracts & RFPs
3. Standard Risk mitigating tools
4. Standard Marketing collateral
5. Standard Bench-mark tools to measure added value to clients
6. Standard Case-study proofs (to resell the firm on new project opportunities)

Benefit These standards make us more cost effective at delivering services and capture larger project margin while differentiating us from the competition.

Impact #4 MANAGING PROJECT RISK – Mitigate risk through a management process that anticipates problems and eliminates wasted time/cost.

Contribution – Trusted advisor to CEOs, Heads of Corporate Real Estate Departments, Chairmen/ Principals of development companies through all project phases in order to maximize their profitability and optimize the ***price - value - quality equation***.

Page 1 of 2

Impact #5 TECHNICAL COMPETENCY – possess unique depth and breadth of knowledge regarding the following competencies as applied on 125 projects, ranging from Class A office to high-rise residential and mixed-use developments.

Owner Representation Handle communications between ownership, design professionals, contractors, building management and marketing to conceptualize a project, resolve problems, coordinate the process, and successfully implement the project.

Project Coordination Develop long term strategic plans, track progress, ensure schedule compliance and coordinate all associated disciplines.

Budget Analysis/Planning Develop and qualify proformas, monitor/manage costs to attain profitability goals (ROI, P&L, and cash flow projections).

Site Selection/Entitlements Conduct extensive land evaluations and due diligence focusing on product requirements, user needs and long term opportunities (residual value).

Negotiations Manage RFP and bidding processes, negotiate contracts and perform contract administration.

Value Engineering Evaluate program, design, constructability and operational issues to improve efficiencies, enhance real estate design characteristics and manage costs.

Project Development Develop proforma and pre-design schedules; provide entitlement management, design and on-site management, and construction oversight to control changes, improve production and achieve schedule objectives.

1988 - 1990 **EVERGREEN CONSTRUCTION INC.**, Atlanta, GA
Project Manager - $22MM, 290,000 RSF bank renovation.
- $300MM, 237-acre, 1,200,000 RSF corporate facility (preconstruction).

1982 - 1988 **HOLDER CONSTRUCTION COMPANY**, Atlanta, GA
Overview
Development Manager - $100MM, 1.2MM RSF Corporate HQ project.
Owner Representative -$5.7MM luxury condo renovation. Managed AE groups, contractor and sales agents.
Project Engineer -$30MM, 4 story, 290,000 RSF Bank HQ with underground parking.
Project Manager - Involved in core/shell and tenant buildouts in a 71-story and 50-story high-rise. Managed 60 subcontractors during base building and interior phases.

1981 - 1982 **HARDIN CONSTRUCTION COMPANY**, Atlanta, GA
Development Manager – $10MM, 10-story corporate office, with a structured garage.

1976 - 1981 **AAGAARD-JUERGENSEN**, Orlando, FL
Project Engineer – $30MM phase of a $300MM waste water treatment plant.
Asst. Superintendent/Field Engineer – Supervised 65 union tradesmen erecting 2,000 tons of precipitator steel and installing an underground electrical system for a 500 MW power plant.

EDUCATION

1978	Pursued MBA [night school]	Univ. of Florida, Gainesville, FL
1976	BS, Construction Management	Minor Economics, Univ. South Florida, St. Petersburg, FL

References Available on request.

CHRISTOPHER GELMAN

7891Fairview, Palos Heights, IL 60463 ✆ **847-324-0252**

OBJECTIVE

To continue a successful maintenance or facilities management career.

SUMMARY

Knowledge of building maintenance, construction and property management principals (including mechanical repair and system installation). Experienced in negotiating contracted maintenance agreements, securing repair bids and evaluating quality of completed work. Building rehabilitation experience covers the following strengths:

STRENGTHS

• Plumbing	• Electrical	• Landscaping	• HVAC
• Carpentry	• Furnace/Boilers	• Dry walling/plastering	• Tile
• Buildouts	• Decorating	• Floor installation	• Roofing

EXPERIENCE

1984 - present

BANK OF AMERICA PALOS HEIGHTS

Building Superintendent **-** *note: Bank of America purchased Old River Bank on 10/98*

Overview Manage a staff of 3 responsible for repairing and preventative maintenance efforts on a group of 8 facilities with an aggregate of 1,200,000 sq/ft of built space and grounds.

Actions The goal is on preventative maintenance to minimize major repair costs (50% of all maintenance was conducted in-house), in this capacity we ensure proper operation of all equipment including HVAC, water boilers, bank appliances and structural maintenance (i.e. Elevators, Drive up Teller Equipment, Lawn Care, and Parking Lots, etc.).

PROJECT **BANK BRANCH REHAB & BUILD OUT**

Focus After building a new bank facility, the old property was abandoned. I analyzed economic feasibility of property teardown or rehabilitation.

Results With minimal investment we rehabbed property and then rented it in a 5 year lease that paid for all rehab costs (saving $120,000).

PROJECT **BUILT A NEW CAFETERIA FOR BANK**

Focus After studying existing plans of other bank cafeterias, I chose the building contractors, oversaw the development and conducted final walk through.

Result Built a full service cafeteria that served 300 employees.

Specialized work: **Voice & Data Network** - by 1988, I was involved with the bank's telecommunication and data networks. Specifically, I cabled, processed feature changes and installed new systems.

1982 - 1984

KIMBALL CONSTRUCTION - exclusively new home construction

Carpenter

1978 - 1982

MAJESTY BUILDERS

Construction Foreman

Overview Directed building crews averaging 4-12 employees for an aggregate of 250 projects that included high-rise rehabbing, new church and warehouse construction, condo roofing, and casement repair.

PERSONAL

Mayoral Appointment: Oak Lawn Planning & Development Commission 1994 - present

Chairman of building and grounds for Kedvale Christian Reformed Church

♦ *References available on request* ♦

CHAPTER 3

EXECUTIVE CAREERS

The Executive Category Has

4 Client Examples

23 Job Titles

94 Years of Work History

NAME	JOB TITLES COVERED
1. JONATHAN GREY	................VP International Development
	............VP Senior Counsel/International
	..................Senior International Counsel
	...........Associate, Corporate Department
	....Associate
2. TIMOTHY KRAMER*	..................................Chairman & CEO
	....Principal
	....................................President & COO
	....E.V. P./G.M.
	....President
	................................Vice President/G.M.
3. DAVID OLSON	................................Aquisition Manager
	....................................Business Analyst
	..........................Senior Business Analyst
	..................Supervisor Accounts Payable
	........................International Coordinator
	............................Accounting Supervisor
	....Accountant
4. JENNY EVANS	.............................VP Investor Relations
	.....................Manager Investor Relations
	......................Associate Media Manager
	.........................Membership Coordinator
	.........Assistant VP of Human Resources

* Find the "before resume" in chapter 35

JONATHAN GREY

425-993-7561 • jongrey@.com
321 Juniper Lane, Redmond, WA 98052

1999 – Present **MSN WORLDWIDE,** Redmond, WA
VP, International Business Development & Strategy

Overview Structure and implement deals impacting all global operations, where MSN Worldwide, currently a $4 billion division, is expected to produce 25% of subscriber growth and 65% of EBITDA growth for the parent organization, Microsoft, during the next 5 years.

Actions
- Develop and implement long-range strategic plans for MSN Worldwide.
- Launched MSN in new international markets and developed new strategic partners.
- Negotiate joint venture media, communications, Internet, M&A, and strategic partnerships.
- Negotiate content, marketing, e-commerce and infrastructure relationships and investments.

Examples
- Wireless data
- Interactive TV
- DSL
- Internet on-demand video
- Cable/Pay TV
- Satellite
- Broadband
- New TV channels

Execution Member of senior management team charged with restructuring existing businesses, reducing costs and improving efficiencies to turn around MSN Worldwide. Lead 5-15 professionals in negotiating and closing deals and in developing new product strategies for global markets.

STRATEGY #1 **GOALS** • Led development of new technology platform for international markets.

Challenge Worked with MSN Technologies, MSN International Finance, MSN Member Services, and the individual country operations to build the business model and finalize the technology platform.

RESULTS Rolled out in Australia, Japan and Brazil. The lower rollout costs delivered a product to the consumer at a 16% lower price which helped reduce customer turn-over by 33%.

STRATEGY #2 **GOALS** • Migrate MSN from narrowband to broadband in the UK.

Challenge Create a strategic relationship with NTL (the UK's largest broadband carrier) by convincing NTL's senior mamagement that it was more advantageous to partner with MSN than make us their competitor. ***Solved by*** - Proved that our market strength as the #1 Internet Browser could significantly, and adversely impact NTL's business.

RESULTS Closed the ***largest-ever*** international deal for MSN with an internet browser company.

STRATEGY #3 **GOAL** • Elevate MSN Internet Explorer, from 3rd largest to single largest brrowser in Latin America.

Challenge Convincing MSN to accept a multibrand strategy for Latin America and potential partners. ***Solved by*** - Persuading executive teams that the merger benefits far outweighed the cost of competition.

RESULTS Until my resolutions were accepted, negotiations had collapsed with Latin Americas #1 ISP.

Pg. 1 of 3

1993 – 1999 **DISNEY** Burbank, CA
VP, Senior Counsel/International **1995 – 1999**
Senior International Counsel **1993 - 1995**

Overview Upon Disney's acquisition of ESPN, became chief international lawyer for Disney and its business units:

• Miramax	• ABC Entertainment	• Disney Land & World
• Disney Channel	• Mammoth Records	• Buena Vista
• Lifetime & History Channel	• A&E Channel	• Walt Disney Records

Actions

- Advised senior executives on strategic and legal issues of international development and operations.
- Structured and negotiated acquisitions and divestitures, joint ventures, financing and licensing arrangements for Disney business units globally.

Example – Structured, negotiated and closed a European joint venture with a financial partner for Disney Channel and ESPN's English channel businesses.

Example – Sold TeleMundo, a Spanish general entertainment channel via auction to Viacom at a price 30% greater than projected.

STRATEGY #1

Goals Negotiated a 50/50% joint venture between ESPN and Prisa, Spain's 2nd largest media company.

Challenge Overcoming Prisa's constitutional law which prohibits ***any*** foreign ownership of broadcast networks. ***Solved by*** - Creating a production company, not a broadcast company, that wasn't subject to foreign ownership laws, but where all Disney economic interests resided.

Results Disney spent only $20 million to close the ESPN Spanish joint venture which was structured to deliver $500 million in anticipated revenues over the term of the agreement.

STRATEGY # 2

Goals Capture multimillion dollar financial incentives for Miramax Pictures by using a French tax law to create a shelter for Disney's slate of films.

Challenge Structuring the deal under French law to protect Disney from potential law suits that could originate if a new government administration overturned the shelters.

Challenge Setting up the deal structure with a French Banking partner that met all French tax requirements and then applying the structure to 14 new Miramax films.

Result Saved Miramax $225 million over three years and became the only US studio to gain an economic benefit from the French tax scheme.

STRATEGY #3

Goals Help Disney close a $4.6 billion sale of the Simon & Schuster professional, educational and reference book publishing business.

Challenge Prove to the competition authorities of the Europe, Brazil, Canada and Australia that selling Simon & Schuster to our competitor, Pearson PLC, was not anti-competitive.

Result The deal was approved in every jurisdiction without undue cost or hindrance.

KEY ROLE During '97, served as **Acting General Counsel** of ABC Entertainment, a $4 billion division of Disney.

- Managed and reorganized a legal department of 17 professionals.
- Advised senior management on reorganizing and redeveloping ABC Entertainment.

Result Offered a permanent ABC Entertainment General Counsel role, but declined to continue working at corporate headquarters.

1993-1995 **MIRAMAX** **Los Angeles, CA**
Senior International Counsel

Overview Managed all legal activities of Miramax and its subsidiaries outside of the US. Structured and negotiated 18 deals including joint ventures, acquisitions and divestitures, development agreements and franchise relations ranging from $500K to $65 million each.

Deals
• Restructured Miramax's international movie operations.
• Launched or expanded Miramax in: Argentina, Australia, Brazil, Venezuela, Israel, Spain, Italy, Colombia, France, Ecuador, UK, Japan, Chile, Germany, Thailand and Mexico.

1986 - 1993 **CASE & WHITE** New York, New York
***Associate*, Corporate Department** Paris, France
Prague, Czech Republic

Prague **1992-93** Launched firm in the Czech Republic. Structured, negotiated and closed the following deals:
Deals
• $200 million project finance to reconstruct Prague's International Airport.
• Restructured Czech companies anticipating privatizing and competition in Western markets.
• Developed the first-ever ESOP poison pill defense in the Czech Republic.
• International tax planning for foreign investments.

Paris **1989 - 91** Structured, negotiated and closed transactions of $2M to $1.5B in Europe and Latin America
Deals
• Cross-border M&A and divestitures of public/private companies, divisions and subsidiaries.
• International joint ventures in service and manufacturing sectors.
• European-wide multi-currency commercial lending facilities.
• International intellectual property licensing.
• Corporate tax planning, i.e. tax-efficient structuring and international operations.

New York **1986 - 88** Structured, negotiated and closed transactions from $2M to $2.7B (including the leveraged buyout of American Standard).
Deals
• LBOs, M&A, divestitures, corporate reorganizations, IPOs, private debt placements.
• Limited partnerships; aircraft leases; term loan agreements and revolving credit facilities.

1983 – 1984 **JENNER & BLOCK** Chicago, IL
Associate Corporate & Litigation Departments

PERSONAL Member, New York and California Bars

EDUCATION
1983 **J.D. YALE LAW SCHOOL** Cambridge, MA
Yale International Law Journal, Senior Editor
1980 **B.A.** Economics/Political Science, **DEPAUL UNIVERSITY, Chicago**, IL

TIMOTHY W. KRAMER

67 Brook Ln., St. Louis, MO 63129 314-273-7410 • wk544@att.net

SUMMARY

20 years of domestic and international operating experience in executive level positions. Proven track record in motivating and building a strong organizational climate through personal involvement and a proactive leadership style. Ability to rationalize businesses, reset strategies and streamline operations to achieve revenue and profit goals in a leveraged operating environment.

1998 - 2001 **SEMCO PLASTICS COMPANY INC. CHAIRMAN & CEO** St. Louis, MO

Overview Recruited by Aurora Capital Group to execute an acquisition strategy and rapidly build a $300-$500MM plastic injection molding company by integrating multiple acquisitions into a homogenous multinational manufacturing platform capable of sustained growth.

Phase I Identify target companies to acquire.

Actions
- Conducted due diligence on 80 companies serving 4 market segments (electronics, consumer, medical and industrial/automotive) during first 12 months.
- Negotiated with targets which led to acquiring 5 companies ranging from $7MM -$160MM.

Phase II Rationalize the businesses while expanding product and service offerings to the marketplace.

Actions
- Established a common corporate culture and built an executive management team with CFO, VP Engineering/Technology, VP HR, VP Operations/Integration and 3 Divisional Presidents.
- Closed 2 manufacturing plants that saved $4.2MM annually and implemented cost reduction initiatives that saved $9.5MM annually.
- Expanded value added services (clean room manufacturing and assembly, in-mold decorating, painting and global assembly capabilities).

Result Created a $400MM plastic injection molding company with 14 US, Mexican, Canadian and UK facilities, reduced operating expenses by $13.7MM and expanded products and services.

1997-1998 **DARSON GROUP PRINCIPAL** (expected to become CEO)

Overview Recruited to execute a private equity investment strategy to build a $200-$300MM precision machining business focused on medical products, aerospace and semiconductor industries. Goal was to acquire 3-5 platform businesses as part of an industry consolidation of manufacturers into a single-source solution provider for OEMs.

Phase I Due diligence evaluations of target companies.
Actions Analyzed 57 companies ($15 to $135MM) and negotiated Letters of Intent with 12 prospects.
Result Darson acquired a single medical components manufacturer with $30MM in sales, a significant departure from the original platform strategy.

1994 - 1997 **CALVERT INC. PRESIDENT/COO, INTERNATIONAL WIRE GROUP (IWG)** 1995-97
E.V.P./G.M., ARROW ELECTRONICS 1994-95 Europe

Overview Initially hired by Calvert to take over Arrow Electronics division after the acquisition of Dupont Connector Systems. At Arrow I managed a $180MM European operation with 1,100 staff in France and the Netherlands serving the electronics, computer and telecom industries. By 1995, I formed a $230MM business unit (IWG) and then added companies (ECM and Omega) that became a $450MM company needing to be rationalized to grow profits and compete in a price sensitive market.

At International Wire - Rationalized and consolidated 29 manufacturing plants into 17 plants to capture efficiencies and respond to our largest customers who demanded price cuts of 5-10% each year.

Actions
- Instituted a unified corporate culture with new Executive Management Team.
- Organized business units into 3 market driven divisions (bare wire, insulated and harness).
- Evaluated P&L performance of each division to identify opportunities to reduce costs.

Result Created a top-5 US producer of copper wire and wire harness products.
Result Reduced prices 10% yet increased EBITDA by 5% worth $8MM - all accomplished while absorbing $10MM in closing and relocation costs.
Result Reduced inventories by 20% in 1996 thereby increasing cash flow by $13.5MM.

— Pg. 1 of 2 —

As EVP/GM Arrow Electronics - Improved speed to market product delivery, by focusing on design, development and restructuring of the sales marketing organization.

Actions
- Instituted the American culture into the existing European system.
- Completely re-engineered product development cycle time through process mapping.
- Re-engineered manufacturing operations into highly focused factories.

Result Increased sales by 22% within year one - worth $35MM.
Result Reduced design development cycle time from 180 days to 70 days.

1987-1994 **LARSEN MANUFACTURING** Ft. Lauderdale, FL

PRESIDENT — *Larsen Packaging Systems*	1993-94	Ft. Lauderdale, FL
PRESIDENT — *Larsen Construction Equipment Group*	1992-93	Ft. Lauderdale, FL
PRESIDENT — *Rockford Steel Building Systems*	1988-92	Waterboro, SC
PRESIDENT — *Precision Equipment*	1987-88	Fargo, ND

Overview Recruited by the CEO of this Fortune 500 company to help execute new initiatives to consolidate a conglomerate of 38 companies into 7-9 global market leaders ranging from $50MM-$500MM in sales.

Phase I **Market integration -construction manufacturing group**. Successfully integrated 2 manufacturing companies and an acquisition into a business unit with $60MM in sales and was poised to grow to $150MM through new sales of branded products.

Phase II **Market integration -packaging group**. Took over project after an initial attempt was made to create a single integrated market provider from 6 Larsen packaging companies - Larsen spent $50MM to consolidate 4 plants yet sales dropped by $85MM.
Strategy to salvage the integration is as follows.

Actions **At Larsen Packaging Systems** – Managed worldwide operations of 6-operating units with manufacturing centers in the UK, Italy, Brazil, Mexico, Australia, and the US (sales of $150MM with over 1,000 employees). Implemented a recovery plan by meeting with global customers, building a new executive management team and working with plant management to resolve a order backlog and push sales management to meet expectations.
Result Expanded sales and distribution by $5MM in the Pacific Rim.
Result Accelerated R & D to meet the current and future demands in Asia and the Eastern block.

Overview **At Larsen's Manufacturing** – Managed 3 manufacturing companies and a distribution company. Targeted sales were approximately $150MM. Successfully created Larsen's first global market leader platform.
Result Streamlined marketing, sales, and distribution to focus on customer expectations.
Result Consolidated four manufacturing plants into a single highly automated facility.

Overview **At Rockford Steel Building** – Managed an $85MM company with 2 manufacturing facilities, 34 branch locations and over 800 employees. Expanded market presence into all tier-1 markets in the US.
Result Increased sales by 55% and profit by 115% from 1989 to 1991.
Result Expanded branch operations from 22 locations to 34.

Overview **At Precision Equipment** – Senior Executive of a $17.5MM manufacturer of construction and road building equipment. Rationalized products by pruning under performers and reduced organizational overhead.
Result Realized $1.5MM in new profit from successful turnaround of this division.

1980-1987 **ORERCO SYSTEMS** **VICE PRESIDENT — GM** Southerlin, OR
Managed a specialized manufacturing and distribution company. Additionally, was Executive VP of a $17MM international division that was in partnership with S.A. White Martin's in Brazil.

EDUCATION Business Administration - University of Miami, Miami, FL

DAVID OLSON

5432 Pinewood Dr.
Northfield, IL 60093
davido@Aol.com • 847-572-3296

Senior Management • Strategic Planning, Negotiating, Financial And Analytical Expertise •

Skills focus on reviewing industries and markets to identify new businesses, evaluate joint venture alliances and M&A opportunities. Financial skills include qualitative and quantitative due diligence of investment strategies, cost factors and financial forecasting to structure deals that ensure a profitable ROI. Experienced at presenting to senior management and leading teams responsible for new business opportunities and acquisitions. Aggressively and creatively identify key challenges then choose strategies to solve these problems while at the same time designing deals that are structured to minimize risk.

1997 - present **DUPONT** ***Acquisition Manager*** **-** Corporate Development 12/98-present

Enhance value in a growth-oriented environment where ambiguity and change must be resolved to meet corporate objectives. I identify targets, execute business plans, conduct due diligence, negotiate deals and facilitate post-closing integration. I evaluated 100+ deals for 5 business segments, values of $2M-$65M each, of which Dupont entered into negotiations on 20, leading to $200M in acquisitions or divestitures. ***The Challenge*** is navigating a strategy that is defensible to the CEO, the Board and meets the objectives of the operating managers.

SAMPLE OF COMPLETED DEALS

1. **Acquired Food Machinery Manufacturing Plant** ($8M) – led financial and due diligence team. Resolved numerous risk factors to complete deal. Successful acquisition despite pending bankruptcy, inaccurate financial statements and unstable workforce.
2. **Technology Acquisition** – led Dupont's first pure software company acquisition ($3M). Structured the agreement to ensure the founders and key application engineers remained captive to Dupont until software was tested, rolled-out and perfected in the market place.
3. **Manufacturing Divestiture** – led a $4M plant divestiture that saved Dupont $2.5M in shutdown costs. Qualified a buyer willing to continue to supply Dupont with manufacturing capability and arranged their financing.
4. **Acquired Food Machinery Manufacturer ($45M)** – as second lead, created valuation model, conducted due diligence and negotiated transition services agreement with seller. Lead in divesting one product line ($lM) and associated manufacturing capacity, avoiding $500K in severance costs.
5. **Leveraged a Weak Stance into the Dominant Position** – led post-closing/breach of contract negotiations with a major chemical company after a recent Dupont divestiture. Changed adversary's position, where Dupont owed $2M, into the resulting position, where Dupont received $2.5M.
6. **Acquired a Norwegian software firm** – a leading-edge developer of software for offshore oil production control systems. As second lead, developed a valuation model and led due diligence that uncovered risks that strengthened Dupont's position and ultimately reduced the acquisition price from $4.8M to $3.8M.
7. **Acquired a Texas based Energy Measurement Company** ($6M) – as second lead, created valuation model and led due diligence team that uncovered significant inventory issues resulting in a $2M reduction in price.

Business Analyst, Energy & Transportation Measurement Division 5/97-12/98
Financial & Project Management - assignment in Norway to develop reporting standards, project management procedures and financial controls to help senior management accurately understand their cost structure.

8. **Restructured an International Business Contract** - a $10M agreement between Mexico's PEMEX and Dupont's Norwegian subsidiary. Created a Mexican entity, hired local management and instituted tax strategies to enhance contract value. Once the business model was refined we exported it to the Venezuelan market.
9. **Helped Develop Dupont's Global Strategy** - led the divisional team to work with Boston Consulting group, as well as senior management, in identifying growth opportunities and strategies.
10. **Negotiated $2M Construction Contract** - secured site, arranged financing and oversaw the building of a high tech manufacturing center.

1982-1994 **MARATHON CORP.,** Houston, TX

Senior Business Analyst 1989-94

Financial analysis, reporting and budgeting for the Permian Oil Basin, a $300M domestic business unit.

Corporate profitability analysis - Created the first true portfolio analysis of a 150 field basin with 5,000 wells. The key was to model productivity and compare cost structures with nearby competitors and industry data as well as provide senior management detailed reports to optimize their resource allocation.

Impact Engineers, once I trained them to apply the financial analysis, could benchmark individual field productivity and profitability. Management could determine whether to retain, expand or divest individual fields.

Supervisor Accounts Payable 1987-89

Supervised 12 accountants/clerks responsible in processing 50,000 monthly checks to 2,000 vendors. Led team to centralize AP from 12 locations into the newly created Tulsa data center. Brought Electronic Data Interchange into the AP process for the first time and reduced headcount by 60% from 80 to 32.

International Coordinator- Chicago Corporate office 1985-87

Coordinate financial and personnel issues for staff in Algeria, Gabon, United Arab Emirates and Egypt.

Accounting Supervisor - Permian Basin Plant Group 1984-85

Managed a group of 6 accountants responsible for recording all plant revenue in the Permian Basin.

Accountant-Natural Gas Group 1982-83

Resolved NGPA pricing issues.

1974 - 1980 ***Nurse*** - Specialized in Critical Care and Burn Therapy (3 Texas based hospitals)

MILITARY US ARMY - ***Clinical Specialist*** (Nurse)

- Brooke Army Burn Unit

EDUCATION

1995-1997	Texas Southern University	MBA Concentration - Finance
1980-1982	University of Houston	B.S. Business Administration - Major, Accounting

JENNY W. EVANS

310 First Street, Plymouth Meeting, PA 19462 610-553-2186

OBJECTIVE To continue a career as an investment relations executive for a consumer goods manufacturer.

SUMMARY Investor management expertise has been executed in two completely disparate markets, rail road transportation and real estate. My strategies apply to all industry segments and focus on improving cost of capital and shareholder value while minimizing volatility. Success is a result of researching business peers, identifying industry trends, shaping corporate messages to win favor and executing strong IR programs structured to adapt to dynamic market conditions.

EXPERIENCE

1995 - present **V.P. INVESTOR RELATIONS** **BRANDYWINE REALTY TRUST** [Ticker BRT]

Overview The first VP of Investor Relations for this $2.7 billion REIT after they had experienced a 33% drop in share price. My focus is using PR, marketing, analytical and financial skills to articulate our business strategies to Wall Street Analysts. Manage a staff of 3 and $1.3M budget.

Need To change Wallstreet's erroneous view that Brandywine was overleveraged, had a poor balance sheet and had little upside growth potential.

Strategy ***Create Company's Investor Relations Infrastructure.*** Goal — Improve stock price by identifying Wall Street's reward mechanisms and preparing key executives to communicate a convincing message so that we could meet our objectives and attain their expectations.

Step 1 **ESTABLISH COMPANY'S FIRST INVESTOR RELATIONS PROGRAM**

Actions
- Wrote ***an IR business plan*** with measurable goals.
- Created ***a shareholder diversification plan.***
- Designed ***a multimedia investment presentation*** for retail brokers & institutional analysts.
- Identified 500 key investor targets and then communicated long-term strategies to win continued support from existing shareholders and initiate interest from growth oriented investors.

Step 2 **CREATED AN MFM MODEL (MOST FAVORED MESSAGE) TO WIN WALLSTREET SUPPORT**

Actions
- Analyzed the closest 17 industry competitors and tracked the top 10 sell-side analysts to identify the ***MFM's*** that the street rewarded.
- Conducted a rigorous valuation comparison of 2 peer groups based on:
  1) P/FFO Dividend Yield 2) Price to NAV 3) NOI 4) FFO Growth
  4) Operating Strategies 5) Balance Sheet 6) Management Capability
- Prepared our CEO to address corporate vision, strategy and messaging on:
  1) Management Quality 2) Capital Structure 3) Growth 4) Value Creation

Step 3 **CREATED A TOP-LEVEL MESSAGE MODEL TO ENSURE EXECUTIVE COHESION**

Actions
- Identified and crystallized a set of ***core executive messages*** that complemented the CEO's strategies and also clarified, simplified and repeated our strategic plan to the investment community.
- Once messages were shaped, ***the challenge*** was to prepare all executive officers to communicate a cohesive strategy and ensure the right message hit the right target audience.

Step 4 **SHAREHOLDER DIVERSIFICATION & EXPANSION PROGRAM**

Actions Developed a 2-phase diversification and expansion program to alleviate downward pricing caused by an investor shift favoring high-tech, blue chip and S&P 500 stocks.

Phase ① ***Capture non-REIT-dedicated institutional investors.*** Retained a consulting firm to match our characteristics to those of our investment peers.

Phase ② Marketed to stock brokers and investment groups to appeal to a broader retail investor.

Result 1 Institutional investor holdings **increased 220%.** Sell-side analyst coverage **increased 120%.**
Result 2 Contributed to 3 successful add-on stock offerings totaling **$446 million.**
Result 3 17 new institutional investors and 12 of the top 20 institutions added us to their positions.
Result 4 Eliminated Wall Street confusion on our approach which gained a stock price premium.

Pg. 2 ⇨

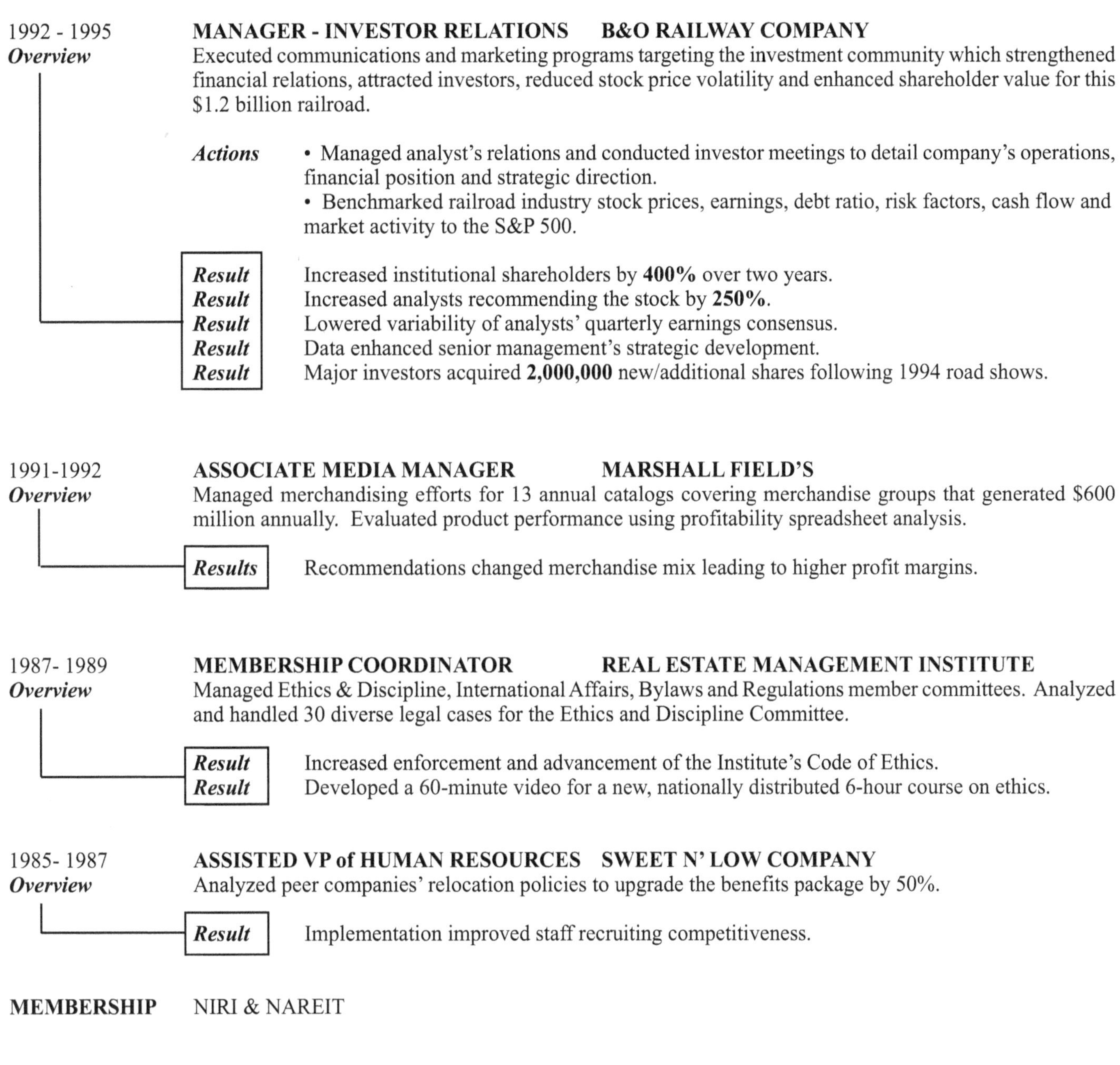

1992 - 1995 **MANAGER - INVESTOR RELATIONS B&O RAILWAY COMPANY**

Overview Executed communications and marketing programs targeting the investment community which strengthened financial relations, attracted investors, reduced stock price volatility and enhanced shareholder value for this $1.2 billion railroad.

Actions
- Managed analyst's relations and conducted investor meetings to detail company's operations, financial position and strategic direction.
- Benchmarked railroad industry stock prices, earnings, debt ratio, risk factors, cash flow and market activity to the S&P 500.

Result Increased institutional shareholders by **400%** over two years.
Result Increased analysts recommending the stock by **250%**.
Result Lowered variability of analysts' quarterly earnings consensus.
Result Data enhanced senior management's strategic development.
Result Major investors acquired **2,000,000** new/additional shares following 1994 road shows.

1991-1992 **ASSOCIATE MEDIA MANAGER MARSHALL FIELD'S**

Overview Managed merchandising efforts for 13 annual catalogs covering merchandise groups that generated $600 million annually. Evaluated product performance using profitability spreadsheet analysis.

Results Recommendations changed merchandise mix leading to higher profit margins.

1987- 1989 **MEMBERSHIP COORDINATOR REAL ESTATE MANAGEMENT INSTITUTE**

Overview Managed Ethics & Discipline, International Affairs, Bylaws and Regulations member committees. Analyzed and handled 30 diverse legal cases for the Ethics and Discipline Committee.

Result Increased enforcement and advancement of the Institute's Code of Ethics.
Result Developed a 60-minute video for a new, nationally distributed 6-hour course on ethics.

1985- 1987 **ASSISTED VP of HUMAN RESOURCES SWEET N' LOW COMPANY**

Overview Analyzed peer companies' relocation policies to upgrade the benefits package by 50%.

Result Implementation improved staff recruiting competitiveness.

MEMBERSHIP NIRI & NAREIT

EDUCATION Kellogg Graduate School of Management, Northwestern University 1991
M.M. (MBA), Marketing, Organizational Behavior and Management Strategy

University of Wyoming, B.A. in Journalism/Public Relations 1984

Internships Nevada Legislature - Assisted Senator Feinstein, Chair of the Ways & Means Committee.
News Reporter -KRWN TV, Las Vegas, Nevada

CHAPTER 4

ENGINEERING & SCIENTIFIC CAREERS

The Engineering & Scientific Categories Include

4 Client Examples

15 Job Titles

62 Years of Work History

NAME	JOB TITLES COVERED
1. JOSHUA SMITH*	......Senior Mechanical Project Engineer .....Supervisor, Information Management ....Project Engineer Thermal & Hydraulic Program Engineer
2. JOHN REEVES	...........................Senior Design Engineer ....Manager Manufacturing & Products ....Senior Design Engineer ....Design Engieer ....Electrical Engineer
3.SAMANTHA RAMSEY	...................................Research Scientist ....Technologist ....Ajunct Faculty
4. JASON CHANDLER	......................................Design Engineer ....Research Assistant ....Engineer

* Find the "before resume" in chapter 35

JOSHUA SMITH
Registered Professional Engineer

421 Roberts Rd., San Francisco, CA 94105
415-328-7979 • Jsmith@sbcglobal.net

OBJECTIVE Engineering career in the area of mechanical, electrical or instrumentation and controls.

SUMMARY Lead teams, direct subcontractors and ensure that my project involvement is totally acceptable to the client. I create plans to account for contingencies, execute actions quickly and oversee activities to meet cost, quality and deadline objectives.

STRENGTHS

- Project Management
- Process Reengineering
- Team Leadership
- Strategy Execution
- Process System Design
- Technology Management
- Client Support
- R & D

EXPERIENCE

1981 - 2003 **BECHTEL CORPORATION** ***Senior Mechanical Project Engineer*** San Francisco, CA

Overview I supported Bechtel efforts to remain a global Top 3 management consulting and engineering design services leader for new and operating fossil-fuel and nuclear power plants and power delivery systems.

Mandate Work profitably, with a high degree of quality. Guarantee that specifications were adhered to on projects budgets of $2 million to $1 billion each.

Contribution 1 **RECOVER A BEHIND SCHEDULE PROJECT**

Need: Took over mechanical engineering efforts on a severely behind schedule $300 million project (Redhawk 1080 MWe Merchant Plant) where CPI was .68 at my appointment.

Challenge I was not given new manpower, yet was expected to bring project in on time.

Solution Reassigned project workload and coached 7 mechanical engineers to move beyond engineering analysis into actual physical design.

Result: Within four months the project was on schedule with a CPI of 1.05

Result: Protected Bechtel from **$500,000** in additional engineering manpower.

Contribution 2 **MEETING NRC FEDERAL REGULATORY REQUIREMENTS**

Need: To prove that ComEd had control of the design basis on 12 nuclear power plants.

Challenge Create an acceptable Design Basis Documentation Program.

Solution Developed a 5-year program that met all NRC requirements.

Result: Delivered **over $5,000,000** in billable work hours.

Contribution 3 **NEW PRODUCT DEVELOPED**

Need: To diversify Bechtel's business offerings by helping customers use computer technology to improve productivity of design engineering.

Challenge Took in-house expertise in CAD technology and created a saleable product.

Solution Conceived and sold an interactive 3D-CAD system to ComEd.

Result: Generated **$1,000,000** in new revenues, year-1 and over **$1,000,000** more by program end.

Contribution 4 **WINNING $35,000,000 PROJECT - CONSUMERS ENERGY**

Need: Supported the RFP effort to make Bechtel the contractor of choice to decommission and dismantle Big Rock Point Nuclear Power Plant.

Challenge Creating an economical solution to remove a highly radioactive, 120 ton reactor pressure vessel.

Solution I engineered an upgrade to the existing crane, the one used originally to install the vessel, rather than rent a new larger, more costly crane.

Result: We became the low price vendor of 5 RFPs submitted, which won the bid.

Contribution 5 **REDESIGNING VENDOR'S SYSTEM TO MEET PROJECT SPECIFICATIONS**

Need 1 Discovered late in the project that operating temperature on one of four coal units was trending higher than allowable maximum temperature for the system fans.

Challenge Avoid costly schedule delays to upgrade new fans to handle higher temperatures.

Solution I calculated how much pipe insulation should not be installed to reduce temperature sufficiently on hot days, but not too much on cold winter days.

Result Saved over **$100,000** plus incalculable schedule delay costs.

Need 2 Discovered a supplier's error who improperly sized the cooling tower.

Challenge To ensure that all systems and equipment would meet the performance guarantee on net electric output and heat rate (i.e. 6342 BTU per KWe)

Solution Proved to the vendor that our calculations warranted redesign of their system.

Result Enabled Bechtel to meet performance guarantees on plant output and avoid a **$2,400,000** penalty.

1992-1994 **Supervisor, Information Management Section - Computer Services Division**

Helped project and administrative staff better use computer resources and provided a dedicated staff (18 persons) for client projects requiring information management expertise.

Project Conceived idea and managed installation of a WAN TCP/IP and Novell link with a major client.

Project Managed implementation of an internet connection with SMTP and X400 electronic mail.

Project Participated in data base migration strategies for major client and employer.

Project Engineer - Control & Instrumentation Division

Directed 5 engineers and 2 technicians in control and instrumentation systems design and specifications. Wrote equipment specifications for service water, radiation monitoring, and emergency core cooling systems.

Previous Experience

GENERAL ELECTRIC CO. Pittsburgh, PA

Overview Bettis Atomic Power Laboratory **Thermal & Hydraulic Programs Engineer**

Conducted hydraulic and thermal test research for reactor cores for the Navy's Trident Submarine. Designed an upgrade for all instrumentation systems (neutron monitoring and primary plant controls and instrumentation) for a submarine-prototype nuclear power plant.

Contribution 6 **IMPROVED LAUNCH OF THE TRIDENT SUBMARINE**

Need Identified and solved an early stage design problem on the Trident submarine thermal core, which if it remained undiscovered would have cost hundreds of millions in wasted production.

Challenge Developing tests to prove the extent, root cause and significance of the problem.

Solution Presented findings to the Head of Experimental Engineering which won his support.

Result Changed all data gathering methods to protect project schedule and budget.

EDUCATION BSEE, University of California Berkeley, Berkeley, California (Dean's List)
BA, Monmouth College, Monmouth, Illinois (physics major)

MEMBERSHIP Registered Professional Engineer (PE) in Arizona, California, Illinois, North Carolina and Pennsylvania

JOHN REEVES

7156 Valleyview Rd., Burbak, CA 90230 310.585.4598 • jrevve@aol.com

SUMMARY

Manufacturing, engineering and project management expertise focuses on problem solving, communications and team support to attain goals. I manage operations by promoting accountability, developing standards and delegating duties as appropriate. Overall, my efforts center on balancing human and capital resources to achieve efficiencies and reduce costs.

2000 - present **MACLEAN POWER SYSTEMS - MPS** • ***Senior Design Eng.*** [Div. of MacLean-Fogg Co.]
Engineering support for a manufacturer of power transmission suspension and post insulators.

Project 1

New Product Launch – took over development of "**Stacked Sheds**", a product expected to increase global market-share from 15% to 20% and grow revenues 22% (from $45M to $55M).

Focus Electromagnetic stresses caused by "water droplet corona" could drop high-voltage power lines resulting in huge economic consequences.

Actions Used **SOLIDWORKS** to design different transmission scenarios (tower, insulator, cable, and hardware) and used **COULOMB,** electric field modeling software, to determine where critical field density occurred.

Results The new product gives MPS a competitive advantage in the marketplace since our key competitors have yet to respond with a design solution for the problem.

Project 2

Re-engineering a Product Configurator to make finished drawings from generic part drawings.

Focus Our customers use unique engineering specifications that our configurator could not handle, forcing MPS to make many of the customer drawings, process sheets and BOMs by hand.

Actions Reprogrammed, in COBOL, a large portion of the product configurator and wrote the structure for changes in an Excel/Visual Basic program I created and ported to COBOL.

Results The enhanced configurator increased design capability from 4,500 designs to 120 million designs, reduced engineering techs to .25 staff from 2-3. Our product configurator automatically produces customer drawings, process sheets, and bill of materials.

Project 3

Research & Development - ACSS Cable w/ High Temperature Clamp Testing.

Focus MPS did not have a suspension clamp on the market proven to withstand 250°C continuous. Our chief competitor had a new product design to meet this condition.

Actions Designed and conducted the testing of our clamps for qualification at 250°C .

Results Determined what clamps we could market and helped maintain a key customer who was concerned over this problem.

Project 4

Integration of a New Business Acquisition

Focus MPS bought a competitor, Sediver, and became the world's largest seller of polymer insulators.

Actions I learned their product design and manufacturing processes, moved the design engineering from their York, SC plant to our Franklin Park, IL facility, modified our procedures to include their designs and trained a new technician to manage it all.

Results Engineering staff at the other plant were eliminated and I assumed responsibility for Sediver, as well as MPS' designs. My efforts also cut time to create new designs by 50%.

Project 5

ISO 9001 Certification - Chosen for an interdepartmental team to write MPS' new design procedure.

Focus MPS was only ISO 9002 certified and desired the more esteemed ISO 9001 certification.

Actions I co-authored the new design procedure and was it's principle trainer for 300 personnel.

Results MPS received ISO 9001 certification.

1994 - 2000 **JARRED MANUFACTURING** • ***Manager of – Manufacturing & Product Engineering*** • ***Senior Design Engineer*** • ***Design Engineer***

Managed 9 direct and indirect reports who supported design and manufacturing for 3 product groups in the electrical apparatus division, a business unit that produces $25M a year (25% of all revenues).

Project 6 ***Line Extension - ZSP Surge Arrester***

Focus A competitive strategy to extend products to an untapped portion of our market segment.

Actions Designed and tested to ANSI/IEEE standards and teamed with manufacturing engineering to develop production machinery for product rollout.

Results Added 12 new SKU's which increased net revenues for this product by 30%.

Project 7 ***Process Automation-Bill of Materials***

Focus The old system was manual and demanded 340 hours a year of an engineer's time.

Actions Completely redesigned and automated Jarred's process for generating Bill of Materials.

Results Reduced engineer's time commitment by 85% which saved $50,000 annually.

Project 8 ***Product Introduction of* ZForce**

Focus ZForce was Jarred's single most important new product development and was expected to grow market share from 30% (FY '97) to 50% by FY '02.

Actions Created all bills, routings and assembly drawings for the product launch.

Results By 2000 this product generated $13.5 million and has grown market share by 10%.

Project 9 ***Strategic Alliance***

Focus Selected by the President to salvage our partnership with an Italian manufacturer after our product failed at the independent test lab and jeopardized our contract with Passoni & Villa.

Results Corrected a problem with Passoni & Villa's prorated design and helped modify the future design of their product to achieve certification, thereby saving the partnership.

1990 - 1993 **CALIFORNIA POWER COMPANY** • ***Electrical Engineer***

Member of the Instrumentation Engineering Team responsible for designing metering for high-end industrial customers such as Texaco, Archer Daniels Midland (ADM) and Solo Cup.

• ***Recognition***: Received customer service awards for my 2 largest projects.

Project 10 ***Cost Cutting***

Focus Existing meter readers cost IPC $1.2 million a year due to meter estimation inaccuracy.

Actions Part of a team that changed IPC from proprietary meter readers to a PC environment.

Results My suggestions conservatively saved $300,000 annually.

EDUCATION

1990 B.S.E.E., **UCLA**, Los Angeles, CA GPA 4.8 of 5.0

Honors Henneman Scholar (Power and Energy Award)

Research Assistant Department of Electrical Engineering in the field of Power and Energy Systems.

SAMANTHA RAMSEY

3117 Plimpton Dr., Rancho Cucamonga, CA 91729 • 909-334-1079 • samram@yahoo.com

OBJECTIVE — **RESEARCH SCIENTIST**: where I can bring new products to market or enhance existing products.

STRENGTHS

- Report Writing
- QA/QC Standards
- Process Management
- Product Launches
- Team Support
- Project Development

EXPERIENCE

9/98-present — **UNISOURCE SCREENING & INFORMATION INC.**, Cucamonga, CA

9/99 - present **Research Scientist, R&D Group**
9/98-9/99 **Technologist**

Overview.............. Started as a production technologist testing specimens for drug abuse. Within a year, I was promoted to Research Scientist in the newly created R&D group.

My Goal Help Unisource become the US market leader of noninvasive drug testing by integrating our GC/MS capabilities for rapid drug testing programs and adding a hair drug-testing product line to our oral-screening line.

My Value Improved 3 key products, a pair of drug tests, Oral•Screen and Hair•Screen, and MecStat-EtOH, an infant test we conduct for Pediatric MD's to identify fetal alcohol exposure. These products account for 65% of total company revenues.

Challenge Unisource's initial product was manufactured at a detection level commercially unusable (initially we were at of 5000 ng/ml, where commercial detection needs to be 5 ng/ml in accordance with NIDA, National Institute of Drug Abuse standards).

Solution Screened numerous antibodies and antigens by EIA. I conjugated 3 antibodies to gold to identify which one worked well with the chosen antigen in the final test.

Result Within 10 months I improved the level of detection 100 fold from 5000 to 50 ng/ml. Currently, I am testing 3 new antibodies that can better conjugate to gold while also testing a brand new technology defined as conjugating antibodies to magnetic particles.

R&D Duties

- Develop solid phase extraction methods for oral fluid
- Specimen extraction for analysis
- Analyze samples by GC/MS for drugs of abuse
- Set up and run EIA
- Conduct experiments for FDA 510K submission
- Conduct clinical trials for rapid flow immunoassay
- Analyze data and write upper management reports and laboratory documentation

Project Change off-site manufacturing to in-house: Between 5/01-7/01, I helped the manufacturing department replicate the process to make Oral•Screen.

Results Costs were reduced by 33% (saving $500,000+ a year)
Production was increased 750% (from 8,000 units per month to 60,000)
Efficacy of the test was increased 100 fold

1/02-5/02 — **ADJUNCT FACULTY -Biology** — **SAN JOAQUIN VALLEY COLLEGE**, Cucamonga, CA

10/98-1/02 — **TUTOR** — **TUTORING ASSOCIATES**, Cucamonga, CA
Tutored high school students in biology, chemistry, and mathematics.

LAB SKILLS — Animal testing and maintenance, gold conjugation, GC/MS and rapid test development.

EDUCATION

University of California Irvine	Forensics Certificate	6/02
University of California Irvine	M.S. Biology	3/99
University of California Irvine	B.S. Biology	5/96

Language: Fluent Greek

JASON CHANDLER ——— 1623 Trenton Way, Chicago, IL 60611, 312-726-0569, jchand@att.net

OBJECTIVE Engineering position where my experience and formal academic training will be fully utilized.

SUMMARY Design, specification, verification, and debug of ASICs/FPGAs/PCBs for high performance products using state of the art silicon technologies and EDA tools.

EXPERIENCE

1/97-10/03 **NORTEL NETWORKS - DESIGN ENGINEER - IC Hardware Development** Chicago, IL

Member of Technical Staff-Intellectual Property System on a Chip (SOC) 2001 - Present

Overview Part of a team of 8 design engineers tasked with using IBM's PowerPC 405 on a CoreConnect bus architecture to shrink technology and collapse 7 FPGAs and an embedded microprocessor core onto a single device.

Actions Designed/simulated/synthesized master/slave blocks for the Processor Local Bus (PLB) and the On-Chip Peripheral Bus (OPB).

Result Nortel's first complete design of multiple FPGAs on a single IC chip with an embedded microprocessor core.

Result The new SOC/FPGA design decreases circuit size 50% and is projected to save $30-$35MM on manufacturing costs annually since it is central to numerous telecom applications in development.

Member of Technical Staff-Device Maintenance/IC Hardware Development 2001 - Present

Overview Inherited a Packet Switching Unit FPGA design (PSU) from a retiring engineer 5-months before drop dead date with 40% of the design remaining. The goal was to design a device on the Protocol Handler of the PSU for wireless applications using a Xilinx Virtex IIe FPGA package.

Actions Simulations in register transfer level (RTL) and timing.
Synthesizing of the device and place and route

Result Delivered a fully functioning system with new functionality to Lucent's System Lab on deadline.

Result Doubled channel capacity from 64 to 128 channels, 400% increase from original design.

Member of Technical Staff-Intellectual Property/Reuse Methodology 1999- 2002

Overview Nortel's first Reuse Methodology application team. We designed a Packet Bus Multi-Access device using in-house PCI Core, Packet Bus Interface and Direct Memory Access Controller (DMAC) that was reused in other designs.

Actions Assisted in design and simulation of the PCI Core.
Performed gate simulations, synthesizing the device and using FPGA place and route tools.

Results The new PCI core has been used 5 times and the DMAC twice within 2 years.

Results Created Nortel's first-ever Reuse Library with web site (currently has 100 IP core elements).

Member of Technical Staff-Network Clock Control Circuit Pack Verification Testing 1999 - 2001

Overview Supported the circuit pack designer with lab testing prior to initial delivery of the next generation communication module to the field.

Actions Wrote C based verification tests of the circuit pack using the Multi-ITS test system.
Updated firmware loads on all circuit packs.
Supported the environmental chamber and compliance lab tests.
Replaced flash devices on packs so that the memory would be segment protected.

Result All packs were delivered on time to system lab and the field office with full software transparency.

Nortel Networkss Experience Cont'd...

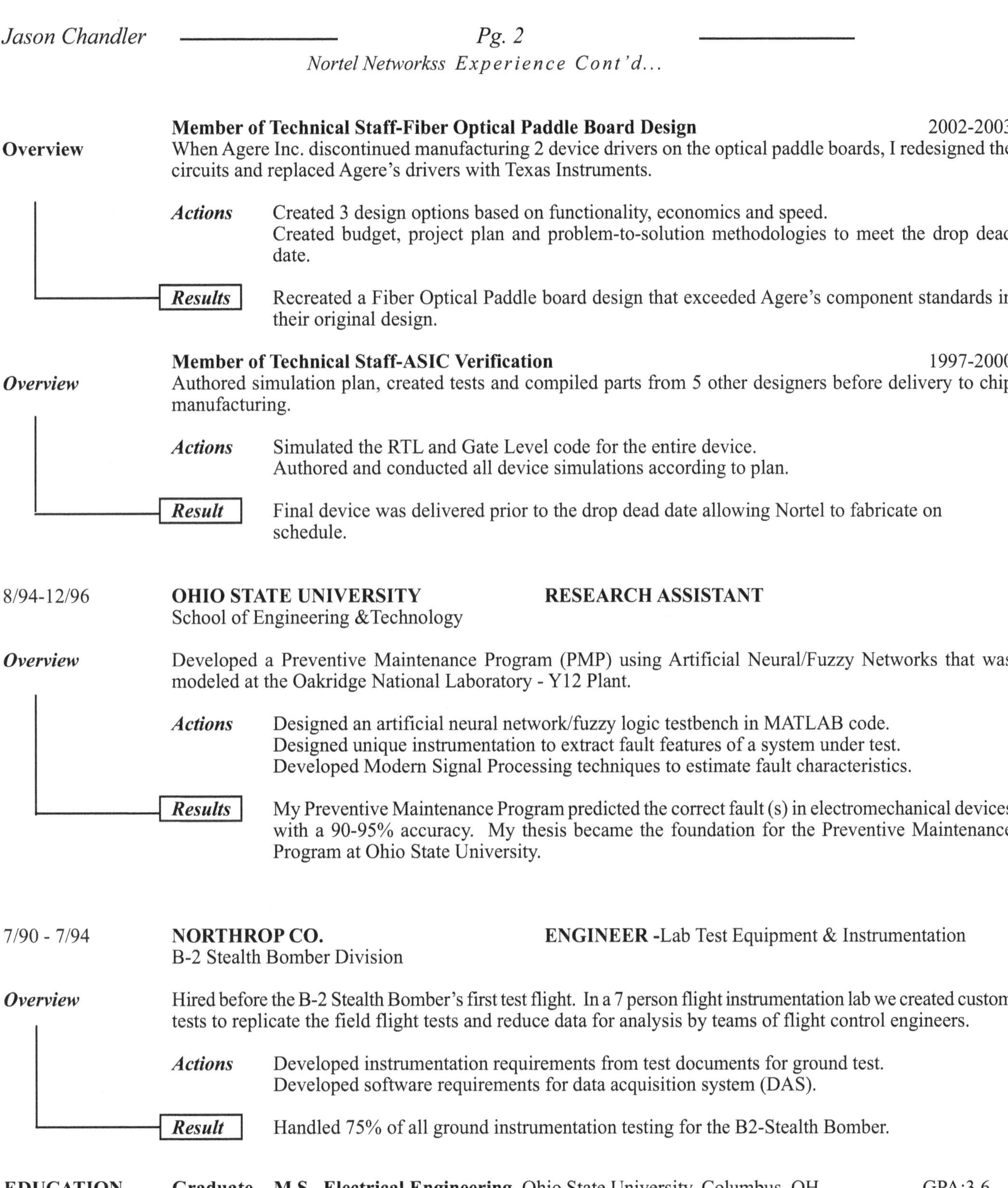

Member of Technical Staff-Fiber Optical Paddle Board Design 2002-2003

Overview When Agere Inc. discontinued manufacturing 2 device drivers on the optical paddle boards, I redesigned the circuits and replaced Agere's drivers with Texas Instruments.

Actions Created 3 design options based on functionality, economics and speed.
Created budget, project plan and problem-to-solution methodologies to meet the drop dead date.

Results Recreated a Fiber Optical Paddle board design that exceeded Agere's component standards in their original design.

Member of Technical Staff-ASIC Verification 1997-2000

Overview Authored simulation plan, created tests and compiled parts from 5 other designers before delivery to chip manufacturing.

Actions Simulated the RTL and Gate Level code for the entire device.
Authored and conducted all device simulations according to plan.

Result Final device was delivered prior to the drop dead date allowing Nortel to fabricate on schedule.

8/94-12/96 **OHIO STATE UNIVERSITY** **RESEARCH ASSISTANT**
School of Engineering &Technology

Overview Developed a Preventive Maintenance Program (PMP) using Artificial Neural/Fuzzy Networks that was modeled at the Oakridge National Laboratory - Y12 Plant.

Actions Designed an artificial neural network/fuzzy logic testbench in MATLAB code.
Designed unique instrumentation to extract fault features of a system under test.
Developed Modern Signal Processing techniques to estimate fault characteristics.

Results My Preventive Maintenance Program predicted the correct fault (s) in electromechanical devices with a 90-95% accuracy. My thesis became the foundation for the Preventive Maintenance Program at Ohio State University.

7/90 - 7/94 **NORTHROP CO.** **ENGINEER** -Lab Test Equipment & Instrumentation
B-2 Stealth Bomber Division

Overview Hired before the B-2 Stealth Bomber's first test flight. In a 7 person flight instrumentation lab we created custom tests to replicate the field flight tests and reduce data for analysis by teams of flight control engineers.

Actions Developed instrumentation requirements from test documents for ground test.
Developed software requirements for data acquisition system (DAS).

Result Handled 75% of all ground instrumentation testing for the B2-Stealth Bomber.

EDUCATION **Graduate** 1996 **M.S., Electrical Engineering**, Ohio State University, Columbus, OH GPA:3.6
- Concentration: Communication and Signal Processing Systems
- Fellowship: Oakridge National Laboratory

UNDERGRAD **B.S., Electrical Engineering**, Ohio State University, Columbus, OH
1990
- AT&T and Lockheed Scholarships
- Most Outstanding Senior, School of Engineering

TECHNICAL
- Exemplar's Leonardo Spectrum
- Mentor Graphics High Speed Electrical Design using IS
- Xilinx Advanced FPGA Implementation
- Mentor Graphics Signal Integrity & High Speed Methodology
- Altera's Quartus II Software
- Xllinx Embedded Systems Development
- 'C' / VHDL / Verilog HDL
- Matlab Tools

CHAPTER 5
FINANCE, BANKING & ACCOUNTING CAREERS

The Finance, Banking & Accounting Category Has

5 Client Examples
22 Job Titles
111 Years of Work History

NAME	JOB TITLES COVERED
1. PETER WATERS	..............................Director of Finance
2. LAURA STERN	....Accountant
3. SANDRA JOHNSON	.................................Finance Manager ....Business Development Manager ....Customer Account Manager ....Customer Account Supervisor ....Credit Analyst-Sr. Asset Recovery ....Team Leader ....Customer Account Representative ....Customer Service Representative
4. RICHARD WALKER	.......Assictant V.P. Relationship Manager ....Corporate Bank Officer ....Credit Analyst ....Management Training ....Manager /Owner
5. AARON SCHULER*	.......Managing Director-Private Banking ....Managing Director ....Vice President ....Senior Vice President ....Managing Director ....Vice President ....Assistant Vice President

* Find the "before resume" in chapter 35

PETER WATERS

832 Jenner Dr.., New York, NY 10001 • pwater@earthlink.net • 212-735-8558

OBJECTIVE Increased responsibilities and new challenges in audit and accounting, the opportunity to exercise financial management vision within the professional environment of a consulting/legal firm.

SUMMARY 10+ years of solving strategic problems and creating action plans to improve efficiencies in the areas of finance, accounting, and internal audit. I create programs that give measurable results which surpass corporate objectives.

FINANCE & ACCOUNTING EXPERIENCE

9/98 -present **Director of Finance** **S&S Public Relations, Inc.** **New York, NY**

Overview I essentially act as CFO reporting to four co-CEO's who hired me to implement strategies for this privately held PR agency. My mandate was to modernize the accounting, billing and financial management systems. ***Challenges:*** due to the joint ownership by 4 partners with limited financial and systems management experience, the company needed new computerization and operating standards to enhance revenues, staff efficiency and profitability.

STRATEGIES

Boost Revenues	***Goal 1***	Recaptured 3%-5% of the staff's work-hours. Client billings had been left unreported due to an inefficient reporting system which cost PCI $312,560-$523,900 a year.
Financial Controls	***Goal 2***	Customized billing to improve the Time & Billing reports in order to prove that S&S over-services the clients. Partners can now leverage negotiations on future contracts. Custom billing improves client trust, reduces disputes and promotes long-term associations rather than "one-time" projects.
Performance Tracking	***Goal 3***	Simplified work-tracking standards to improve staff reporting to management. This recaptured more billings by each employee and identified underperforming staff.
Effective Staffing	***Goal 4***	Helped this 40 year old company with 21 staff in 1985, grow to a peak of 43 employees, while average revenue per employee grew 43%.
Human Resources	***Goal 5***	Purchased a more cost effective corporate health insurance plan. Managed the profit sharing accounts, which included loans and pay-outs. Conducted company-wide benefits interviews for new and departing employees. Established training and cross-training programs.
Broadening Client Mix	***Goal 6***	Originally S&S operated as a small PR agency with poorly integrated billing standards and poor reporting to customers which were 65% local. My systems helped attract a large national and multinational customer base where 67% of our clients are national corporations.
Streamlining	***Goal 7***	Simplified the line-item billing reports to help speed the supervisor review process and improve accuracy of the final client bills (12 supervisors review 36,000 custom AP/AR bills a year).
	Results	Helped S&S grow 310%. It now serves 220 large corporations, associations, non-profits and Fortune 500 customers including large pharmaceutical and medical companies.

EDUCATION	B.A., Literature, with Honors	University of Connecticut
CONTINUING EDUCATION	Auditing, Accounting Theory I/II	Central Connecticut State University
	Financial Accounting	Albertus Magnus College
	Cost Accounting	Western Connecticut State University

LAURA STERN

812 Westwood Ave, Medford, MA 02155, 781/530-4242 • lstern2@aol.com

OBJECTIVE

Accounting management career where my skills will provide management continuity, leadership direction and accountability.

SUMMARY

I impact corporate operating and financial objectives by analyzing our strengths, accurately projecting expectations based on these strengths and indicating areas for improvement to capture efficiencies. The organizations I've assisted developed my ability to diplomatically resolve disputes, improve effectiveness and accountability standards across broad categories. Overall, I set direction, then create step-wise action plans with tracking mechanisms to ensure results are achieved.

STRENGTHS

Management	• Problem Solving • Organization • Strategic Planning	• Enhancing Operational Infrastructure • Staff Coaching • Management Collaboration	• Project Leadership • Managing Change • Leadership Vision
Accounting	• Payroll • Auditing • Cost Justification	• Planning & Forecasting Budgets • Financial Statement Analysis • Financial Reporting	• Month-end Closings • General Ledger (GL) • Applying Technology

ACCOUNTING EXPERIENCE

2/98 - Present **Accountant** **GENERAL INSULATION COMPANY INC.**

***Overview*...............** Organizationally, I report directly to the CEO and an outside auditor. Prepare monthly financial statements, handle A/P and journal entries as well as provide monthly GL analysis.

MY VALUE & IMPACT These 6 areas conservatively saved or earned my company over $265,000.

Revenue Consulted with the CEO on improving billings and collection controls as well as revamping the billing policy, especially the 10% retention hold (retentions are balances due at final project walk through), in total we had over $200,000 outstanding (between 2-4 years old).

Result Quickly captured $100,000 on the outstanding retention hold and our system now attains a quicker cash turnaround, with potential savings of $40,000 in write-offs per year.

Insurance Reviewed the last workers comp. insurance audit from our insurer and discovered they were calculating our audited additional premium with incorrect classifications and rates.

Result Gained a credit of $2,300 instead of $10,500 additional due (a turn-around of $12,800).

Union The workers union sent a notice that payments for health & welfare benefits were short. I researched records and substantiated our figures were correct and defended the company before the union.

Result Recovered $13,000.

Taxes Created audit procedures to optimize the recovery of tax exemptions for job materials used on tax exempt projects. This addresses 80% of all projects annually and involves over 40 vendors.

Result Eliminated a $50,000 potential loss.

Systems Implemented a new accounting system in 1999, Computereaze (construction centric), and oversaw the parallel operation of the legacy system for 6 months to ensure smooth integration.

Result Saved $36,000 off the project budget by personally managing the program. System also reduces the GL end-of-month reporting cycle for both companies by 50%.

Inventory Implemented a reporting process and audit trail between shop and inventory staff and my office to account for all inventories.

Result Reduced shrinkage by 90%, saving over $22,000 a year.

EDUCATION 4/98 B.S., Accounting, College of Business and Public Administration, Adelphi University

TECHNICAL Lotus, Excel, Dbase, Foxpro, Word and Computer Ease

SANDRA JOHNSON

631 Sandpiper Ln., Woodcliff Lake, NJ 07642, 201-326-5500
sj2000@bmwcredit.com

OBJECTIVE To continually add value to the company's profitability, staff productivity, and operating efficiency goals.

EXPERIENCE

8/92 – Present

BMW FINANCIAL SERVICES Woodcliff Lake, NJ

Financial Manager - Credit Services	11/03-Present
Business Development Manager - Management Cross-Training Program	11/02-11/03
Customer Accounts Manager - Collections & Recovery	11/00-11/02
Customer Accounts Supervisor - Collections & Recovery	1/97-11/00
Credit Analyst - Sr. Asset Recovery - Sr. Customer Accounts Representative	8/92-1/97

Overview Led 2 of the 3 core areas of Credit & Financial Services as the portfolio grew from $8-$14 billion. Contributed to profitability, servicing the customer base, and mentoring 80 subordinates. Personally noted by Gallup's Manager Survey as ranking in Top 10% of all BMW corporate managers.

Financial Manager Lead 3 teams and 54 staff during the fastest expansion of AR in BFS's history.

Leadership Style Set forth clear and measurable expectations. Created individual performance standards and outlined expectations from staff, vendors and management.

Concurrently manage three business operations -

Financial Care Accounts Receivable operations with 530,000 loans.
Title & Registration Processing dealer and customer checks ($116MM month).
Document Imaging Digitally scan 33,000 documents per month.

- ***Impact 1*** Profiled all of BMW's 1,100 US dealers to identify fraudulent performers and uncovered 2% needing rehabilitation. At the risk of personal reputation, I exercised a contract recourse option for the first time in BMW's history to force dealers to payoff bad loans (**and recovered $1MM**).
  Results Reduced AR delinquency to industry's lowest level (.97%) from a historical rate of 2.5%. This saved **$14.7MM** in FY 03 and **$30.7MM** since FY01.

- ***Impact 2*** Audited our Title Service Vendor which led to shifting 50% of the business to a competitor. This pushed the original title agency to reduce their delivery schedule 75% (from 20 to 5 days).
  Result Saved **$525K** on unwarranted depreciation costs due to slow title distribution.

- ***Impact 3*** Wrote a business case approved by management to charge customers with title services fees.
  Result Earned **$733K** in fees between '03-'04.

- ***Impact 4*** Reorganized Financial Care & Title departments after visiting Bently, Mercedes, Audi and VW's Credit groups to benchmark their best practices and implement them into BFS.
  Result Saved **$486,000** in payroll by reducing headcount 50% even as checks processed doubled.

– Total Value – Delivered **$33,444,000** in cost savings, efficiencies, reduced waste and optimized performance since 2001.

Customer Accounts Section Leader – Managed 84 staff - 6 supervisors, 3 team leaders and 75 analysts. Oversaw legal reviews and complaints. Tracked insurance and coordinated with I.T. and Risk Management. Reduced turnover in the department from 23% to 7% by mentoring and guidance.

- ***Results*** Improved First Payment Default and Fraud handling processes which increased profitability. Ranked among Top 10% Best Performing Managers, Gallup results for 2000.

Customer Accounts Unit Leader – Managed 12 analysts, resolved customer disputes and approved customer payoffs. Evaluated work performance, coached employees and hired new staff.

- ***Results*** Maintained low delinquency rate and reduced losses.
  Led team to win 75% of all department performance contests out of 6 teams.

Credit Analyst (8/94-1/97)

Actions
- Analyzed credit applications and provided an assessment of applicant's credit risk.
- Effectively delivered the individual credit decisions to the dealership personnel.
- Demonstrated willingness to listen to dealers' opposing viewpoints with an even disposition.
- Responded to all dealership inquiries in a timely and consistent manner.
- Traveled to designated dealerships on a regular basis.

Result Evaluated 125 applications daily and approved 50% or $1.87 million in loans.

Senior Asset Recovery Representative (4/94-8/94)

Actions
- Resolved repossession accounts and processed deficiency balances.
- Reviewed in-house charge-off accounts.
- Assigned accounts to outside collection agencies.

Senior Customer Accounts Representative (8/92-4/4)

Actions
- Effectively trained employees for collection department.
- Approved retail extension agreements and lease deferrals to assist customers.
- Followed up on pending repossession assignments.
- Approved default notices to be sent to customers.
- Skip-traced accounts to locate customers.

5/85 – 8/92 **SEARS CREDIT SERVICE CENTER** ***Team Leader*** Hampton, NJ

Customer Account Representative

Customer Service Representative

Overview Managed one of four East coast teams in collections where the operation included Auto-Dialers in Customer Accounts, Skiptracing and staff training.

Result Led team to collect an average of $300,000,000 in annual receipts.

EDUCATION

MBA	Monmouth University	**2003**	
	International Program	**2002**	Oxford University, UK Student consultant for Druck, a subsidiary of GE
B.S. Business	Monmouth University	**2001**	
B.S. Accounting	Monmouth University	**1983**	

References available on request.

RICHARD WALKER

428 Lakeview Ave., Chicago, IL 60610 ✆ *312-726-5300*

OBJECTIVE

Financial career using analytical, strategic planning and financial markets expertise.

SUMMARY

Financial skills include evaluating investment strategies to identify opportunities and structuring loans that ensure ROI. Analytical skills drive actions to meet profit targets. Aggressively and creatively identify key challenges to my corporate clients then choose strategies to solve these problems and grow their revenues while at the same time helping my bank design deals that are structured to minimize risk.

EXPERIENCE

1992 - present

BANK ONE Chicago, IL

Assistant V.P. Relationship Manager - Agribusiness Group ***1997-present***

Overview Manage a **$300+ MM** portfolio of leveraged and investment grade relations as the administrative agent for these syndicated transactions. Agribusiness is the fastest growing group and represents **30%** of divisional earnings.

I've analyzed financials and assessed risk profiles of 65 clients representing ***$1.75 billion*** in commitments. Participated on 15 major transactions (***$75MM to $750MM***) underwrite mergers, acquisition financing, and recapitalizations.

Corporate Bank Officer ***1994-1997***

Overview Handled covenant structuring, pricing, credit analysis and negotiations to help senior managers underwrite transactions. Efforts included analytical support during each transaction.

Credit Analyst ***1993-1994***

Overview Monitored performance of industry groups within portfolio. Created economic models to analyze supply and demand implications. Developed sensitivity scenarios using probability distribution of historical variables.

Management Training ***1992-1993***

Training covered

- Secured Lending, Term Lending and Corporate Lending
- Financial Forecasting • Credit-Structuring • Cash Flow Analysis

DEAL EXAMPLES

Dean Foods - Divestiture of Bird's Eye & Veg - All to Agrilink Foods 8/98

Focus Bank One underwrote ***$750MM*** and completed the deal in 10 days. My role involved financial analysis of cash flow, balance sheet, and P/L to structure senior and bridge loan facilities.

Results Bank One's most profitable transaction to date and largestr underwriting of subordinate debt.

Mid America Dairymen's Acquisition of the Borden/Medow Gold Dairies 5/97

Focus Bank One underwrote ***$650MM***. I created a sophisticated financial model reflecting the combined operation and worked to formulate a capital structure with acceptable leverage targets and adequate liquidity to support seasonal capital fluctuations.

Results This represented Bank One's largest underwriting to date.

Rosen's Diversified Inc.'s Purchase of Skylark Meats 1/97

Focus Arranged a **$75MM** senior facility to fully finance the acquisition and recapitalize the company on a more attractive structure than other capital sources.

Results Rosen's now represents a Top 10 client relation within the group on an annuity basis.

1985- 1992

Manager/Owner **WALKER FARMS** Monroe, WI

Managed purebred cattle operation along with a corn and soybean farm. Analyzed herd efficiency ranked against national average then implemented breeding programs to improve yield. Managed all marketing and financial operations.

EDUCATION

BA, *Agriculture & Economics*, **UNIVERSITY OF ILLINOIS AT CHICAGO**, Chicago, IL 1992

DEPAUL UNIVERSITY, Evanston, IL Advanced coursework in Accounting 1992

UNIVERSITY OF CHICAGO, Chicago, IL Advanced coursework in Corporate Finance 1992

AARON SCHULER

334 Jargos St., Houston, TX 77042 713-262-7959

OBJECTIVE To continue in a management role within the financial services industry.

EXPERIENCE

11/99 - present **BANK OF AMERICA** ***Managing Director - Private Banking***

Overview

As 1 of 8 US Managing Directors, I manage the Central Region, a team of 30 staff based in Chicago and Houston offices and total assets under management of $2.5BB.

Revenue Challenge To grow top-line revenues by 15% a year in a region that had seen 2% or less annual growth for three years straight prior to my appointment.

Tactic Corrected an unbalanced revenue model where 75% of income originated from lending fees and 25% from asset management/banking fees, to where it is now a more rational 60/40% split.

Tactic Repositioned staff to pursue ultra high-net worth clients, i.e. individuals with assets of $10MM-$75MM - historically we pursued clients with $500K-$3MM to invest.

Tactic Building relationships with centers of influence to find referrals, i.e., CPA firms, Corporate Attorneys, and Advisors who consult with closely held companies.

Management Challenge Reducing staff size although I managed he largest geographic territory of 15 states with clients in tier-one cities across the Midwest and Texas.

Tactic Restructured and upgraded talent at Houston and Chicago offices, this included hiring a new Chief-of-Staff to handle internal operations as I focused on business development activities.

Tactic Travel 50% of the time to meet with top clients, to make presentations to prospects and to lend the credibility of senior management involvement.

Results Achieved 18% growth in revenues each of the past 3 years. Reduced operating expenses 26% (from $6.4MM to $4.7MM). Attained a net margin of 25% a year.

1994-1999 **CENTRAL BANK** ***Managing Director***
Vice President

Overview

As Managing Director of the Midwest and Southwest markets, I managed a team of 5 private bankers and oversaw efforts to build assets under management as well as expand the total client base supported.

Management Challenge Implement sustainable strategies that could grow business revenues by a minimum of 10% a year.

Tactic Recruited new staff who could meet aggressive business goals and used coaching/ mentoring techniques to enhance personnel performance.

Results Achieved an average year-over-year revenue growth of 15%.

1993-1994 **COMPASS BANK** ***Vice President***

Overview

Responsible for developing and managing a base of institutional accounts.

Selling Challenge Grow the account base under management.

Tactic Used business development techniques to present long-term fixed income investment strategies to institutional funds managers.

Results Gained 5 new accounts which grew the portfolio 33% and added $1MM in new revenues.

Experience Cont'd...

1991-1993 **HARRIS NESBITT CORP.** ***Senior VP***

Overview Managed the Mortgage Backed Security desk which consisted of a team of 10-12 trading professionals.

1980-1990 **ATLANTIC TRUST** ***Managing Director***
Vice President
Assistant VP

Overview Managed a team of 18 fixed income sales professionals for the global markets group spread across two regions - Midwest and Southwest.

EDUCATION

1980	MBA - Finance	University of Baltimore	Baltimore, MD
1974	BBA - Finance	University of Houston	Houston, TX

References available on request.

CHAPTER 6
NON-PROFIT & ASSOCIATION CAREERS

The Nonprofit & Association Category Has

5 Client Examples

18 Job Titles

61 Years of Work History

NAME	JOB TITLES COVERED
1. CHARLOTTE MAXWELL	.... Assistant Manager Visitor Services & Volunteers ...Coordinator/Associate Visitor Services
2. WILLIAM DOBBINS	..........................National Service Officer ....Fire Team & Squad Leader
3. ALEXANDRA STEINBURG	....President ....VP Campaign VP Community Development &Education
4. JEFF REYNOLDS*	............................Development Associate ....Customer Service ....Quality Control ....Marketing Assistant ....Consultant
5. JOANN WILLIAMS	.......Associate Director Member Services ....Manager Member Services ....Sr. Coordinator Member Services ....Member Services Coordinator ....Marketing Assitant ....Legal Assistant

* Find the "before resume" in chapter 35

▪ CHARLOTTE MAXWELL ▪

823 Westland Dr., New York, NY 10028 212-919-3215 email: cmax24@aol.com

SUMMARY

Focus on training and developing staff, strategic planning, meeting objectives, conserving resources and maintaining quality standards. Leadership skills are used to identify opportunities to improve and positively impact the organization. Good judgment complements a high-energy and outgoing personality.

STRENGTHS

- Interpersonal Skills
- Client Relations
- Team Leadership
- Problem Solving
- Group Training
- Resource Coordination

EMPLOYMENT

1/97-3/00 **THE METROPOLITIAN MUSEUM OF ART**
Assistant Manager - Visitor Services & Volunteers
Assistant Manager - Visitor Services
Coordinator/Associate - Visitor Services

Overview ——— A challenging role where I received three promotions in two years and impacted the museum's functional as well as financial success. Managed a staff of 85 (25 paid employees and 60 volunteers). Implemented operating policies and training programs by partnering with department heads to provide volunteer support that was critical to this nonprofit's existence.

Actions

Consulting · Served management as an internal consultant to create policies, procedures and practices
Planning · Developed strategic plans to identify trends, challenges and opportunities
Recruiting · Interviewed applicants to select 250-300 volunteers per year
Training · Implemented training programs and wrote the MCA's first training manual
Counseling · Maintained open door policy to counsel all staff

Challenge ——— With an unpaid volunteer force of 40-60 employees and a turnover rate of 15% each month, I thought of creative ways to recruit and maintain volunteer support.

Result Volunteer staff grew 1,000% (from 6 to 60). Volunteer hours averaged 17,500 hours a year (saving nearly $80,000 off the capital expense budget).

1996	**Photography Assistant**	Studio Z	New York, NY
1995	**Sales & Lab Technician**	Photo Emporium	Boston, MA
1993-95	**Ski Instructor**	Breckenridge	Breckenridge, CO

College Employment

1991	**Marketing Intern**	Hubbard Street Dance	Chicago, IL
1990/91	**Club Leader**	Club Med	Virgin Islands

EDUCATION

1995	Photography	Art Institue of NYC	New York,NY
1993	B.A., Art History	Art Institue of NYC	New York,NY
1991	Study Abroad	Syracuse University	Florence, Italy

ACTIVITIES

Professional Ski Instructors of America.
Volunteer: Arts Organization and Variety Club

WILLIAM DOBBINS

3002 Sandalwood Ct. Washington, DC 20024 202-549-7851 wdobbins@aol.com

SUMMARY

Expertise in project support and leadership areas such as administration, service integration and management reporting demonstrates analytical capabilities that made me an asset in my past roles. Research skills complement communication strengths and ensure smooth continuity whether I interface with management or the client directly. To ensure success of my responsibilities, I maintain personal involvement and accountability at all operational levels.

Strengths

- Communications
- Managing Relations
- Project Leadership
- Multi-tasking
- Research
- Management Reporting
- Time Management
- Mediation

1/98 - present *National Service Officer* **Disabled American Veterans**, Washington, DC

Overview..............Part of an 8 person team supporting 12,000 disabled veterans and 20,000 dependents, where my focus is counseling them in the areas of legal, psychological and medical issues.

➨ Impact — Personally manage a pipeline of 4,000 individual clients representing 1/3 of the total DAV client population in Illinois although 8 staff are assigned.

➨ Impact — Attain positive judgments on 55% of cases I advocate (a significant statistic since it is mandated to advocate all claims regardless of validity or merit).

➨ Impact — Over the past 38 months, I've secured final determinations on 2,500 unique cases.

➨ Impact — The gross monetary value to my clients provided $400 million in new benefits.

➨ Impact — Rank Top 33% in the nation (of 276 officers) on each of the following categories
- Awards Validated
- Members Recruited
- Hearings Held
- Veterans Interviewed
- Files Reviewed
- Claims Submitted

Challenge — Handle 30 calls, personally assess 6 Veterans and initiate 25 claims per day.
For each denied claim with merit that is appealed, I write arguments covering:
- History of Claim and Medical Evidence
- Outline regulation applicable to the claim found in the code of Federal Regulation.

ACTIONS

Document Control — Prepare and coordinate documents to ensure integrity of all phases from case outline to final outcome.

Communications — Integrate information between project leaders and global teams. Revise presentations, exhibits, agreement drafts, product listings and disclosure schedules.

Legal — Abstract incoming legal data; docket project deadlines; maintain confidentiality.

TRAINING

Sponsored by the University of Pennsylvania

Courses Anatomy & Physiology | Speech Communication | Legal Writing

MILITARY

UNITED STATES MARINE CORPS Fire Team and Squad Leader: 4-man teams.
- ***Meritorious Combat Promotion***
- ***Meritorious Mast for Duty in Desert Shield/Desert Storm***

Significant Event **Desert Shield/Storm**

Member of the first battalion unit to penetrate Iraqi border defenses in Kuwait. **Day 1** First of 500 soldiers to forge through 7 mine fields. **Day 2**, Fire fight: Iraq's 8 armored carriers and 120 troops attacked our 3 Amtracks and 45 soldiers (zero US losses). **Day 3** Middle of burning Kuwaiti oil fields, constant skirmishes from enemy frontline. **Day 4** Helped secure Kuwaiti International Airport.

Significant Event **Survived Helicopter Crash**

A fast roping drill 100 miles off Somalian coast in the Indian Ocean onto a ship's deck when an engine blew up, 16 soldiers fell into the sea, only 12 survived. Survived 20% body burns, instant pneumonia, and 15 minute treading among sharks until rescue.

EDUCATION Pursued B.S., Business Finance, University of Pennsylvania

ALEXANDRIA STEINBURG

175 Remmington Ave., New York, NY 10021 stein223@aol.com 212-389-9015

OBJECTIVE

To use management, organizational and leadership skills in fund raising, membership development, special event planning and volunteer coordination.

STRENGTHS

- Non Profit Management
- Fund-raising
- Public Speaking
- Training/Education
- Volunteer Recruiting
- Problem Solving
- Task Management
- Capital/Gift Campaigns

EXPERIENCE

NON-PROFIT & FUND-RAISING MANAGEMENT

1988-1996 UJA FEDERATION — NEW YORK, NY

President — Women's Campaign Board
VP Campaign — Women's Campaign Board
VP Community Development & Education — Women's Campaign Board

Overview Initially joined the Women's Campaign's Board in its 8th year of existence. Within a year, I went from a volunteer to an executive, and led the organization through critical changes to broaden our membership base, donor pool and deliver a more valuable program of services.

My Challenge Lobby and win support to shift WCB's focus from exclusively recruiting new members from New York's affluent communities to a more democratic organization that would appeal to a larger geographic region, yet still capture the affluent member.

Strategies Refocused the WCB mission and purpose to:

1. Add — New Member Education components
2. Add — Significant Spiritual/Nurturing/Emotional Support elements
3. Continue — To deliver an exciting social outlet for the members

Results • WCB grew from approximately 1,000 members to 3,000 active members and added chapters in 5 new towns.

Results • We captured members nearly 15 years earlier in their life, this is worth an additional $20,000-25,000 per person in donations - $40-$45 million in total donation value.

Results • Delivered an experienced donor to The Women's Board at an average annual contribution of $2000 vs. the historical level of $365.

Results • My member development plan strongly supports UJA's new Endowment Program.

Results • Recipient: *Womens Leadership Award* (only 2 people a year selected), 1995

DUTIES

Management	Managed an Executive Board with 44 members.
Volunteer	Managed, recruited, trained and motivated work effort and commitment.
Special Events	60+ fund-raisers, galas, dinners, phon-athons, lectures and conferences.
Public speaking	To groups of up to 250 attendees as well as choosing local and national speakers.
Training	Ran public speaking workshop for Women's Leadership Division. Trained volunteers in fund-raising techniques.
Fund-raising	One-on-one solicitations, caucus settings, major gifts and large groups.

EDUCATION

RN, Monmouth University, West Long Branch, NJ

JEFF REYNOLDS 124th St. #2., New York, NY 10022 212-349-7717
jrey@aol.com

OBJECTIVE To manage, organize and facilitate success as a leader of a group or department.

EXPERIENCE
8/98 - Present *Development Associate* THE NEW YORK COMMUNITY TRUST [NYCT]
The fourth largest community foundation with $1.3 billion in assets.

My Challenge Develop NYCT's endowment assets under management (expectations are to raise $2-3 million a year).
Key goal: change the structure of philanthropy according to the following two strategies.

Strategy 1 Create a new breed of "***Venture Philanthropist",*** like Venture Capitalists, these donors want their charitable dollars to work like investments rather than one-time gifts.
Tactic 1 Work with VPs to identify which of 150,000 national non-profits match their goals and then coach them to be board members, consultants or volunteers.
Tactic 2 Administrate, recruit, set budgets, correspond and manage events.

Strategy 2 Direct grant making and manage fund development, disbursement and audit controls.
Tactic 1 Provide back-office support to our 200 existing funds.
Tactic 2 Maintain integrity of the money trail.
Tactic 3 Define benchmarks to justify continued investment in a charity.

Result • Enhanced donor trust and the perception of fund mismanagement.
Result • Created active lifetime donors and significantly increased endowments at the trust.

Project **Young Leaders Fund** **MY ROLE**: *Program Coordinator*. Support New York's young community and business leaders, 350 members, whose donations are matched 2-to-1.
Springboard Foundation **MY ROLE**: *Trust Liaison*. Each group member contributes $5,000 a year to after-school and summer youth programs.

Actions
• Manage correspondence, budgets, organization, staffing, and member contributions.
• Manage 9-10 events a year, including one with Playboy CEO, C. Hefner as keynote speaker.
• Directed planning for the annual dinner hosted by the CEO of Chicago Public Schools.

Result • Springboard now makes more than $200,000 in grants annually.
Result • Granted $450,000 to 126 organizations.
Result • Manage capital campaign drive to make the fund self-sustaining ($1,000,000 over 4 years).

Project **James Brown Award** **MY ROLE**: *Project Coordinator/Organizer*. In its 29th year, this award offers a $50,000 grant to an outstanding non-profit.

Actions Handled the entire project for 2002.
1. Created award application materials and mailing list of 1,900 organizations.
2. Created a candidate pool for selection committee and then evaluated subsequent proposals.
3. Organized yearly meeting and gave report to Trust Executive Committee on results.

Result I cultivated the Award Selection Committee, an elite group of donors, encouraging them to make greater contributions and motivated their contacts to become active in the CCT.

Project **Basic Human Needs Fund** **MY ROLE**: *Point Person/Organizer*. The Trust's one annual campaign drive.

Action Worked closely with the VP External Relations and the Board Chair of the Trust.

Result In 2001, as point person, I wrote the campaign letter which generated $255,000, 10% better than 2000, despite the post September 11th fund-raising difficulties.

NYCT Experience Cont'd....

Project

Newman Policy Dinner: $50,000 budget
October Donor Dinner: $25,000 budget

Action Point Person/Coordinator/Organizer. Designed the program around a social issue (health) used to educate and engage donors.

Result I coordinated budgeting and contracts for two successful donor cultivation events.

Project

Actions Create "Snapshots" - short written summaries on organizations w/ pictures and specific data, for donors to read in order to determine which organizations to fund.

Result My snapshots have directly led to $250,000 in new grants.

6/95-6/98 **ADECCO STAFFING,** Temporary Roles

INDUSTRIES

Customer Service, Microsoft — Technology 12/97 - 6/98
Client liaison on shareholder accounts.

Customer Service, State of New York Dept. of Insurance — Insurance 11/96 - 10/97
Quality control support of various projects.

Quality Control, Anderson Consulting — Consulting 3/96 - 9/96
Input and analysis of database documents.

Customer Service/Correspondence, Citicorp Bank — Banking 6/95 - 1/96
Client calls and correspondence as service representative.

6/93 - 8/96 ***Marketing Assistant***, Digital Technologies
Conceived marketing strategy, promotions and advertising as well as acted as client liaison.

1991 - 1993 ***Consultant***, Waste Management Disposal
Conducted field research on competitors to target revenue building opportunities for WM.

EDUCATION

1991 Marshall University, Huntington, WV
B.A., Social Sciences Emphasis in Communication

JOANN WILLIAMS

7146 Benton Way #38A, Washington, DC 20036 • 202-569-4592
adamssm@msn.com

EXPERIENCE

8/91 - Present — **National Restaurant Association -NRA** — Washington, DC

- ***Assoc. Director -Member Services*** — 12/99 - present
- ***Manager - Member Services*** — 12/97 - 12/99
- ***Sr. Coordinator - Member Services*** — 7/95 - 12/97
- ***Member Services Coordinator*** — 3/94 - 7/95
- ***Marketing Assistant*** — 8/91 - 3/94

Overview Progressed through 5 titles for a national association that serves 900,000 restaurant and foodservice outlets in the $430 billion foodservice industry.

Key Challenge Executing programs to grow membership while serving the association's existing members at a high-level of quality to ensure they remain active dues paying contributors to the organization (dues range from $2,000-$65,000 per company).

Responsibility Manage 107 members or 35% of NRA's membership base.

- Darden
- McDonald's
- Lettuce Entertain You
- Lawry's
- Pepsi
- RJ Gator's
- Damon's Grill
- Ruby Tuesdays

Member Focused Actions

- *Recruiting/Retention* — Execute retention and attraction programs to meet budget goals.
- *Event Management* — Coordinate all membership events, company visits, presentations, conference receptions, and member dinners.
- *Research* — Provide market research and general information to members.
- *Customer Service* — Follow-up with the membership on association projects via conference meetings, phone calls and correspondence.
- *Special Assignment* — Small Business Advisory Committee Liaison.

Business Focused Actions

- *In-house Publications* — Produce the annual membership directory and created a new in-house desktop format to eliminate outsourcing costs.
- *Reporting* — Report on: Member Analysis, Call Logs, Staff Assignments.
- *Technology* — Manage the Association's membership database.
- *Marketing* — Create marketing plans, solicitation letters and direct mailings to member prospects.

Result Added $1,463,087 in dues since '02 by attaining an 84% retention rate.
Delivered $568,167 in new revenues by adding 310 members since '94.

Project #1 Conference Sponsorship Program – Worked with the VP of Member Services to implement NRA's first monetary sponsorship of the annual conference.

Result Sponsor revenues grew from $190,000 in '02 to $400,000+ in '04.

Project #2 Managing the Educational Foundation and "Cornerstone" Fund which awards $50,000 in scholarships.

Result Successfully moved all foundation training programs from Notre Dame to the Culinary Institute of America.

6/88 - 7/91 — **Jenner & Block** ***Legal Assistant*** — Washington, DC

Liaison between legal staff and State and Federal Courts. Assisted in preparing court documents, researched cases and filed pleadings. Prepared daily reports for attorneys.

EDUCATION 1988 B.S., Public & Environmental Affairs: Major Criminal Justice, Trinity University

CHAPTER 7

MUNICIPAL CAREERS

The Municipal Category Has

3 Client Examples

10 Job Titles

92 Years of Work History

NAME	JOB TITLES COVERED
1. STEVEN MCGUIRE	....Firefighter
2. PAUL MORRIS	..........................Patrolman Public Transit
	....Patrolman
	............USMC Light HelicopterSquadron
3. WILLIAM ZUCKERMAN	..............First Deputy Fire Commissioner
	...............................Deputy District Chief
	....Battalion Chief
	....Captian
	....Lieutenanat
	....Fire Fighter

STEVEN MAGUIRE

399 Twin Peaks Rd., Boston, MA 02118 617-279-5461

OBJECTIVE To continue a successful career as a Fire Officer in a capacity where I can better serve the general public and capitalize on leadership, operational support, and administrative management skills.

SUMMARY Commitment is expressed by a tireless work ethic, a desire to constantly challenge my assumptions, to improve effectiveness and seek opportunity to foster *esprit de corps* with team members. I exceed expectations and give management the confidence to increasingly use my capabilities. My integrity is defined as taking ownership of all assigned duties and being personally committed to the best ideals of the fire service in helping the department remain a vital community asset.

FUNCTIONS

Training	Integrate the changing trends involving the relationship between training needs and the widening role of fire fighters.
Administration	Prioritize action steps to attain program goals and coordinate concurrent project responsibilities to achieve stated objectives.
Management	Participate with building a professional, disciplined and motivated staff prepared to handle pressure, maintain morale and peak performance on the fireground.

EXPERIENCE

1994 - present *Fire fighter* **BOSTON FIRE DEPARTMENT** Boston, MA

Overview Member of a 20 man fire fighting team responsible for performing fire suppression, specialty rescue and hazardous materials mitigation.

Assignments		
	Public Education Officer	Create and present public education programs.
	CPR Instructor	Teach American Heart Association curriculums.
	Asst. Training Officer	Train department in classroom and live field exercises.

Actions

- ☑ Recreated — ***New Fighter Training Program***; an 8 week curriculum using 20 modules.
- ☑ Co-created — ***Saving Our Seniors*** a Fire Safety Program delivered to 300 seniors.
- ☑ Maintain — Firehouse Computer Information System and Support Help Desk.
- ☑ Member — Committee to select ***Onboard Computer Systems***: My research and report to Fire Chief protected department from buying obsolete systems from a Fortune 500 vendor.
- ☑ Member — Committee to create station's ***First Internet Web Site***: a community information tool.
- ☑ Member — Committee to redevelop stations - ***Target Hazard Pre-plans.***
- ☑ Rewrote — All public education lesson plans for primary school fire safety education.
- ☑ Created — ***The Boston Hazard Hunters*** A new multimedia interactive fire safety and prevention Program: Targeting juvenile fire starters.
- ☑ Created — ***Home Escape Brochure***: given to elementary students for use with parents.
- ☑ Created — ***Quick Reference Guide:*** to help Paramedics gauge correct dosage of Pediatric drugs.
- ☑ Created — The ***Tactical Check List***: a reference tool outlining 8 categories of activities that incident commanders track during fire suppressing efforts.
- ☑ Developed — The ***High-rise Evac Plan***: A public education program.
- ☑ Leading — P.R. and media relations efforts to support our participation with NFPA's ***Great Escape*** - North American home fire drill.

Special Project **Created a Multi-Department Training Exercise**: *Rescue Extrication*
Result 1-day event attended by firefighters from Cambridge, Charlestown and Somerville Fire Protection Dist. along with representatives of General Motors and Amkus Rescue Systems. I secured 8 donated vehicles from Burkhill College and Don's Towing.

EDUCATION

Pursued M.A.	Cognitive Psychology, SUFFOLK UNIVERSITY, Boston, MA	1992
B.A., Psychology	*Magna Cum Laude*, Boston University, Boston, MA	1990

PAUL J. MORRIS

107 111th St. #301A, New York, NY *10013* ✉ pmorris@aol.com
✆ *212-277-5797* (Home) • 212-721-1313 (Message) • 212-752-6789 (Work)

OBJECTIVE

To continue a successful career as a Police Officer in role where I will endeavour to exceed the expectations of my supervisors as well as the general public.

STRENGTHS

• Public Relations	• Communications	• Reporting
• Investigation	• Witness/Criminal Interviewing	• Team Support
• Time Management	• Fair Minded	• Persuasion

SUMMARY

Professional Provide organizational assistance and support to help the group attain stated objectives. Possess strong analytical, written, organizational and interpersonal skills. Excellent management sense and commitment to developing effective plans.

Personal I'm conscientious of my work quality and use self-discipline to exceed expectations. I'm a problem solver and clear communicator able to articulate, persuade and reach consensus.

EXPERIENCE

7/94-present — **NEW YORK POLICE DEPARTMENT**

Patrolman	Public Transportation	7/98 to present	
Patrolman	District 012	5/95 - 7/98	Supervisor: Lt. Johnson
Patrolman	District 010	1/94- 5/95	Supervisor: Lt. Freidman

Overview Preserve peace, protect life and property, detect and investigate criminal acts, arrest law violators in compliance with state and municipal laws. Collect evidence and secure crime scenes for processing. Skilled in physical techniques to safely complete arrests and knowledge of the deadly force policy. Communicate (verbal/written) in a clear, concise manner and experienced in court-of-law proceedings.

Recognition Numerous Honorable Mention Citations for Professionalism.

7/85 - 1/92 — **UNITED STATES MARINE CORPS** - Light Helicopter Squadron

Overview Advanced repair, inspection and readiness for flight of UH-1N helicopter. Repaired airframe and powerplants. Configured aircraft for flight operations, search and rescue missions, bomb delivery, VIP transportation and medevac missions.

Accomplishments

• Letters of commendation	• National Defense Service Medal
• Marine Corps Reserve Ribbon	• Sea Service Deployment Ribbon
• Rifle expert Badge	• Pistol Marksman Badge
• Letters of Appreciation	• Marine's Physical Fitness Award

Special Squadron activated in support of **Operation Desert Storm** in 1/91. Provided disaster relief to citizens after Mt. Pinatubo erupted in the Republic of Philippines.

EDUCATION Presently Pursuing B.A., Criminal/Social Justice, St. Peters College, Jersey City, NJ

References available on request

WILLIAM ZUCKERMAN, JR.

2550 St. Peters Dr., New York, NY 10001

212-569-0874 Home • E-mail williamzucker@aol.com • 212-569-8874 Work

OBJECTIVE Continue a successful career in the New York Fire Department by providing management continuity, leadership vision and operational accountability.

SUMMARY

PROFESSIONAL 30+ years of fire service experience, fifteen in upper management (thirteen as the 1st Deputy Fire Commissioner and Chief of Staff). Possess a fundamental understanding of maintaining fiscal responsibility and improving accountability to the citizens of New York while increasing visibility and interaction with fire safety programs. Skilled in dispute resolution by using diplomacy, sensitivity and comprehensive knowledge of local/state policies and procedures.

PERSONAL Lead by example and use organization skills to improve operational effectiveness. Build a cohesive staff management program by setting specific goal criteria, articulating targeted objectives and encouraging staff input and participation.

EXECUTIVE STRENGTHS

- Leadership
- Organization
- Report Management
- Logistics Support
- Research & Planning
- Program Coordination
- Public Relations
- Problem Resolution
- Finance/Budget Management

FUNCTIONAL RESPONSIBILITIES

STAFF DEVELOPMENT - Emphasis is to build a professional, disciplined and motivated staff that is prepared to resolve problems, maintain moral excellence and peak performance standards.
ADMINISTRATIVE MANAGEMENT - Prioritize action steps to attain complex program goals and coordinate concurrent project responsibilities to achieve mission objectives.
FISCAL ACCOUNTABILITY - Outline budgetary guidelines to each bureau manager to ensure efficient resource utilization and fiscal restraint.
PROBLEM SOLVING - Implement procedural guidelines to improve system operations, enhance operational quality, contain costs, maximize resources and reduce administrative problems.

EXPERIENCE

1965 - Present **NEW YORK FIRE DEPARTMENT**

First Deputy Fire Commissioner	[1/84 - present	9 years]
Deputy District Chief	[1/81 - 1/84	3 years]
Battalion Chief	[4/80 - 1/81	1 year]
Captain	[1/78 - 4/80	2 years]
Lieutenant	[1/73 - 1/78	5 years]
Fire fighter	[12/65 - 1/73	8 years]

ACTIONS

- Chief advisor to the Fire Commissioner in establishing policy, performance and operational goals.
- Supervise deputy commissioners of five bureaus (Fire Suppression, EMS, Fire Prevention, Administrative Services and Support Services with 102 firehouses).
- Oversee operational programs and serve as interim Fire Commissioner as needed.
- Compile all financial reports to justify annual resource needs of $286 million.
- Attend and/or chair hearings, social events, and community meetings.
- Coordinate Department participation in major city special events.
- Manage contract labor negotiations and advise on legal dealings and governmental affairs.

RESULTS Over the past fifteen years, by maximizing resources, focusing on educating the general public regarding fire prevention and properly training fire fighters, our accomplishments include:

- Decreased number of structural fires by 45% — Result: 2nd lowest total since 1980
- Decreased number of fatalities by 117 people — Result: 66% decrease since the high of 1980
- Increased incident responses by 80% — Result: 400,000 ambulance & fire runs
- Oversaw department staff restructuring — Result: Decreased head count by 472 positions since 1989, saving $22M annually

EDUCATION	Medical Specialist Electronics Executive Development III	U. S. Army Medical Service School, San Antonio, Texas Coyne Electrical, Chicago, Illinois National Fire Academy, Fredericks, Maryland
RECOGNITION	Fire Commissioner's Award of Valor	New York Fire Department Unit Citation - 2

VISION: A.D. 2000+

In order to meet the New York Fire Department's goals and community mission objectives for the foreseeable future, I am outlining key issues that will take priority at the Office of Commissioner (if given the opportunity to fulfill this role).

☑ *Improve Community Relations and Public Awareness*

FOCUS To complement the City's existing P.R. efforts and to build public awareness of the New York Fire Department's presence & value to the surrounding community.

BENEFIT Increased community support reduces public concern over budgetary demands, improves community morale and enhances quality of life perceptions.

☑ *Staff Restructuring*

FOCUS Evaluate and justify to the satisfaction of Union Executives and department members, within the context of FLSA guidelines, the need to reduce the 5-man engine policy to the nationally accepted 4-man model.

BENEFIT Save New York over $30,000,000 annually and remove the public perception of fire fighter inactivity.

☑ *Implement Accountability Guidelines and Exempt Staff Recognition Programs*

FOCUS Reintroduce performance reports for exempt personnel using a non-biased review process.

BENEFIT We will be able to give an incentive to managers, to meet or exceed department objectives using official recognition by peers and the prestige of the Fire Commissioner's Office.

CHAPTER 8

HEALTHCARE CAREERS

The Healthcare Category Has

3 Client Examples

8 Job Titles

49 Years of Work History

NAME	JOB TITLES COVERED
1. KAREN MCKENZIE	.....................................Clinical Manager
	.................................Clinical Coordinator
	....Staff Nurse
	....................................NICU Staff Nurse
	....Charge Nurse
2. SCOTT WOODMAN*	........................Vice President of Hospital
3. JANET CROW	....................................Dental Hygentist

* Find the "before resume" in chapter 35

KAREN S. McKENZIE

5791 Princeton Ln. , Atlanta, GA 30074
404-313-7987 kmack3@aol.com

OBJECTIVE To apply my management background and medical education toward a professional clinical specialist position in the biotech/pharmaceutical market. To participate in marketing products or services in a team based environment.

SUMMARY Healthcare expertise includes hospital, clinical and home care settings. Results are illustrated by achieving performance improvements and successfully directing organizational change. The challenges I've meet include simplifying complex processes and motivating staff to achieve mission or program objectives.

Strengths
- Strategy Development
- JCAHO/CMS Standards
- Report Writing/Presentations
- Multitasking
- Client Management
- Team Building/Training

CLINICAL MANAGEMENT EXPERIENCE

1998 - Current **Clinical Manager** **FULTON REGIONAL HOSPITAL**
Home Care Department Atlanta, GA

Overview Manage operations for a large Southeast home care provider. As clinical and business manager, I oversee Registered Nurses, Social Workers, Occupational, Speech and Physical Therapists, who conduct over 25,000 annual visits. This is an increase of nearly 20% since FY 2002.

Challenges Ensuring the business operates profitably and that good clinical outcomes are attained.

Actions
- Added computerized Point of Care technology with Horizon, McKesson software.
- Manage department operating budget, set yearly goals and ensure service quality.
- Determine all clinical and operational policies and procedures.
- Subject Matter Expert: Joint Commission (JACHO) Standards & Regulations
  Medicaid & Medicare Reimbursement Regulations
  GA/FL/AL state certified home care therapy

Result ***Quality*** The Clinical Quality Indicators (Outcome Based Quality Improvement) CMS reports (Centers for Medicare and Medicaid Services) show 23 of 27 indicators improved from '02 and 18 indicators outpace national levels.

Result ***Production*** Overtime during implementation of Horizon, McKesson software, 7/02 -12/02 averaged 52 hours per pay period, by 1/03 this was reduced to 14 hours per pay period.

Result ***Profits & Revenues*** Delivered a 33% gross profit margin in 2003
Revenue goal = $2.05MM, delivered $2.4MM

1993 - 1998 **ACCESS HOME HEALTH CARE** **Clinical Coordinator** (1995 - 1998) Atlanta, GA
Staff Nurse (1993 - 1995)

Overview Coordinated a team of 4 Respiratory Care Practitioners and 12 RNs for the care of complex pediatric patients with specialized equipment.

STAFF NURSE EXPERIENCE

1989 - 1993	***NICU Staff Nurse***	Memorial Hospital Neonatal intensive care and relief coordinator for a tertiary unit (level 3).	La Jolla, CA
1985 - 1989	***NICU Staff Nurse***	St. Marys Medical Center	Miami, FL
	Charge Nurse	St. Mary's Medical Center	Miami, FL

EDUCATION

BS – Health Arts	Argosy University	Atlanta, GA
RN – Registered Nurse	Atlanta Christian College	Atlanta, GA

CERTIFICATION Neonatal Intensive Care from 1990 – 1998.
LICENSURE Georgia, Florida & Alabama (current), California (inactive).

——— *References available on request.*

SCOTT R. WOODMAN, M.D.

566 Twinpeaks Tr., Laguna, CA , 92651 760-761-3515, email: bayermd@aol.com

Professionally, I focus on communicating vision to the teams I lead and acting as a technology catalyst to adopt leading-edge medical and computer systems that enhance patient care and capture economic efficiencies. As an executive, I constantly seek innovative ways to save resources and maximize staff productivity. The programs I champion typically achieve immediate results, but are designed to be refined on an incremental basis so that they stand up over the test of time. On a personal level, flexibility and persistence are the cornerstones I use to modernize infrastructures that were resistant to change.

EXECUTIVE OVERVIEW

11/93 - 3/99 **VICE PRESIDENT - NAVAL HOSPITAL CAMP PENDLETON (NHCP)**

Created and managed a $57 million multi-disciplinary health care operation consisting of –

- REMOTE MEDICAL CARE CLINICS / EMERGENCY SERVICES / WELLNESS CENTER
- OCCUPATIONAL HEALTH / INDUSTRIAL HYGIENE / PREVENTATIVE MEDICINE
- OPTOMETRY SERVICES / IMMUNIZATION SERVICES / SPECTACLE MANUFACTURING

NHCP, led a medical staff of 29 physicians and 324 medical personnel who provided health care services for 90,000 new students each year and 21,000 permanent employees.

Remote Medical Care Operation, oversaw 4 medical clinics spread over 4 states.

Occupational, Industrial and Preventative Medicine, created programs to enhance workplace health and safety in a 13 state region.

Optometry Services, modernized a military operation to a civilian styled service that grew patient visits 270%, reduced cost of spectacles to consumer by 90% and reduced wait time from 2 weeks to 1 hour.

Wellness Center, attracted $100,000 from corporate and public sector sponsors to build a 10,000 sq/ft state of the art center dedicated to teaching and promoting healthy life-styles.

■ ***AS EXECUTIVE DIRECTOR*** ■

Championed the *Camp Pendleton Plan* through Senate & House congressional committees. Won a $23M contract to build the Navy's first centralized medical hospital clinic (80,000 sq/ft) which transformed a 50 year old operation of three centers into a single hightech facility serving 400,000 patient visits annually (635% increase).

COST CUTTING DIRECTIVE

Restructuring Led a three year process to restructure, outsource, close and consolidate 3 medical clinics: San Diego, Los Angeles, and San Jose.

Result Efficiencies saved $13 million a year.

TECHNOLOGY INNOVATIONS

Smartcards & Barcoding Launched automation technologies used to collect data on a dozen health related programs, this technology also provided electronic currency.

Result The largest US demonstration and first mass medical use of Smartcards -150,000+ cards.
Barcoding saves 5 staff or **$250,000 year**

Computerized All clinical operations with 300 PC's tied to an internet WAN/LAN architecture.

Result Attained 99.9% prescription order accuracy and a 95% reduction in life threatening anaphylactic reactions.

Paperless Office Introduced document scanning and CD storage.

Result Consolidated laboratory filing system saves **$2.3 million/year**

Scantron Computerized, automated and databased all new student health information.

Result System processes 4,000 new patients per week at peak periods and **saves 11 FTE/$600,000 year**.

HEALTH CARE PROGRAM INNOVATIONS

Established "Total Health" for new Managed Care Patients

Result Enrolled 57,000 new patients annually into **TRICARE**. Services included screenings, health risk appraisals, medical testing, wellness lecture, lab evaluations, immunizations and treatment.

Introduced Family Practice Teams

Result Created a group of 3 family practice teams dedicated to student patients, decreased average visit time from 3 hours to under 40 minutes while visits jumped from 4,000 to 16,500.

Established Women's Health Clinic

Result The first gynecology clinic for 12,000 female students annually who were screened for chlamydia and cervical cancer using a Fast-Track PAP system.

Developed Tobacco Cessation Program

Result Attracted **$1 million** to create a national anti-tobacco model program that attained a 60% success rate of participants who remained non-tobacco users 1 year later.

Consolidated Quality Assurance Programs

Result Combined a group of 10 different QA programs into one unified directorate-wide quality program which met all JCAHO and hospital requirements.

Founded NHCHS Research Council

Result 20 research and scientific papers were written-7 received awards for "**Best At Conference**".

Founded National Scientific Symposium

Result Attended by an average of 350 participants, now in its 7th year

Established Primary Care Symposium

Result Saved hospital $40,000 by bringing in-house the required continuing medical education credits.

MANAGEMENT INNOVATIONS

Established Community Public Relations Program

Result Naval staff became classroom teachers, participated in sports programs, and student tutors at area schools which in turn improved publicity and public image.

Served Staff Attrition Task Force- Executive Member

Result Assigned by the Navy's CEO to work with a team of 20 executives to stem the loss of recruits due to medical reason. Overall our findings have a annual saving of $120 million.

Originated
- Weekly medical news column, *Your Health Matters*
- Quarterly wellness letter, *Lifestyle 2000*
- Tobacco cessation film and web site
- Booklet, *Home Health Care*

Papers
- "Evolutionary Revolution, Total Quality Leadership Faces Major Change...60,000 Recruits" at the JCAHO Health Affairs symposium, Leadership into the 21st Century
- Lessons from the Influenza Epidemic of 1918, at the Recruit Symposium

FUND RAISING Chairman- NMC Relief Society: Led a 2-month campaign to raise $450,000 in donations and established a method that increased giving to $600K level.

MILITARY US Navy, Honorable Discharge, O-6 rank

HONORS Legion of Merit, Meritorious Service, Bronze Star, Navy Commendation and the Purple Heart

LEADERSHIP Trained by Edward Demming on total quality management principles of leadership

EDUCATION

MD	School of Medicine	Temple University, Philadelphia, PA
BA	Arts and Letters	Pennsylvania State University, University Park, PA

JANET CROWE

7171 Johnson St., #307, San Francisco, CA 94102 415-879-3178

OBJECTIVE

A sales position using existing selling skills which I have honed at three dental practices by helping improve revenues, increase patient counts and make each one more profitable.

STRENGTHS

- **Client Management** — Build successful customer relationships that allow me to sell additional services, generate referrals and ensure client satisfaction.
- **Sales Assessment** — Determine needs and present service options for a wide array of treatment plans that ensure the practice's profitability.
- **Key Skills**
  - Program Introduction
  - Consultative Sales
  - Clinical Knowledge
  - Customer Service
  - Value Added Sales
  - Client Education
  - Organization
  - Suggestive Sales
  - Vendor Relations

EXPERIENCE

DENTAL PROFESSIONALS OF BERKELEY, Berkeley, CA — 1995 - present

Practice Focus: Dental Hygienist for a general practice specializing in cosmetic work and implants staffed by two Dentists, two Hygienists with a base of 3,000 ongoing patients that generate **$65,000** in monthly revenues (**$800,000** annual).

My Focus: Personally generate **$80,000 -$90,000** annually and screen patients by presenting treatment programs for both cosmetic and necessary dentistry including: restorations, bleachings, crowns, veneers, bridges, etc. priced from **$700-$4,000** per program.

Results

- Program sales recommendations increased total practice revenues 33%.
- Bleaching sales increased by 571% (increasing from **$700** month to **$4,000**).
- Cosmetic veneering & bonding increased 600% from 6 per year to 3 per month.
- 90% of the clients that buy my periodontal management programs now return to the office an additional 1-2 times annually, increasing billings **$34,000-$68,000.**

DR. JOHN GOULD, San Francisco, CA — 1991 -1994

Practice Focus: Dental Hygienist for a single primary care dentist in a busy office of 3,000-4,000 patients. This was the first practice offering a revenue based bonus program.

My Focus: Maintaining customer satisfaction for a rapidly growing practice of new patients that we turned into steady clients.

Result

- Attained bonuses for production over **$600**/day, 50% of the time.

BAY DENTAL WORKS, San Francisco, CA — 1988 - 1991

Practice Focus: Dental Hygienist for an established practice that pioneered cosmetic dentistry staffed by 5 Dentists, 2 hygienists and 3 administrative employees supporting 10,000-12,000 ongoing patients.

Overview: Personally generated **$85,000** annually while learning to sell cosmetic dentistry and accessories as well as bruxism appliances with prices ranging from **$350 to $3,000.**

Results

- Broke a production record for month (**$7,000**) by selling deep cleaning periodontal management programs and prophylaxis services ranging from **$50-$600.**

EDUCATION

B.S., Community Health, Universityof California Berkely — 1988

AAS, Dental Hygiene, Azusa Pacific University — 1987

CHAPTER 9
IT & TECHNOLOGY CAREERS

The IT & Technology Category Has

4 Client Examples

14 Job Titles

69 Years of Work History

NAME	JOB TITLES COVERED
1. ALEX DONAHER	........Systems Officer & Project Manager ....Product Support Project Manager ....Product Support Loan Analyst ....AVP Loan Operations Manager
2. KENNETH BALLARD*	...............................Managing Consultant ....Senior Network Specialist
3. TONY WALLACE	...............................Senior Staff Engineer ....Group Program Manager ....Staff Program/Project Manager ....Senior Consultant
4. BRYCE ARMSTRONG	......Director of Provisioning & Networks .Manager, Network Technology Services ....Senior Telecommunications Analyst ....Technical Director

* Find the “before resume” in chapter 35

ALEX DONAHER | 1122 N. Clark, #3201, Chicago, IL 60610 • 312-504-0450 • wljacobs@aol.com

OBJECTIVE **BANKING:** Loan Operations or Commercial/Retail Loan IT Management. Expertise: Loan Processing/Loan Accounting Systems, Centralized Project-Release and System Conversion/Integration.

EXPERIENCE

1997-2003 **BANK ONE CORP.** Chicago, IL

- ***Systems Officer & Project Manager*** 1999-2003 (Retail Consumer Loan division)
- ***Systems Officer -First Chicago NBD Bank*** 1997-1999 (Prior to the Bank One merger)

Initially at First Chicago, I helped integrate the $122 billion merger between Detroit NBD and First Chicago. Two years later, Bank One acquired First Chicago-NBD and made me IT Project Test Manager reporting to the SVP of Retail IT.

Focus #1 Completed a SAP GL conversion on-time and on-budget and then led implementation of an Alltel Advanced Loan System that Bank One uses to create new products to build the customer base and capture market share.

Result Led a team of 10 analysts that grew to 65 during the launch of 22 new product types and 32 enhancements (with a $12MM budget, the Alltel software package was Bank One's 2nd largest I.T. project in the year).

Focus #2 Strategic Integration Officer for the $68 billion Retail Consumer Loan division (at **$10 billion in annual profits** this is Bank One's second largest profit center).

Result Built a team of 20 project managers, testers and coders who installed a new **Consumer Loan System** that improved on-time/on-budget and quality goals covering dozens of corporate-wide IT projects.

Enterprise Impact Created the **first-ever CPRM** (Centralized Project Release Methodology) to reduce project cost and schedule length. **Goal** - Use CPRM to hold Line of Business Managers and IT Project Managers accountable to time and money budgets while ensuring the projects that go to production don't harm existing system operation.

Introduced

1. Staff Accountability — Compared actual to expected results which made programmers write cleaner code and forced Line-of-Business mangers to write clear requirements. Linked project bonuses to member participation.
2. Streamlined Test Processes — Consolidated 6 test regions into 1 corporate test region.
3. Benchmark Tracking — From requirements sign off, to testing to regression to production.
4. Project Documentation — Wrote test plans, implementation check lists and line-item result analysis.

Result Delivered 29 corporate-wide projects under budget (alone saving $500K) and reduced schedules by 33 weeks. For Bank One, Consumer Loans now meet the 3-year goal of increasing contribution to profits by $2.2 billion.

Result My CPRM model became the preferred methodology used by the following corporate systems:

- Consumer & Commercial Loans
- Demand Deposit
- Regular Savings Systems
- Central Information System
- Lock Box
- Credit Cards

1986 - 1997 **FIRST OF AMERICA BANK** Kalarnazoo, MI

- ***Product Support Project Manager*** 1994-1997 (Corporate Headquarters)
- ***Product Support Loan Analyst*** 1993-1994
- ***AVP - Loan Operations Manager*** 1986-1993

Managed all corporate consumer loans and system support, supervised 6 analysts, documented system upgrades and liaison between users and programmers. Wrote work requests for product changes or new business lines. Created custom reports for Corporate SVPs/Regional Presidents and Branch Managers.

First of America Experience Cont'd... on Pg. 2

First of America Bank Experience Cont'd...

Focus #1

By 1990, First of America had acquired 16 banks and needed me to manage the integration of each bank's loan platform to the corporate ACAPS loan origination system.

Result

Consolidated 20 offices into 4 regions and reduced back-office staff by 66% which saved $2.5MM a year.

Focus #2

Installed Fair ISACCS credit scoring cards into ACAPS to automate 75% of ***indirect*** lending decisions and give loan officers systematic recommendations for ***direct*** loan requests.

Result

The new system automated approval/decline on 75% of 50,000 indirect loans a month (i.e. auto loans). It also flagged loan officers who took undue risk by overriding the system excessively - ultimately reducing charge-offs by 30% which saved over $20 million a year.

Focus #3

Managed teams that were responsible for the Consumer Loan portfolios and Commercial Loan Floor-Plans in excess of $250 million.

Result

Converted the Kirchman Floor Plan system to the Shaw Commercial Loan system and reduced headcount by 30%. Also converted the Kirchman Consumer Loan system to the AMS system which reduced headcount by another 20%.

As Product Support Loan Specialist (Loan Analyst)
Introduced new and enhanced bank products to make computer systems more efficient with less staff.

As Assistant VP & Loan Operations Manager
Managed a team of 18 professionals for the Consumer Loan/Commercial Floor Plan portfolios of $250 million.

FINANCIAL SYSTEMS

Alltel ALS	Hogan Loan System	SAP GL	AMS ACAPS
Shaw Commercial Loans	Kirchman Loan Systems	MS Office Suite	AMS ALS

EDUCATION University of Wisconsin — Prochnow Graduate School of Banking (3 year program) — Madison, WI

Seminars/Workshops:

- Bank One Seminars: Advanced Project Management, Diversity and Delivery Process Simulation
- First of America Seminars
- American Management Systems Classes
- American Bankers Association Programs
- National Installment Credit School, University of Oklahoma

References available on request.

KENNETH BALLARD 132 Granger St., Austin, TX 78757, 512-656-2127 • kballard@aol.com

8/96-Present **BURNETT & ASSOCIATES** **Managing Consultant** Austin,TX

Overview Help corporations develop the technology environments that sustain their business growth needs, eliminate inefficiencies and enable true collaboration between IT, branch management, corporate executives and technology vendors. The following projects are a sample of the results and leadership challenges I've met.

• **PROOF OF CONCEPT FOR NOVELL** ——— Industry **ACADEMIC INSTITUTIONS**

Mandate Handpicked by Novell 5 months after a competitor failed to implement a clustered server network in a 100% fault tolerant environment for Austin Township School District.

Technical 3 site, 10-server network migration: Netware 5.1 to 6.0; GroupWise 5.5 to 6.0

What's New

• Servers on Clustering Services • 3 New Compaq Storage Area Networks (SANS)
• Novell's e-Directory • WebAccess

Result Finished project 3 months under schedule and at 65% of budget. Network saves $250K in reduced paper and 40,000 man-hours a year which includes cutting IT staff 33%.

• **NOVELL NETWORK OS TO MICROSOFT NT** ——— Industry **CHIP MANUFACTURING**

Mandate Help VisionTek move into high-end computer graphic board manufacturing and win Microsoft orders once they migrated to an NT environment. The move kept VisionTek from bankruptcy as memory chip prices, their core product line, dropped 90%.

What's New

Technical • Migrated 300 users to Win NT Domain Structure • Novell Groupwise to MS Exchange
• Novel Remote Access to MS Remote Access • Novell File-Print to MS File-Print

Result

For B&A	1st Novell to Microsoft NT Migration (leading to $2M in same-type projects)
For Microsoft	An early Proof of Concept - 1998, helping them build their business
For Client	Seamless migration, reduced total cost of ownership and -0- productivity loss

• **CENTRALIZING AN IT INFRASTRUCTURE** ——— Industry **LOGISTIC/TRANSPORTATION**

Mandate Hub Group, Americas second largest logistics broker, suffered IT downtime of 15-20% due to decentralized IT systems at 35 offices, resulting in lost productivity, missed shipments, and erroneous billing as noted by their CIO.

What's New

Technical Implemented a ***Corporate IT Network Management System*** on Novell Netware 5.1 with Zenworks 3.0 which enabled remote control of desktops, software distribution and asset management.

Result

For Client	Reduced IT headcount by 35 staff (133% over projections) this saves $2 million a year. The system is maintaining a trackable up time of 99%.
For B&A	First multi-state implementation of a Central Network Management Package.

• **SAVING CLIENT FROM TERMINATION** ——— Industry **MANUFACTURING**

Mandate Brought in on a IT contract to support Chamberlain Inc., the largest manufacturer of residential and commercial doors in the world and a business unit of Duchossois. My goal was to reposition their infant Novell network to where it could sustain the huge growth it was experiencing.

What's New

Technical Helped the IT Director launch a new technology strategy using a Citrix Thin Client Architecture.

Implemented	***Aurigin, a Patent Tracking System*** to protect Intellectual Property Rights.
Implemented	***Abra*, an *HR Employee Management Package*.**
Implemented	***Hyperion, Cash Flow And Budget Tracking System*** for Director of Finance.

Result

For Client	Elevated Chamberlain to the 21st Most Innovative Technology User (of 500 manufacturers) noted by Information Week, Sept. 17, 2001.
For B&A	Grew this client to the #1 billable relationship in the company.

1992-8/96 **PC SERVICES INC.** **Senior Network Specialist** Austin, TX

Hardware and software maintenance on PCs and networks. Quoted, designed and implemented network installations to increase workplace efficiency. Resolved multi-vendor hardware and software incompatibilities.

Progression of Business Role evolved from being a contracted engineer who focused on supporting LAN/WAN implementations for PC Products & Services to where I became a full-time employee for the company.

Results: I successfully marketed our networking capabilities and grew the business from under $100,000 in annual billings to over $700,000 by the time I left.

TRAINING & CERTIFICATION

- Group Wise Administration
- Compaq Hardware
- Novell E-Directory
- MCSE
- Cisco Router Training
- Compaq Server Configuration
- Citrix Winframe Certified Administrator
- Stephen Covey: 7 Habits of a Highly Effective Manager
- Charles Deming: Total Quality Management

TECHNICAL

Network OS	• Novell 2.x-6.x • Terminal Services	• NT 3.5-Win 2000 • Citrix Metaframe	
Email	• Exchange	• Novell Groupwise	• Lotus Notes
Infrastructure	• Cisco and Intel switches/routers		
Network Mgt.	• LanDesk Management	• Novell ZENWorks	
Enterprise Backup	• Arcserve	• BackupExec	

EDUCATION

Devry Institute of Technology - Telecommunications
University of Wisconsin, Oshkosh, Pursued B.S., Business Administration

——— *References available on request* ———

TONY WALLACE

764 Randall Ave., Marlborough, MA 01752 508-456-8192, twall@aol.net

A project director with experience managing full-cycle multi-technology, multi-platform software development teams up to 50+ people, consulting and advanced technology development. Received numerous Key Contributor awards for performance, innovation and business development. Knowledgeable business partner to senior managers and key customers across industries such as communications, consumer products, medical, publishing and petroleum.

1999 – 2003 **3COM** *Senior Staff Engineer* *2002-2003*
Group Program Manager *1999-2002*

Overview Member of the Advanced Technology Team, 5 senior staff tasked with working ahead of 3com's development organization to remove financial and technical risks from the development path and meet the following mandates:

Mandate 1 Advise Executive Team (CEO, CTO, Divisional SVPs) on how to:

- Reduce 3Com's R&D cycles
- Protect 3Com's intellectual property with domestic and international patents
- Grow Market presence via M&A activities
- Compete Internationally in the hyper-competitive technology arena

Mandate 2 Access talent in Asia (i.e. India and Singapore) that could

- Reduce Cost of development while also increasing development capacity
- Shift Product maintenance offshore to free engineers to focus on new products

Impact Enabled 3Com to optimize software development on 4 product groups impacting $500MM-$600MM in revenues (50% of all company income) and $1.0BB in R&D expenditures.

Contribution 1 **Help 3COM reduce cost and cycle time on product development**

Goal Reduce new product R&D time frame for market launch to under 2 years.

Actions Defined due diligence criteria used by the Business Development Team to evaluate acquisition targets. Researched technologies at 50 companies and features of 75 competitive products.

Result Contributed to a $135,000,000 acquisition of Vivace Networks.

Contribution 2 **Protect 3COM's multimillion dollar R&D Investments**

Goal Create a "Patent Scrub" process to permeate the engineering organization that would a) Preserve 3Com's IP rights, b) leverage additional licensing agreements.

Actions 3Com's Patent Committee member who evaluated 33% of all corporate patents of which 80% proceeded to patent filing. Coordinated technical, legal and capital resources.

Result Reduced patent backlog to zero within 4 months (prior to involvement, 25% of patent applications had languished for over 6 months).

Contribution 3 **Increase 3COM' s software development capacity while lowering development costs**.

Goal 1 Form a new international business unit to access global software development talent, (became 3com's Communications ***India***, 3CI).

Actions Directed US efforts in collaboration with 3Com's Denmark to create a software R&D center in New Delhi, India. Led a matrix-team of 25+ and managed multiple budgets ($4,000,000).

Result 1 Launched facility within 15 months of inception while remaining under budget.

Result 2 Recruited & formed software project teams and drove projects to first product release in 9 months at a reduced engineer cost of 40% (products are expected to deliver $50MM a year).

Goal 2 Planned and directed a global program to train ***Singaporean*** engineers in optical networking technology and seed a new software R&D center in Singapore.

Actions Negotiated a $1.4 MM grant from the Singapore Economic Development Board.

Result Improved product software integration testing time frame by ~20%.

Page 1 of 2

1983 – 1999 **CONSULTANTS INTERNATIONAL CORP.** *Staff Program/Project Manager: 1990-99*
Senior Consultant: 1983-90

Overview A multifunctional role as technical consultant, project manager, revenue producer and account executive. Authored project proposals to win new business and managed project execution for Fortune 500 and mid-sized companies.

Mandate 1 Optimize staff contributions to the bottom line for this publicly-held corporation.
Mandate 2 Increase new business development and ensure quality of project execution

Impact Added $40MM in revenues to the company as Project Manager, won dozens of individual awards for performance and business development efforts, and contributed to hiring over 200 technical staff who as a group delivered another $25MM in revenues to the branch.

Contribution 1 **Dallas Branch consistently ranked #2 among 25 branches in revenues and profits for 9 straight years**
Goal Project Leadership and New Business Development
Actions Authored proposals, won new business and directed software/hardware project engineering and IT teams for a diverse range of architectures, technologies and computing platforms.
Challenge Defining project scope, managing risk, staffing, schedule, timeline and budgets on projects such as: communications, automated testing, order fulfillment, customer product returns, embedded systems and point-of-sale.
Result Achieved a 25% revenue growth year-over-year, from $2 MM to $6 MM with 90% repeat business.

Contribution 2 **Develop "Best-In-Class" multifunctional/multi-talented project teams**
Goal Full accountability for teams of 50+ software development consultants assigned to client base of 25 accounts.
Actions Served clients such as AT&T, Ameritech, Lucent, Motorola, BP Amoco, Panasonic and Discover Financial.
Result Drove process improvements for interviewing, performance reviews and employee retention, resulting in lowest turnover rate (10%-15%) in a corporation experiencing over 33%.

As ***Senior Consultant*** led full-cycle software development projects & national product rollouts.

Result 1 Contributed to successful national rollout of AT&T's Enhanced 911 system which doubled product revenues for a $1.2BB product line.

Result 2 Conceived and developed a new product for AT&T, the "Call Stalker Integrated Management and Reporting System" used by fire/police emergency call centers to replace paper records with a PC-based system. Product generated over $3.6 M in revenues over life span.

EDUCATION

- Graduate coursework toward MBA, Management Concentration; University New Hampshire (1984/5)
- **BS** Computer Science – High Honors; University of New Hampshire (1980)
- **BS** Electronics Engineering

CONTINUING Business courses, negotiating techniques, conflict resolution, Internet marketing, 7 Habits of Highly Effective People, excellence in customer service, Project Management principles, Theory of Constraints & Critical Chain, software risk management.

TECHNICAL C++, HTML, Perl, Pascal, DEC Assembler, IBM Assembler, ESQL/C, PL/SQL, Unix, VMS, RSX-11, MVS, Dreamweaver, Informix, Optical Networks, T1/E1, SONET: ClearCase, UML, Object-Oriented Analysis/Design (RUP), Rational Rose Fundamentals, Oracle (SQL, Forms), Fiber Optic Fundamentals,

BRYCE ARMSTRONG 420 Benson Ave, Oak Park, IL 60130
708-721-5694 • barmstrong@earthlink.net

STRENGTHS

- Project Management
- Change Leadership
- Client Representation
- Technology Implementations
- Persuasive/Diplomatic
- Systems Architecture

EXPERIENCE

8/00 – 2002 **DIRECTOR,** ***Provisioning & Networks*** **TELSTRA.,** Chicago, IL

Overview Hired by the US CEO of Telstra, an Australian teleco, to execute a North American Business Development plan, initially in Chicago as the 1st office rollouts in 14 tier-1 cities. As Director of Provisioing my mandate was to support the corporate revenue, customer acquisition and profit goals of the company.

Challenge Make Chicago's rollout the model for NYC and LA openings to be added in a year.

My Value Within 4 months of hire, I completely changed Davnet's go-to-market strategy by replacing our existing T-3 technology with a networked Cisco optical switch.

Benefit Allowed Telstra to provide a data feed 10x faster and twice as secure with fewer single points of failure, all accomplished at a lower build cost, meaning we could keep a flat fee structure of $1,000/month with a better offering to win customers and yet protect profits.

Actions Designed and installed infrastructure for: Chicago & LA & NYC
Managed sales, engineering, provisioning and support teams. Engineered and implemented a SONET dark-fiber Metro Area Ethernet Network that supported Internet connectivity, VPN, VOIP, disaster recovery and business continuity.

Result Increased customer base from 2 to 99.
Result Exceeded building penetration rate of 15% in first 6 months.
Result Increased number of on-network buildings from 1 to 25.

1997 – 2000 **MANAGER,** ***Network Technology & Services*** **MARSH MCLENNAN CO.,** New York, NY

Overview Recruited by VP, Network Technology to help integrate Marsh's 21 business acquisitions which had made them the 2nd largest insurer in the world. Headcount grew from 12,000 to 50,000 staff, global reach went from 60-120 countries and worldwide offices increased from 400 to 600.

Initiative ***Business Integration*** Marsh needed to integrate multiple technologies and business functions, such as sales, marketing, accounting, administration to a single corporate intranet. **The goal was to save over $200,000,000** by capturing economic advantages of the acquisitions.

Result Physical and logical restructuring of Marsh's intranet to integrate new businesses onto a single corporate platform. Integrated mail systems, IP/IPX network addressing, and traffic routing schemes.

Initiative ***Network Mgmt.*** Introduced HP OpenView, VitalSuite and CiscoWorks 2000.
Result This is the ***new enterprise network management platform*** to manage growth.
Supported ***PeopleSoft implementation*** (first-ever client/server app. on the network).

Initiative ***Internet Integration*** Consolidated nearly 2 dozen locally-managed Internet portals.
Result Centralized all traffic to one corporate firewall and reduced 22 portals to 3.
Saved Marsh over $200,000 operational expenses (staff and maintenance).

Initiative ***International WAN*** To increase traffic for email and application access between the international entities, which had doubled from 60 to 120 countries.
Result Implemented global WAN for 7 business units. Used public frame relay for network connectivity, routing and firewalls in Chicago, London, Sydney and Toronto.

1994 – 1997 ***Senior Telecommunications Analyst*** **RITE AID PHARMACY,** San Francisco, CA

Overview Recruited by the Director of Network Services to design, provision and operate the company's **FIRST-EVER** intranet for this 350 store chain spread over 6 states.

Need Rite Aid's existing systems infrastructure couldn't meet daily business volumes and store operations were failing, i.e. pricing updates were delayed, credit card confirmations were slow and replacement hardware for legacy architecture was impossible.

Need Rite Aid's was on a rapid expansion spree that resulted in buying its competition and increasing their number of stores by 25%.

Need The central profit business, filling prescriptions, grew from 92 million to 110 million, nearly a 20% gain.

Actions

- Engineered a WAN to a frame relay with 350 Cisco routers, replacing X.25 network.
- Designed, implemented and supported Cisco Pix Internet firewall.
- Implemented network management environment and of business-to-business connectivity.
- Deployed HP OpenView and CiscoWorks for enterprise network management.

Result As sales grew by 20% from $2.5BB to $3.0BB, the IT infrastructure could now scale properly to meet this increasing business demand and consumer volume.

1983 – 1994 **Technical Director** **PACIFIC BELL (now SBC),** San Francisco, CA

Overview Handpicked by the Director of Data Center Operations to lead technology project teams on the following assignments.

Result I put email into Pacific Bell (the same system that is in use today,.

Result Implemented and operated Pacific Bell's ***First Ever*** intranet to connect their 65,000 staff and 16,000,000 customers.

EDUCATION

Certified Computing Professional (CCP) - Institute for Certification of Computer Professionals
Cisco CCNP - In progress, Tech Skills, Chicago, IL

Specialties in:

- Business Information Systems
- Communications Management
- Office Information Systems
- Systems Security
- Systems Development

1050+ hours of data communications and computer training, (224 hours of Cisco training as CCIE candidate)

1985 A.A. Business Administration, California State Long Beach, Long Beach, CA
Plus a certificate in Industrial Relations

References available on request.

CHAPTER 10

LEGAL CAREERS

The Legal Category Has

3 Client Examples

6 Job Titles

64 Years of Work History

NAME	JOB TITLES COVERED
1. JENNIFER HANSON	....Attorney
2. ERIC STAMOS*	....Senior Associate ....Associate
3. DEBI LABERGE	..........Paralegal -Real Estate Department ....Title & Closing Officer ....Sales Associate

* Find the "before resume" in chapter 35

JENNIFER HANSON

8709 Janet Ave., Overland Park, KS 66211 729-548-0559 jhanson2@aol.com

OBJECTIVE To pursue a consulting/sales career that will allow me to use my negotiation, public relation, business management and strategic planning skills.

SUMMARY Expertise in administration, staff development, service integration and project management enables me to achieve strategic objectives, resolve complex issues and defend organizational position. Use leadership abilities to achieve results and network with both management and clients to solve problems.

STRENGTHS

- Training
- Research
- Writing
- Client Relations
- Due Diligence
- Graphic Design
- Project Leadership
- Staff Management
- Contract Negotiations
- Cost Management
- Project Finance
- Operational Planning

EXPERIENCE

10/86 - present **BLACK & VEATCH**

A Fortune 250 worldwide construction and engineering company specializing in energy, power and environmental markets.

CORPORATE ATTORNEY

Overview • • • • • This is a general business management role that dictates I handle 40-50 concurrent multi-phase projects lasting between 1-5 years each that are staffed with teams of 5-15 professionals. On average, I retire approximately 20% of these projects annually, so the mix is constantly changing. The fact that I control a total annual budget of $400-$600K, along with the pressure associated with meeting stringent state and federal regulatory guidelines, drives performance standards and has challenged me to exceed internal expectations. Since the core business is highly technical, I am tasked with simplifying our business activities by setting up audit trails and corporate record keeping protocols to ensure that we hit specified business targets.

FUNCTIONS

Bid Oversight • Prepare contract documents and oversee the bid process (RFP/RFQ) to ensure integrity of all phases from project outline to final award. Key issues include determining requirements to comply with state and federal regulations, meeting deadlines and defining project specifications.

Project Lead • Focus on selecting team leaders from a large pool of technical experts, i.e. senior engineers, geologists, hydrogeologists and project managers as well as negotiating contracts awarded to vendors that average $75,000 per project.

Litigation Support • Counsel business parties and mediate disputes involving construction, commercial, real estate and environmental law issues. Dispute analysis includes reviewing all incoming contract documentation to determine case complexity and urgency.

Administrative • Implement quality initiatives to ensure accuracy and timeliness as well as meet contract provision stipulations.

Personnel • Build and supervise project teams of 4-5 by matching skills with functional needs to improve efficiency and attain appropriate manpower levels. Personnel actions include hiring, assessment and conflict resolution.

Project 1 **MERGER & ACQUISITION PARTICIPATION-** Over the past ten years, I have been involved with the due diligence, planning and execution phases of several acquisitions and divestitures averaging $100-$200 million each.

Project 2 **BUSINESS PROJECT** - Internal consultant to the Commercial Business Group Team Leader. As a team player I helped create a strategy to capture tax credits and government price concessions by integrating an eco-friendly farming operation in conjunction with our newly built $90 million cogeneration plant in Pennsylvania.

EDUCATION J.D., New England School of Law, Boston, MA

B.A., with *magna cum laude honors*, Political Science, Montclair State College, Upper Montclair, NJ

ERIC STAMOS

13 Trenton Way, Menneapolis, MN 55438 952-429-8951 erics14@aol.com

OBJECTIVE To continue a successful legal career as a lawyer for a medium to large firm.

SUMMARY ***Over 50 tort law trials*** - Litigation expertise combines elements of client screening to discern case potential, selecting expert witnesses capable of supporting the case and pre-litigation preparation to win favorable outcomes without undue expense. For 20 years I have been dedicated to building a legal track record of results in environments where high performance and quality are essential to success.

STRENGTHS

Client Representation Build client relations, successfully meet their needs and build good will in order to generate referrals.

Trial Preparation Experience, instinct and litigation skills have won the majority of jury cases.

Negotiations Apply specific justification techniques and psychological insight to gain leverage and to attain favorable settlement.

Legal Research Extensive case law research to determine controlling precedent, to substantiate trial or appellate positions, and to win cases.

EXPERIENCE

9/93 to present *Senior Associate* **HUER & ASSOCIATES** Minneapolis, MN

Overview Lead the personal injury litigation efforts to position H&A as an aggressive well respected law firm. Successfully argue cases, choose juries and outline evidentiary information to win positive judicial opinion and justify large damage awards in the areas of medical malpractice and product liability.

Result The firm as a whole has hit record income for two of the past three years, of which my practice generates 50% of all fees received in this five-lawyer firm.

Actions Expert in all phases of litigation development and resolution including investigations, 213 (g) interrogatories, pretrial motions, as well as:

- Pleadings
- Discovery
- Negotiations
- Research for Case Precedents
- Voir Dire
- Client Relations
- Case Assessments

9/87 to 8/93 *Senior Associate* **SEIBEN,GROSE, VON HOLTEN & CAREY LTD.** Minneapolis, MN

Tort law practice concentrated in medical malpractice and product liability.

8/80 to 8/87 *Associate* **GALLAGHER LAW FIRM** Little Cananda, MN

Practice divided between defense work for Farmers Insurance and plaintiff's medical malpractice, product liability, auto accidents, worker's compensation, and premises liability.

▪ CASE EXAMPLES ▪

MEDICAL MALPRACTICE

Hamden/Giovanni v. Assa-Ottoman – Failure to timely diagnose and treat a bowel infarct.

Key to case In foresight, obtained favorable 2-622 reviews against ***both*** the attending physician and the consulting surgeon.

Discovered The two physicians disagreed on what was said about whether the consultation was urgent, and by the time the consultation took place, it was too late to save the patient's life.

Dameran v. Sanders – Sciatic nerve injury during abdominal surgery resulting in foot drop.

Key to case Naming both the surgeon and the assistant surgeon in the complaint and the 2-622 review.

Discovered The two physicians switched their names in the operative report, with the listed assistant actually being the physician who performed the surgery. Developed alternative theory of injury to the sciatic nerve as a result of a nurse's postoperative Demerol injection which led the hospital to contribute toward the settlement.

Puttman v. Dynamic Foundation Osteopathic – Failure to timely treat post-operative complications following anterior decompression for osteophytes with resulting paraplegia.

Key to case Keeping both the surgeon and the hospital in the suit, as the surgeon's liability insurer went bankrupt.

Developed Criticism of hospital's failure to keep surgeon advised kept the hospital in for substantial contribution.

PRODUCT LIABILITY

Brennnan v. Culticare Products – Plaintiff developed reactive airways dysfunction syndrome with hypersensitivity to everyday irritants caused by a new ***toxic*** solder in the workplace.

Key to case A creative investigative strategy obtained the European Material Safety Data Sheet for the product that substantially differed from the U.S. version. Retained Chief of Toxicology at County Hospital as an expert witness.

Discovered Aldehydes and other irritants were not listed in the defendant's American Material Safety Data Sheets.

Johnson v. Schaffer Manufacturing – Inadequate grounding instructions caused static electric discharge and ignited combustible vapors causing burn injuries.

Key to case Developed a theory that the machine operators should be grounded in addition to the manufacturer's specification that only the machine needed to be grounded.

Discovered Lack of operator grounding caused a static electric arc to ignite the combustible vapors.

APPELLATE LAW

Pelman v. Caruso – In a case of ***first impression,*** it was held that a preexisting mental condition may conceal wrongful causes of one's injury so as to fall within the discovery rule.

Key to case Plaintiff believed her suicide attempt was the result of long-standing depression, and only suspected negligence in her psychiatric care and/or medication when she saw a news report on the dangers of Prozac.

Result Summary judgment for defendant physicians and drug manufacturer reversed.

Neher v. Dicks' World of Sports – In a case of ***first impression,*** it was held that skiing is not a contact sport to which common law immunity from negligence applies.

Key to case Successfully contended that while collisions of skiers can occur, these are rare and unintended aspects in the sport of skiing.

Result Summary judgment for defendant reversed.

MEMBERSHIPS • American Bar & Minnesota State Bar Associations • Admitted to the U.S. Northern District Court

EDUCATION University of Minnesota College of Law, Minneapolis, MN 1979
Law school admission test score: 672 of 700

B.S., *Cum Laude* - Political Science, minor English, St. Mary's University, Minneapolis, MN 1976

▪ *References available on request* ▪

DEBI LABERGE

924 Jennings Dr., San Diego, CA 92105 • 619-245-2004

OBJECTIVE

To continue a successful career that capitalizes on improving operations, attaining objectives and helping a company meet the dynamic challenges of a rapidly changing business environment.

SUMMARY

Proficient at creating and using standards and procedures to accomplish goals. Work diligently to solve problems and apply organizational skills to maximize the effectiveness of my efforts. Overall, a sincere interest in the quality of my work ensures the company minimizes operating costs, sustains profitability and grows efficiently.

STRENGTHS

- Troubleshooting
- Communications
- Project Management
- Persistence
- Strategic Planning
- Resourceful
- Client Service
- Self Starter
- Team Building
- Responsiveness
- Accountability
- Dedication

PARALEGAL EXPERIENCE

HASKIN & ASSOCIATES — ***Paralegal - Real Estate Department*** — San Diego , CA

Overview.............. Assisted in representing lenders, land developers, purchasers and sellers on multimillion dollar commercial office/industrial buildings, shopping centers/malls, multifamily as well as residential real estate transactions nationwide. Other departments supported included: Litigation, Estate Planning and Corporate law.

Challenge Single-handedly supporting a group of 11 law partners and 8 associates.

Actions

- Reviewed contracts, prepared closing check lists and tracked contingency dates.
- Ordered title commitments, surveys, payoff letters and performed title clearance.
- Prepared closing documents, strict joint order escrows and deed and money escrows.
- Attended commercial closings, sometimes acting as first chair and always without an attorney at residential closings.
- Prepared 1031 Tax Deferred Exchanges.
- Performed ownership searches and tax work on properties.

Liaison Contact with title companies, brokers, lenders, attorneys, clients, land trusts, surveyors and exchange companies. Familiar with procedures and personnel of title insurers.

Impact Contributed to closing 138 transactions - a total monetary value of $845 million.

RMC REAL ESTATE CORP. — ***Title & Closing Officer*** — San Diego, CA

Overview.............. Part of a team of two who assisted 7 sales staff with closing property transactions on land previously owned by the bankrupt Chicago-Milwaukee R.R.

Impact Closed over 30 deals in one year.

ARMSTRONG & ARMSTRONG — ***Paralegal - Real Estate Department*** — San Diego, CA

Overview.............. Provided comprehensive paralegal support during real estate transactions for single-family residential buyers.

Impact Helped close over 250 deals in 5 years.

BOYD & BRIMMER APC — ***Sales Associate*** — San Diego, CA

Assigned to sell residential property in La Jolla area.

EDUCATION

Certified Paralegal, California Western School of Law — San Diego, CA
University of Southern California San Diego — San Diego, CA
BA Sociology - Minors: Psychology/Social Psychology. Graduated with highest honors.

CHAPTER 11

INSURANCE CAREERS

The Insurance Category Has

2 Client Examples

8 Job Titles

43 Years of Work History

NAME	JOB TITLES COVERED
1. CHRISTOPHER THOMAS	Assistant Secretary/Corp.Claims Analyst ....VP Claims Manager ....Litigation Manager ....Claims Manager ....Claims Specialist ....Claims Representative
2. MICHAEL FELDMAN*	.......International Underwriting Manager ....Assistant Product Line Manager

* Find the "before resume" in chapter 35

CHRISTOPHER THOMAS

336 Westmoorland, Seattle, WA 98109

cthomas@aol.com • *206-766-3233*

EXPERIENCE

1999 to Present — **Pemco Insurance** *Asst. Secretary/Corporate Claims Analyst* — Seattle,WA

Overview

Supervise Pemco's highest exposure claims as follows: technical oversight of 3 managers, 13 lawyers and 6 claims examiners for Lawyers E&O and Director's and Officers Liability Litigation.
As Chief Technical Claims Officer for Professional Liability, I oversee risk and litigation issues impacting 3 lines of business, 2,300 open files with aggregate reserves of $82 million.

Key contribution — **Extra Contractual Liability Claims** - on 7/99 I analyzed all 200+ existing claims and recommended changes in department structure as well as claims evaluation and resolution processes.

Result — Reduced bad faith claims by 40% (this yielded the lowest payout and lowest total open cases in the past 9 quarters).

1985 - 1999 — **Employer's Reinsurance** **Div. of GE Capital**

1993 - 1999	***VP Claims Manager***	(Coregis, div. of Xerox Corp.)
1991 - 1993	***Litigation Manager***	
1988 - 1991	***Claims Manager***	
1985 - 1988	***Claims Specialist***	

Overview

In 1985 hired by a subsidiary of Xerox, which in 1993 became Coregis. In 1997 Employer's Reinsurance Corp. bought Coregis.

As VP Claims Manager — Oversight of the largest exposure Lawyers & Accountants claims with total reserves over $100M, 9 Claims Supervisors and 20 Claims Technicians. Conducted quality control audits and drafted reports. Made CEO presentations on high exposure cases. Liaison to Actuarial and Reinsurance departments.

As Litigation Manager — Managed large exposure Professional Liability and Extra Contractual Liability claims. National Coordinator for failed financial institution litigation.

As Claims Manager — Directed claims staff in investigating and adjusting Accountants Professional Liability claims. Hired and trained new claims technicians, wrote performance appraisals, managed clerical staff and made quarterly presentations to the AICPA Professional Liability Insurance Plan Committee.

Key contribution — **Reducing Claims Overpayment**- worked with McKenzie & Co. to identify and measure causes of overpayment which resulted in implementing a ***Claims Cost Management System*** to address a 9% leakage rate.

Actions — Part of 5-person claims management team that reviewed core skills of Coverage, Investigation, Evaluation, Litigation Management and File Resolution.

Results — Saved $10M by reducing claim overpayments from 9% to 3.5%.

Key contribution — **Large Claims Resolution** - Personally responsible for the company's largest cases from initial claim receipt to resolution.

Actions — Applied alternative dispute resolution on large cases such as:

• FDIC v. Cherry, Bekaert & Holland (reduced a $46M claim to a $2.5M settlement and saved litigation costs), see Wallstreet Journal, March 8, 1991.

• Identified a dispositive motion issue overlooked by counsel which saved Coregis $2MM on a large exposure Professional Liability Claim.

Result — Effective management of large exposure cases resulted in reducing overall claims payment.

ERC Experience Cont'd...

Key contribution	LITIGATION RISK ANALYSIS - Introduced the first corporate use at ERC of methodology to evaluate complex cases with high exposures.
Actions	Created decision trees to consistently evaluate multiple variables in a graphical format that leads to rational decisions on when to continue or settle claims.
Result	Consistent application of these methods helped drive down claims leakage.

1984 -1985 **State Farm Insurance** ***Claim Representative*** Seattle, WA

Overview Received initial claim notices from insureds, verified coverage, established reserves, conducted field investigations, analyzed medical reports, attended pretrial conferences and negotiated settlements.

RECOGNITION

2001	Panel Speaker: Lawyers Malpractice, American Bar Association Meeting, St. Petersburg, FL
1999	Panel Speaker: Professional Liability; Defense Research Institute Convention, Boston, MA
1992	Recipient of Xerox Financial Services Chairman's Award
1983	Admitted to Practice Law in Washington

EDUCATION

1982	J.D.	Seattle University Law School, Seattle, WA
1978	B.A.	With Honors, Seattle Pacific University, Seattle, WA

References available on request.

MICHAEL FELDMAN

179 W. Trenton, New York, NY 10036 mfeld210@yahoo.com 212-468-6844

SUMMARY

I have the vision and professional seasoning to contribute as a leader of a corporate team or member of an aggressive consulting force. I am a goal oriented solution provider who maintains integrity and personal accountability at all times.

SKILLS

• Risk Assessment
• Growing Revenues • Forensic Investigation
• RFP Evaluation • Reviewing & Auditing
• Negotiations
• Research
• Client Relations
• Team Management
• Contract Development

1987-1998 **International Underwriting Manager** **GUARDIAN LIFE INSURANCE**, NY, NY
Overview Worked in the energy segment for the most profitable division of a multibillion/multinational corporation.

Actions Set business strategies to bind $3.0 billion in complex technical risks for corporate clients in North American, London and European markets. Negotiated contract limits of $10-$600MM each on 33 accounts consisting of chemical plants, petroleum refineries and power generators. Audited compliance to corporate standards for Hong Kong, Bangkok, and Melbourne offices.

Clients e.g.
- Japan's Tonen Energy
- Philippine Petroleum
- Jamaica's Petrojam
- Nigeria's Nafcon
- Mexico's Groupo Alfa
- Southern Companies

Challenges Engineering - The highly technical client base demanded intimate working relations with internal and client side engineers to adequately identify the assumed risks.

Risk Management - The value of each account to its representative country demanded delicate negotiations to ensure that the client and Guardian's goals were both accomplished.

Networking- Covering risk up to $7 billion per contract, dictated that I create complex syndicates of 5-10 participants per contract in order to completely protect our corporate assets.

Results

1. Delivered **25% profit** on portfolios which generated $5-$11 million in revenues.
2. Increased revenues **BY $4,000,000** after troubleshooting 20 neglected accounts.
3. Laid the foundation to **profitably re-underwrite A $9,000,000** portfolio.
4. **Produced $1,000,000** in new power generation business during short London assignment.
5. Executed US selling trips which generated **$1,500,000 in new business** in 2 years.

1983-1987 **Asst. Product Line Manager** **ZURICH NORTH AMERICA,** NY, NY
Overview Specialized in Electric Utilities as this business line grew 50% from $30 to $45 million in three years.

Actions Worked with branch personnel and HQ executives to determine price rates and Zurich corporate going-forward strategies on 300 business opportunities involving special risks or unique trends.

Results

1. Delivered profitability of 25% on a $30 to $45 million business line.
2. Part of a three manager team that developed a System Performance that earned $1,500,000 in new business within a year.

EDUCATION M.A, New York University, NY, NY
B.A., Baruch College, NY, NY

SEMINARS Dale Carnegie Course: Advanced Negotiations
Wheaton University: Creating Customer Value/Essential Principles of Marketing

LANGUAGES German Fluent & French Functional.

CHAPTER 12

PR & ADVERTISING CAREERS

The PR & Advertising Category Has

3 Client Examples

11 Job Titles

39 Years of Work History

NAME	JOB TITLES COVERED
1. DEBRA JACKSON	VP Associate Director of Local Broadcast ....Partner/Client Services Supervisor ....Senior Broadcast Negotiator ....Junior Broadcast Negotiator
2. ELIOT FISHER	.....................Director Of Golf Marketing ....Director Of Sales & Marketing ....Account Executive ....Director Of Ticket Sales
3. DENISE DREMAN	.....................................Media Supervisor ....Media Planner ....Assistant Media Planner

DEBRA JACKSON

729 S. Oakhurst St., Houston, TX 77027 713-295-7878

SUMMARY

Execute regional advertising campaigns, negotiate rates and create media buys for local tv, cable and radio. Manage staff to ensure buys meet schedules, purchases attain plan goals and accurately post. Maintain client relationships by clearly presenting buying strategies and explaining complexities relevant to the account.

Strengths

- Staff Development
- Client Management
- Posting
- Ratings Research
- Cost Estimations
- Market Research
- Negotiations
- Communications
- Presentation

EXPERIENCE

6/97 - present **DDB NEEDHAM** *V.P./Associate Director of Local Broadcast*

Overview

Handle all Chicago office operations, oversee 16 buyers conducting $60M in spot tv, cable and radio purchases spread over 42 markets representing 600 annual schedules. Team with account representatives and media planners to represent media buying to client.

- Built an effective team of buyers (replacing 75% of existing staff).
- Ensure accurate pre-post, time period and affidavit posting.
- Train on: estimating, negotiating, posting and maintaining schedules.

Managed, supervised accounts and negotiated rates for every major category of advertiser. The list represents an aggregation of client representation over the past 10+ years.

Industries	*Clients*	*Clients*	*Clients*	*Clients*
Business/High-Tech	• Hewlett Packard	• Carter Wallace	• Motorola	• Page-Net
Package Goods	• Kraft Foods	• Reynolds Metals	• Best Foods	• Kellogg
	• M&M/Mars	• Procter & Gamble	• General Mills	• Gerber
	• Warner Lambert	• Oscar Mayer	• Heinz	• Lipton
Quick Serve	• Burger King	• Chuck e. Cheese's	• Wendy's	• Red Lobster
Retail	• Kohls	• Bally Health Clubs	• Orkin	• Florsheim
Automotive	• Ford Dealers	• Lexus Dealers	• Toyota Dealers	
Entertainment/Toys	• 20th Century Fox	• Saban Entertainment	• Bandai Toys	
Weight Loss	• Jenny Craig	• Weight Watchers		
Hospitality	• La Quinta Inns	• Princess Cruise Lines		
Pro Bono	• US Marine Corps	• Office of National Drug Partnership		
Auto After-Market	• Car-X	• Midas		
Airlines	• Northwest Airlines	• Delta		

7/87 - 6/97 **OMD WORLDWIDE**

Partner/Client Service Supervisor 1/94 - 6/97
Senior Broadcast Negotiator 1/91-1/94
Junior Broadcast Negotiator 7/87-1/91

Overview

Controlled a $30M local market spot tv, cable and radio budget. Managed communication and quality control of client's needs. Analyzed costs and presented media schedules to client. Analyzed media schedules from pre-buy to post-buy and presented to clients. Reviewed overall market performance to identify under deliveries. Trained new associates.

- Ensured media buys posted to industry standards of 90-100%.
- Ensured our standard of buying at 15% less than industry average.
- Participated with the new business development team to present buying plans to potential clients.

AWARDS

- OMD, Best Non-Metered Market Buyer, 3rd qtr, 1999
- OMD, Best Non-Metered Market National Buyer, 4th qtr 1998

EDUCATION

1992 M.S. Integrated Communication — UNIVERSITY OF HOUSTON - SCHOOL OF JOURNALISM
1987 B.A. Graphic Design, Minor Advertising — RICE UNIVERSITY

ELIOT N. FISHER

1610 W. La Quinta Ave, San Hosea, CA 95160 408-377-7725

OBJECTIVE

An event marketing opportunity that capitalizes on creating excellent profit results, improving client development efforts and enhancing overall product delivery.

SUMMARY

An established professional capable of building strong business relationships, developing innovative ideas to improve market share and handling the logistics of large scale national/international events. Marketing insights focus on identifying trends, creating effective strategies and planning promotional programs to achieve sales growth targets. Advertising and product/branding experience is balanced with client communications, sales, and staff development skills.

FUNCTIONS

MARKETING	Identify potential markets and product segments to target consumer interests.
ADVERTISING & PROMOTION	Formulate advertising strategies to build brand awareness, product distinction and consumer loyalty.
TEAM COORDINATION	Ensure project success by selecting and managing human resources.
CLIENT DEVELOPMENT	Ensure coordination and relationship development efforts are centered on helping clients attain corporate goals.

EXPERIENCE

1995 - Present

CALIFORNIA SPORTS MARKETING

Director of Golf Marketing

Recruited to manage marketing support and overall event coordination for CSM's portfolio of major sports programming. Supervise a staff of 4 professionals responsible for developing strategy, communicating vision to client representatives and planning advertising execution.

CONCURRENT SPORTS PROJECTS

⊙ ZURICH CLASSIC OPEN PGA TOUR

Overview Developed the proposal which was submitted to Zurich's Director of External Affairs and won CSM the rights to oversee sales, marketing and advertising for three years ('96, '97, '98). Sold $1.1M in hospitality, advertising and sponsorships (81% increase over '95 revenues). Developed a $400K public relations, advertising and creative event promotional campaign to purchase tv, print and radio time.

⊙ CALIFORNIA OPEN PGA TOUR

Overview Provide national sponsorship sales support to this Pebble Beach TOUR stop. Increased sales by 10% to $1.8M.

⊙ ASSOCIATION OF VOLLEYBALL PROFESSIONALS (AVP)

Overview Contracted with Jerry Soloman and the AVP to market the season-ending Miller Lite Tour Championship in Los Angeles. Procured $50,000 in new sponsorship for the event, plus an additional $40,000 in print coverage through a trade with the L.A. Times.

⊙ NCAA BASKETBALL - MAUI INVITATIONAL

Overview Direct sponsorship and promotional initiatives (Web site) for the nation's premiere pre-season college basketball tournament. Assist ESPN's tv producer with production.

1991- 1995

INTERNATIONAL MANAGEMENT GROUP (IMG)

Director of Sales and Marketing

Overview Directed the opening of IMG's San Diego office and established a significant market presence. Managed a staff of 8.

IMG Experience Cont'd...

SPORTS PROJECTS

Account Executive/Client Management

⊙ **IMG MOTORSPORTS DIVISION**

Overview Helped Indy-Car drivers Emerson Fittipaldi, Bryan Herta, Danny Sullivan, Tom Kendall and the Chip Ganassi Target and Tony Bettenhausen racing teams obtain sponsorship and appearance money. Liaison between major motor sports marketing corporations and IMG Motorsports.

⊙ **ITT AUTOMOTIVE INDIANAPOLIS GRAND PRIX**

Overview Sold over $300,000 in new sponsorship and hospitality in a three month period. Supervised the day to day operations of the ticket managers in Indianapolis and Daytona. Responsible for $2.6M in ticket revenue for both events. Devised and implemented an organizational system to improve the credentialing of clients and guests at the event.

Director of Ticket Sales

⊙ **BUDWEISER GRAND PRIX OF DAYTONA**

Overview Responsible for $1.2M in ticket revenue for IMG's first major Indy-Car event. The race experienced a sell-out for the first time in the 14 year history of the event.

BUSINESS PROJECTS

⊙ **OPERATION CAPE HORN** [Coordinated with Jason Freidburg, IMG's CEO]

Overview Corporate effort involving 18 sales executives traveling to South and Central America to promote IMG products and services. IMG secured over $1M in new business and established two regional offices.

INTERNSHIP

⊙ **TRANS INTERNATIONAL (DIVISION OF IMG)**

Overview Project Accountant Interned for the world's largest producer of tv events. Learned all financial aspects of tv production and sale of broadcast rights. Prepared client reporting statements.

EDUCATION

BS: **Sports Management/Marketing** [1992] UNIV. OF SOUTHERN CALIFORNIA, LA, CA

References available on request.

DENISE DREMAN

2215 Whiewater Dr., San Fransisco, CA 94102 • 415-347-7794

OBJECTIVE To apply skills in marketing, brand management, and advertising.

SUMMARY Execute national advertising campaigns, negotiate rates and create media buys for TV, print and other media. Skills impact consumer communications, increasing client sales and staff development. Ensure buys meet schedules, purchases attain planned goals and accurately post. Support the client relationship by clearly presenting buying strategies and explaining complexities relevant to the account.

STRENGTHS

• Staff Training	• Ratings Research	• Negotiations	• Cost Estimations
• Communications	• Postings	• Market Research	• Presentations
• Forecasting & Projections	• Client Management	• Product Launches	• Strategy Development

EXPERIENCE
1/98 - present

OMNICOM
Media Supervisor 6/01-present

CLIENT QUAKER OATS

Overview.............. Execute multimillion dollar advertising campaigns for TV, print, outdoor and newspaper that focus on effectively using budgets to capture the client's key target audiences.

Develop product launches and product tests prior to national distribution in new categories (ie. Propel Fitness Water). Train and manage Media Planners and Assistant Media Planners

DIVISIONS SUPPORTED	**Products Represented**
Hot Cereals	Instant Grits, Oatmeal
Snacks	Gatorade Energy Bar
Golden Grains	Rice-a-Roni, Near East
Beverages	Propel
Fortified Foods (Altus)	Take Heart, WIN

Budget Snap shot	**Total ($) Planned**
As Supervisor	$39MM over 15 months
As Media Planner	$53MM over 24 months
As Asst. Media Planner	$40MM over 14 months
Total	$132MM

As Media Supervisor
Prepared and presented or contributed on client presentations to support TV, Print and other media buying decisions.

Plan media buys to capture a client's marketing and sales objectives by executing tactical media strategies.

Key Contribution

Client Presentations	***Include***
• Objectives & Strategies	8 each
• Media Plan Recommendations	15 each
• Competitive Analysis	9 each

Media Planning Focus

• Penetrate new markets	• Build brand equity
• Increase product consumption	• Launch new product
• Heighten product awareness	• Increased sales

Media Planner 2/99-6/01 ***Products*** Hot Cereals, Propel Fitness Water

Overview.............. Developed media plans and executed buying strategies based on ratings projections, program content and audience mix. Managed brands to ensure maximum effectiveness. Analyzed competition and wrote business overviews to support Quaker Oats' marketing plan. Managed media, planning, cost database for 18 planners who spent $250MM. Trained new staff on the Competitive & Buying IT systems.

Asst. Media Planner 1/98 - 2/99 ***Products*** Hot Cereals at $600M year

Overview.............. Assisted in the planning process for Quaker Instant and Standard Oatmeal.

COMPUTER Adviews, IMS, SQAD, Mediatools, Telmar, MS Excel, PowerPoint and Word

EDUCATION 12/97: B.S., Marketing & Finance, UNIV. OF CALIFORNIA SAN FRANSISCO

CHAPTER 13

ENTERTAINMENT CAREERS

The Entertainment Category Has

2 Client Examples

3 Job Titles

25 Years of Work History

NAME	JOB TITLES COVERED
1. SARA COHEN	..............................Reporters Assistant/PA
2. CHRISTY ADAMS*	................................Production Manager ....Senior Account Coordinator

* Find the "before resume" in chapter 35

SARA COHEN

310-772-9132 • coe323@aol.com
3131 Appletree Ln., Sherman Oaks, CA 90212

OBJECTIVE **TV News Reporter -** to help improve ratings at a major-market broadcast affiliate.

MEDIA EXPERIENCE

	CBS-2 TV, L.A.	**PROGRAM FORMAT**	
①	**Bogey's Corner**	Consumer advocacy	Worked on 40 programs over 5 months
	My Role	Reporter's Assistant/PA	Fraud investigation for show host/reporter
②	**Women 2 Women**	Daily female-topics show	Worked on 130 shows over 6 months
	My Role	Reporter's Assistant/PA	Supported 2 reporters on 30 minute prograı Set appointments and called guests
③	**McCain Brothers**	2 hour daily mornings	Worked on 80 shows over 4 months
	My Role	Reporter's Assistant/PA	Meet/greet guests, track arrival, call/confirm
④	**E! Entertainment**	Fashion & Style	Worked on 12 shows over 3 months
	My Role	Reporter's Assistant/PA	Helped producer and pre-show planning Topics: celebrity & designer interviews.

Bogey's Corner

"Woman 2 Woman"

ACTING

Television

Telemundo: Tiranos Del Norte Video
Dreamworks: Dancer-Henry Rollins Band
Access Hollywood-Guest
Sony: Dancer - Weezer Video

Commercials/Print

AirTouch Communications
Wella Hair Products

MEDIA EDUCATION

DEGREES				
	BA TV/JOURNALISM	COLUMBIA COLLEGE	Chicago, IL	2004
	AS LIBERAL ARTS	MOORPARK COLLEGE	Moorpark, CA	2000

✓ Key knowledge	**What I learned...**	
CORE COURSE	*PRINT/BROADCAST REPORTING*	Interviewing, news gathering, and lead-writing for print and broadcast. Reporting with accuracy and objectivity.
CORE COURSE	*NEWS WRITING/EDITING*	Writing radio and tv news scripts, checking errors, inconsistencies/redundancies improving clarity and editing in AP style.
CORE COURSE	*INVESTIGATIVE REPORTING*	Methods to track a story to its roots, gathering relevant news info for presentation on radio, tv and newspaper.
CORE COURSE	*COMPUTER AIDED REPORTING*	Technology-based news reporting techniques, database research reporting applications, such as Internet search engines and analytical software.
CORE COURSE	*THE TV NEWSPACKAGE*	Shooting, interviewing and editing news package material. Stand-ups, voice-overs sound bites, cut-aways and writing to video.
CORE COURSE	*PRODUCTION & EDITING*	Field production, concept development, planning, storyboarding, project editing with DVCam and Avid Express editing.
CORE COURSE	*MEDIA ETHICS & LAW*	Issues confronting journalists; First Amendment history and interpretation.

Christy Adams

19255 Western Ave., Brooklyn, NY 11238, 718-544-2170, cadams@Aol.com

OBJECTIVE A successful creative career that capitalizes on my ability to successfully manage complex projects or accounts.

SUMMARY I emphasize a personal and responsive approach to business needs, budget constraints and staff management. Skills include client service of programs that impact consumer communication, creating sales support collateral and project leadership. I attain objectives by executing national/regional radio, print and direct mail advertising campaigns. To ensure success of my responsibilities, I maintain personal involvement and accountability.

FILM, MUSIC VIDEO & COMMERCIAL PRODUCTION MANAGEMENT

EXPERIENCE Production manager/coordinator on 16 pop music videos, 2 commercials and 4 movies for 8 different production companies. I've managed 80 person crews and budgets of $60,000-$1,800,000. I've participated on creating the initial concept, pitching it to the artist and label (RCA, MCA, Universal), customizing concept to fit budget and final edit. I've brought value by negotiating favorable rates, meeting deadline and ensuring final product quality.

10/97 - present ***Production Manager***

Managed pre-production, filming, and post-production teams for pop music videos aired on **BET, MTV** and **VH1** as well as feature films and tv commercials**.** Negotiated film crew pay rates and managed vendor relations covering pricing and budgets.

PROJECTS	**FILM**	Chicago	[bought by Entertainers Tonight, distributed by SONY Entertainment]
		Freida	['00 Women in Film, Honorable Mention at Film Festival]
		Teaching Anna	[45 minute short]
	VIDEO	Shania Twain	[$1.2M budget music video with heavy special effects]
		Britney Spears	[$575K budget - Production went from Chicago-to-NYC-to-Atlanta]
		Puff Combs	[Grammy Winner/Grammy Producer, $250K budget, 1999 release]
	TV	Absolute Vodka	[European distribution, $800K/Crew of 50]
		Verizon Wireless	[European distribution $1M budget/**Spike Lee** Directed]

EXPERIENCE

ADVERTISING & ACCOUNT MANAGEMENT

1/95- 10/97 ***Senior Account Coordinator* - Kellogg Account** **Global Advertising**

Within 6 months of hire, I created the company's first corporate brochure with individual components for the four divisions: P.R./Advertising/Medical Education/Medical Solutions. After brochure completion, I was assigned to the advertising department's new Kellogg account for: • Wheat Bran • Oat Bran • Bran Buds

Planning Formulate strategies, identify time targets and determine executable actions to improve reach, build brand awareness, product distinction and helping create loyalty.

Budgeting Evaluate program cost efficiencies to meet constraints and deliver best value to client.

Campaign **Kelloggs:** Advertising campaign with heavy PR spin targeting Medical Doctors, where we linked Kelloggs' claim that their wheat bran diet reduces the risk of colorectal cancer.

Results Two medical journals, JAMA and the New England Journal of Medicine wrote positive articles.

Web Project Launched Kelloggs' Nutrition University web site *www. kelloggsnu.com (70 pages). Note!* SWA's first web page application and template for other projects including, Exceddrin Aspirin.

Campaign ***American Red Cross, Focus:*** Launched two products using classic movie personalities Marilyn Monroe, Rock Hudson and Edward G. Robinson

EDUCATION B.A., Modern Dance, University of Wisconsin Madison

CHAPTER 14
MARKETING CAREERS

The Marketing Category Has

2 Client Examples

6 Job Titles

26 Years of Work History

NAME	JOB TITLES COVERED
1. MEREDETH CANNESTRA	.............................Marketing Coordinator
2. SUZANNE KATZ*	......................Public Information Officer ......Deputy Director Of Communications ....Communications Specialist ....Media Relations Specialist .....Employee Communications Specialist

* Find the "before resume" in chapter 35

MEREDITH CANNESTRA

4987 JENNER LANE
ATLANTA, GA 30339
770-338-1645

OBJECTIVE

Creative support in a Media/Advertising/Promotions environment.

SUMMARY

Expertise includes designing and producing print collateral such as identity systems, logotypes, reports, corporate publications, brochures, advertisements and direct mail. Experienced at managing projects from conceptual development through production stage to final piece.

STRENGHTHS

- Lead/Direct Teams
- Multitasking
- Set Objectives
- Organization
- Project Coordination
- Client Relations
- Client Support
- Promotional Launches

EXPERIENCE

8/98 - present **ADAMS OUTDOOR ADVERTISING** Atlanta, GA
Marketing Coordinator - Report to Southeast Marketing Manager

Overview Sole creative marketing support for Atlanta (a top 3 office which generates $33 million a year). Create custom visual presentations for 15 Sales Representatives during pitches to corporate clients and advertising agencies.

On a project basis, I support 30 National Sales Representatives spread across 60 US offices who are proposing to Fortune 500 clients or executing national campaigns that include an Atlanta presence.

Challenges Increased presentation volume due to:
1. Adding 6 new media forms which required creating 6-times more visual mock-ups.
2. Sales staff used marketing tools as their key strategy to generate new media buys.

Responses
1. Developed branches' first priority scheduling strategy based on level of urgency and taught the 15 sales reps how to use it effectively.
2. Redesigned entire Promotions Program
3. Created a showcase for Account Executives to present our capabilities to clients.

Result Produce 15-25 client presentations a week versus 1-2 per week before my hire. This 600% increase helped grow billings $12 million a year (35%) without adding new marketing staff.

Actions

Create	Visual Boards & Specialized Media Kits.
Manage	A staff of 3 interns.
Conduct	Field research by accompanying sales staff on pitch/presentations.

COMPUTERS MS Office, Adobe Illustrator, Photoshop

EDUCATION

Bachelor of Fine Art	SCHOOL OF THE ART INSTITUTE *Emphasis*: PAINTING - DRAWING - PERFORMANCE
Internships	Administrative Intern, Fox Theatre Administrative Intern, Georgia Arts Council

Suzanne Katz

729 Eastern Ave., New York, NY 10013 212-232-4897 skatz@aol.com

PUBLIC SECTOR	6/99-12/00	***Public Information Officer***	**City of Chicago**
	2/98 -6/99	***Deputy Dir. Communications***	**Park District**
	3/96 -2/98	***Communications Specialist***	**Park District**

As Public Information Officer - increased visibility and public appreciation for the Mayor's Workforce Development program. - Challenge - balancing conflicting demands by different political constituents while communicating how our efforts were fair to a broad political constituency.

As Deputy Dir. of Communications - Official spokesperson for media, public & community group inquiries coordinated press conferences and special events. - ***Challenge*** - building appreciation for Chicago's leading tourist draw (552 parks, 64 miles of lake beaches and 46 museums). A $200M annual city investment into the community to build tourism and quality of life for the residents and that adds billions to the economy.

Media Relations Management
- Coordinate news conferences and interviews
- Edited newsletters, brochures and generated publicity
- Establish standards on release of information

Creative
- Wrote speeches, PSAs, brochures and promo materials
- Executed special events and public image promotions

Collaboration
- Field Museum
- Soldier Field
- The Art Institute
- Shedd Aquarium
- Planetarium
- Museum Science & Industry

Results ———— Secured 300+ local and national media placements. Formed a partnership with the Bozo TV show on WGN that became a cornerstone strategy to promote the Chicago Park District nationally on 100+ segments.

HEALTH SECTOR	6/90 -3/96	***Media Relations Specialist***	**St. Francis Medical Center**

Promoted key discoveries impacting scientific, cultural and medical topics for a $2 billion integrated healthcare network to national and local medias. - ***Challenge*** - competing for media attention in a glutted healthcare market and positioning complex, scientific or medical stories so consumers would perceive St. Francis as a leading healthcare and research institution.

Results ———— Secured 1,000 local & national mentions in broadcast and print mediums (sample below).

National Media	**Topics Covered**
AP	Violent acts committed by children (carried in 300+ US newspapers)
Prime Time Live, ABC	Dreams and Violence
US News & World Report	Changes in the field of obstetrics and gynecology
Good Housekeeping	Risks and benefits of alcohol consumption among women
Newsweek	On site daycare facilities (in wake of the Oklahoma City bombing)
UPI	Pregnant women face greater risk for rejecting heart transplant
People	Suicide Q & A
Family Circle	Cryotherapy
World News Tonight, ABC	Essential tremors
USA Today	Psychosomatic medicine
New York Post	Artificial bone transplants
CNBC/20/20	Smell and weight loss
Time Magazine	Spiritual healing and holistic medicine
The News Hour, PBS	Effects of the Norplant contraceptive
NBC Nightly News	Using sleep as a legal defense
Dateline, NBC	Dreams (friend of OJ Simpson testifies that OJ told him he'd dreamed about killing his wife)
Newsday	The life of serial killer Jeffrey Dahmer
Wall Street Journal	Physical exams
Newsweek	Child abuse

BUSINESS SECTOR 5/86 -6/90 ***Employee Communications Specialist*** **Spiegel, Inc.**

As Employee Communications Specialist - Supported the initial effort to build a Spiegel Community using communication channels to connect all corporate divisions and bridge the gap among the executive headquarters, branch operations, order fulfillment centers and sales staff. - Challenge – Use information to boost morale and build cohesion in the organization, i.e., maintain open lines of communication between upper management and 10,000 front line employees.

Communication • Co-edited employee newsletter, wrote articles for internal publications, memos, speeches and correspondence for CEO and VP of Human Resources.

Special Events • Helped plan and coordinate meetings, state of company addresses, media extravaganzas (huge galas and professional fashion showcases that presented seasonal product lines).

Multimedia • Assisted in developing video concepts and supervising production for employee orientation and United Way campaign videos

PR • Handled all requests for information about the company.

Results ——————— Built a community between Spiegel staff, the various target audiences (media representatives, fashion experts, and investor representatives) to help Spiegel continue to be a leader in its market category.

EDUCATION 1986 B.A. Journalism Roosevelt University, Chicago, IL

REFERENCES AVAILABLE ON REQUEST

CHAPTER 15

PLANTS & MANUFACTURING CAREERS

The Plant Manufacturing Category Has

4 Client Examples

20 Job Titles

98 Years of Work History

NAME	JOB TITLES COVERED
1. GARY GRAVITT	......Quality Manager
	......Manufacturing Engineer
	......Product Development Engineer
	......Production Manager
2. ANDY CHAMBERLAIN*	......Production Supervisor
	......Chemical Operator
	......Project Superintendent
	......Project Meneger
	......Project Estimator
3. CHARLES CONWAY	......Plant Superintendent
	......Production Supervisor
	......Production Manager/QC
4. CARL SCHUPAK	......VP & GM
	......Acting Works Manager
	......Mill Superintendent
	......Rolling Mill Trainer
	......Manager Small Bar Mill
	......Systems Manager 10" Bar Mill
	......Shift Manager Bar Mills
	......Plant Engineer

* Find the "before resume" in chapter 35

GARY GRAVITT

722 Benton Grove Ct., Milwaukee, WI 53516 414-729-3840

OBJECTIVE – Manufacturing Management.

Strengths

- Product Development
- Product Quality
- Designing for Manufacturing
- New Business Development
- Industry Research
- Staff Training

1989- Present

REMY BATTERY

Milwaukee, WI

Quality Manager • 1999 - present
Manufacturing Engineer • 1995 - 99
Product Development Engineer • 1992 - 95
Production Manager • 1988 - 92

Overview

Worked on 33 key products, 13 launched from scratch and 20 redesigned for easier manufacturing. These 33 products proliferated into 100+ iterations sold to various niche markets. Overall, I helped Remy grow from a $1 million to a $30 million company in 8 years. At peak times, I managed staff up to 15 and directed purchasing decisions of up to $2 million.

Engineering Focus

Setup assembly lines, took new products from engineering to production and implemented processes to improve outgoing product quality. The following challenges define my impact on the bottom line.

Challenge 1 **OVERCOMING PEAK PRODUCTION LIMITS**
A $3.8 million General Motors order (largest ever) overwhelmed production capacity. For under $10,000, I implemented a simplified manufacturing process that reduced assembly steps from 10 to 3. Overall this increased production capacity by 800%.

Results

1. Saved **$500,000** by eliminating the need for outsourced manufacturing.
2. New process saves **$2.5-3.0** million based on annual production of 50,000-70,000 units per year.

Challenge 2 **CHRYSLER CONSULTING ASSIGNMENT**
Chrysler Automotive was experiencing a 20% failure rate for batteries after cars were shipped from their Sterling Heights Assembly Plant. Teamed with a product manager to design a battery tester that could withstand the stress union personnel put on it.

Result

Package was sold for **$150,000** (our highest single package price).

Challenge 3 **IMPROVING CUSTOMER SERVICE LEVELS**
Created a 12 step process that reduced turnaround delays lasting 2-5 days for repairs into a guaranteed 24 hour turnaround period.

Result

Maintained the 24 hour benchmark 99% of the time.

Challenge 4 **MANUFACTURING PROCESS REDESIGN**
Remy developed a one of a kind high tech charger using patented conductance technology. My role was to redesign and simplify the manufacturing process and allow for a smooth transition from engineering to production.

Result

Saved **$1,500,000** annually from improvements that reduced assembly labor 75% (4/hrs to 1/hr).

Challenge 5 **HELPED LAUNCH 2 NEW BUSINESS SEGMENTS**
Remy won a 30 year contract to re-manufacture John Deere's hightech crop yield instruments used on high-end tractors. Worked with a team to create a viable 40 step process flow.

Result

New business segment was profitable in first year and volume doubled by second year.

Projects Continued

Challenge 6 **WINNING A LARGE FORD MOTOR COMPANY CONTRACT**
Involved with the development process to build product prototypes for testing at Ford's Atlas Labs during a 3 year period.

Result The $1,200,000 contract doubled Remy revenues and put our product in every North American Ford dealership.

Challenge 7 **PRODUCT LINE CONSOLIDATION**
Consolidated 6 product lines, all with individual printed circuit boards, into one universal PCB that could be easily configured into any of the 6 product types. In addition the new PCB incorporated several quality enhancement, i.e., better switches, overvoltage protection that reduced warranty repairs.

Result Reduced inventories by $125,000 and reduced warranty repair costs by $40,000.

Challenge 8 **PRODUCTION FACILITY CONSTRUCTION**
Oversaw layout of office, production area and warehouse and coordinated construction for a new $5 million production plant.

Result Coordinated move into new building that tripled operation from 20,000 to 60,000 sq/ft.

EDUCATION

1990 A.A.S., General Science
University of Wisconsin Milwaukee, Milwaukee, WI

1997 - 1998 Pursuing B.S., Business Administration
Marquette University, Milwaukee, WI

PROFESSIONAL TRAINING

Cost of Quality
TE Supplement to QS-9000
Statistical Process Control
Advanced Quality Planning
MS Access/Word/Excel/Outlook
Project Management
Bench Marking

CERTIFICATIONS RAB ISO-9000 Accredited Lead Auditor

ANDY CHAMBERLAIN

5378 Hampton Ct., Cleveland, OH 44115 216-879-3658 achamber22@hotmail.com

Strengths

- Materials Management
- Production Planning
- Preventative Maintenance
- P&L Labor Costing
- Waste Water Treatment Systems
- Lean Manufacturing Practices
- Problem Solving
- Union Negotiations
- Motivating Staff
- Quality Control
- Staff Training
- Change Mgt.

PLANT MANAGEMENT EXPERIENCE

1992-1/02 **PRODUCTION SUPERVISOR** **THE EUCLID CHEMICAL CO.** Cleveland, OH

Overview Supervised 100 staff in a 24/7 chemical processing plant that generated $70 million in revenues by producing 30 million pounds of Paracresol and its derivatives (US' largest producer). The $85 million in equipment and facility value of my operation was spread over 10 buildings, 500,000 sqft on a 32 acre campus.

My Role Solving plant problems, enhancing productivity, scheduling work flow, maximizing staff contribution, promoting accountability, creating standards, production reporting and delegating as appropriate.

Summary of production, process and staff management responsibilities.

Staff Managed	Plant Operators Safety/Security	70 each 5 each	Maintenance Power House Engineers	30 each 4 each
Processes Managed	Sulfonation Springing	Sodation Distillation	Fusion Reactor Phases	Compressing Cooling
Products Created	Paracresol Dinitro PC	Orthocresol DNPC Solution	Isophthalonitrile (IPN) Mono-nitrated PC	Blue Ink
End Users	Este Lauder Avery Labels	Frito Lays Good Year/Firestone	Wrigley Gum Purdue Chicken	

Duties

- Quality Inspect lab sample data/testing using SPC program.
- Scheduling 100+ production staff, maintenance field supervisors and craftsmen.
- Training Emergency response, industrial hygiene, chemical production, site safety.
- Reporting Production, inventory, materials purchasing, shipping and receiving.
- Production Identify goals, measure performance, control labor costs.
- Maintenance Directed facility shutdown/start-up and equipment turn around/upgrade.
- Negotiations Company/union contract disputes (i.e., 5 trade and PACE union contracts).
- Operations Safety management, personnel development, and regulatory compliance.

Results Increased productivity 29% without adding staff overtime or purchasing new equipment. Improved safety program that reduced work injuries by 50%.

Challenge 1

New Plant Start-up Lost 40% of seasoned chemical operators who were reassigned to start a blue ink plant.

Response Hired 30 new staff, selected 5 lead trainers and created programs to teach the new staff all 10 plant production processes.

Result We maintained production capacity and met increased volume demand.

Challenge 2

Biological System Euclid spent $12.5 million to install a world-class Biological waste water treatment system to meet stringent EPA discharge laws. ***Problem***: Euclid lacked the experience to integrate the bio and production processes, output dropped 33%; cost = $12 million in lost revenues.

Response Implemented a rigorous testing and monitoring plan to identify appropriate affluent levels. This eliminated emergency shut downs and stabilized wide swinging ppm counts.

Result Production grew 28%, worth $10 million in added volume.

Challenge 3

Purity & Quality In 1998, two key issues (competitive pressure and customer demand) forced us to reevaluate our product purity levels and devise a strategy to increase purity from 98.5% to 99%+.

Response Used SPC and Jouran guidelines to chart the deviation of temperature in the distillation to fit a much more narrow tolerance.

Result Improved purity to a consistent 99.1% which met all customer expectations and protected our accounts from competitive erosion.

1992 - 1996 **Chemical Operator**

Managed the following processes:

- Sulfonation of Toluene
- Acid springing of crude
- Operated fusion pots
- Distilled crude Cresol using fractionation

Overview Applied refining techniques; monitored temperature; vacuum pressure; condensers; heat exchangers; cooling towers; and reactors.

- Interpreted lab data to adjust chemical processes to meet customer expectations and OSHA regulations.
- Performed QC of in-process and final product. Capable of start-up and shut down of all process phases.
- ***Special Assignment*** - Trained all new production line employees.

1985-1992 **C & P DEVELOPMENT LLC** Cleveland, OH

Project Superintendent ——— ***Project Manager*** —— ***Project Estimator***

Overview Led 200+ construction projects spanning residential, commercial and industrial jobs. Crew size from 3 laborers to 20 skilled construction staff responsible for concrete flatwork, building store fronts, remodeling property and industrial construction.

Results

Profitability: of 200 projects all averaged 15-20% profit margin.
Scheduling: of 200 projects we met the projected schedule 97%.

Equipment Operated

- Bobcat
- Front-end Loaders
- Backhoe
- Lifts-all types
- Any Size Truck
- Rollers

Duties

Negotiations	Contract values between $15,000 - $300,000.
Inspections	Arranged for building, electrical and code inspections.
Staffing	Recruited and interviewed subcontractors.
Supervision	Project crews, contract staff and managed contract documents.
P&L	Created budget estimates and controlled costs.
Blueprint	Reading, structural and mechanical design and layout.

Challenge 4

Safety Handled quality control testing and technical safety to comply with OSHA, DOT, EPA, Air and Water, and Uniform Fire Codes.

Response Developed company wide safety compliance training and education program for the project crews.

Result The new safety audit program reduced incident recurrence 33%.

CERTIFICATES

- US DOT, Hazardous Material
- 29 CFR 1910 - 120 HAZWOPER Emergency Response
- 146 Confined Space - Rescue/Entry
- Emergency Response Contingency Trainer
- High Performance Work Team Trainer
- Lockout-Tag out Trainer
- Confined Space Trainer
- OSHA Safety Management -Hazardous Chemicals
- HAZMAT Certified
- Hazardous Communication
- EPA Regulatory Information
- Material Safety Correspondence (EPA Reporting & Regulations)

COMPUTER Win 2000 MS Office Lotus MS Project Timberline Estimator

EDUCATION Pursued B.A., Operation Production Management University of Phoenix

CHARCHARLES CONWAY ———————— 738 Oakhurst La., Cincinatti,OH 45242 • 313-729-8801

OBJECTIVE To continue a successful manufacturing/factory management career that capitalizes on my ability to build efficient operations, develop strong employee relations and improve production efficiencies.

SUMMARY I implement process improvements into daily operations to increase productivity. I'm committed to exceeding objectives, attaining excellent results, managing shift staff and solving problems. I set priorities, track staff response and build teams who contribute to their full capacity. Essentially, my efforts center on merging human and technology resources to achieve optimal production efficiencies.

STRENGTHS

• USDA Standards	• Quality Control	• Manufacturing Systems	• Logistical Management
• Scheduling	• Maintenance	• Troubleshooting Machinery	• Production Planning
• Staff Training	• Cost Controls	• Good Manufacturing Practices	• Process Improvements

MANUFACTURING EXPERIENCE

7/03 - present — ***Plant Superintendent - Custom Blending & Packaging*** **THE WARNICK COMPANY**

Overview.............. This $170MM contract manufacturer of dry food products, serves the Fortune 500 such as: Hills Bros., Dunkin Donuts, Nestles, ADM, Superior Coffee, Starbucks, Weider (pharmaceutical) and Dean Foods.

Manage 2 Supervisors, 3 Team Leaders, a QC Supervisor (with 12 technicians), Shipping/Receiving & Warehouse Manager (with 7 staff), 60 packagers on 20 packaging lines that create 50+ items or 250,000 lbs of product per shift in a 150,000 sq.ft. production facility.

Result Since hire we successfully added 5 major customers (Del Monte, Starbucks, Nestles, Dunkin Donuts and the Military) which increased production volume 25%-50% per shift.

Result Oversee the highest quality standards in the industry without a single product recall ever (monitor production output by checking for taste, flowabiltiy, brix, disolvability, texture).

9/99 - 4/03 — ***Production Supervisor - Ben Myerson Candy Co.*** **SUNKIST CANDY**

Overview.............. Took over a struggling first-shift production line with an 8 member team consisting of machine operators, stack operators and cooks using an NID Mogul System that produced 70,000 pounds of product per day.

Result ***Productivity*** Attained 26 batch production average on a 24 batch a day standard (115% of quota).

Result ***Operations*** Achieved a machine run-time of 99.5%, which meant that we had down time only 3 times in 40 months (the few repairs were always under 6 hours).

Result ***Product Launch*** Rolled-out 2 new products that increased productivity 5%.

Result ***Quality Increase*** Product consistency and flavor quality led to a 20% increase in sales for two years in a row worth $2 million in new sales annually.

Result ***Team Building*** Improve staff morale, lead by example, remain courteous, fair and respectful to:
• Improve Product Quality • Increase Production • Minimize Machine Downtime

1/97 - 9/99 — ***Production Supervisor - Culinary Foods Division*** **KRAFT FOODS**

Overview.............. Supervised 100 workers and 4 team leads for a USDA Certified food processing facility which produced 200,000-250,000 assorted items per shift (omelettes, french toast, pancakes, pre-plated airline entrees and crepes) on 7 open flame ovens across 4 different product lines.

Results ***Productivity*** Managed the spiral freezer system to increase productivity 20% year to date comparable. This delivered over 40,000 units in new daily volume worth $4,000,000 in sales.

Results ***Setting Records*** Formally recognized by the Plant GM as setting production records 3X within 1 year.

Results ***Revenue Value*** My contribution represents 15% on the corporate revenue stream of $300 million, meaning my lines add $45 million to Kraft Food's bottom line.

11/95-11/96 — ***Production Supervisor*** **COOL AID**

Overview.............. 3rd shift supervisor of 25 staff making a children's soft drink. Averaged 4,500-7,000 cases per shift. 3 APV Pasteurizing systems, 22 Automatic liquid packing machines (ALPs), 3 Krones Labelers, 3 Mead folding carton machines and 3 Douglas Case Makers.

Result ***Setting Records*** Exceeded company production records 2x by attaining 8,463 cases in one shift.

1978 - 1995 ***Production Manager/QC*** **PASITANO'S FOODS, INC.**

***Overview*..................** Supervised 3 kitchen lines: • Sausage Kitchen • Prepared Foods & Salad Kitchen • Pasta Kitchen
Managed 30 employees for a food products manufacturer with over $4 million annual revenues. Operational duties included hiring, firing, scheduling, negotiating union contracts and resolving grievances. Developed new products and improved existing products and redesigned packaging.

ROLES • Purchasing • Formulation • Production • Cooking • Packing
• Pricing • Distribution • Freezing • Inventory Control

IMPACT..............DEVELOPED NEW REVENUES
In '90, I was handpicked to develop a pilot catering test program with 3 Brown's Chicken franchises. A year later, the corporate franchise organization rolled-out our program throughout their 100 stores.

Result Increased Brown's purchases to over $900,000 annually and they became our single largest account.

IMPACT.............WON USDA CERTIFICATION & EXPANDED SALES OUTSIDE OF ILLINOIS
In 1989 we began the arduous process of becoming approved as a USDA facility. Three years later we achieved USDA status and began to pursue new business accounts outside of Illinois.

Result Institutional business (prisons, mental institutions and school lunch programs) added $1.2 MM annually.

IMPACT.............MAJOR ACCOUNT SUPPORT - Jewels, Dominicks, Centralla & Certified Groceries
The core existing accounts demanded constant product change, new item suggestions and updated packaging to remain our partners.

Result ***Introduced*** 7 new products or line extension and revised packaging on dozens of items.

Special Skills
Polish and Spanish language skills
Computer literate
Purchasing
Accounts Receivable
Bills of Material

EDUCATION
B.S., Manufacturing Engineering, Indiana, University, 1978
Studied Fundamentals of Baking, American Baking Institute, 1980

References available on request.

CARL SCHUPAK

529 Marshall Ave., Charlotte, NC 28211
704-322-8976 • cschupak@sbcglobal.net

9/02- present **NUCOR** **VP & GM** Charlotte, NC

Overview Recruited to restart a 500K tons/year specialty steel mill Nucor bought from Sumatomo Heavy Industries. Charlotte was to be the flagship plant fed by Nucor's network of 2 Canadian and 1 US steel mills. Together, the new plant group would boost productivity, optimize efficiency and reduce operating costs.

Challenge Build an organizational culture using values, principals and ethical behavior as well as a performance based wage system within an empowered union-free culture.

Challenge With half the budget ($50MM, 5-year capital improvement) and only 68 staff, I began accomplishing what Sumatomo, a multi-billion dollar company could not do with 400 staff – which was to achieve profitability (Sumatomo lost $40MM from 1999-00).

Actions
- Recommissioning, repairing, improving and facility start-up.
- Created the 5 year business plan and capital expansion plans.
- Team hire process, handbook, policies, safety and housekeeping programs.
- Accounting and purchasing systems. Polices to meet OSHA, EPA legal requirements.
- Hired 64 staff & 4 key leaders (Mill, Material, HR managers & Maintenance Engineer)

Result Executed plan 6-months ahead of schedule and entered 4 quality steel markets: aircraft, auto, specialty steel and stainless steel bar products.

Result Won product trials at • Remington • Boeing • Harley Davidson • John Deere • Caterpillar

Result Production output was achieved at 70% of budget.

4/96-9/02 **QUANEX CORP.** **Temroc Metals**

Acting Works Manager, 6/01-9/02 St. Paul, MN
Mill Superintendent, 10/98-6/01 St. Paul, MN
Rolling Mill Trainer, 4/96-10/98 Hamel, MN

Overview Recruited to Temroc Metals, a Quanex company, for construction and start-up of a green-field steel mill in the Hamel plant, which led to two management promotions at the St. Paul, MN mill.
As Works Manager, 2nd in-charge in preparation to become Plant GM of a full-line melting and rolling, unionized mini-mill that produced 650,000 tons/year with 480 staff and annual sales of $170MM.

Challenge Execute a ***Value Enhancement*** plan to boost profits and enable St. Paul, which had historically underperformed, to meet Quanex's return on gross investment expectation of 12-18% annually.

Actions
- Enhanced margin by changing product mix.
- Re-engineered the manufacturing processes to reduce costs.
- Negotiated new terms with suppliers to leverage Quanex's buying power.
- Implemented an effective asset reliability/maintenance program.

Actions
- Safety education, enforcement and new housekeeping standards.
- Review scrap-purchasing requirements to reduce inventory.
- Implement Quanex Quality process and ISO 9002:1994 into daily plant activities.
- Helped develop HR policy, resolve staff relation issues/disputes, staff retention policy.
- Worked with Financial manager on division's P/L.
- Contract interpretation/grievance response.

Result Within one quarter, Temroc realized 68% of the annual goal and was tracking at 162% of goal by year's end, worth an additional $4.9MM ($12.6MM vs. goal of $7.7MM).

Result Drove OSHA reportable safety incidents from 50/year in 00' to less than 10/year by 02'.

Temroc Experience Cont'd - pg. 2

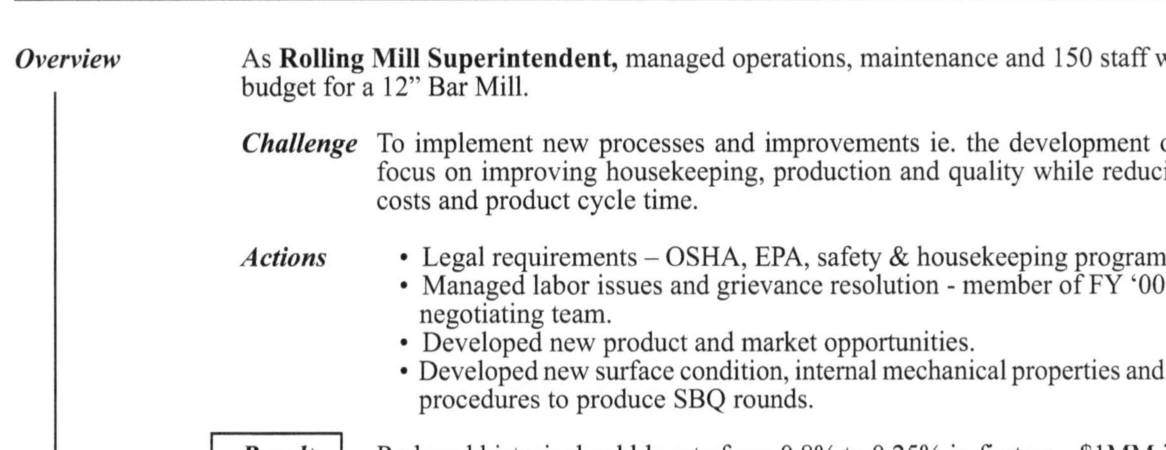

Overview

As **Rolling Mill Superintendent,** managed operations, maintenance and 150 staff with a $20,000,000 budget for a 12" Bar Mill.

Challenge To implement new processes and improvements ie. the development of ISO 9002; with focus on improving housekeeping, production and quality while reducing manufacturing costs and product cycle time.

Actions

- Legal requirements – OSHA, EPA, safety & housekeeping programs
- Managed labor issues and grievance resolution - member of FY '00 labor contract-negotiating team.
- Developed new product and market opportunities.
- Developed new surface condition, internal mechanical properties and heat lot separation procedures to produce SBQ rounds.

Result Reduced historical cobble rate from 0.8% to 0.25% in first yr. - $1MM in annual savings.
Result Decreased off spec material from 1.7% to under 1% - saving $250K a year.
Result Reduced rolling cycle time from 60 to 45 days via pass design and process changes - an additional $1.3MM in revenue.

Overview

As Rolling Mill - General Trainer, managed operations of a 13" Bar Mill and a wire/rod outlet with 48 staff that produced 500,000 tons annually.

Challenge Construction and start-up of green field facility that was the first high performance team culture, empowered workforce at Temroc. The facility was union free and anti-unionization.

Actions

- Developed safety, training & housekeeping program (as well as actually training staff).
- Developed Union Free labor/management relationship.
- Developed product production standards as well as design/redesign of mill equipment.

Result Conversion costs for the rolling mill was second lowest in Temroc.
Result Cobble rate 0.6% = 50% lower than goal. Rolling mill operations = 0.38 man-hours/ton of steel produced. Yield = 93% of goal established. Efficiency = 92% of goal established.

1989-1996	**AK STEEL**	**Manager Small Bar Mill**	1994-1996	Rockford, IN
	(3,500 employees/4MM Tons)	**Systems Manager 10" Bar Mill**	1993-1994	
		Shift Manager Bar Mills	1991-1993	
		Plant Engineer	1989-1991	

Overview

Started as a plant engineer for this joint venture and 6-months later was hand picked by the VP - Operations for the 5 Engineer Lead Team executing a $750MM mill modernization project. Subsequent promotions included 3 management roles in preparation to become VP of Operations.

As **Manager Small Bar Mill** - Design, construction, start up and operations of a brand-new, first-of-its-kind precision tolerance 9" Small Bar Mill.

Challenge To serve the US automotive industry and the growing transplant Japanese automotive market which required highly precision steel product.

Actions

- Teamed with Morgan Construction Company, G.E. and mill personnel to design and install an $80MM mill projected to produce 500,000 tons a year at quarter tolerance.

Result Created the best tolerance mill in the world for its time, the first mill in the world to apply reducing sizing block technology and the first US mill to produce cold-wound springs.
Result Increased productivity by 400% on sizes from 1/2 inch to 11/16 inch.

AK Steel Cont'd - pg. 3

Carl Schupak — *Experience Cont'd...* — *Pg. 3*

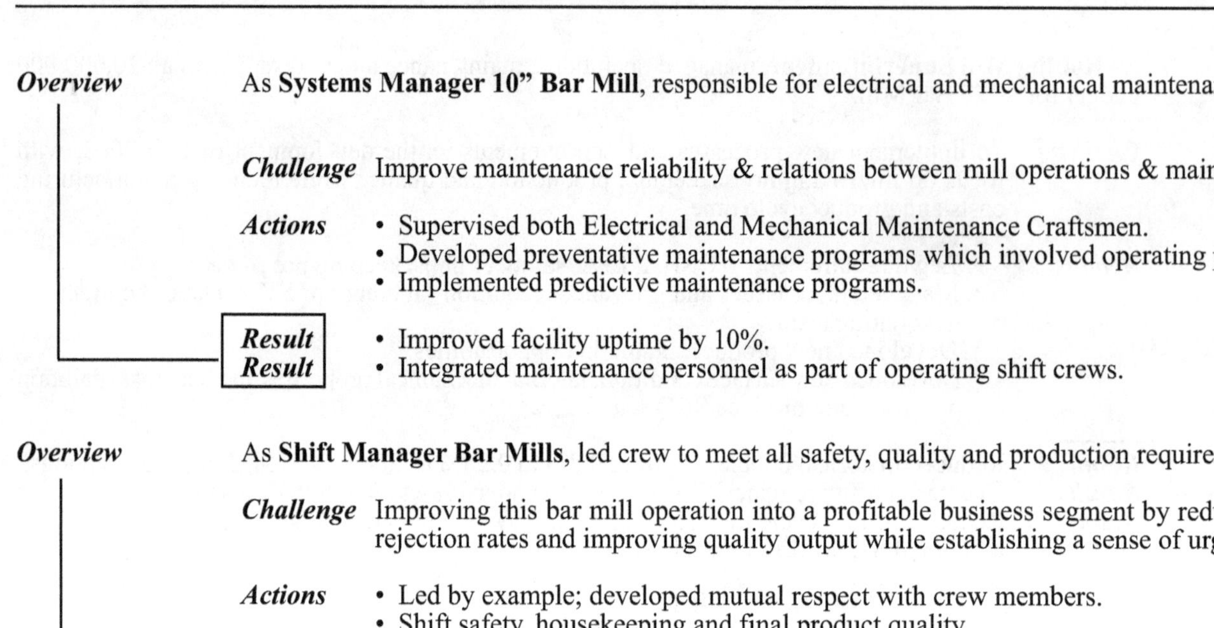

Overview As **Systems Manager 10" Bar Mill**, responsible for electrical and mechanical maintenance.

Challenge Improve maintenance reliability & relations between mill operations & maintenance staff.

Actions
- Supervised both Electrical and Mechanical Maintenance Craftsmen.
- Developed preventative maintenance programs which involved operating personnel.
- Implemented predictive maintenance programs.

Result
- Improved facility uptime by 10%.

Result
- Integrated maintenance personnel as part of operating shift crews.

Overview As **Shift Manager Bar Mills**, led crew to meet all safety, quality and production requirements.

Challenge Improving this bar mill operation into a profitable business segment by reducing product rejection rates and improving quality output while establishing a sense of urgency.

Actions
- Led by example; developed mutual respect with crew members.
- Shift safety, housekeeping and final product quality.

Result Developed new one-piece delivery guide to improve surface quality and eliminate product scratching.

Result Developed new rolling practices to reduce cobble on 11XX and 12XX grade steels as well as leaded steels- realized a $400K annual savings.

Overview As **Plant Engineer/Central Maintenance,** supervised electrical high voltage repairmen, electrical linemen and maintenance utility personnel.

Projects:
- Design & construction team member to completely rebuild a "new" 4,500-ton-a day blast furnace.
- The *Quality Technology Center*, a fully functional state of the art testing and research lab.
- The Bloom caster design & conception team & the #4 Butler mill modernization conception team

Result My effort to salvage equipment from AK Steel's shuttered mills and to use new engineering techniques saved AK Steel **$21MM**.

Affiliations
- American Iron and Steel Institute – Rod and Bar Technical Committee
- Association of Iron and Steel Engineers – SC – 42 Bar and Shape Rolling Division
- Youth sports coach

Quanex Management Seminars
- Quality Award – Auditing and application of the CQA process to enhance business unit value. (Quanex's version of the Malcolm Baldrige Award Criteria).
- Reliability Centered Maintenance – Develop, implement and education of criticality defined reliability centered maintenance process.
- Environmental compliance – Understanding legal environmental requirements and compliance.
- Production & Inventory Control – maximize productivity while managing inventory & working capital.
- Managing Worker Comp –Seminar on managing care, rehabilitation & worker's comp claims costs.
- Leadership Seminar - applying principals of the book "*Good to Great*" within business units.
- Safety and Loss Control Seminar - developing a safe, effective and responsible work environment.

Education 5/89 B.S. Electrical Engineering, **Queens University of Charlotte** – Charlotte, NC
Completed- University of Wisconsin,, Madison, WI
Wisconsin Executive Management program - Executive Leadership Program

CHAPTER 16

SERVICES & HOSPITALITY CAREERS

The Services & Hospitality Category Has

5 Client Examples

16 Job Titles

42 Years of Work History

NAME	JOB TITLES COVERED
1. AMANDA FARNHAM	..............................Server/Floor Manager
	....Server
2. DONALD DECARLO	...............................Restaurant Manager
	...................................Assistant Manager
3. DARREL CROMWELL	......Assistant GM/ Dir. of Housekeeping
	......Assistant G.M./Rooms Div. Manager
	Exec. Housekeeper/Asst. Front Office Mgr.
	............................Front Office Supervisor
4. RACHEL CARUSO*	......Manager: Special Events & Training
	................Account Rep. & Event Planner
	.....Outside Sales Rep./ Accounts Payable
	................................Sales Representative
5. JOHN TREVINO	..............Assistant Front Office Manager
	.............Asistant Housekeeping Manager
	....Project Manger
	....Night Auditor

* Find the "before resume" in chapter 35

AMANDA FARNHAM

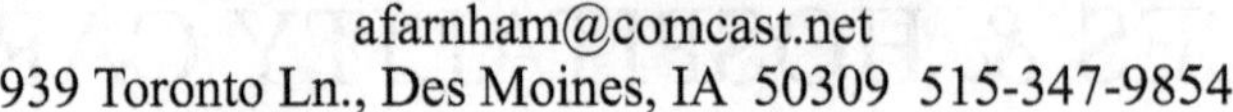

afarnham@comcast.net
939 Toronto Ln., Des Moines, IA 50309 515-347-9854

STRENGTHS

- Public Relations
- Up-selling
- Multi-tasking
- Customer Management
- Loyal & Dedicated
- Dynamic & Ambitious
- Team Work
- Problem Solving
- Love to Learn

SUMMARY

Over the past 5 years I've contributed as both a leader and as a team player. My key as a professional is that I want to add value whether I am selling product, serving customers or solving a complex problem. Ultimately, I want to work as a member of a team where I can impact a company's goals and mission objectives.

10/03 - present

HACIENDA'S [privately owned/managed fine Mexican restaurant]
Server/Floor Manager Des Moines, IA

Overview

Act as floor manager for this fast-paced, fine-dining establishment. The challenge is to work as a cohesive team (where only two servers are employed for a property with 20 tables). I also am the bartender concurrently with my serving duties.

Actions

- Orchestrate quality of service and speed of food delivery.
- Attention to building loyalty with patrons in order to grow repeat business, word-of-mouth referrals and increase average daily revenues.

Results

Generate, with only one other server, $3,000-4,000 per night.

8/00 - 5/03

RED LOBSTER [privately owned hospitality franchise]
Server Des Moines, IA

Overview

Hired at one of the most popular F&B properties in Des Moines. High performance expectations by the GM included: professional appearance, presentation of product, quality of personality and promptness of service.

Actions

- Focus on providing excellent customer service and generating top sales revenues. Relied on attention to the customer in order to build traffic volume and repeat patronage.
- Responsibilities encompassed all areas of waiting duties, including:

• Hostessing • Cash Management • Recommending Food Promotions to Customers

Results

Averaged $700-1,000 in nightly sales.

COMPUTER

Skilled with MS Word, Excel, Access and PowerPoint.

EDUCATION

5/03 Drake University, Des Moines, IA Note: self financed college tuition
B.A., Anthropology
B.B.A., Economics
Minor, Psychology

References available on request.

DONALD DECARLO

1348 Sunset St., Forest Park, IL 60130 708-554-2398

OBJECTIVE

To continue a successful hospitality management career that capitalizes on the ability to:
• Streamline Operations • Increase Profitability • Improve Staff Performance

SUMMARY

A proven leader who can solve complex business problems, provide personalized customer service and administratively manage large-scale operations. As a continual student of the art of hospitality management, my emphasis is preparation, execution and consistency of efforts. I make complex processes simple and develop approaches that can be replicated to save time and improve efficiency.

EXPERIENCE

3/01 - present **RED ROBIN** ***Restaurant Manager***

3/03-present	• Schaumburg	Yearly Revenues $1.8MM	30 Staff
11/01-3/03	• Warrenville	Yearly Revenues $500K	12 Staff
3/01-11/01	• Wheaton	Yearly Revenues $500K	12 Staff

Overview Regional troubleshooter assigned to 3 Chicago locations where I team with the GM to align restaurants to meet corporate sales, cost and service quality goals.

Duties

1. Lead the team to attain revenue and profit objectives in the market we serve.
2. Enforce standards to maintain proper food, payroll, and utility costs.
3. Hire staff as well as conduct local-store marketing and promotions.
4. Create an inviting atmosphere that is balanced with the speed of fast food service.

Result Oakbrook Mall — Maintained Top 7 rank in the Central Region of 38 stores on controllable profit. Reduced Cost of Sales to 18.6% from 23% (the corporate average is 20%).

Result Northbrook Court Mall — Reduced labor as percentage of food costs and increased YTD sales growth of the property which resulted in achieving 130% of goal on controllable profit, worth $35,000 in pure profit added.

Result Old Orchard Mall — Led property to become a *Training Store* for the first time, meaning that we scored 97% or better on the following Performance categories.
• Quality • Food Costs • Labor Percentage • Controllable Profits

1/97 - 3/01 **BAKERS SQUARE** ***Assistant Manager*** (Acting GM during last 2 months of 2001)

Overview Managed a $1.8 million property with a staff of 36-40 employees. The key focus was to turn an average property into a Best-In-Region performer by building good practices that the staff followed.

Action During the last two months of employment my GM quit and I became acting GM and began to implement change throughout the organization.

Result As GM, my store became the No. #1 restaurant in the Area for 5 weeks straight, by achieving a 97% Quality Inspection rate on 27 performance categories, i.e. Food Standards, Kitchen Cleanliness and Overall Image of the Front-of-the-House.

3/91 - 12/96 **BARNES & NOBLE** ***Assistant Manager***

Overview One of 3 managers for a $3.25MM property, where I was First Assistant Manager in-charge of the store's second largest profit section, ***Book Publisher's Remainders***, which is B&N's low price-high profit/offering.

Focus Remainders represented 35-40% of all store revenues, $1,137,500-$1,300,000 on a volume of 275,000-330,000 books sold annually. The key was to build the category and make it the profit center for the Oakbrook location.

Results Ranked #1 of the region's 8 stores in gross volume and profitability.
Ranked #2 in the entire corporation's 80 stores on gross volume and profitability.

EDUCATION

Completed 50% of an A.A.S. in Computer CAD/CAM Design, Columbia College, Chicago, IL

DARREL CROMWELL

1625 Beachview Ln., Miami, FL 33124 • 305-445-9833 • dcromwell@yahoo.com

OBJECTIVE To continue a successful hospitality management career that capitalizes on the ability to: Streamline Operations, Increase Profitability, Improve Staff Performance, Generate Profits and Reduce Costs.

HOSPITALITY EXPERIENCE

2000-2001 ***Assistant G.M./Dir. of Housekeeping*** **HOLIDAY INN MIAMI,** Miami, FL

Overview Managed, trained and evaluated 35 employees spread across housekeeping, banquets and recreation departments in a 240 room, mid-range, corporate travel hotel. Operationally I forecasted occupancy, managed ongoing renovations and assisted the GM on P&L reports.

Challenge Recruited by the GM after Miami Hotel Corp. bought the property. My mandate: resurrect the Guest Service Index (GSI). Before acquisition, the hotel suffered a severely declining GSI rating for 8 years and was on the verge of loosing it's franchise flag. Since Holiday Inn uses a merit system on referring reservation inquiries to the highest rated GSI properties in a region, being 16th of 17 properties adversely impacted revenues.

Response Hired a number of new staff, trained them on providing extremely high service and implemented a bonus program to motivate exceptional performance.

Results Increased GSI from 900 to 925 (a significant increase).
Gained a 100% satisfaction on the Corporate Audit.
Reduced supply expenses 30% by renegotiating with suppliers.

1999-2000 ***Assistant G.M./Rooms Div. Manager*** **HAWTHORN HOTEL & SUITES**, Miami, FL

Overview Hired as the Executive Housekeeping Manager and within two months was promoted to Assistant GM for the grand opening management team of this new, 11 story, $30 million, full service corporate hotel. Managed and scheduled 47 staff in Housekeeping, Banquets and Front Office departments.

Challenge Since this was the Hawthorn's Flagship in their 130 property portfolio it was expected to generate $9 million a year, so there was incredible corporate pressure to ensure that it would perform excellently on both financial and operational levels. Finally, this was Hawthorn's first effort to bridge from extended stay to a full service, corporate hotel.

Response Executed an aggressive business marketing campaign with the GM and Sales Manager. Additionally, I trained the staff to treat each guest as if they were part of our family

Results Grew occupancy from under 1% on the first night to an average of 40% within 8 weeks.
Passed our first inspection with flying colors by scoring 980 of 1000.

1997-1999 ***Exec Housekeeper/Asst. Front Office Mgr.*** **HAMPTON INN**, Carmel, CA

Overview Managed and scheduled shifts for 35 staff. Performed budgeting and inventory control, purchased housekeeping supplies from vendors. Made reservations and performed check-in/out service for guests.

Result Selected: Manager of the Year 1998

1995-1997 ***Front Office Supervisor*** **CROWN PLAZA**, San Jose, CA

ww Performed reservations and check-in/out services for hotel guests. Overseeing nightly operations and handled guest complaints.

SYSTEMS Encore, Holidex, PMS, Image 12 (Best Western), and Jaguar.

EDUCATION 1998 BS, Hotel/Motel Management **SAN JOSE STATE UNIVERSITY**, CA
Won a $5,000 Fairmont Hotel Scholarship - 200+ competitors

1993 AAS, Hotel/Motel Management **MONTEREY PENINSULA COLLEGE**, CA

RACHEL V. CARUSO

1152 Sudown Ln., Nashville, TN 37203 615-335-8972 • rcaruso@aol.com

OBJECTIVE To continue a successful special events management career for a hotel.

SUMMARY

Professional Skilled at building relationships and managing client expectations and providing timely reporting to meet management's need for accurate feedback. I have a sharp business sense and use organizational skills in the hospitality, catering, amusement and entertainment industries.

Personal Lead by example, delegate appropriately and motivate personnel to work as a team. Creative factors include an intuition to find options that optimize or enhance value to the client.

Strengths

- Program Development
- Budget Management
- Client Support
- Event Planning & Management
- Contracts
- Team Leadership
- Systems & Controls
- Logistical Coordination
- Marketing Support

EXPERIENCE

1996 - Present

- **Manager: Special Events & Training, SANDRA'S CATERING**
- **Account Representative & Event Planner**

Business Overview... One of the Top 3 largest special event/catering vendors in Nashville. We bridge between large corporate events where I manage service for up to 4,000 attendees and direct as many as 40 servers as well as provide full catering for smaller private parties averaging 100 guests where I interact with the event sponsors to deliver exceptional service.

My Impact Supported all key accounts for the company, an average of 50-60 ongoing clients, and as Sandra's only manager of special events I execute a high-season schedule of 6-8 events per day (with peak volume of 15 events in one weekend).

CHALLENGES

Operational Orchestrate various departments such as sales and customer service as well as directly interact with client representatives. Determine event strategy and logistical planning. Manage event staff training programs.

Planning Conceptualize project execution with attention to accuracy, timeliness and ensure detailed data is available for management and client review.

Management Analyze and track actions to ensure seamless program flow throughout all event stages. Hire and train service staff and manage payroll.

Creativity I've managed over 4,000 events since 1996 and possess the creative vision to design decor, site layout and thematic appointments for all staging, production and entertainment elements (in 2003, I recreated the corporate brochures - first redesign in 20 years).

Reporting Prepare post event detailed reports for senior management that includes outlining event menus, entertainment, staff size, equipment and schedule compliance.

— ***Top Customers Served***

- AT&T
- Pepsi
- United Airline
- U.S. Postal
- Coca-Cola
- Chicago's Mayor's Office

— ***Sample of Events***

- Mardi Gras
- Grand Opening
- Hawaiian Luaus
- Company Picnics
- Western Cook Outs
- Employee Appreciation

RESULT I manage the profitability of each event. With budgets up to $50,000 and an average of 650 events I manage a year, I deliver over 50% of Sandra's revenue stream, and more importantly, 60% of their profits.

RESULT I completely restructured Sandra's business from 25% corporate events, 75% private to 75% corporate (much more profitable) and 25% private.

1994-1996 **Outside Sales Representative/Accounts Payable, MCBROOM CO.** (A Miller Beer Distributor)

Business Overview... Cold called perspective clients as well as managed 60 existing accounts. Pre-sold non-alcoholic products such as Arizona Ice Tea to chain retail accounts. Merchandising and promotions for Miller Beer, maintained accounts payables, sales, staff expenses, tracked accounts sales, and created Point of Sale for Sales Department.

1993-1994 **Sales Representative, PORTILLO'S CATERING**

Business Overview... Specialized in off-premise catering, conducted inside/outside sales presentations to perspective customers, scheduled and coordinated special events for corporate and private affairs.

JOHN TREVINO

5623 123rd St., New York, NY 10013 212-632-1884

OBJECTIVE To continue a successful hospitality management career as a department head where I can enhance service, streamline operations, increase profits, improve staff performance and reduce costs.

SUMMARY A proven leader and hospitality professional able to resolve complex business problems, maintain focus on personalized customer service and cross functional skills in employee development and training. As a proven self-starter, I enjoy creating profitable operations to surpass corporate objectives. Use organizational, interpersonal and communication skills to network and determine solutions to problems or guest concerns.

SKILLS

✓ Strategic Planning ✓Discipline ✓Staff Training
✓ Revenue Building ✓Project Management ✓Controling P&L, Labor Costs
✓ Personal Motivation ✓Public Relations ✓Purchasing Control

EXPERIENCE

9/97 - 12/99 **THE RITZ CARLTON CHICAGO -** 16 floors, 435 rooms — New York, NY
[Top 5 hotel in the world, Best City Hotel in the U.S., *Travel & Leisure*,]
AAA 5 Diamond Award, 19 years.
Assistant Front Office Manager — **4/99 - 12/99**
Assistant Housekeeping Manager - *Managed a Staff of 100* — **5/98 - 4/99**
Project Manager - Acted as the Ritz' on-site manager during 3 construction projects

Overview A month after hire, I was picked by the GM to help JMB Realty Co. (the property owner), with 3 renovation projects (total budgets $3,640,000). At project completion I became Assistant Housekeeping Manager for a year and then Assistant Front Office Manager. Managed 11 receptionists, personally responded to all VIP needs and oversaw hotel operations to ensure the integrity and reputation of a world class luxury hotel.

Project **Upsell Program**: Led the Upsell Team in a program that was the most successful in the history of the Four Seasons Hotel and Resort properties.
Impact: Generated new revenues of $224,000, exceeding budget by 12%.

Project Manager ***Acted as the Ritz' on-site manager during construction projects***

① Premier Level **Budget**: $3,200,00
Upgrade conversion of a 17 room floor from permanent apartments to luxury suites. The renovation is now key to promoting the hotel in print marketing literature.
Impact Generates revenues $1,200,000/first year.

② Boardroom **Budget**: $140,000
Conversion from a suite to a corporate business setting.
Impact Generates revenues $45,000/first year.

③ Presidential Suite **Budget**: $300,000
This upgrade raised the average room rate 45% from $2,500 to $3,500/night.
Impact: Generates revenues $175,000/first year.

1/95 - 7/97 **COURTYARD BY MARRIOTT** - 3 floors, 150 rooms — New York, NY
Night Auditor
Overview Charge of total hotel operations from 11-7. Balanced all transaction including hotel and restaurant.

TECHNICAL • Word for Windows • Word Perfect • Lotus 123 • Fidelio

CERTIFICATES ***Corporate Training***
• Quality Service Seminar • Guest Relations Seminar
• Marriott 5 Star Service Advantage • KSL Leadership 2000
• Four Seasons 12 week Management Development Program

EDUCATION B.S. Hotel Administration **ADELPHI UNIVERSITY, Garden City, NY** **5/97**

HONORS
1996 Hyatt Hotel Lodging Management Scholarship
1996 People Pleasure Award, Radisson
1996 Team Member of the Month, Courtyard by Marriott
1994 Las Vegas Strip Scholarship

CHAPTER 17

RETAIL CAREERS

The Retail Category Has

5 Client Examples

19 Job Titles

77 Years of Work History

NAME	JOB TITLES COVERED
1. JANET SCHULTZ*	........Buyer
	........Assistant Buyer
	........Replenishment Analyst
	........Executive Account Coordinator
	........Assistant Visual Manager
2. ERIN TURNER	........Store Manager
3. REBECCA SANDERS	........Manager
	........Grand Opening Manager
	........Manager & Founder
4. RAFAEL RICCIO	........Department Manager
	........Store Director
	........Regional Manager
	........Store Manager
	........E.V.P Sales & Marketing
	........National Sales Manager
5. LAUREN MCCARRON	........Sales Manager
	........Asistant Buyer
	........Fashion Merchandiser
	........Department Manager

* Find the "before resume" in chapter 35

JANET SCHULTZ —— 555 Martinez Dr., San Jose, CA 95110, 408-336-7982

SUMMARY

Results-driven professional with retail industry experience, proven vendor relations, sales analysis, and forecasting skills. Possess the initiative to excel in challenging environments. Skilled at building relationships with vendors and staff across organizational channels. Develop creative strategies to increase profitability and efficiency.

STRENGTHS

- Operational Support
- New Product Introductions
- Industry Research
- Inventory Management
- Trending
- Sourcing
- Project Oversight
- Staff Management
- Financial Analysis

EXPERIENCE
1999 to present

ULTA San Jose, CA

Buyer - 11/01-present **Prestige Cosmetics**

Overview
Handpicked by the SVP of Merchandising & Marketing to optimize profitability and sales of a underdeveloped category representing $22M in annual revenues, 20 vendors and 10,000 line items.

Tactics

Inventory Management
Turned $1.8M overbought inventory that I had inherited into $1M in credits. Increased turns from 1.12 to 1.72.

Product Launches
FY02: launched 4 new brands which represent 30% of category revenues.
- Tested ***Bourgeois*** line in the California market. Projected $3M, results trend toward $10M or a 333% increase over projections when fully implemented.
- Launched ***Neostrata,*** then doubled the shelf space and negotiated an extra $110K in profit, in total the product has increased by 47.3% YTD 01-02.
- Launched Cosmasuetical brands: Borghese, Peter Thomas Roth, Ellen Lange.

Co-Op Revenues
After successfully securing $500K in FY01, the goal increased by 160% to $1.3M (I have attained 85% YTD or $1.1M as of 9/02).

Optimizing Lines
Exited 2 unproductive brands and expanded 1 line.

Results
- FY 02 sales increased 15%, as comparison, FY01 results (before my hire) were 0% growth over FY99.
- Profitability across the category increased 28.5%

Assistant Buyer - 12/00 to 11/01

Overview
Marketed, merchandised, promoted, maintained vendor and store relations for 5 categories: Prestige Cosmetic, Fashion Hair Accessory, Hosiery, Sunglass and Cosmetic Bag with annual sales $35M.

Tactics

Advertising & Marketing
Analyzed advertising results and featured-item performance to set strategy. Managed co-op goals and collected obligations averaging $500K.

Forecasting
Selected merchandise for planogram; developed new item forecasts, wrote opening orders and authorized returns on discontinued products.

Negotiating
Interacted with vendors to secure collateral, gift-with-purchase or samples.

Promotions
Developed directives and sales scripts for staff during promotions or product launches.

Management Reporting
Prepared P&L report summaries for SVP of Merchandising & Marketing.

Training Support
Delivered a key training module across the US to educate Beauty Advisors.

Created
Promotional programs to drive sales.
- *Winter Rescue*
- *Murad's Results You Can* 'C '
- *Consultation Kit*
- *Hip On Hygiene*

Results
- Designated by Ulta's President as a *'Passionate Entrepreneur"*.
- Created the company's first formal ***"product tester program"*** deployed corporate wide by 2,500 beauty consultants at 100 locations. Conservatively this increased sales by 10% or $15M.

—— ***Pg. 1 of 2***

Ulta Experience Cont'd....

Replenishment Analyst - 12/99 to 11/01

Overview Purchased and maintained in-stock position for 5,000 line items in Popular Cosmetic, Professional Haircare and Salon Supply categories. Determined stock levels for 80 stores. Analyzed sales histories and trends to develop forecasts for advertised items and buyers.

Results Researched and analyzed history of salon supply movement and established replenishment standards that reduced inventory by $150K.

1998 to 1999 **LANCOME** New York, NY

Executive Account Coordinator - *Lord & Taylor*

Directed 5 business managers and 18 sales associates in 5 Manhattan' stores that generated $3.5M. Educated staff on products and strategies to increase sales. Hired, trained and evaluated staff. Evaluated monthly competitive, daily business and class analysis reports. Coordinated promotions for Saks Fifth Avenue, Neiman Marcus, Bloomingdales and Nordstroms in total sales $4.0M annually.

Results Generated a 10% sales increase worth $350K in added revenues.
Only coordinator of 6 in the region to exceed sales goals.

1996 to 1998 **Assistant Visual Manager** - *Neiman Marcus*

Organized promotions and worked with vendors to develop selling strategies, presentations and marketing tactics. Worked with PR and advertising to execute large scale functions for Harpers Bazaar, Tahari, etc.

Results Increased sales for all product lines.

EDUCATION 1996 Southern New Hampshire University, Manchester, NH Associate of Science Degree

References available on request

ERIN TURNER —————— 31363 Kemmer Ln., Jackson, MI 39202 • 601-334-7721 • eturner12@aol.com

OBJECTIVE

To continue a successful management career that capitalizes on the ability to:

- Streamline Operations
- Increase Profitability
- Improve Staff Performance
- Increase Customer Loyalty
- Reduce Costs
- Implementing New Programs

EXPERIENCE

5/89 - Present **KIDS "R" US** ***Store Manager - Northpark Mall*** Jackson, MS

Overview Oversee all store operations of multiple locations, control P&L accounts on annual sales of $7.5MM, act as regional trainer, work with corporate planning to ensure merchandise stock and visual presentation reflect sales trends as well as supervise HR functions to recruit and train 25-35 hourly/management staff a year.

GOAL **Reduce Shrinkage**

ACTIONS Implemented aggressive loss prevention measures.

RESULT Decreased shrink by 41%, worth a total savings of $344,542 since 1998.

GOAL **Enhance the Customer's Buying Experience**

ACTIONS As a "***Manager of Delight***", I trained staff to engage the buying customer as well as lead their children into the buying process thereby delighting them and building stronger customer loyalty.

RESULT Rank # 1 in customers who rate their experience as ***"delightful"*** (44% versus the region's 33%).

PROJECT Launch the "***Combo-Store***" plan: 1 of 3 company managers picked to pilot a program where Kids "R" Us boutiques were created inside existing Toys "R" Us stores.

CHALLENGE Managing the largest volume store in the region while launching and subsequently managing 2 combo-sites in Louisiana.

RESULT Success led to 100+ new combo sites nationwide.

PROJECT Launch "***Magic of Service***": 1 of only 10 managers selected to train staff and change selling mentality from a passive retail selling position to an active feature & benefit selling approach.

CHALLENGE Initially I recruited a new 'breed' of retail sales associates then taught them aspects of product knowledge and feature/benefit selling techniques.

RESULT Average sales revenues per staff increased from $90K/year to $144K/year and I traveled to other markets to train district mangers and store managers on the program.

PROJECT Launch "***Life Styles***" 1 of only 10 managers selected to implement hard-line products such as bedroom and home decor into the soft-goods retail mix.

CHALLENGE Increase incremental sales and use my urban store, to help the chain differentiate product for urban market rollouts.

RESULT Attained the corporate goal of 5% sales generated from the Lifestyle product group.

TOTAL IMPACT

- Grew property to the #1, highest volume store in a 15 state region of 71 stores.
- Deliver $500K to $1.48MM more in revenues annually than my closest 3 peers on a sales per square foot comparative average.
- As 1 of 5 Regional Trainers, I deliver train-the-trainer "Essential Leadership Skills Training" (note 2 of my staff are now District Managers and 5 became Store Managers).

4/87 - 5/89 **THE CHILDREN'S PLACE** ***Store Manager*** Jackson, MS

Achieved $2MM annual sales volume. Controlled operating expenses, total store operations, P&L, merchandise flow, sales, bookkeeping, maintaining inventory and delivery of guest service.

RESULT Reduced turnover by 35% and reduced shrinkage by 47.8%

Developed and implemented a chain-wide guide to recruit and retain staff in hard to hire locations.

EDUCATION Pursued, BA, Economics, Finance Minor, Jackson State University, Jackson, MS

REBECCA L. SANDERS

1622 Sherman Oaks Blvd. #13, Sherman Oaks, CA 90212 310-442-7796

EXPERIENCE

1992 - present **STARBUCKS COFFEE COMPANY**

Manager	Beverly Hills	Beverly Hills, CA
Grand Opening Manager	Universal City	Universal City, CA
Grand Opening Manager	Sherman Oaks	Sherman Oaks, CA

Overview **February '92** the start of my tenure, when Starbucks had only 6 properties in the Los Angeles Metro and was about to complete an IPO that would expand their Los Angeles presence to 115 units. Of the 6 original stores, I held supervisory positions at 3, managed staffs, ensured compliance to corporate standards and participated with the management team in growing business revenues.

By 1997, I had grand opened two properties, handled HR efforts for operations of up to 25 employees (reviewing performance, hiring/terminating and promoting), helped attain P&L budget goals up to $1,000,000 annually and conducted store promotions/merchandising programs for both retail and restaurant components.

Actions

Recruiting Hired 100+ employees and shift supervisors.

Training ***Classroom Learning Coach***: Teach 6 different classes twice monthly at the regional headquarters.
Management Coach & Mentor: Developed and trained 5 managers.

Programs As a ***District Specialist***, I rolled out ***Sacred Grounds*** - a program used to educate managers/staff on techniques to increase product sales. This program was customized to each property's individual operation.

① PROJECT ***International Expansion - London, UK***
Focus: Part of a global strategy to extend the Starbucks brand reach.
Challenge: A national posting generated 300 applicants from existing managers, of which I was 1 of only 12 appointments.
Result: Grand opened the 4th UK property while also writing a staff training tool used during the changeover of the 55 UK based Seattle Coffee Co. properties into Starbucks.

② PROJECT ***Concept Store - Sherman Oaks & Universal City Properties***
Focus: These two properties represented the 1st and 5th stores in Los Angeles Metro to apply the new corporate focus on customer driven business growth.
Challenge: By implementing business communication and operational programs we reduced employee work area 50% and yet created an environment that increased customer comfort and satisfaction.
Result: Increased traffic flow and sales by 30%.

③ PROJECT ***Customer Management - Service Deployment***
Focus: A multimillion dollar program to increase customer service and employee efficiency.
Challenge: My Beverly Hills property was selected as 1 of 10 national test sites.
Result: Property has increased customer counts and overall sales while at the same time maximizing resource utilization of staff and equipment.

1994-1995 **SANDRA'S BISTRO AT USC-BUSINESS START-UP**

Overview **Manager/Founder**. Spearheaded project to create a coffee house on campus. Selected vendors.

EDUCATION B.A., Business Management: Marketing Concentration, Univ. Southern California, LA, CA 1996

ACTIVITIES

President, International Studies Group & President of USC Business Club
Chairman and Co-Founder, USC Student Planning Commission 1993-1996

AWARDS

Who's Who Among Students in American Universities and Colleges 1994-1995/1995-1996
St. Andrews Madden Service Award 1994-1995
USC Outstanding Leadership and Special Service Awards 1993- 1994

RAFEAL J. RICCIO — *111 153rd St., New York, NY 10012 212-334-9868 • rriccio@aol.com*

OBJECTIVE Management role that capitalizes on 15+ years of retail jewelry experience for both privately and publicly held companies where I drove sales and profits, developed staff and created branding as well as consumer marketing programs to maximize revenues and net income.

EXPERIENCE

7/01-Present **NEIMAN MARCUS** ***Department Manager - Precious Jewels*** New York, NY

Recruited to reinvigorate a top-tier retailer's highest-profit margin department and introduce a variety of new blended marketing strategies that integrate luxury brand sales with fashion and couture.

Sales Challenge Integrate fashion luxury lines covering 14 key designers (Armani, Chanel, St. John, Roberto Cavalli, etc.) with Neiman's fine-jewelry designer sales (Henry Dunay, Jean Mahie, Roberto Coin, etc.) to increase our share of a customer's discretionary spending.

Response Personally trained all couture department staff to compliment their fashion sales with a fine jewelry accessory purchase.

Result 33% of fine jewelry sales now come from leads initiated via the fashion departments.

Market Challenge Win significant new deals in a competitive market of international jewelry designers.

Response Combine community involvement (social-selling that leverages my expertise on art/travel/entertainment) with personal follow-through i.e., "priceless customer service" to win client trust and loyalty.

Result 40% of all department sales originate from contacts I make in the community.

Coaching Challenge Transform employee's attitude to that of an excited team eager to come to work.

Response Motivate staff by teaching them their vital role to Neiman's bottom line and, equally as important, their personal role in contributing to a customer's positive buying experience.

Result Customer satisfaction dramatically improved and sales are growing correspondingly.

5/00 - 6/01 **BLAUWEISS BERKOWITZ** ***Store Director*** New York, NY

Recruited to build brand value, grow sales and open 2 properties as Blauweiss Berkowitz reemerged onto 5th Avenue. Worked with the architect and construction contractors on the $1.2MM build-outs, recruited all sales staff, determined merchandising strategies and grand-opened Hamptons location on 10/00 and 578 5th Ave. on 12/00. Executed the following operational, branding and selling programs to build revenues.

Branding Challenge Blauweiss Berkowitz was bought out of Chapter 11 in the early 90's.

Response Executed the reemergence of a forgotten brand on New York's most competitive retailing market - 5th Avenue. Built a network of social, professional, charitable, philanthropic and business contacts to reestablish Blauweiss Berkowitz with New York organizations.

Result Opened 2 stores in 3 months to build a New York presence.

Sales Challenge Launch an aggressive clienteling program to achieve $2,800 and $1,000 per sqft at the 2 stores.

Response Recruited 16 sales professionals, only 3 with prior retail jewelry experience and delivered an 8 module, 80 hour intense selling skills training seminar.

Result Conversion rate of inbound client prospects was above 10%, average sell was $1,100 and I personally closed a $175,000 corporate sale to Trump International.

3/97-5/00 **TIFFANY'S** ***Regional Manager***- East Central Region 7/98-5/00
Store Manager - Greenwich 3/97-7/98

After a year as store manager, I was elevated to Eastern Central Regional Manager of 10 properties, 90 staff and $30M annual sales plan.

Profit Challenge Delivered an aggressive profit margin by motivating all store managers to take ownership of the business and by revealing how discounting and variable expenses negatively impacted their compensation and bonuses.

Response Coached staff on how to use feature and benefit selling techniques, alternative financing tools and strategies to redirect sales to higher margin branded product lines.

Result Delivered $7.5M in profits or a 25% margin.

1986 -1996 **GEM STONES, LTD.** ***Executive VP of Sales & Marketing***
National Sales Manager

Directed a team of 150 sales, operations, manufacturing and administrative staff.

Budget Challenge Optimized 35 sales teams (consisting of a sales rep and a jeweler) that conducted 10,000 remount shows a year at 2,000 jewelry stores in North America.

Response Created an extremely efficient master schedule that tracked every show, team travelling downtime and minimized conflict with peak selling seasons of our 6 corporate accounts.

Result The new master schedule reduced per show costs from an average of $750/show to $500/show which delivered $2.5M to the bottom line.

As National Sales Manager
Sold and directed sales of jewelry remount services to leading national specialty and department stores such as Zale's, Marshall Field's and Service Merchandise. Personally generated annual revenues of $5.5MM.

Sales Challenge Execute a pull-through sale, meaning the sales professionals at the retail sites had to generate appointments prior to the shows by maximizing their customer's interest and enthusiasm.

Response 1 Conducted 150-200 motivational speeches a year and created GEM's first-ever team of District Sales Coordinators who took my selling strategies and executed them at both store level and at regional level.

Response 2 Created a ***Kickoff Sales Training Program*** that I took on the road (250,000 miles of travel annually) to each region prior to that regions show schedule in order to guarantee sales-staff enthusiasm and to build peak sales potential.

Result Sales spiked 25-40% on YTD comparisons across all regions, and overall revenues grew from $16M in 1989 to $38M in 1995.

PERSONAL INTERESTS

- Art collecting, symphony, literature, and domestic and international travel.

MEMBER/DONOR/PATRON

- Opportunity Village-New York
- Guggenheim/Hermitage-New York
- Metropolitan Museum of Art -New York
- Candlelighters for Childhood Cancer
- Art Donor: Indiana University Art Museum
- The Art Institute of Chicago-Chicago

References available on request

LAUREN MCCARRON 334 Burberry Ct., New York, NY 10022 • 212-644-6611 • 212-547-9087

OBJECTIVE Retail sales management using business, customer relations and staff development skills.

SUMMARY As a sales professional, I grow revenues by creating and maintaining profitable client relations. My communication skills are used to identify referrals, assess need and explain product value. My focus is building client confidence by quickly responding to needs and monitoring details that ensure loyalty.

Strengths
- Sales Presentations
- Relationship Management
- Direct Marketing
- Product Promotions
- Consulting Sales
- Business Development

RETAIL MANAGEMENT EXPERIENCE

1/00 to Present **SAK'S 5th AVENUE** New York, NY

Sales Manager - $12MM Volume
- Men's Designer Collections
- Men's Shirts, Ties, Accessories & Furnishings

(previously)
- Boys/Girls Apparel, Children's Accessories & Shoes

Overview.... Originally managed the $7MM Children's apparel business lines until promoted to manage selling efforts in the Men's departments (recently added designer collections) where I lead a team of 50 associates who sell $10MM-$12MM annually.

Noteworthy! Negotiated with buyers to add new lines: Mount Blanc Assortment - Ghurka men's leather goods - Burberry Accessories.

Noteworthy! As regional ***Credit Marketing Captain*** in 2003, built credit penetration to meet YTD goal for the first time since 1999 (compare FY02 - they hit 85% of goal).

Noteworthy! Manage the largest Polo shop in the Eastcoast.

Result Tracking to exceed the corporate YTD growth of +20% (industry average -3%).

Result Department sales growth at my store ranks #1 of 60 Marshall Field's in the US.

8/93 1/00 **BLOOMINGDALES** New York, NY

Sales Manager - $7MM
- Men's Tailored Clothing
- Home Christmas Shop
- Young Men's Denim
- Designer Sportswear
- Men's Outerwear
- Men's Big & Tall

Overview...... Concurrently worked with corporate buyers to extend lines and assortments while aggressively working with Asset Protection to reduce a severe shortage/shrinkage problem that had grown to 5% of sales.

Noteworthy! Developed a men's tailored clothing clearance event with advertising which generated $110,000 per week or 130% over previous best clearance results.

Noteworthy! Launched first-floor new men's shops for – Polo Nautica Hilfiger

Noteworthy! Tracked and helped Asset Protection catch 50 shoplifters and 10 employee thieves.

Result Grew tailored business from $2MM to $3MM or 50% within 2 years.

Result Decreased shortage to -$0- dollars (a value maintained 6 years straight).

Ranked #1 of 60 FDS stores on shortage results (6 years straight).

1/91 -8/93 **MACY'S** New York, NY

Assistant Buyer [4/92-8/93] $30 Million Sales Volume
- Infant & Toddler
- Girl's 4-14 Outerwear
- Toys

Fashion Merchandiser [1/91 -4/92] $16 Million Sales Volume
- Infant & Toddler
- Outerwear
- Sleepwear
- Basics

Experience cont'd on pg. 2 —

1/91 -8/93 **MACY'S** New York, NY

Overview..... ***As Asst. Buyer*** – Helped senior staff buy for 350+ stores. Planned and placed Spring outerwear and toy buys. Directed merchandisers and planners with assortment and inventory issues. Liaison to vendors, distribution centers and support staff.

Noteworthy! Responsible for the children's advertising including copy writing, frequency, budgets and quality on new advertising strategies.

Noteworthy! Independently created the Toy product line for Spring and Easter seasons which led to working with 20 vendors such as Mattel and Fisher Price to modify lines to meet Macy's profit goals.

Noteworthy! Independently created, bought and designed styles, sizes and colors for children's cold whether accessories: hats, gloves, scarves for infant/toddler 4-6x.

Result Won corporate award for maintaining the best in-stock average for my lines (99% in stock) when buying for 5 volume tiers across 5 climates.

As Fashion Merchandiser – Coordinated and allocated store receipts by sales volume, climazone, and customer profile.

8/85 -1/91 **BLOOMINGDALES** New York, NY

Department Manager - $6 Million Sales Volume

- Women's Accessories & Hosiery
- Cold Weather Shops

Overview... Negotiated with buyers and key resources to improve stock levels and productivity.

Noteworthy! Organized and supervised the grand-opening of Lincolnwood Store.

Noteworthy! Worked with VP of Store to design and develop new first-floor layout.

Result Manager of the Month 3 times.

Result Received the Chairman's Board Award for Best Sales Performance

Department Manager [4/87-4/91] - $4MM Volume

- Moderate
- Update
- Active Sportswear

Department Manager Trainee [10/85-10/87]

- Better Sportswear
- Update
- Petite Women's Sportswear

Overview... Trained executive trainees and sales associates for promotion, taught retail selling skills program and completed quality education system for management.

EDUCATION 1981 New Jersey City University, Jersey City, NJ, General Studies & Liberal Arts Program

CHAPTER 18
SALES CAREERS

The Sales Category Has

8 Client Examples

36 Job Titles

109 Years of Work History

NAME	JOB TITLES COVERED
1.JIM WILSON	......................Urology Product Specialist
	................................Sales Representative
2. ZOE YOUNG*	.......................Pharmacuetical Sales Rep
	....Store Manager
3. RICK ISLEY	............................National Sales Manager
	..............................National Sales Director
	....Sales Manager
	....Sales Executive
	............................National Sales Manager
	.................................Area Sales Manager
	....................................Team Sales Leader
	.........Project Manager/Managing Partner

* Find the "before resume" in chapter 35

CHAPTER 18
SALES CAREERS CONTINUED

NAME	JOB TITLES COVERED
4. ALEX BROOKS	....Sales Engineer
	..............................Production Supervisor
	....ISO Auditor
	....Laser Technician
5. RANDY JOHNSON	......Intl' Business Development Manager
	...............................Senior Sales Manager
	....Sales Manager
	...........................National Sales Manager
	..........................Regional Sales Manager
	.......................Senior Account Executive
6. HANK REDMAN	........................Team Leader/Sales Group
	........................Senior Account Executive
	..................................Account Executive
	................................Telemarketing Sales
7. BRENT NICHOLSON	....................................Sr. Sales Manager
	....Sales Manager
	...............................Account Coordinator
	....Owner Operator
8. ADAM HAUSMAN	............................Senior Sales Executive
	....Sales Executive
	..................................Credit Investigator
	..........................Bankruptcy Coordinator
	...............................Contract Coordinator
	....................................Accounting Clerk

JIM WILSON

1710 Faircrest Ln, Houston, TX 77251
713-555-2384 • jwilson2@sbcglobal.net

OBJECTIVE A challenging outside sales role for an aggressive industry leader.

EXPERIENCE

4/00-Present
Overview

BAXTER HEALTHCARE, *Urology Specialist* - Ethicon Endo-Surgery Division Houston, TX

Market a full-line of capital surgical equipment costing $15,000-$60,000 per unit along with single-use disposable laser fibers for surgical procedures conducted by Urologists. Manage a territory spanning Houston, Arizona and parts of Southern California.

Challenge 1 Capture and then maintain market-share dominance relative to other solution providers selling BPH thermal therapies.

Challenge 2 Changing clinical perception to grow the entire market by persuading doctors to replace the prevailing, drug centered medical management therapy, which represents 95% of current treatments, with thermal therapy.

Products Laser Optic system for treating enlarged prostates, TVT for female stress incontinence, PD 103 radioactive implants (Brachytherapy) to treat prostate cancer, and a device for laborscopic surgery.

Actions
As Market Specialist Attended 2,000 procedures in the OR, ASC or doctor office, where I help identify the right to cases that fit our modality and work with doctors during trial use.
Grew Houston market share for thermal modalities from 5% to 85% (national average is 25% share).

Actions
As Sales Specialist 6 times in the past year I flew to major selling opportunities in other regions where I took the lead during the sales presentation.
Impact Closed 5 of the 6 deals worth a total of $2,400,000 in capital and disposable product revenues.

Actions
As Staff • Taught 88% of the 55 sales reps the Indigo Sales Mastery Course (SMC). Conducted 1-2 week field training with 22 sales reps. Trained 3 Territory Assistants in a 6-12 month mentorship.
• Part of the corporate team that created the division's first-ever performance standards criteria for the Urology Sales Representative.
Impact The first TA I trained is now #10 ranked sales rep.
I coached the 43rd ranked rep to where they are now the #9th ranked rep in the company.

Results

- Capital and disposable sales are worth $8,360,000 (grew territory revenues by 1000%).
- My capital sales represent 21% of the entire divisions output (from a field of 55 sales reps) and disposable sales represent 14% of the division's gross revenues.

Awards

- Member, Baxter Healthcare *President's Club* (only the Top 2% of 800 national sales reps are selected).
- Sales Rep of the Year 2001. In 2002, finished #2 ranked rep in the country (currently #2 for FY03).
- Received the Sales Excellence Award 2001, 2002 and 2003.

4/98-4/00
Overview

ABBOTT LABORATORIES, *Sales Representative* Houston , TX

Sold drugs to specialists including CNS, Cardiovascular, Pulmonary Cardiologist, Psychiatrist and Allergists. Used strong closing skills and relationships with doctors to sell 5 different pharmaceuticals. Worked with Formulary Committees to achieve formulary status in hospitals.

Results

- Grew territory to 47th out of 311 after starting out at 307th.
- Ranked as high as #1 of 60 regional territories for pulmonary drug, Aerobid.
- Ranked as high as # 4 of 60 regional territories overall.

EDUCATION 1998 B.B.A, Marketing, Iowa State University, Ames, IA

ZOE YOUNG

1633 Madison St. #16B, Whitehouse Station, NJ 08889 908-337-2315

OBJECTIVE A sales career with strategic planning, business relationship & project execution responsibilities.

SUMMARY Maximize profits and meet revenue objectives by building effective relationships, seeking referrals and ensuring that my clients remain satisfied. Able to close profitable sales and provide meaningful service to meet demanding and specialized needs.

STRENGTHS
- Consulting Sales
- Presentations
- Relationship Management
- New Business Development
- Public Relations
- Problem Solving

6/99 - Present *Pharmaceutical Sales Representative* **WYETH-AYERST** Whitehouse Station, NJ

Overview Starting in June, 1999 I was employed by Innovex, a contract sales force used by Wyeth-Ayerst until I was hired directly onto Wyeth's elite Lederle selling division in April, 2001. I sell a portfolio of pharmaceutical products to a client base of over 100 primary care and specialty physicians.

PRODUCTS SOLD

Drug	Mechanism of Action	Indications Addressed	Competitors
Altace	ACE Inhibitor	Risk Reduction of Cardiovascular Events	10 each
Effexor XR	SNRI	Depression, Anxiety	4 each
Premarin	HRT	Menopause	5 each
Protonix	Proton Pump Inhibitor	GERD, Maintenance of Healing of EE	5 each
Sonata	Sleep Aid	Insomnia	8 each
Zosyn	BLIC	Skin Infections, Surgical Staph Wounds	7 each

Challenge 1 **Building A Territory** Identify sales targets: physicians, clinics and medical centers.

Solution Cold call to setup initial meetings where I deliver product information pertaining to the indications, dosage and formulary coverage as well as address customer service problems.

Challenge 2 **Account Protection** As territory develops and revenues stabilize, my focus shifts to adding value to existing customers and reducing competitive threats.

Solution Act as a partner to my clients by consulting with them on product developments that are relevant to their core speciality.

Challenge 3 **Grow Market Share** Convert non-prescribing doctors, i.e. Endocrinologists, Cardiologists, Primary Care Physicians, Gastroenterologist and Nephrologist.

Solution Leverage clinical research from medical journals to support our product features and benefits. Turn existing clients into Product Advocates and train them to speak at round-table events.

Result Ranked top-3 in sales for 8 straight months out of 136 representatives.

Result Grew market share against the competition for a key product by 55%.

7/95 - 11/98 *Store Manager & Co-manager* **GAP** Whitehouse Station, NJ

Overview Shaped young Sales Associates into a team who could exceed corporate expectations for sales, customer satisfaction and ability to build loyal clientele. Created a working environment where camaraderie and team chemistry among staff to create a top performing store.

Result Attained a 79% increase over previous year's sales, earning Regional Medallion

Result Achieved Best Year-to-Date statistics for district.

EDUCATION 1992 B.S. Human Resources & Family Studies, Rutgers, Camden, NJ

RICK ISLEY

1511 N. Hudson Ave., #4, Chicago, IL 60610 312-751-0182 rickl@aol.com

1998-present **DUNN & BRADSTREET** ***Nat'l Sales Manager*** 8/02-present
Nat'l Sales Director 2 years
Sales Manager 4 months
Sales Executive 1 year, 4 months

Overview

Convince C-level executives of IT, Security, Government, and Consulting companies to attend business summits that I help create. The summit's focus is to arrange meetings between vendors and pre-qualified buyers (known as delegates) who control budgets of $1-$100MM each. To build participation, I close 90% of sales with a CEO and 10% with a CFO, COO or EVP of Business Development or Sales.

Challenge • Average 100+ CEO presentations to generate 10-12 sales for each summit.
Challenge • Conveying credible urgency to generate 48-hour opt-in/opt-out windows to CEOs.
Challenge • Explaining our ROI value-proposition convincingly to a CEO so that they add an unexpected line-item costing up to $250K to their predetermined fiscal budget.

Actions

Selling Strategy Present solutions to Fortune 500 and Global 2000 clients in terms of enhancing shareholder value, meeting critical business-development goals and outmaneuvering the competition.

Market Analysis Learn competitive environments and study market changes, growth opportunities and trends.

Leadership Manage and develop inside sales teams of up to 35 staff. Evaluate performance, goal alignment, career planning, motivation, training and reward/recognition.

Results
As Sales Executive
- Closed 6-figure deals with Siebel, Northrop, Lockheed Martin & Lucent.
- Closed Cisco & Computer Associates who had declined for 2 & 5 years each.
- Largest-ever single event booking in company history with Worldspan.
- #1 Conference Sales Representative (2000 & 2001 & 2002).

Results
As Sales Manager
[Led 2 teams]
- Reduced headcount 40% (from 25 to 15 AE's) yet increased revenues as follows:
- Record sales-months & exceeded past highs by 165% (12/98) & 157% (1/01).
- Elevated teams from #8 and #11 of 48 worldwide teams to #1 and #3 respectively.
- Moved team from the #3 team to # 1 rank, continued from 5/00 to 8/02.
- Pushed team to be the # 1 profit center in the world (2000-2001).
- Top Delegate Sales Manager for 1999.

Total Impact As a Sales Exec, closed $1.88MM from 3/00 to 6/02, including a record $310K in one month (previous high was $188K) As a Sales Manager, led the team to close $6.8MM.

1/97-7/98 **PRONOMICS** ***National Sales Manager*** South Africa

Overview Assisted CEO in building an extremely successful Hewlett Packard consumables reseller business from startup.

Challenge Creating an attack strategy in a competitive market which included teaching sales reps how to negotiate price and quantity discounts to meet a target of 11% profit margins.

Action

Building a Team Interviewed, recruited and trained 20 telesales staff. Established short and internal procedures, sales strategies and customer evaluations to reach revenue and profit goals.

Result
- Grew customer base 400%, from 100 active accounts to over 400 clients.
- Pronamics became HP's #2 reseller in S.A., in the first year (of 31 competitors).

Total Impact Within one year, total revenues had grown 500% at an average profit margin of 15%.

1994-1997 **CINEMA METRICS** ***Area Sales Manager*** ***1996-1997*** South Africa
Team Sales Leader ***1995-1996***
Sales Executive ***1994-1995***

Overview Cinema Metrics, a $60MM division of the $500MM CNA Gallo conglomerate, is the largest distributor of music and videos in the country. I sold Warner Brothers, Disney, 20th Century Fox and New Line Cinema video product to 140 retail clients consisting of independent operators and franchises.

Challenge 1 Selling Hollywood media products in a country with 11 national languages and broad income range, education and cultural demographics.

Challenge 2 The speed of changing movie trends and the variety of genres as well as the need to launch an average of 35-40 new titles per month.

Actions

- Sales Strategy Became a client's business partner and media consultant by recommending key selections, pricing and local marketing initiatives tied to their customer base profile and profit margin expectations.
- Management Led a team of 4 Sales executives by setting goals, reviewed performance and worked with other regional mangers to share information in order to improve the group's selling results.

Results

- Grew business at 30% a year.
- Most Improved Sales Executive-1994 (of 16 staff).

1989-1993 **GRACE CONSTRUCTION** ***Project Manager/Managing Partner*** South Africa

Overview Directed and controlled multiple projects, as many as 6 at a time, from design bid to completion & final delivery.
Clients Types: Public Schools, Government Contracts, and Industrial Sites

Actions • Project Mgt.

- Managed subcontractors, consulting engineers and client expectations.
- Secured city/municipal approvals and permits.
- Procured materials, vendors and managed daily construction schedules.
- Ensured quality and company standards were met per specification to avoid penalties.
- Contained costs by resource planning, cost estimating, budgeting.
- Estimating, take actions to meet milestones and to ensure project P&L as well as cash flow.
- Hired and trained staff, prepared management reports and corporate reviews.

Results Captured 7 of the 9 projects I had prepared bid quotes.

EDUCATION 1989 Diploma-University of Cape Town - Electrical Engineering
1997 Diploma-Damelin Management School-ICM Business Management

References available on request.

ALEX BROOKS

147 Buena Vista Dr., San Marcos, CA 92069
Abrook@aol.com • 760-367-2154

OBJECTIVE A sales role where I develop revenues, build client relationships and earn bonus based on performance.

EXPERIENCE

1984-9/02 **AUGUILA TECHNOLOGY CORP.**, San Marcos, CA

Sales Engineer [10/90-9/02]
Production Supervisor [6/86-10/90]
ISO Auditor [3/98-9/02]
Laser Technician [6/84-10/86]

Overview.............. Led a team of 12 manufacturing sales reps through all stages of business development; defining new opportunities, quoting for RFQs, working with production on prototype design, and promoting product lines in a business segment that generates $9,700,000 annually or 50% of all corporate revenues.

Challenge Cradle to grave project management (350 total projects) for a company that custom laser welds and cuts OEM metal, plastic or glass product for industries such as:

Industries & Clients

• Automotive	• Aviation & Aerospace	• Consumer Products	• Medical
• Military	• Telecommunications	• Food Service	• Energy
• IBM	• Ford	• Motorola	• Beltone
• SC Johnson	• Seimens Gammasonic	• Litton	• Rockwell
• GE Nuclear	• Delco Electronics	• AirGun Design	• Ericcson
• Medtronic	• Abbott Labs	• Baxter	• Snap-on Tools

Products Created

• Audio System	• Fuel Regulators	• Satellite Batteries	• Contact Lens
• Orthopedics	• Paint Ball Gun Parts	• Vascular Cutters	• Hearing Aids
• Surgical Tools	• Nuclear Hardware	• Reactor Fuel Rods	•Ignition System

Project **Internal** Created the first cost-based RFQ system to standardize the quoting process and help Aguila win more profitable orders.

Result Reduced quoting costs 20% and time from 3 to 1.5 days

Project **Team** Member on: ***Continuous Improvement JIT Team,*** of manufacturing, purchasing, shipping, QC, and sales to create a ***flexible factory*** of independent ***work cells***.

Result Reduced order processing 56% (from 12 to 7 days then to 5 days)

Project **Client** **Barringer Technologies**—Worth $1.6M to Aguila (largest new client in 2002) Created the Trace Detector, a vacuum cylinder & gas spectrometer to capture samples.

Result The technology will be used in drug detection and life science applications (i.e. pharmaceutical product manufacturing).

Project **Client** **Delta Faucet**—Worth $3.4M annually (Aguila's #3 client out of 200): Originally started as a prototype production project with an order for 50 parts.

Result Client grew orders to 173,000 per month.

Supervisor Managed 15 technical staff and 55 machine operators working 24/7 in an advanced production environment. Oversaw a manufacturing plant with 42 work centers on a 30,000 sqft site. The custom nature of contract business demanded that I execute small batch orders from simple prototype design up to mass production orders of thousands of parts produced per day across every conceivable industry application.

ISO Auditor Led monthly internal audit teams to comply with ISO 9002 standard. Presented audit reports to senior management. Company rep. for external audits from both independent ISO registrars and customer quality auditors.

Laser Technician Setup laser welding and cutting workstations for prototype and large-scale production runs of customer parts. Helped implement the *CAD/CAM* systems used to cut and weld metal, plastic, and ceramic parts.

EDUCATION

2001	B.A.	Business Management	Cal State San Marcos, San Marcos, CA
1984	A.A.S.	Laser Technology	San Diego Dity College, San Diego, CA

RANDY JOHNSON

435 Princeton St., Jackson, MI, 49202 517-389-2331

OBJECTIVE Sales management for an original equipment manufacturer.

SUMMARY Sales and marketing strategist with a history of innovating corporate programs that gain competitive advantages, are foundational to sustaining profits and meeting quarterly objectives. The key is effectively solving problems to improve my company's image and confidence with our customer base.

STRENGTHS

- Consulting Sales
- Technical Sales
- Negotiations
- Sales Training
- Value Added Selling
- Product Promotions
- Territory Development
- New Business Development

EXPERIENCE

5/00 - Present **International Business Development Manager** proxima 

***Overview*................** Recruited by Proxima prior to their merger with Infocus on 8/00. My mandate was to build revenues in the PC channel for a line of multimedia projectors ranging in price from $3,000-$28,000 each.

Strategy 1 Implemented ***The Proxima Exclusive Reseller Program,*** a partnership plan to motivate resellers to focus on our product lines. The key is to creatively use co-op dollars, product trainings, VIRs and exclusive promotions as sales drivers.

Strategy 2 Once InFocus bought Proxima thereby creating the $1 billion market leader (70% share), the Director of Sales wanted me to create a new selling program for InFocus and train sales staff on how to execute the plan.

Results

• Sales — Grew from $18MM to just over $24MM a year.

• Landed

Boise	PC Nation	Pomeroy	Educational Resources
GE	Comark	Sayers	Sarcom

• Examples — Grew Comark from $484K, 1st Q00 to $920K 1st Q01 during a down market
Grew CDW from $500K per month to a consistent $1MM per month
Opened D&H Distributing and built it to a consistent $450K a month

Final ....Impact Won the "Award of Excellence" for highest over quota in the PC channel

5/99 - 6/00 ***Senior Sales Manager***
Sales Manager

NOKIA
CONNECTING PEOPLE

Overview*................** Recruited by the VP of Sales as the channel expert to create Nokia's first-ever ***National Reseller Program and rebuild the Monitor/Display product line which had lost $50MM off the peak US sales of $200MM.

Strategy Created an exclusive reseller partnership program (Team NOKIA) to separate Nokia from the 10,000 other computer technology manufacturers. An invitation only program with tangible participation rewards to motivate VARs who signed-on to focus on Nokia over the competition.

Results Signed 10 VARS worth $9MM on their way to $15MM (based on a POS fiscal year run rate analysis). As the program grew, an East coast sales rep was hired, whom I taught the program, she added 7 new accounts and increased sales $6MM.

Partnerships created

• Comark	• Westcon	• Woodfield	• GE
• Pomeroy	• Sayers	• All-Star Systems	• Boise
• Computech	• Arlington	• Compucom	• CDW

Final ....Impact Nokia sold division to Viewsonic- 1/00 for $800MM who bought our success and eliminated us as a competitor. For Nokia the benefit was divesting a non-core business unit.

1993 - 1999 **National Sales Manager** PANAMAX
Regional Sales Manager - Central Region

Overview................. As ***National Sales Manager*** of a $10 million computer channel, I directed 6 Regional Sales Managers, personally handled Panamax's Top 4 accounts and implemented two new programs:

1. Implemented ***Points for Panamax*** (a national marketing program)

Strategy To duplicate my regional sales efforts at the national level, I created a selling platform for my sales team to follow and a marketing plan to differentiate Panamax from the other 4,000 peripheral manufacturers.

Result Increased revenues 28% or $4 million annually, signed 1,500 VARs to Points for Panamax, and became the largest revenue producer of Panamax's 3 business channels.

Final ....Impact

- Won new accounts
  - Raytheon
  - Bank One
  - Discover Card
  - CNA Insurance
- Grew accounts
  - ENTEX
  - Micro Age
  - CompuCom
  - GE Capital
  - Comark
  - Pomeroy

- Recaptured Tech Data, increasing sales from $20K -$140K+ per month.
- Closed Nationwide Insurance, generating $1.5MM in sales.
- Landed First Chicago Bank and CNA Insurance, generating $150K.
- Closed PC Wholesale and grew business 532% to became a top 10 account.
- Landed Raytheon generating $200K in sales.

Overview................. As ***Regional Sales Manager*** my challenge was to grow Central Region revenues (1 of 6 US regions), a 14 state territory worth $3.6MM annually.

Strategy Within my first 3 months, I pitched Comark on carrying our products, secured their $65K initial order and won a $10K market development investment from Panamax to build a relationship.

Result By year-end, Comark became a Top-10 account, grew to $500K a year, became a model that I used to build other selling programs that led to signing 1,500 VARs once the programs were adopted company-wide.

Final ....Impact

- Ranked #1 in individual sales as a result of creating #1 sales territory out of 6 regions.
- President's Club 3-years straight
- 2-time winner of Best Sales Presentation/Training Award.

1991 - 1993 ***Senior Account Executive*** Sams Computer, Chicago, IL
1989 - 1991 ***Senior Account Executive*** PC Transition, Benseville, IL

EDUCATION 1987 BA, Psychology with Minor in English, Drake University, Des Moines, IA

HANK REDMAN

100 W. Current Ct., #10B, Palo Alto, CA 94304 • hred@aol.com

1994 - present **HEWLETT PACKARD** Palo Alto, CA
• ***Team Leader - Sales Group*** • ***Senior Account Executive*** • ***Account Executive***

Overview Independently maintain 100 top level accounts (43% are Platinum or Platinum Elite) worth $10-12 million annually, while leading a team of 6 sales representatives. Market 30 major product lines and over 50,000 technology items to small, medium and Fortune 500 companies, governmental institutions and universities. Develop new business, grow opportunities from existing relations and set profit margins on each sale.

Challenge As a selling-sales manager, my profit goal increased from $1,500 to $3,600 a day (240%) between 1995-02, representing the highest profit goal of any HP sales rep.

The following actions outline how I achieved revenue results even as the technology sector declined by nearly 50%.

Actions

Vertical Selling Initiate and cultivate relations with contacts in order to move up the chain of authority and win opportunities to sell directly to MIS Directors and heads of IT purchasing.

Penetration Probe to learn quarterly fiscal budgets. Provide pre-planning and technology consulting support to ensure that HP becomes the technology partner.

Pursuit Execute an ongoing pipeline of quotes on biddable projects, then relentlessly pursue opportunities until decision is reached (maintain a 90% bid-to-closure rate on 15-20 bids a week).

Regeneration Consistently pursue new opportunities in order to maintain a fresh account base (over the past 7 years, my top accounts have been given to peers at least five times).

Winning Beat competitive bids by combining: 1) strong knowledge of competitors, 2) leveraging HP's value-added benefits and, 3) building customer loyalty via personal integrity on all sales.

Result
Result
Result

• Regular member of ***Million Dollar Sales Club***-only top 10% of staff hit this mark.
• Top 15% on gross revenues generated past 4 years (out of 2,100 reps).
• Closed 20 individual contracts above $100,000 in value.

Projects As team member, launched the following HP corporate selling initiatives:

CRM Beta Test - Worked with IT to create the initial data infrastructure used to track critical customer information.
HP WinSales - Databasing strategies used to make product substitutions.
HP@Work - Automate sales by putting HP@work on customer desktop and creating evangelists who could then help penetrate their company.
Big Pushes - Initiated HP's migration to higher margin brokering sales. Brokered warranties, data storage and telephony with Tier-1 companies.

1993-94 ***Tele Sales*** **AMERICAN FAMILY INSURANCE** , Madison, WI (part-time)
Sold advertising products to national insurance agents.

EDUCATION 1994 BA, English & Political Science University of Wisconsin - Madison
College Work: 1992-94 ***Legislative Page*** **State of Wisconsin Assembly**, Madison, WI

BRENT NICHOLSON

932 San Gabriel Way • Valencia, CA 91355 • 661-777-2475, bnichols@yahoo.com

Objective

To continue a sales career that capitalizes on strategic strengths as applied to marketing and business development.

Summary

Business strategist and sales executive with a focus on maximizing profits, improving market performance and meeting corporate revenue objectives. Effectively manage human and capital resources with insight to overcoming barriers to business growth and marketing strategies to expand market share nationally. Leadership vision is to build teams who are prepared to compete and win, where customers are assured of personal attention and executive management is 100% confident in my performance.

Sales Mangement Experience

12/98 - Present **MARZOCCHI SUSPENSIONS**

Sr. Sales Manager-OEM Channel 4/00-now
Sales Manager-OEM Channel 9/99-4/00
Account Coordinator 12/98-9/99

Overview............... Selected by a new VP-Sales & Marketing to help turn-around and revive a failing brand. Marzocchi had suffered 4 years of declining revenues prior to my appointment to Sr. Sales Manager (from $106MM in '97 to $70MM in '00) and had lost 25% of their market share to their two major competitors.

Duties Defined quotas, budgets and evaluated performance for an 8-member sales team. Improved sales forecast accuracy and managed sales orders to help manufacturing increase on-time deliveries by 12% and reduce write-offs of obsolete inventory by 60%. Overall we minimized on-hand inventory from $17M to $10M. Managed orders, communications and customer satisfaction for 31 international distributors.

The following challenges explain how I led sales and marketing to grow revenues and win market share.

Challenge 1

Segmentation In 1997, our key international competitor discovered and dominated the Xtreme Sport segment, a $20M high-end market with margins 25% higher than standard lines. By FY '99 the competition held 85% share versus our 15%.

Response Created the Psylo line - unveiled the product launch strategy during a global sales and marketing meeting with European and US sales groups. Key determinations included: setting price points and refining product features and image on the new platform.

Result Psylo is now Marzocchi's flagship product line and has attained first year revenues of $8MM representing 40% of the total Xtreme Sport marketplace. Psylo enhanced sales for the entire Marzocchi brand as a beacon product that attracted wide consumer appeal.

Challenge 2

Market Share A key US competitor improved their product to where we could no longer demand premium prices. They gained 70% and 40% of our #1 and #2 customers respectively (historically, we owned 80% of each account) costing Marzocchi $30M. The past sales team responded to price competition by quoting our lowest price regardless of volume commitment.

Response Profiled all accounts to identify where price vulnerability existed and designed a multi-tiered pricing plan based on:
1. Dollar volume commitment by the customer.
2. How much a customer used us in their full product line.

Result Taught sales team to negotiate price breaks with clients well enough that margins grew from 26% to 32% and gross sales went from $70M-74M (first revenue increase in 5 years).

1990 -1997 **NICHOLSON CYCLES** **Owner/Operator** Valencia, CA

Overview................ Responsible for sales, purchasing, AP & AR. Established city's first bicycle patrol unit. Promoted over 30 national bicycle events. Awarded "Citizen of the Year" for work in the community.

EDUCATION 1983, Pursued B.A., **Advertising,** College of The Canyons Valencia, CA

ADAM HAUSMAN —— 17 Donnelly Dr., Lake Success, NY 11042, 5176-335-2910 • ahaus2@yahoo.com

OBJECTIVE Sales career for a company that needs seasoned, aggressive and motivated staff.

EXPERIENCE
1997-present

CANNON			Lake Success, NY
	Senior Sales Executive	2001- Present	
	Sales Executive	1999-2001	
	Credit Investigator	1997-1999	
	Bankruptcy Coordinator	1997-1998	
	Contract Coordinator	1997	

Overview

As Senior Sales Executive - 1 of 21 New York sales representatives in the largest district of 90 US regions. Manage a base of 425 diverse customer accounts that generate $1.998MM in annual revenues.

Tactic

• Prospect 3 Client Types — 1. Network within existing large-business accounts, 2. Take-away or win-back from competitors 3. Identify and capture brand new business.
Combine research (i.e., using a national competitor data base) with mailers and sales blitzes to uncover opportunities.

Result — Increased average account revenues by 20% with add-on sales. Displaced over 40 competitors and initiated 80 new accounts.

Tactic

• Managing Client Relationships — Make client calls to cycle through every account at least once every 3 months (average 8-10 drop-by or courtesy calls a day).

Result — Maintain a 95%+ retention rate among extremely strong competition.

Tactic

• Product Introductions & Extensions — Represent a group of 35-40 products costing from $2,500-$65,000 each. Present hardware and software business solutions that range from simple modifications to entirely new automated systems.

Result — Rolled out 20 new products or extensions since '00 including the launch of the first Logistics Tracking System at a Chicago Hospital (U of C).

Tactic

• Customer Satisfaction — Write Statements of Work (SOW) outlining Cannon obligations and service level responsibilities relative to client expectations.

Result — Of 20 SOWs written to date, 100% of my clients are completely satisfied relative to their expectations as defined in the SOW (noteworthy since we charge 20-30% premium prices for our offerings).

Total Impact

Year End Performance Results: FY '00 102% • '01 87% • '02 106% • '03 101%
Awarded Top Honors Twice -'00 & '02 (for total dollars, new business and technology sales).

As Credit Investigator - Processed high dollar commercial and government leases. Created a training manual for future staff on credit investigation procedures. ***As Bankruptcy Coordinator*** - Filed all Chapter 7 & 11 bankruptcy claims of our customers with US Bankruptcy Courts. Analyzed legal documentation and assessed the best process to recoup lost revenue. Liaison between US courts and Cannon.
As Contract Coordinator - Processed and approved 60-100 daily commercial and government leases.

Result The sole Credit Investigator of 30 in the US recruited into Sales.
Result Member of New Business Mailing Credit Investigation team which increased dollar volume and lease volume 20% over 2 years.

1990-1997 **GABLES & HAUSMAN** ***Accounting Clerk***
Performed various accounting functions while balancing and preparing client accounts.

EDUCATION

2002	MBA, Management, Syracuse University
1995	B.S., Political Science, Syracuse University

CHAPTER 19

EDUCATION CAREERS

The Education Category Has

4 Client Examples

17 Job Titles

109 Years of Work History

NAME	JOB TITLES COVERED
1. ALECIA JONES	....Professor
	......................................Dean of Students
	......................Chairperson of Counseling
	...................................Assistant Principal
	....Counsellor
	....Teaching & Acting:Assistant Principal
2. LEE FONG	......................................Program Director
	................................Program Coordinator
	.................................Program Facilitator
	.........................Director of Cosmetology
	......Instructor in Advanced Cosmetology
	.............................Manager & Instructor
3. VANESSA RODRIGUEZ*	....Teacher
	......................................S.A.T. Instructor
	....Tutor
	...................................Research Assistant
4. VIVIAN GRAHAM	....Teacher K-9

* Find the "before resume" in chapter 35

ALECIA JONES, Ed.D.

177 Forest Lake Rd., Atlanta, GA 30302
404-399-1598 • ajones@worldnet.att.net

EDUCATION

1995	**Ed.D.**	**Educational Leadership**	Florida Metropolitan University
1992	**E.B.D.**	**Guidance & Counseling**	Georgia State University
1980	**M.A.**	**Guidance & Counseling**	Georgia State University
1978	**M.A.**	**Reading**	Barry University
1977	**M.A.**	**Cultural Studies**	Georgia State University
1971	**B.A.**	**Education**	Barry University

EXPERIENCE

2000-present — **Professor of Reading** — CLARK ATLANTA UNIVERSITY, ATLANTA, GA

Overview — As a full-time Academic Developmental Reading Professor, I prepare students to read at the university level (75% are non-native US).

The Need — 50% of 7,000 freshmen are identified as needing developmental reading from their academic reading assessment scores.

Goals —
1. Perfect the student's ability to write compelling research papers.
2. Improve the student's ability to summarize their reading assignments.
3. Teach students how to comparatively analyze lead characters and conflicts.
4. To perfect higher order thinking skills (i.e. recall-synthesis-evaluation).

Solution — Implemented the school's ***first-ever*** Literary Circle Discussions.

Solution — Integrate cultural diversity by selecting reading materials that expose the majority culture to minority authors and vice-versa.

Result 1 — Average student completion rate is 95% although the dropout rate, apart from my classes, is over 50% in the Developmental Reading program.

Result 2 — Took over class rosters from other professors 3 times (after they had excessive dropouts).

Result 3 — The Department Chair considers my teaching methodology the program model.

1998-2000 — **Dean of Students** — NEW TRIER H.S., WINNETKA, IL

Overview — Supported a top 5 high school by learning each one of my 350 assigned students, relative to their special needs, academic standing, career aspirations and personality type.

The Need — New Trier parents have some of the highest expectations in Illinois public schools and demand exceptional student support and counselling. As the only Dean (of 9) with an MA in Guidance and Counselling, I was given the hardest student group to counsel.

Goals —
1. Provide inspired guidance that respects the innate ability and individual self-worth of every one of my 350 students in order to motivate them to excel.
2. Fully integrate into, believe in and empathize with each of my 350 students.

Solution — Spent up to 16 hours a day calling parents, notifying all special issues, keeping detailed anecdotes on progress, personality, personal feelings of each child.

Solution — Created the first-ever group counselling plan in order to increase the number of students I could personally visit with and allowed the students to not feel isolated.

Result 1 — Logged an average of 60 hours of counselling per week.

Result 2 — Received hundreds of verbal statements of appreciation from students for my personal interest and for going beyond expectations.

Result 3 — My counselling efficacy led parents to request individual counselling for themselves.

1986-1998 NORTH ATLANTA HIGH SCHOOL

Chairperson of Counseling 1991-1998
Assistant Principal 1991-1998
Counsellor 1986-1998

Overview Over 12 years as counsellor and department Chair I personally counselled 5,000+ students as well as managed a team of 8 counsellors. In addition, I completely reorganized North Atlanta's standardized testing process by gaining support and then coordinating 70 teachers to reduce the testing cycle from 5 to 3 days.

Need — Enhance the education quality of this public high school by creating programs that captured student and teacher enthusiasm for academic excellence.

Goal — Initiated North Atlanta's ***First-ever*** participation in the *National Academic Olympic Competition.* The key was to use the competition to build student academic strength in areas such as:
- math
- history
- science
- spelling
- current event
- geography
- art

Solution — Recruited teacher volunteers willing to give over 60 hours of their own time to prepare competitors during the 3 month Olympic cycle.

Solution — Convinced students of the benefits and rewards of dedicating themselves to the rigors of competitive preparation (i.e. 1 hour long before/after school practices).

Result — The program grew each year to include 250 students and 10 participating teachers.

Other Roles

Coordinator	Homebound Medically disabled students
Coordinator	Curriculum School Planning
Chairperson	New Hire Interview Committee
Coordinator	Scholarship Committee

1984-1986 MONTGOMERY ELEMENTARY

Teacher & Acting Assistant Principal

Overview Originally hired to teach 3rd grade until the Principal requested that I become the intermediary between African-American students who were being bussed from south/ west-side communities in order to integrate into this largely Polish-American school.

Need — Identify triggers causing low morale among teaching staff and offered stress-management monthly workshops to improve their ability to work with the new student population.

Goals — Give African-American students voice to their frustration regarding racial, cultural and academic hurdles to assimilating into the student body. Reduce tension, improve communication and modify negative behaviors that were escalating to the point of danger.

Solution — Held weekly stress management counselling sessions with both teachers and students.

Result — Tensions were ameliorated, teacher complaints were reduced by 66% and student incidence of misbehavior reached normal levels.

CIVIC
1980-1999 Mayoral Election Committee of Atlanta
1981-1999 Atlanta Beautification Organization
1985-1995 Secretary-Atlanta Public Relations Committee

PROFESSIONAL
Georgia Education Associations - National Education Association
American Association for Counseling and Development
Georgia Association of Counseling and Development
Association for Supervision and Curriculum Development

LEE FONG

5531 Scenic Dr., Los Angeles, CA 90230 310.667.2160

OBJECTIVE To continue a successful career in corporate training.

5/98 - present **UNIVERSITY OF SOUTHERN CALIFORNIA** Los Angeles, CA

Program Director 7/01-present

Program Coordinator PULSE (Pre-University Lab School Endeavor) 4/01-7/01

Program Facilitator 5/98-4/01

Goal ***Reform how teachers teach.*** Use PULSE methodologies to teach teachers who teach at-risk students to prove the model and then elevate it to the general student population. Ultimately, we are solving the problem of schools socially promoting underperforming students to higher grades.

Actions

- Supervise PULSE staff
- Report on progress to Provost
- Recruit Educational Facilitators
- Coordinate curriculum development
- Chair meetings
- Coordinate schedules

Challenge 1 Deploy PULSE to underserved student populations (low income, ethnic or foreign nationals) who perform an average of 5 grades below their age in reading, writing and math.

Challenge 2 Totally reversing the "Top-Down" teaching approach with a "Bottom-Up" learning system. ***Meaning*** – students actually direct the teacher and identify what they ***need*** to learn vs. the teacher force-feeding a packaged curriculum.

Challenge 3 Elevate PULSE to the standard adopted by Los Angeles metropolitan school systems. Build internal consensus and awareness at USC to gain momentum and evangelists who communicate PULSE's methodologies as they graduate and become active teachers.

Tactic 1 Rigorously track student performance to prove our program efficacy.

Tactic 2 Create teaching standards and guidelines used by 120 educational facilitators and student teachers who test these programs in the classroom (100 students in 10 schools).

Tactic 3 Broaden PULSE as follows:

Internal Work with USC's Educational Department, the Los Angeles Teaching Center and the Senior Administrative Staff (University Provost and President).

External Create partnerships with Los Angeles Public Schools (Area Instructional Officers), City Colleges of Los Angeles and suburban school districts.

Result Won the support of USC's illustrious board of CPLP Professors to adapt PULSE standards into the curriculum and syllabi.

Result 33% of Los Angeles Public School administrators are promoting PULSE to 350 school principals.

Result 100% of PULSE students go onto high school (vs. only 30% of average at-risk student population).

1992 - 2000 **L.A. SCHOOL OF COSMETOLOGY** [LASC] ***Director of Cosmetology*** ***Instructor in Advanced Cosmetology*** Los Angeles, CA

Goal To leverage my 10+ years of industry expertise and businesses contacts in order to make LASC the #1 cosmetology school in the US.

Challenge 1 To be better than local and national competition (over 10,000 estimated schools) who possess strong reputations due to their longevity in the marketplace.

Challenge 2 No formal career path: ie. internships, testing programs, or official degree status that could make the program a stand-out.

Challenge 3 Marketing to students while building industry feeder-referrals.

pg. 1 of 2

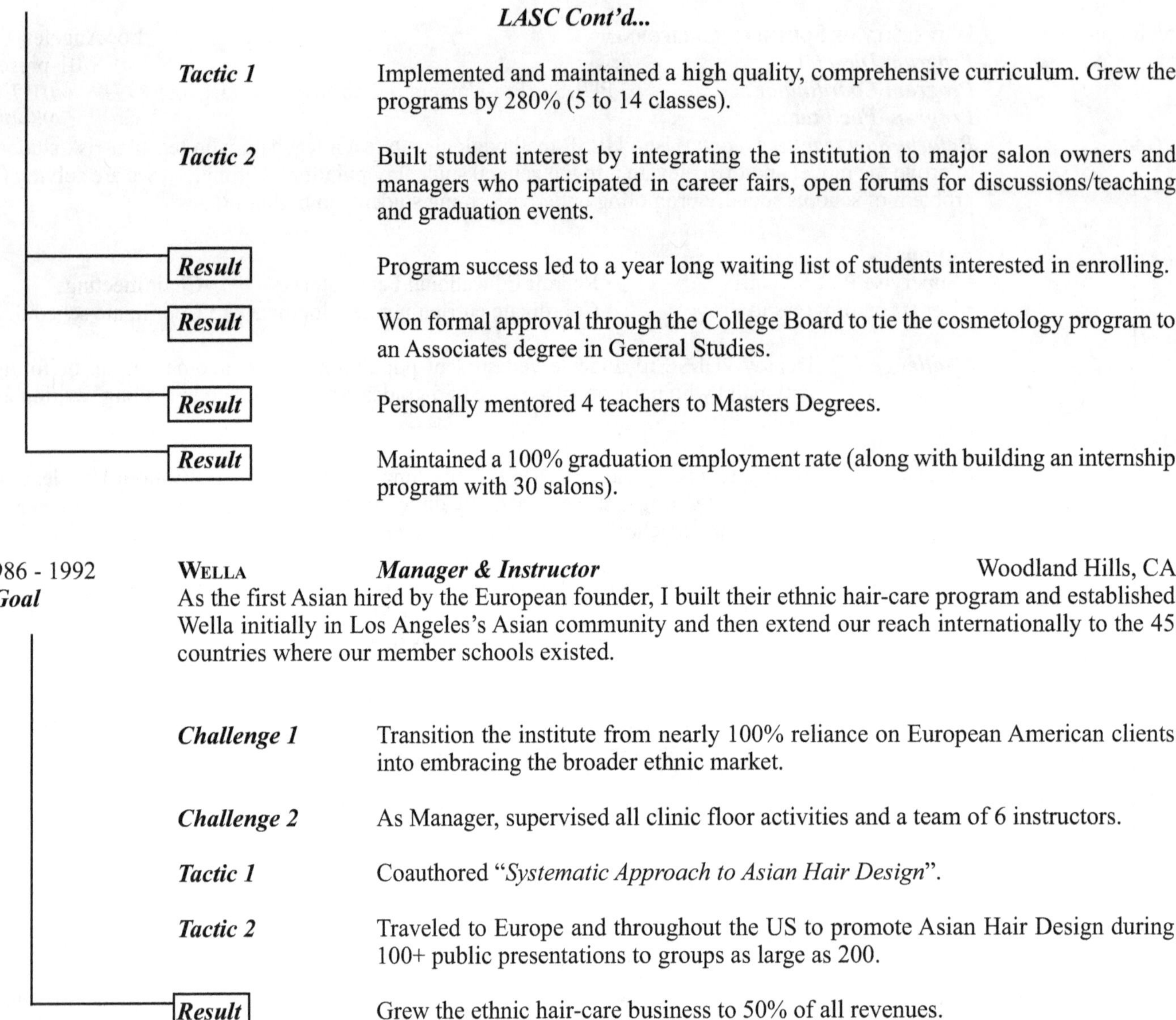

LASC Cont'd...

Tactic 1 Implemented and maintained a high quality, comprehensive curriculum. Grew the programs by 280% (5 to 14 classes).

Tactic 2 Built student interest by integrating the institution to major salon owners and managers who participated in career fairs, open forums for discussions/teaching and graduation events.

Result Program success led to a year long waiting list of students interested in enrolling.

Result Won formal approval through the College Board to tie the cosmetology program to an Associates degree in General Studies.

Result Personally mentored 4 teachers to Masters Degrees.

Result Maintained a 100% graduation employment rate (along with building an internship program with 30 salons).

1986 - 1992 **WELLA** ***Manager & Instructor*** Woodland Hills, CA

Goal As the first Asian hired by the European founder, I built their ethnic hair-care program and established Wella initially in Los Angeles's Asian community and then extend our reach internationally to the 45 countries where our member schools existed.

Challenge 1 Transition the institute from nearly 100% reliance on European American clients into embracing the broader ethnic market.

Challenge 2 As Manager, supervised all clinic floor activities and a team of 6 instructors.

Tactic 1 Coauthored "*Systematic Approach to Asian Hair Design*".

Tactic 2 Traveled to Europe and throughout the US to promote Asian Hair Design during 100+ public presentations to groups as large as 200.

Result Grew the ethnic hair-care business to 50% of all revenues.

EDUCATION

1995 - 1998	M.A., Educational Administration	University of Southern California	Los Angeles, CA
1987 - 1995	B.A., Education	University of Southern California	Los Angeles, CA

MEMBERSHIPS Los Angeles Cosmetology Association American Association of Cosmetology Schools

Vanessa E. Rodriguez

1710 W. Trails End Rd., Albuquerque, NM 87131 505-884-2121 vrode6@vahoo.com

OBJECTIVE

Teaching role at a school needing staff who can contribute to the mission of the school.

TEACHING EXPERIENCE

1997 - present **TEACHER** **ALBUQUERQUE HIGH SCHOOL** Albuquerque, NM

Taught 5 English classes (2-American Literature and 3 World Literature). Teaching dynamics covered presentations, skills assessments, time management, communication and interpersonal techniques.

By the second year, I was recruited by the Principal to roll-out a model program titled, AVID (Advancement Via Individual Determination), where I taught world history to 20 at-risk students with the goal of rehabilitating them to function in a mainstream class. I was expected to set up the teaching model that was to be used school-wide after my initial period. After a 5-day boot-camp to learn AVID, I met the following challenges.

Challenge 1. Leading a class of marginally motivated incoming freshmen (note: I was the youngest teacher for all 3 years at Albuquerque).

Challenge 2. Personally learning world history (from the renaissance to the present day - 600 year span) quickly enough to teach the class, although my degree is in English.

Result Motivated students by maintaining a high expectation level and taught them how to prioritize, organize and plan study time.

Result Boosted a majority of students GPA significantly who then reentered mainstream classes.

1997 **TEACHER** **DEL NORTE HIGH SCHOOL** Albuquerque, NM

Recruited by a new principal for a school that recently lost accreditation and was instituting academic changes and tougher standards in order to recertify.

Challenge 1. Took over a class of seniors in their second semester who were the first to graduate under the new requirements: their GPA must be above C to pass and they must complete a QUEST senior project (a daunting challenge since QUEST consisted of 25 hours of community service).

Challenge 2. Maintained grading integrity although in two classes, a total of 60 students, 33% were either below or near the failing threshold.

Result Implemented teaching strategies that helped 85% of the class pass, and as importantly, created a document trail to validate the integrity and fairness of the grading that was applied to each student (to ensure that the 15% who failed was justifiable).

1997-2000 **S.A.T. INSTRUCTOR** **POWER SCORE** Albuquerque, NM

Taught 18 classes to an average of 20 students per class. The population was characterized as medium to high achievers. This was an intensive training program that addressed Math, English and Reading comprehension.

1999-2000 **TUTOR** **SCORE LEARNING CENTER** Albuquerque, NM

One-on-one tutor for an average of four learning impaired students per semester for an entire year.

1996 **TEACHER** **RANDALL HIGH SCHOOL** Albuquerque, NM

Taught 2 classes of 11th grade English with 30 students each. My first teaching assignment after graduating. The challenge was taking over a class 2 weeks after it began without a Master Teacher to provide guidance.

EDUCATION

1996	**University of New Mexico, Albuquerque**	BA English
1997	**New Mexico State University, Carlsbad**	Teaching Credential

VIVIAN R. GRAHAM

1310 Old Sauk Rd *Madison, WI 53705* *608-234-6952*

OBJECTIVE To continue a successful career using teaching, administrative and management strengths.

SUMMARY

Professional Deliver academic programs to maximize student retention and personal potential. I maintain effective interpersonal relationships as well as use organizational and planning skills to build excellent student performance results.

Philosophy Capture and develop a child's learning capabilities by evaluating their skills to discern how best to elicit peak performance without inducing stress. Use a concerned approach to provide positive guidance that stimulates interest and develops intellect.

STRENGTHS

- Verbal Communications
- Interpersonal Skills
- Lesson Planning
- Organization
- Public Relations
- Student Relations
- Directional Planning
- Leadership

1987 - 1998 **TEACHER K-9** **Crestwood Elementary School,** Madison, WI 1995 - 1998
Marquette Elementary School, Madison, WI 1987 - 1995

OVERVIEW Create lesson plans to meet a pupil's daily educational requirements. Curriculum design helps children reach their full potential. Build 1-on-1 relationships to track progress and meet special needs.

PROJECTS Develop thematic mini-units averaging 3-8 weeks in length (the bar graphically illustrates the degree of the learning challenge for the child).

ARCHITECTURE UNIT

Degree of Difficulty
0 2 4 6 8 10

Focus Taught students independent and group research techniques regarding significant architectural structures and their designers.

Detail Students built scale models, presented biographical reports on the architects and displayed their work in a culminating activity.

ADVERTISING UNIT

Degree of Difficulty
0 2 4 6 8 10

Focus To learn creative and persuasive writing techniques. To become aware of factors that influence behavior (hidden or obvious) and to develop creative ideas.

Details Students created advertisements, selected actors and scripted messages for video taping.

GEOGRAPHY UNIT

Degree of Difficulty
0 2 4 6 8 10

Focus Taught global geography, report researching and writing skills.

Details Students researched population, natural resources, religion, indigenous foods, music and economic structure. Culminating event included fashion/music show, foods, and staging in the classroom.

CIVIL WAR UNIT

Degree of Difficulty
0 2 4 6 8 10

Focus Taught students independent and group research techniques on American history and issues of multicultural diversity within the Civil War context.

Details Reviewed the entire four year war, created a diorama, a live battle reenactment, an underground railroad and historical maps.

MATH & SCIENCE FAIRS

Degree of Difficulty
0 2 4 6 8 1(

Focus Enhanced student's creative thought processes using math and science projects.

Details Culminating activities: Invention Convention and Carnival where students created math/ science games (Wheel of Fortune/Jeopardy) and entertainment (Rube Goldberg).

EDUCATION

1987 M.Ed., University of Wisconsin, Madison, WI
1985 B.A., Criminal Justice/Psychology, University of Wisconsin, Madison, WI

CHAPTER 20
TRASPORTATION & LOGISTICS CAREERS

The Transportation & Logistics Category Has
5 Client Examples

20 Job Titles

59 Years of Work History

NAME	JOB TITLES COVERED
1.ANGELO FIGUEROA	............Assistant Manager Dist. Services
	...........................Supervisor Frozen Food
	Supervisor Engineer & Educational Supplies
	...................Supervisor Mail Distribution
	..............................Equipment Dispatcher
	.................................Motor Truck Driver
	Supervisor -Frozen Food & Cold Storage
2. PATRICIA KEENAN	.................Senior Supply Chain Analyst
	...........................Expeditor/Junior Buyer
3. EDWARD WALSH*	.....................................General Manager
	....Associate
4. DEVIN LEWIS	....Fleet Manager
	.....................................Fleet Coordinator
	....Parts Manager
	....Parts Person
5. JEFFERY MOORE	...........................Account Representative
	.................................Operations Manager
	......................................Dock Supervisor
	....Coordinator
	.....................................Dock Supervisor

* Find the "before resume" in chapter 35

ANGELO FIGUEROA

622 Worth St., New York, NY 10067 | *212-619-1979* | *afig67@hotmail.com*

OBJECTIVE Traffic management, mass transit, logistics, or operational management.

SUMMARY Skilled traffic manager of distribution operations, personnel, facilities and equipment logistics. Experienced at solving complex problems with inventory control and order processing. Monitor distribution systems to improve customer service performance. Established controls and standards to improve tracking of inventory.

STRENGTHS
- Vendor Management
- Transportation Logistics
- Forecast Planning
- Master Scheduling
- Production Planning
- Warehouse Management
- Purchasing
- Cost Control

EXPERIENCE

1981 - 5/00 **NEW YORK CITY DEPARTMENT OF EDUCATION** *Department of Warehousing Distribution*

Assistant Manager - Distribution Services	8/96 - 5/00
Supervisor-Frozen Food & Cold Storage	2/95 - 8/96
Supervisor - Engineer & Educational Supplies	8/94 - 8/95
Supervisor - Mail Distribution Services	7/93 - 8/94
Equipment Dispatcher	3/90 - 7/93
Motor Truck Driver	12/81 - 2/90

Overview Managed ***warehousing*** (10 forklift drivers, 15 stock-handlers and 15 day-to-day), ***distribution*** (7 supervisors, 68 drivers, 80 helpers/substitutes) and an ***office staff*** of 12 for an operation that distributed 1,500+ shipments daily to 600 New York schools.

Duties

Labor Relations Adjudicated labor disputes, set policy and procedure regulations to work cohesively with labor unions and management.

Legal Compliance Coordinated workman's compensation claims, vehicle accident and liability cases with law department.

Facility Management Coordinated with building security for facility and vehicle fleet on a continual basis.

Scheduling Scheduled all personnel and management for daily work, personal days and vacation.

Routing/Dispatching Knowledge of New York city and suburban transportation demographics with focus on enhancing logistics of distribution. Supervised mass distribution of educational publications, mail and payroll checks to 600 schools and administrative departments.

The following 5 projects outline special efforts or assignments I was given to restructure, capture efficiencies and modernize the NYC Public Schools distribution services.

Project 1 **PRIVATIZE NYC DEPARTMENT EDUCATION WAREHOUSING & DISTRIBUTION OPERATIONS**
In 1996 NYC Dept. Ed. privatized warehousing and distribution as well as maintenance and repair trades. Overall savings to NYC Dept. Education was greater than **$20 million** (33% of the total operating budget).

Actions - A year before privatizing, I journalized every management and operational job function. This was used to negotiate the department fiscal budget and became a central element of labor relations during the actual downsizing. Worked with the legal and purchasing departments to annul leases with Ryder and Carmichael trucking. Worked with labor unions to notify and transition the 70% reduction in staffing (from 100 staff to under 34). Once Aramark was picked to replace NYC Dept. Ed. staff, Got it - Thanks! I think that we would like to go forward next week. I am just doing some last editing and working on the cover. I may have some questions early next week. My husband would like to get this printed as soon as possible. He also has two other books in the "Red Hot Careers"I setup their delivery programs and staffing programs.

Project 2 **RESTRUCTURED ALL NYC DEPT. EDUCATION DELIVERY ROUTES** - 6,600 daily traffic miles to 600 delivery sites. Analyzed city demographics, load patterns, employee man hour per vehicle/delivery, traffic patterns, mileage, cargo type, vehicle volume capacity to capture cost efficiencies and optimize manpower and equipment usage. Reduced unnecessary mileage by 16%.

Project 3 **GLOBAL POSITIONING TECHNOLOGY ROLLOUT**- Coordinated the installation of the Teletrac vehicle locators ⇨ for the NYC Dept. Ed. truck fleet and student school buses and supervised the command center.

Project 4 EXECUTED ROLLOUT OF THE: *NEW YORK EDUCATOR,* A MONTHLY NEWSPAPER
A very complex project that touched on managing relations with the vendor, creating a formula to label, package and print **600,000 issues** per month distributed to every staff member, student and parent in every school.

Project 5 INAUGURAL SAFETY PROGRAM: Led efforts to comply with a new federal law that all commercial transportation operators become CDL compliant, to this end, I oversaw an employee random drug testing program and retrained all supervisor and operational personnel under the new safety first guidelines.

Project 6 STAFF RECRUITING: Experienced at searching for and retaining top quality staff. Key on discerning loyalty, issues affecting long-term stability as well as potential for professional growth.

1995 - 1996 ***Supervisor-Frozen Food & Cold Storage***
Supervised facility with 8 forklift drivers, 4 stockhandlers, 6 daily help. Oversaw picking of items, product staging, inventory staging, location storage and warehouse equipment management. Oversaw distribution of routing and conveyance of product to all 600 school lunchrooms. Coordinated with municipal health department facility sanitation inspectors and interacted with La Grou Cold Storage Management, whom the New York Department of Education leased dock and warehouse freezer space.

MASS TRANSIT Develop revenue producing routes, manage service restoration, overseeing customer service and passenger volume conveyance commensurate with equipment safety and scheduling.

LICENSURE CDL with Air Brake and Passenger Endorsements

References Available on Request

PATRICIA KEENAN, *CPIM*

961 Principal St., St. Louis, MO 314-699-7348

OBJECTIVE Optimize Supply Chain-Logistics, reduce costs and attain outstanding service levels.

SUMMARY Management expertise includes production planning, coordinating schedules, marketing/sales forecasts, providing operational support and resolving problems. My efforts are team focused with emphasis on executing corporate projects to ensure profitability or decrease the cost of doing business.

STRENGTHS

Logistics Develop strategic distribution plans, track progress, and ensure schedule compliance.
Forecasting Coordinate between marketing and sales to create ideal production cycles.
Problem Solving Resolve non-compliant products, plant disruptions and overly large inventories.

EXPERIENCE

1992 - present ***Senior Supply Chain Specialist*** ***EARTH GRAINS,*** St. Louis, MO
Establish master plans and production schedules for Bread and Bakery plants ($35MM and over 350 SKU's) shipped to a 6 warehouse network supplying 100,000 customers.

FOCUS **PRODUCTION PLANNING**

Optimize ....Plant transportation costs (i.e. full truck vs. LTL, pig vs. truck).
Analyze ....Product selling histories with Marketing/Sales departments to forecast volume and inventory requirements.
Determine ....Production priorities refined to seasonal fluctuations, demand volatility and new product introductions.
Coordinate ....Between Purchasing, Finance, Sales & Marketing departments.
Balance ....Short term and long term volume requirements between in-process and finished goods inventories.

FOCUS ....**DISTRIBUTION PLANNING**

Analyze ....Transportation cost options in the network and resolve out of stock issues with Customer Service.
Review ....Inventory levels and resolve code date discrepancies, damaged products and quantity variances.
Document..........Freight claims and communicate shipping and receiving priorities to the Traffic department.
Monitor ....Disposition of damaged products, code dates, donation/destruction or repackaging of materials.

PROJECTS

COST SAVINGS

Focus — Changed primary ingredients for 150 products sold to 100,000+ customers without production time loss, inventory waste or lowered customer fill rate.
Results ——— Saved $500K/year and won the 1997 Chairman's Award for Excellence.

BRAND INTRODUCTION & PRODUCT EXTENSION

Focus — Integrated Boboli bread products into Earth Grains after it's acquisition from Sara Lee Corporation and then helped successfully roll-out a newly created Boboli Bread Stick for Applebees (our #1 chain account).
Result ——— The extension value to Earth Grains is $14M annually.

ENTERPRISE RESOURCE PLANNING USING SAP TECHNOLOGY

Focus — As a Supply Planner I coordinated and oversaw a two- phase integration.
Result ——— Successfully implemented SAP's application impacting Supply Chain Management

1991 - 1992 **Expeditor/Junior Buyer** ***DRAKA USA,*** Franklin, MA
Used a military contract procurement system. Ensured vendors met delivery schedules and conformed to federal standards. Liaison with sales, manufacturing and management to ensure uniform production scheduling.

EDUCATION B.S., Business Management, **BOSTON UNIVERSITY** - 1991
APIC Certified CPIM

EDWARD WALSH

7521 Battle Creek Rd., Detroit, MI 48226 • ewalsh77@hotmail.com
Cell 313-556-2190 • Ofc. 313-220-5477 • Hm. 313-667-2154

OBJECTIVE

To increase profits, motivate staff & build operational cohesion in a transportation or logistics management role.

SUMMARY

Build sales, improve net profit and meet the challenges of developing market presence by eliminating account base erosion and responding to competitive pressure quickly. As a business manager, I remain involved at all operating levels and prepare staff to deliver exceptional customer service. Leadership and logistics management experience includes business development and account management with P&L oversight.

STRENGTHS

Sales
- Sales Management
- Feature-Benefit Selling
- Sales Training
- Business Development
- Employee Motivation
- Negotiating

Operations
- Business Plan Execution
- Territory Development
- Logistics
- Budgets/Forecasting
- Strategic Planning
- Purchasing

TRANSPORTATION INDUSTRY EXPERIENCE

1996 - present — **GENERAL MANAGER** — **WALSH TRUCKING** — Detroit, MI

Overview

Tactical Challenge Turnaround 106 year old, $1.1M family run transportation business that had significant erosion of quality and customer base with an aged union staff of drivers (50% were to retire within a year).

Revenue Challenge Comparing '96 to present

1. Prospected 75 of our top 100 customers since '96 (also retired 60 poor margin accounts)
2. 80% of current revenues come from 4 new industries I discovered
3. Increased staff from 10 to 16 of which only 4 remain from pre 1996
4. Increased company networth from $100,00 in 1995 to $500,000 by 2003
5. All equipment and buyout debt was satisfied by 2003 (a total of $935,000)
6. Revenues per mile increased by 100% since 1996

Solved

• DEBT ISSUES

Took on a $1.7MM debt to buy a company with $120K in profit in '96

Pension Liability	= $400,000	
Equipment Debt	= $625,000	(new trucks/tractors from Ford Motor Credit)
EPA Compliance	= $150,000	(underground removal of tanks)
Owner Buyout	= $300,000	(payback in 6 years)
Infrastructure	= $200,000	(rehabbed building that collapsed twice)

Solved

• BIZ RE-ORG

Optomized corporate assets, restructured staff, replaced bad business and strengthened finacial relations

Customer Diversity	Developed clients in new markets that had higher profit margins and gave us a firm niche presence with key commercial accounts.
Cost Management	Delivered sustainable financial gains by reducing cost, improving productivity, and consolidating staff.
Staffing	Recruited 75% new employees.
Labor Relations	Negotiated contracts with 3 labor unions that changed the flat hourly rate into a percentage of the customer charged rate.
Finance	Developed new bank relations with lenders for equipment financing and line of credit for turnaround costs.

Result Increased profits 300% in 3 years
Result Grew year-by-year sales 20%
Result Paid equipment and buyout debt in 6 years, a total of $935,000.

IMPACT Walsh's Teaming's revenues grew from $1.1MM in 1996 to $1.5MM in 2003

1994 - 1996 — **ASSOCIATE** — **LAW OFFICES OF MICHAEL SANDBURG** — Detroit , MI

Researched and drafted litigation, briefs and memoranda for corporate contract law, real estate and banking law issues. Drafted pleadings, discovery and summary judgment motions. Responded to all forms of discovery, prepared cases for trial, drafted trial motions, briefs and prepared witnesses for trial. Edited and drafted loan and loan workout agreements with corporate counsel. Reviewed and edited commercial lease agreements.

EDUCATION

Juris Doctor	University of Michigan Law School-self financed	1996
BS Business Administration	Eastern Michigan University	1991

Devin R. Lewis

765 Lasalle Ln., Valley, MD 21031 410-287-0032

OBJECTIVE To continue a successful career in operations and fleet maintenance management.

STRENGTHS

- Problem Solving
- Planning/Analysis
- Change Management
- Reducing Costs
- Staff Training
- Program Development

SUMMARY As manager, I create programs that make the company run more efficiently by reducing wasted man hours, overstocked inventory, or sloppy procedures. For 10 years, I've achieved results by consistently improving performance, selecting staff capable of working as a team, maintaining cohesion and looking at the overall success of the organization as if it were my company.

EXPERIENCE
1992 - 1999

DUNBAR ARMORED SERVICES

Fleet Manager	1/98 - 2/99
Fleet Coordinator	4/96 - 1/98
Parts Manager	10/94 - 4/96
Parts Person	11/92 - 10/94

OVERVIEW Manage a million dollar operating budget and staff of 13 mechanics servicing a $15,000,000 fleet of 400 vehicles (275 armored trucks and 125 cars). Operations cover 15 branches in VA, MA, NY, RH, & MD.

Success To date, I've saved over $500,000 in reduced costs, inventory reimbursements, revenues from GM for warranty repairs and increased sell prices for used vehicles.

Challenge Although the fleet grew by 300%, I implemented 7 programs without any increase to staffing.

PROGRAMS

❶ **Initiated a G.M. Certified Warranty Repair Center**
Result Dunbar now earns $40/hr for all warranty repairs of our own trucks (200+ hours within the first 8 months) and we cut the downtime from an average of 7 business days to 1 day.

❷ **Fleet Tracking Information System**
Selected a vendor and a computer product to monitor all operational processes.
Result System now tracks: Inventory, Fleet Maintenance, General Information, Fuel, Prices, etc.

❸ **Preventative Maintenance Program**
Developed a PM checklist covering 25 points conducted at 100 hours or 3000 mile intervals.
Result Truck quality is good enough that we sold 9 vehicles on the secondary market for an average of 50-150% over trade average (i.e. $7,500-$12,000/ea vs. $5,000).

❹ **EPA & Recycling Programs**
Introduced an environmentally friendly program that exceeds all statutory requirements.
Result Program covers • Batteries • Oil • Antifreeze • Scrap Metal
• Oversaw removal and replacement of 3 underground tanks

❺ **Inventory Management Program/JIT System**
Analyzed historical usage on a 500,000 piece inventory to determine minimum stocking requirements.
Result Reduced on-hand inventory by 75% from $400,000 to under $100,000 (securing a reimbursement rate of 80% on returns to the original vendors).

❻ **Vendor Consolidation**
Evaluated a group of 50 vendors to look for ideal product, service and price mix.
Result Reduced final group by 60% to 20 key vendors.

❼ **Parts Replacement Program**
Added AC/Delco to our GM parts inventory and negotiated a large discount.
Result Saved 15-20% per AC/Delco part. Rate for AC parts was 3% over manufacturer's price.

Jeffery Moore

1632 Commerce Way
Cranford, NJ 07016
908-323-6154
jmoore@aol.com

SUMMARY

• An account executive experienced with domestic and international territory development as well as client service support. A self-starter, who enjoys creating profitable client relationships, as well as using organizational skills with management to solve problems.

• MBA education includes coursework in Management and Organizational Behavior, Management Information Systems and Finance.

• A decade of successful management experience challenged me to lead projects and develop staff, resolve operational weaknesses, implement controls to manage costs and improve staff utilization.

• Leadership experience in an extremely competitive industry taught me how to assess, analyze, plan, and direct changes to attain market needs and meet corporate objectives.

• Personal accountability focuses on creating work measurements, establishing procedures and tracking expectations for each job.

References on request.

OBJECTIVE

To continue a successful sales career that capitalizes on territory development, client management and marketing skills.

STRENGTHS

- Direct Marketing
- Territory Development
- Client Management
- Logistics
- Proposals
- Negotiations
- Budgeting
- Customer Service
- Prospecting/Cold Calls

EXPERIENCE

1994 - Present

MAERSK, Cranford, NY
Account Representative 5/99- present
Operations Manager - Sole Midwest Manager 1994-1999

Among the 15 largest container shipping companies in the world with an intermodal system that combines sea, land and air transportation.

Overview

Write proposals and negotiate import/export contracts with traffic and export managers of Fortune 500 multinationals that ship to 100+ international destinations. Manage a base of US accounts in a 4 state territory that generates $5 MM annually.

Help overseas colleagues maintain business relationships with corporations from regions in the:
• Mediterranean • Mid East • Asia • South America

Knowledgeable of tariffs, US customs, railroads, rate quoting, bookings, and documentation practices.

Negotiate 100+ contracts per year ranging in price from as little as $800 per agreement up to $1,200,000 with an average of $150,000 per contract.

PROJECT FOCUS

Business Expansion: New Route - Asia to the Pacific N. West
On 6/99, Maersk added 8 new ships to create a *direct* Asia/Pacific NW route and tasked me with creating a paperless office to handle the 100% traffic increase.

Operations Manager - Sole Midwest Manager 1994-1999

Overview

Directed flow of 16,000 containers between port of loading and 10 Midwest cities servicing 3,000-5,000 customers.

Worked with railroad and trucking companies, analyzed logistics and monitored costs to optimize routing. Interacted with contracted agents and terminals to comply with company performance and quality standards.

1992 - 1994

Dock Supervisor **LGI LOGISTICS,** Houston, TX
One of two mangers responsible for overseeing 8 drivers and a 15 door dock. Dedicated 12 hour days to handle the 24hr operation. Dispatched 2-4 LTLs daily. Supervised all drivers and union dock workers while managing billing and routing.

1988 - 1992

Coordinator **EURO AMERICA,** New Eagle, PA
Hired and supervised a staff of 24 employees for all preload and outbound shipping operations at RPS's the largest terminal.
Coordinated 8-12 trailers with 8,000-10,000 packages per day.

1985 - 1988

Dock Supervisor **IET COMPANY,** New Eagle, PA
Organized freight movement, routing, dispatching and billing.

EDUCATION

M.B.A., **William Patterson University**, Wayne, NY 1995
B.S., Transportation, **Martindale Univ.**, Long Branch, NJ 1985

CHAPTER 15

PURCHASING CAREERS

The Purchasing Category Has

3 Client Examples

14 Job Titles

47 Years of Work History

NAME	JOB TITLES COVERED
1.BRENDA SLOAN	............................Planning & Allocation
	......................................Associate Buyer
	....Assistant Buyer
	....................Executive Training Program
	..................................Sr. Assistant Buyer
	...............................Operations Manager
	....Office Manager
2. SANDRA HAUSMAN	....Buyer
	...........................Assistant Sales Manager
	....Sales Manager
3. HEATHER BURKE	................................Purchasing Manager
	..........................Supervisor of Purchasing
	..........................Senior Financial Analyst
	...................................Financial Analyst

BRENDA SLOAN 777 Liberty Ave, Fleetwood, PA 60611 • 312-337-3209
bsloan16@yahoo.com

2001-present **PAUL FREDERICK CLOTHING**
Planning & Allocation - Fleetwood PA Merchandising Office

Overview Handpicked by the COO for a newly created Planning and Allocation team to help manage clothing products sold at 53 freestanding stores, by internet and via the catalog for this full line, private label men's clothier.

Challenges When hired, Paul Frederick styles were over-assorted and led consumers to think the brand had lost its core focus. This led to unacceptably high non-selling inventory, the need to use liquidators and declining gross margin.

Strategies Execute the following product sell-through tactics to help Paul Frederick remain profitable.

Sales Support ▪ Manage inventory sold via catalog (approximately $18 million a year), cleared on the internet (approximately $2.5 million) and sold directly at store-level (approximately $75 million).

Operations ▪ Support corporate buyers by tracking sales trends and price points that contribute to open-to-buy forecasts. Ensure financial goals are met on sales, markdowns, receipts and inventory levels.

Margin Growth ▪ Increase sell-through rates and minimize out-of-stock periods by recognizing selling trends and researching YTD results of 6 clothing divisions covering 3,500 sku's.

Re-Branding ▪ Helped Paul Fredrick identify trendy urban product with an European influence to appeal to a high-end consumer professionals earning $75K-$100K+ salary.

Impact Paul Fredrick is attaining their 67% gross margin target, completely eliminated use of liquidators, reduced clearance stores from 4 to 1 property, & stopped revenue decline by attaining positive growth in Q1 '04.

1999 - 2001 **JC PENNY'S** Philadelphia, PA
Associate Buyer **Men's Furnishings - basics, cold weather and hosiery lines**

Overview Helped select merchandise for men's basics (6,000 sku's) with annual sales of $60 million that produced $26 million in profit across 246 stores. Independent buyer for men's hqsiery and cold weather lines (3,000 sku's) with annual sales of $20 million where I chose product, negotiated costs and managed assortments.

Challenges To revitalize men's furnishing by introducing aggressive fashion trend tactics to move toward a modern/urban market appeal.

Strategies Executed the following tactics to grow YTD sales results.

Allocation ▪ Distributed merchandise based on climate, customer base and volume potential.

Private Label ▪ Developed and managed Ward's private label brands which included marketing and advertising to appeal to the customer base.

Vendor Relations ▪ Identified 5 new mill/factory sources, worked with them on product selection, negotiated price and co-op advertising support.

Open to Buy ▪ Shifted open-to-buy from 10-15% centered on fashion to what became 33% of product purchased being fashion-focused.

Product Launch Helped create "Real Boxer" men's loungewear that delivered over $1MM a year.

Impact Achieved 27% increase in sales FY 2000 in Cold Weather line and met the corporate margin goal of 36%.

1997- 1999 **CARSON PIRIE SCOTT** Boston, MA
Assistant Buyer

Overview Assisted with merchandise selection for lines selling $40MM a year at 74 stores. Distributed merchandise based on volume, customer base, projected pull and history.

Challenge Contribute to annual margin & growth goals for one of the largest retailers in the US.

Strategies Implemented the following tactics to help the Buyer succeed.

Sell-through ▪ Planned and executed merchandise promotions and markdowns.

YTD Analysis ▪ Analyzed selling trends and negotiated vendor returns.

Planning ▪ Developed seasonal sales and stock plans by department.

Impact Exceeded gross margin plan by increasing annual replenishment sales by 8%.

1995 - 1997 **JC PENNY'S** Philadelphia, PA
Assistant Buyer: Dining & Bedroom Furniture
Executive Training Program

Overview After initially completing an executive training program emphasizing merchandising and marketing, I was promoted to Assistant Buyer responsible for selecting merchandise for lines with annual sales of $75MM at 454 stores.

Challenge Create successful programs designed to drive sales in the Dining & Bedroom departments.

Strategies Supported JC PENNY'S corporate goal of being a market leader targeting the discount-price consumer retail category.

Sales Support
- Helped create customer incentive and multi-purchase programs: i.e., Buy 2-Get-1-Free.

Marketing
- Produced sales tools used by a commissioned sales force of 7,500 employees, i.e., product spec sheets with features and benefits. Oversaw advertising programs including layouts and product photography.

YTD Trending
- Prepared pricing analysis, inventory trends and line reviews. Communicated changes in product lines and marketing programs to store management.

Impact Annual performance review noted that I "*greatly exceed*" expectations.

1994- 1995	**Sr. Assistant Manager**	**ANN TAYLOR**	Philadelphia, PA
1993- 1994	**Operations Manager**	**LIZ CLAIBORNE**	Boston, MA
1989- 1993	**Office Manager**	**JOHNATHAN MCBRIDE LAW OFFICES**	Boston, MA

EDUCATION 1989 B.A., Political Science, Philadelphia University Philadelphia PA

References available on request.

SANDRA HAUSMAN

131 Sunset Blvd. #107
Beverly Hills, CA 90210
310/511-5690

■ OBJECTIVE ■

Retail Management.

■ SUMMARY ■

Professional – Result-oriented, high-energy professional experienced with new product roll-outs, managing clients and leading sales teams.

Management skills in the fields of ***art, fashion, and retail*** encompass dynamic business environments where I built operations to enhance revenues.

Success – To date, I've generated $3MM in new revenues using a creative fashion perceptive and by importing European vendors to differentiate us from our key competitors and penetrate consumer awareness.

■ STRENGTHS ■

Fashion Consulting
Relationship Management
Industry Research
Team Coordination
Marketing/Advertising
Fashion/Trade Shows
Product Promotions
Business Analysis
Public Relations

References Available

EXPERIENCE

1995 -5/00 ***BUYER*** SARAH JONES SHOES

Overview Recruited by the founder in a role that quickly transitioned from floor sales, to management to buying. The creative dynamic was optimizing the product group and vendor mix as well as re-merchandising S. Jones to expand choice and increase revenues.

Challenge Accurately profiling our customer base, which in 1995 was a narrowly defined 28-40 year old urban professional female. After discerning unexploited opportunities, I convinced the founder to broaden product selection as follows.

					Margin
Extended	• **Hand Bags**	Revenues			
1996	10 vendors/50 styles	**Then**	$55K		
1999	100 vendors/2000 styles	**Now**	$378K	⇧ 650%	49.7%
Extended	• **Hair Accessories**	Revenues			
1996	1 vendor/1 style	**Then**	$5K		
2000	25 vendors/20 styles	**Now**	$156K	⇧ 3,100%	49.1%
Extended	• **Jewelry**	Revenues			
1996	15 vendor/25 styles	**Then**	$50K		
2000	25 vendors/20 styles	**Now**	$552K	⇧ 1,100%	51.5%
Extended	• **Miscellaneous**				
1996	10 Items	**Then**	$78K		
2000	30 Items	**Now**	$312K	⇧ 400%	51.5%
Introduced	• **Scarves** (seasonal)				
1997	10 vendors/8 styles	**Now**	$40,000		52.6%
1997	• **Belts**				
	2 vendors/5 styles	**Now**	$41,600		52.0%

TOTAL .... Revenue Increase 787% $188K ⇨ to $1.48 million

DUTIES
Manage operations, budgets, staff training, sales seminars and the following:
- Purchase merchandise and accessories for all retail locations
- Forecast and analyze budgets
- Attend retail trade shows in top markets
- Predict inventory trends
- Create visual displays
- Design and photograph advertisements
- Maintain personal book of business worth $300K year

Assistant Sales Manager CHICO'S BOUTIQUE 1994 - 1995
- Designed retail floor plans
- Created window and jewelry displays resulting in 30% sales increase
- Staff supervision, training, inventory control, stocking, and customer service

Sales Manager RENER GALLERY 1993-1994
- Curator for American and European art exhibits
- Recruiter of new artists
- P.R coordinator—press releases, catalogues, gallery guides and mailing
- Cold-called to create new sales with private corporations

PERSONAL Create and sell abstract oil paintings and photography
EDUCATION B.F.A., The School Of The Art Institute 5/94

HEATHER BURKE

978 Burberry Lane, Atlanta, GA 30301 678-714-7842

PROFILE

Provide financial perspective on corporate and supply chain initiatives. Build strategic cohesion to manage expenditures, improve market share, and reduce cost of goods sold. Management credits my ability to consistently hit goals, complete projects within budget and motivate peers to accomplish a common goal. Maintain relations with suppliers to facilitate product innovations, coordinate product tests and attain cost projections. Evaluate volume reports and industry data to forecast purchases.

EXPERIENCE

1998 - present **COCA COLA BOTTLING GROUP** ATLANTA, GA

Purchasing Manager *Duties*
- financial planning and analysis - $300 million budget
- oversee purchasing budget of $40 million
- development and implementation of SAP purchasing system

Actions Negotiated a processing fee and the first ever grain related purchase, then executed a corn purchase strategy using corn futures contracts to control prices on sweetener.

Result Achieved annual savings of $4 million and migrated the same strategy to the parent.

Project **SAP IMPLEMENTATION**: After leading phase 1 to completion and taking delivery of system from SAP consultants on 8/99, I have focused on rolling out the 2nd phase to 16 sites across the Midwest.

Project **SYSTEMS ENHANCEMENTS**: Configured Purchasing Database, developed training material and led training sessions, developed implementation plans and provide support for the Purchasing and Inventory Management Modules.

1980 - 1998 **GENERAL MILLS**, Corporate H.Q. MINNEAPOLIS, MN

Supervisor of Purchasing - Financial Services
Senior Financial Analyst
Financial Analyst

Provided financial decision support to the VP of Operations and Purchasing Director for **$350,000,000** in annual purchases (note: prior to the divestiture of Snapple, purchasing support encompassed an aggregate of **$600,000,000** annually). Key challenge was to network between R&D, Plant Operations, Marketing and Accounting Functions in order to set strategies and implement cost reduction initiatives.

Actions
- Analyzed past purchasing trends and financial decisions to develop annual plans and quarterly business reviews as part of the corporate reporting requirements.
- Attained corporate financial or profitability goals while increasing competitiveness.
- Sourcing efforts captured benefits from economies of scale, improved market position and offset inflationary pressures.
- Developed financial performance measurement tools and internal compliance controls to track the competitiveness of buying decisions.
- Managed Supply Chain initiatives to meet our financial targets.

Results Strategies implemented reduced costs by $6,500,000 - $12,000,000 annually.
We maintained steady profit margins without ever increasing product price to the buyer.

Project **YOPLAIT INTEGRATION**: In 1995, General Mills purchased Yoplait and integrated their 150 SKU's and 50 suppliers into the General Mills Family.

Project **YOPLAIT COST MANAGEMENT INITIATIVE**: As Purchasing Unit Leader, I oversaw efforts to identify executable projects that were projected to save $50,000,000.

EDUCATION B.S., Business Management, University of California, Los Angeles

CHAPTER 22
OPERATIONS MANAGEMENT CAREERS

The Operations Management Category Has

3 Client Examples

9 Job Titles

41 Years of Work History

NAME	JOB TITLES COVERED
1.BOB STARK	..............................Operations Supervisor
	............................Senior Production Lead
	...............................Bookkeeper/Sr. Clerk
2. NICHOLAS ROTH*	....VP/ Operations
	....Office Manager
	...............................Asssistant Supervisor
	....................................Professional Actor
3. BENJAMIN SHAW	.......Director of Operations & Circulation
	....................................Division President

* Find the "before resume" in chapter 35

BOB STARK

154 Cherry Blossom Ct., Scottsdale, AZ 85260, 480-772-0782

OBJECTIVE

To become a General Manager in an organization that values hard work, integrity and knowledge. I believe in action, accountability and that my contribution is to add operational value to enhance profits.

SUMMARY

Experience in both service and manufacturing environments with expertise in transportation, operations and inventory management along with skills in safety, production, budgeting, HR, change management and capital improvement. Apply a results oriented approach to gain employee involvement in a team framework.

EXPERIENCE
1988-present

ALLIED WASTE

SITES		TITLES	
	Scottsdale Sorting Centers	Operations Supervisor	1996-present
	Scottsdale Sorting Centers	Senior Production Lead	1995-1996
	Corporate HQ	Bookkeeper/Sr. Clerk	1988-1995

Overview

After progressing through two office roles at Allied corporate HQ, I was handpicked by the CEO to help rollout Allied's largest municipal contract ever won, the $550 million Phoenix Sorting Centers; a group of 4 production sites that process 85-90% of Phoenix's residential waste.

My Role Manage 18 staff (union truck drivers and heavy equipment operators), oversee P&L, a $4.5 million operating budget and a plant that generates $18.6 million in revenues. Capital equipment includes 120 conveyors and 50 pieces of rolling stock.

- ***Action*** P&L — Met EBITDA goals by controlling the following line items:
  - Transportation Costs
  - Material Sales
  - Disposal Cost Per Ton
  - Tons Per Load
  - Overtime Labor Hours
  - Landfill Allocation Cost

- ***Action*** Logistics — Schedule 289 inbound and outbound truck shipments a day.
  Result • 100% on-time schedule for a total of 74,750 shipments a year

- ***Action*** Safety — Implemented new safety initiatives code named the ***Near Miss Program***
  Result • Reduced loss time and property damage costs by $290,000.

CONTRIBUTIONS

TO THE DIVISION

Benefit #1 **Maximize tons-per-trailer load** [optimized capacity of 43,000 truck shipment loads A year]

Tactic: Developed a cost-to-benefit analysis I presented to the Director of Operations that outlined how to use time-off incentives (up to 1 day a month) to motivate union operators to carefully pack and maximize tons per shipment hauled by each outbound truck (17,500 shipments a year)

Result 1 Increased average truck loads from 88% full capacity to 95% capacity which reduced my centers hauling expenses by $114,000 annually.

Result 2 When rolled out to the division, saved **$456,654** since '99 (after $282,000 in incentive costs).

Benefit #2 **Operational Efficiency**

Tactic: Worked with consultants at JMY Solutions and used Microsoft Excel's Solver add-on program to create cost effective transportation routes (Solver accounts for varied rates and distances while satisfying physical and contractual constraints ie. turnaround time, trailer availability and tonnage commitments) to distribute 850,000 tons of waste to 6 landfills across a 300 mile radius.

Result Once routes were optimized we saved **$500,000** in transportation costs.

Benefit #3 **Created Top-line Management Reports** governing P&L and operating costs on Landfills.

Tactic: Designed the *Transportation & Disposal Summary* for senior management to meet annual contract obligations with third party operators.

Result The new measuring system has optimized our landfill costs and saved Allied **$500,000.**

Benefit # 4 **Created first ever training program** for Allied Wheel Loader Operators.

Tactic: Collaborated with Caterpillar Inc. to customize the program to our needs.

Result Program success led Caterpillar to rollout a national Training Program charging $1800 per student (worth $520,000 in new revenues to Caterpillar).

Management Actions

Training Created Staff and Supervisor training programs covering the Incentive Plan, Benefits, Introduction to Supervision, Change Management, and Production Reporting.

Staffing Recruited and hired both exempt and nonexempt staff using affirmative action programs to create a truly diverse work force reflective of the local community.
Conducted employee surveys which gave snapshot of employee's perception of the strength of the overall organization, their direct supervision and their team effectiveness.

Union Contracts Managed 3 collective bargaining agreements simultaneously for 100+ contracted employees and direct reports. Created relationships with union agents. Managed policies and procedures relating to benefits, work rules and employment conditions.

Mentoring Conducted Performance Appraisals for all direct reports linking individual and team performance to compensation and growth in the organization. Surveyed employees to learn their perception of the organization, their supervision and team effectiveness. Trained staff to ensure professional growth.

Leadership Participate in Employee Involvement Teams that achieved better work start-times, production scheduling, capital improvements. Created Employee Involvement Teams to address production scheduling to capital improvement allocations.

TRAINING

Principles of Organizational Safety and Health	National Safety Council Phoenix, Arizona
Safety Management Techniques	National Safety Council Phoenix, Arizona
Certified Wheel Loader	Caterpillar, Peoria, Illinois
First Aid/CPR	American Red Cross, Phoenix, AR

References available on request.

NICHOLAS ROTH *337 Kensington Ln., Sherman Oaks, CA 90212 815-332-9955*

OBJECTIVE An executive position in an established film or television production company or studio.

EXPERIENCE

1996- 2000 ***VP Operations*** **TELEPICTURE PRODUCTIONS, INC.,** Los Angeles, CA

Overview Upon hire, TPI had 9 staff, generated $3.8 million annually and produced 30 hours of original programming for one cable channel, A&E Network. Two promotions later, I now oversee a $1.5 million operating budget and coordinate 75 staff who produce 65 hours of content for A&E, The History Channel, The Learning Channel and WGN TV, a revenue stream of $11+ million. Cost controls I've implemented have **saved $1,400,000** to date.

Duties Organize/reorganize, cut costs and create programs to increase revenues.

- Payroll • Human Resources • Benefits Administration (Health, 401k, Dental)
- Budgeting • Event Planning • Corp insurance (Liability,E&O,Worker's Comp.)
- Info Systems • Office Management • Corporate policy planning and implementation

Projects

HEADQUARTERS RELOCATION
Directed real estate agent, negotiated lease, planned construction & executed company move.
Result — Negotiated lease $6 below market rate. Estimated **savings of $1,000,000** over ten years. Flawless office move. Company lost one day of productivity.

CREATED H.R. DEPARTMENT
Employee Benefits Program: disability insurance, dental, 401(k). **Created Staff Review**:
Result — Devised pay analysis templates for personnel. **Staff Handbook**: Documented office policies and standards. **Changed Company Health Plan**: Saving over 2 years is **$173,513.**

CREATED POST-PRODUCTION DEPARTMENT
Integrated a system of 6 off-line/on-line AVIDs, with computer graphics and motion control. At completion of the Audio Suite buildout, we achieved complete post-production capabilities.
Result — **Added $500,000 to bottom line in 1998, projected to grow to $1,500,000 in 1999.**

CREATED NEW BUSINESS DIVISION-CORPORATE VIDEOS
Identified potential revenue stream: producing videos for corporate clients.
Result — Currently in negotiations with Northwestern University, Ivex Packaging Corp. **Estimated '99 gross-$350,000. Projected '00 gross-$650,000**

TRANSFERRED COMPANY INSURANCE
Coverage for Worker's Comp, General Liability, E&O, Employee Practices & Disability Gap
Result — Worked with Mesirow Financial to purchase a blanket policy, saving **$110,000**/year.

CREATED M.I.S. DEPARTMENT
Hired a System Administrator to manage computer and AVID resources. Instituted a complete review of Towers Productions Y2K compliance to upgrade all systems by 3/99.
Result — System Administrator has negotiated price points below average market value.

Office Manager & IT System Administrator **4/96 - 4/97**

Overview Duties included: buying a $100K AVID digital video editing system, consolidating Telepictures from 2 floors to 1, main contact with landlords, hiring the CEO's secretary and pre-interviewing producers. Set up PR/publicity system to furnish press releases. Result: 80 Press mentions & 5 radio interviews.

Changed Vendors

- Negotiated single car rental company Result: Saved money & reduced travelers' confusion
- Moved long distance service Result: Cut rates 35%
- Changed office supply vendor Result: Saved money
- Contracted new shipping company Result: Reduced shipping costs 15%
- Changed telecommunications provider Result: Reduced telecommunications problems

1994-1996 ***Assistant Supervisor*** **ARCHDIOCESE OF BOSTON**

Overview Managed 5 staff during Supervisor's absence. Maintained computer databases, inventories and postage accounts. Assisted the Supervisor when investigating or selecting vendors.

1991-1994 ***Professional Actor*** — Stage, Film and Commercials (i.e. with Michael Jordan for Nike).

EDUCATION 1991 **BFA**, Theatre, SOUTHWEST MISSOURI STATE UNIVERSITY ***Intern:*** US Representative Rod Kind

BENJAMIN SHAW ________ *217 W. Sheridan Ave., Boise, ID 83705 • 208-424-6196 • Ben_shaw@hotmail.com*

OBJECTIVE To contribute as a manager in the areas of cost management, operations and business development.

SUMMARY Focus on improving net profits, penetrating new markets and extending market dominance. As a business developer, I'm involved in the total sales equation by finding new business, sourcing suppliers, developing contacts and satisfying customer expectations. My vision is building business environments where employees compete and customers receive personal attention to their needs.

EXPERIENCE

1986-2001 **JOHNSON NEWS INC.**, Boise, ID — **Director of Operations & Circulation**
Division President – *Read It Book Stores*

Overview Managed operations and P&L for a $36 million wholesale distributor to 700 retail accounts in Idaho and Nevada (magazines, books, comics and trading cards). Oversaw a $3,000,000 operating budget, 50 staff and fleet of 20 vehicles. Negotiated distribution and pricing with publishers and national distributors, ie. Time/Warner, Hearst Corp., Murdoch Publishing, Hachette, National Publishing Services, American Media and TV-Guide.
As President of ***Read It Book Stores***, directed a 10 store chain that generated $6 million annually with 100 employees including 10 store managers and a district manager.

Challenges Led business efforts that generated $157 million in sales (97-01), allocated $9 million in capital expenditures and implemented cost saving initiatives that reduced the operating budget by $1.5 million. Grew revenues in a territory with 0% population growth.

MILESTONES

STRATEGIES	ACTIONS	BENEFITS
Business Building	▪ Acquired 2 of our competitors-distribution companies.	Grew market share from 55% to 80%.
	▪ Negotiated distribution agreement with Fleer, Upper Deck & Topps	Created trading card department that added $800K a year in sales.
	▪ Extended comics into large grocers Target, Walmart, Osco, Safeway, Hi Vee	Increased sales by 125%.
	▪ Grew the ***Read It*** chain of book stores from 2 to 10 outlets.	Added $6M a year (22% of JNI's income).
Cost Management	▪ Introduced new bin picking technology	Saved $50K and cut 2 staff.
	▪ Introduced sealed tote program for returned magazines from retailers.	Saved $90K a year by reducing 2 drivers and 2 trucks.
	▪ Created recycling program to turn a cost (waste paper) into a revenue source	Recycled 50 tons of waste paper a week which added $300K per year.
PR & Media Relations	▪ Built media hype with 10 radio and 4 tv stations.	Daily broadcast exposure worth at least $1,000,000 annually.
	▪ Introduced autograph parties tied to media exposure for author visits such as Louis Lamour and Robert Ludlum.	Improved relations with retailers, increased sales and public awareness for our bookstores.
	▪ Created "***Magazine News***", a local interest sales program to boost revenues with special interest editions.	Boosted special edition sales by 1,000%. Program becamea model for Time Warner special editions.

RECOGNITION Target (Dayton Hudson) — Rated a Top-10 Wholesaler, 1994 & 1995
Walmart — Rated a Top-10 Wholesaler, 1994 & 1995

EDUCATION 1986 B. A., Economics, University of Idaho, Boise

CHAPTER 23

START-UP & SELF-EMPLOYED CAREERS

The Start-up/Self-Employed Category Has

2 Client Examples

6 Job Titles

45 Years of Work History

NAME	JOB TITLES COVERED
1.MITCHELL FREIDMAN	S.V. P. Sales & Marketing
	V.P. Business Development
	Bookkeeper/Sr. Clerk
2. FRANCES LEVINSTEIN*	E.V.P. Sales
	C.E.O. & President
	Export Manager

* Find the "before resume" in chapter 35

MITCHELL FREIDMAN 1390 Princeton Ave., Miami, FL 33010 • mfreidman@aol.com • 305-226-7860

SENIOR MANAGEMENT • BUSINESS DEVELOPMENT, MARKETING, BRAND MANAGEMENT •

SUMMARY

14+ years of business development experience as a strategist focusing on identifying new business markets to penetrate, joint venture opportunities or M&A prospects that fit our core competencies and offer the best ROI. Execute front-end qualitative and quantitative due diligence of investment strategies, and deal structuring as well as the back-end change management responsibilities that are critical to ensuring operational, cultural and fiscal cohesion.

EXPERIENCE

1988 - present

Senior Vice President - Sales & Marketing **THE FREIDMAN COMPANY** **New York, NY**
Vice President - Business Development
Engage in debt and equity placement, direct investment, property development and sales due diligence to appraise investment-grade capital structures up to $200M as well as distressed capital structures.

SKILLS

Reporting — Compose summaries, market feasibility studies and income/expense projections covering current and historical market conditions.

Negotiating — Negotiate partnerships and corporate structures with respect to economics of individual transactions.

Due Diligence — Qualify proformas to attain profit projections (ROI, P&L and cash flow). Lead communications between ownership and equity partners to successfully close deals.

Management — Evaluate opportunity costs to determine long and short-term profitability as well as fit within the total business structure of our organization.

Leadership — Identify staff who demonstrate the ability to lead, who work equally well independently or within team contexts.

DEAL

BC PLACE STADIUM (Vancouver)
Principal in developing the winning bid to purchase stadium, hotel and 300,000 sq. ft. retail/office center for $60 million (US) out of Canadian Bankruptcy (property was originally built for $660 million (US)). Negotiated a 50/50 premium food and catering joint venture with Encore Compass worth $8-10 million in annual sales. Sold adjoining hotel to Hyatt for $33 million plus a $600K annual lease.

DEAL

NORTHWESTERN MUTUAL BUILDING (Milwaukee)
As land owner, contributed a $60 million property in a 50/50 joint venture with Ameritech Pension Fund. Eventually we resold the property to The Herrods Group and netted an additional $36 million (in 1998 the land was developed into the 1,300,000 sq. ft. Northwestern Tower).

DEAL

PRODUCTION SOLUTIONS INC. (Hollywood)
Developed a digital post production company serving DreamWorks, Columbia, Sony, MGM and Warner Brothers TV and film divisions. Acted in an Investment Banking capacity while negotiating a $10,000,000 purchase of the 80,000 sq. ft. headquarters (financed 100% loan to value). Helped develop the business growth strategy and worked with Bank of America to secure $12,000,000 in Series A funding.

DEAL

BAUXBAUM LIQUIDATION (New York)
Recruited as the selling agent for this $30,000,000 liquidation fund. Developed relationships with high networth and institutional investors, created road-show strategic plan and deal structuring (the promoted interest, the preferred return for the limited partners and whether it is a fund investment or a direct investment into the business).

DEAL

SAN DIEGO PADRES MLB TEAM (San Diego)
Part of a 10 member buying group consisting of Bank One, General Electric, Alcoa, etc. that purchased the team with the intention of implementing new branding, ticketing and marketing strategies to grow revenues, fan appreciation and asset value. Participated in subsequent sale for $98,000,000 in 1996.

EDUCATION

1992 — MBA, Finance & Marketing, Anderson School of Business, UCLA
1988 — B.A., Economics, University of San Diego

FRANCES LEVINSTEIN

Ph. +44-020-7672-4730 • flevin1@Levin-online.net

SUMMARY 24 years as CEO of a company that grew from a one-man operation to an employer with 30 staff in 3 countries and listed some of the worlds major retail corporations as clients. I'm a team player with a management style that involves coaching those on my team to deliver the best performance results possible.

STRENGTHS

Global Sourcing	(Compete for business in North America, Europe, Asia and the Middle East)
Building Selling Relations	(Conducted 1000+ presentations to corporate executive decision makers)
Market Development	(Took small initial or test accounts to multimillion dollar key account status)
Executive Presentations	(Negotiated 300 programs ranging from $24,000 to $3,700,000 each)

BUSINESS MANAGEMENT EXPERIENCE

2/03 - present — **Executive VP of Sales** — **ANSUN MULTITECH INDIA LTD.**

Overview Handpicked by the CEO of a 30 year-old, $40MM garment/leather/accessories manufacturer with the mandate to gain new clients, grow sales and drive profitability.

Goal Develop business for both the AMI corporate parent and their At Home divisional startup by introducing this relatively unknown India-based manufacturer to large US retailers.

Actions Within 6 months, made 15 key presentations to US importers, retailers & hotel suppliers.

Results Closed 2 contracts
- Ultimate Dress Inc. — Worth $2MM in fiscal commitment
- US Hotel Co. — Worth $1MM in fiscal commitment

Presented At Home — To Walmart, Umbra, JC Penny, Eddie Bauer and Crate&Barrel

1979—2003 — ***CEO & President*** — **SOMAR AGENCIES**

Overview As founder and entrepreneur, I grew Somar into a $10MM rep-firm of Israli manufacturers and buying agency for North American retailers. Selected vendors, screened credit worthiness and negotiated pricing.

1st Goal Growing a one-man operation to a business with 10 merchandisers, QA and Admin staff. Initiated and cultivated relationships with senior executives at national accounts where I built trust and personally guaranteed to the customer that Somar would deliver quality products, on time and on budget.

Actions Pursued and won over $200MM in business with the following accounts.

• SEARS	• JOHN LEWIS	• NORDSTORM'S
• REITMANS	• DONNA KARAN	• CAUSAL CORNER
• T EDWARDS	• REFERENCE POINT	• BROOKS FASHIONS
• JOHN LEWIS (UK)	• PEACOCKS (UK)	• FOSTER BROS (UK)

Results Represented 11 manufacturers and sold over $200,000,000 in products. Averaged a 50% operating profit margin for the company.

2nd Goal Expand Somar by merging with Fashion Industries, Inc., a $50MM business that focused on European markets yet wanted a presence in North America using the economies of scale of our combined organization. As VP Sales-North America I began penetrating US and Canadian retail opportunities. I setup a Cairo, Egypt office to capture low manufacturing costs and proceeded to grow agency to 20 staff.

Results Doubled sales to $20MM annually, a total of $180MM sold since 1994 which was 33% of all corporate revenues, while maintaining an operating profit of 50%.

Sales Success Examples

1.Sears — Grew account from 1 to 20 departments represented
Launched a new ladies suit program for Egyptian manufacturer (first ever)

2.Nordstrom's — Grew from 1 to 5 departments represented and $50MM in total sales
Won a Private Label Sweater program from an Italian manufacturer and become the #1 Private Label Program in the Men's Category (nationally).

CHAPTER 24

CREATIVE CAREERS

The Creative Career Category Has

2 Client Examples

7 Job Titles

16 Years of Work History

NAME	JOB TITLES COVERED
1.MELVIN HARRIS	.....................................Graphic Designer ....Senior Graphic Designer ....Production Artist ....Freelance Artist
2. LAURA STARK*	........Internet Communications Specialist ....Graphic Designer

* Find the "before resume" in chapter 35

CHUCK ANDERS 933 W. Sweet Valley Ln. , Charleston, SC 29402, 336-765-9589
• canders@hotmail.com

GRAPHIC ARTIST EXPERIENCE

6/02-present **Graphic Designer** **POINTBLANK DESIGN** Charleston, SC
The only graphic designer in a high-volume operation where I produce art for 2 business segments of this national religious publisher.

Challenge I'm the sole creative support fulfilling design/artistic orders for PointBlank's 200 reps who sell display ads, bulletins and calendars to 10,000 churches.

My Value Graphic Designer

• Calendar business	***Volume:***	Create 40 unique calendars a week or 2,500 designed since my hire.
• Display Advertisement	***Volume***:	Create 30-50 ads a day or 15,000 unique advertisements designed since my hire.
• Bulletins	***Volume***:	Designed 300 bulletin newsletters.

Impact Contributed to 50% of '03 revenues, PB's best financial performance in 90 years.

8/99-6/02 **Senior Graphic Designer** **BLUETONE MEDIA** Wilmington, NC
Managed team of 4 graphics designers for a 50 year-old toy-model company that needed my team to creatively add new products into their monthly catalog which was distributed nationally to hobby, toy and game retailers.

Challenge Managing the design team and a department schedule to meet production deadlines.

My Value Graphics Manager
- Monthly catalog (100 pages), flyers, promotional signage and display ads.
- Color correction and image manipulation.

Impact Personally launched 25 new product design campaigns that generated over $350,000.

7/97-8/99 **Production Artist** **CARGO PARK CORP.** Raleigh, NC
Worked directly for the CEO of a rapidly growing employment company that needed a Production Artist to create direct mail, marketing, training manuals and promotion collateral.

My Value Graphic Artist
- Produced flyers, booklets, posters, and display ads.
- Maintained production schedules and met customer deadlines.
- Designed original clip-art and page layout for newsletters and brochures.

5/96-7/97 **Production Artist** **FAST N' COOL GRAPHICS** Greensboro, NC
Produced flyers, posters, direct mail and display ads. Illustrated images for brochures and catalogues.

FREELANCE ARTIST

D&A Comics Illustrated & designed sci-fi/horror comic book. Wrote script for characters.

Women's Sports World Illustrated apparel for catalogues and signage. Created logos for marketing and designed page layout for direct mail ads.

Rising Sun Graphics Illustrated promotional items. Color correction and photo manipulation. Created page layout and marker renderings.

CNA Marketing Led 2 marketing teams. Inventory management and account maintenance.

TECHNICAL QuarkXPress, Adobe Photoshop/Illustrator, FreeHand, CorelDraw, PageMaker, Excel and PowerPoint
TECHNIQUE Oils, marker rendering, watercolor, acrylics, pastels, charcoal, pen and ink

EDUCATION 1996 BFA, Fine Arts, University of North Carolina, Greensboro, NC

LAURA S. STARK 313 Thornton St., Stratham, NH 03885, 603-534-0975 lstark@yahoo.com

OBJECTIVE To use creative graphic design abilities in combination with experience in print & web media.

TECHNICAL • HTML • Dreamweaver • Photoshop • Illustrator • QuarkXpress • Flash • IBM/Mac

EXPERIENCE

4/99 - 4/01 ***Internet Communications Specialist & Graphic Designer*** **TIMBERLAND**

Started on the Advertising team as Graphic Designer until promotion 8 months later to the corporation's first-ever web designer where I supported the launch of Timberland's enterprise site/store.

Launched Timberland.com

As Internet Communications Specialist: Sole web designer working with the IT department to implement web functions and perform the role of marketing liaison to IT department.

As Graphic Designer: Concept-to-finish weekly ROP ads and full color circulars. Directed photographers during photo-shoots at studio.

Actions

Manage Creatives	Created a "style guide" for web product shots.
R&D	Part of e-commerce business team (President, VP-IT, and VP-Marketing).
Vendor Relations	Helped interview design agencies for initial site design.
Statistical Analysis	Tracked, compiled and reported web statistics.
Competitive Analysis	Researched Kohl's, Nordstroms and Footlocker sites to identify features we needed and added a customer loyalty program in our site.
Negotiations	Captured lower cost photography for ongoing project.
Process Controls	Helped implement new web site processes into company work flow.
Sales & Marketing	Researched coupon and marketing strategies for site.
Staffing	Interviewed and hired a web copy writer.

Result Created an e-commerce "click & mortar" business channel that generates millions in annual revenues.

Result Wrote a proposal justifying the value of buying www.shoes.com given to and approved by the VP Marketing and Director Internet Communications which resulted in the acquisition.

Result Created the Timberland.com internet logo.

1998-1999 ***Graphic Designer*** **CREATIVE MARKETERS, INC.**

Created and prepared "camera-ready" art work for promotional business items used by a base of 200 customers including Lands' End, American Family Insurance, and WPS.
Worked with manufacturing vendors to ensure products were fully functioning created to design specification.
Recreated corporate logos when digital copies were unavailable.

Result Helped create or revise 100+ unique products.

EDUCATION

12/98 A.A.S., Commercial Art, Triton College, Chicago, IL
Member: Phi Theta Kappa Honor Society

3/04 Continuing Education: Macromedia Flash, The Art Institute of Boston

Online portfolio
http://stark.com

CHAPTER 25

HR & TRAINING CAREERS

The HR & Training Category Has

3 Client Examples

9 Job Titles

47 Years of Work History

NAME	JOB TITLES COVERED
1.LAWRENCE CARNESI	....Director H.R. ....Manager, HR &Labor Relations ......Manager Corporate Logistics & H.R. ....Human Resources Generalist
2. MARK CHEN	.............Instructor/Instructional Designer ....Cellular Operator ....Training Coordinator
3. PATRICIA TKACZYK	..............................Instructional Designer ....Training Developer & Facilitator

LAURENCE CARNESI

2410 Quaker Ln., LaVergne, TN 37086 • 615-963-2148 • lcar2@aol.com

OBJECTIVE ***Human Resources***

To develop an HR team capable of achieving objectives, improving organizational performance and contributing to the company's profit goals.

SUMMARY

A change agent who engages employees at all organization levels. Proven ability to direct all aspects of the HR function, with results in improved productivity and profitability. A key advisor to senior and executive staff members with a track record of leading corporate initiatives in diverse labor environments.

EXPERTISE

- Multi-Site Management
- Strategic Planning and Partnerships
- Employee/Management Relations
- Change Management
- Mergers/Acquisitions/Closings
- Safety/Workers' Compensation
- Employment Law
- Labor Relations/Labor Law
- Executive Coaching

EXPERIENCE

4/00 – Present **INGRAM PERIODICALS Director, Human Resources** La Vergne, TN

Hired a year after Ingram completed a $550MM acquisition strategy to buy 5 agencies and become the 3rd largest magazine distributor in the US. My role — lead all HR initiatives, manage a $2.7MM budget and supervise 11 HR staff. As chief corporate strategist and spokesperson, I also negotiated 10 collective bargaining agreements.

The Issues Ingram took 100 years to become a $450MM company with 700 staff, by 2000 they were a $1BB company with 4,900 staff. A 210% revenue increase could not sustain a 700% increase in payroll, access to credit was exhausted and Ingram was on the brink of insolvency.

My Mandate Create Ingram's first corporate integration plan, direct restructuring efforts and properly align headcount to sales.

Mandate 1 RIGHT SIZE INGRAM In Nov. 2000 the COO asked me to cut payroll by $6MM within 4 weeks.

- **Need** To meet loan terms and protect access to capital so that Ingram could continue doing business.
- **Tactics** By 1/01 I executed Ingram's first ever non-divestiture Reduction-In-Force and by 6/03, I executed six additional RIF which cut payroll from $102MM to $71MM.

Result Delivered $30MM in savings by reducing headcount 55% without one law suit.

Mandate 2 DEFEND INGRAM AGAINST EEOC CLAIMS – Successfully defended 21 EEOC complaints, six I inherited and the rest by staff trying to protect their jobs during corporate downsizing.

- **Need** To defend against each complaint well enough that 50% of the claims were never investigated by the EEOC, which eliminated the possibility of class action suits.
- ***Tactic*** Prove that complaints were frivolous, irrelevant and unsubstantiated.

Result Won 100% dismissal of all EEOC claims by the Commission.

Mandate 3 MAKE INGRAM'S LARGEST ACQUISITION PROFITABLE – In '91 Ingram bought United News Agency (UNA) for $7MM, hired 2 law firms that worked for 9 years to close UNA's Philadelphia plant and lower union staffing costs -- both firms failed to win union approval.

- ***Need*** UNA cost Ingram $4MM a year, their single largest loss center ($2.5MM came from labor contracts with guaranteed headcount).
- ***Tactics*** Within 2 weeks of hire, I stopped our illegal '*run from the unions*' and won all 4 unions to allow us to close the Philadelphia center and re-open a Lancaster non-union site. I then oversaw hiring 220 new line & office staff, a VP of Distribution & 2 HR generalists.

Result My negotiations saved Ingram $10,250,000 to date ($3,750,000 a year for 3 years).

Eliminated the decision negotiation stage which saved 6 months.

9/97 – 4/00 **GENERAL DYNAMICS Manager, HR & Labor Relations - MSC Division** **Edina, MN**

Member of GD's HR Counsel and Labor Counsel executive teams. As HR Manager I supported a manufacturing division of 1,000+ employees. Reported to VP, Human Resources, managed a $1.7MM budget and led 4 staff. Supervised orientation, recruitment/staffing, compensation and benefits administration.

Actions

Executive Coaching Counseled executive team on organizational planning, promotions, compensation, bonus/options plans and performance issues.
Collective Bargaining Chief Spokesperson and strategist for 18 collective bargaining negotiations. Member of GD Labor Counsel.
Legal Compliance Managed compliance with EEOC, FMLA, ADA, FLSA, OFCCP and OSHA laws.
Labor Relations Initiated, developed and conducted employee and labor relations training programs.

Mandate 1

Write the "Best Practices" Manual - which was adopted by all GD Companies.
Need Standardization of HR practices for all 7 corporate divisions
Tactics Interviewed by Townsend Perrin Consultants to learn my SOPs for the Material Services Division.
Result At presentation to GD's HR Counsel, Townsend's Chief Consultant noted that 80% of the adopted best practices came directly from my existing programs.

Mandate 2

Need **Implement PeopleSoft HRIS**
Goal — Help Alliant grow intelligently (from 27,000-44,000 staff), capture economies of scale and eliminate an archaic payroll system.
Need Implement Criterion & Resumix databases
Goal — Meet Federal Contract Compliance Programs (OFCCP) regulations (e.g. 49-CFR 20).
Need To standardize HR/Payroll for the following acquisition
• Gulf Stream • Lucent's defense business • Nass Co. (a large ship builder)
Tactics HR project management team member tasked with completing the $27M implementation.

Result Completed all implementations in 14 months for 7 divisions, payroll went-live without a hitch and General Dynamics conservatively saves $5MM a year by reducing duplication of efforts.

4/96 – 4/97 **CARTER CHAMBERS** **Manager, Corporate Logistics & Human Resources** **Baton Rouge, LA**
Recruited by the CEO of the south's largest distributor and supplier of engineered valves and piping a year after they had doubled in size and, as a result of becoming joint partner with Amoco and Mobile Oil, would grow headcount another 300% within 12 months and expand into 13 new distribution centers across 4 states.

Mandate 1

Establish Carter Chambers's first-ever Corporate HR department for the 400 employees:
Tactics **Introduced**
1. Benefit & Compensation Package.
2. Annual performance reviews.
3. A $5M, 3-year employee health insurance contract.
4. Government compliance standards

Results Saved Carter Chambers $400,000 by reducing annual turnover from 50% to 10%, created the HR policy manual and all work rule standards.

1985 – 1993 **CROMPTON CORP.** **Human Resources Generalist** **Baton Rouge, LA**
Handled recruitment, compensation, negotiations, benefits, performance/organizational development, training, policy formulation and strategic planning Conducted annual review and bonus process for all employees. Recommended all terminations, disciplinary actions and performance improvement plans.

AFFILIATIONS

Society for Human Resource Management, Member and SPHR Certified
Human Resources Management Association of Louisiana, Member
Louisiana Material Producers Association (LIMPA), Director, 1997 – 2000
Academic Advisory Council for Department of Engineering, Southern University, 1998 – 2000
National Maritime Union, Health & Welfare and Pension, Trustee, 1999 - 2000

MILITARY

U.S. Army - Special Operations

EDUCATION

1995	MBA, Human Resources	Louisiana State Univ., Baton Rouge, LA
1988	BS, Management & Finance	Southern Univ., Baton Rouge, LA
1999	Labor Relations Certificate	Louisiana State Univ., Baton Rouge, LA

Mark Chen

212-685-9612, 63 W. Madison St., New York, NY 10036

EXPERIENCE

10/93 - present **Nokia Americas H.Q.**

7/98 - Present	Instructor/Instructional Designer III	Nokia University
2/96 - 7/98	Instructor/Instructional Designer I	Nokia Cellular Subscriber Sector
11/92 - 2/96	Cellular Operator	Cellular Subscriber Group

Overview.............. After an initial project role where I created and delivered *The Defects in Manufacturing Analysis Report* to the divisional VP and entire manufacturing staff, elevated me to a part-time instructor and training coordinator until 1996 when I became a full-time Instructor/Instructional Designer.

My Impact............. Saved over $1,000,000 by developing courses from scratch or tailoring existing courses to fit department needs. Delivered 15 courses and designed 18 training solutions, a total of 2,000 training hours spread over 265 classes for 7,500 Nokia students.

Areas Taught

- Human Relations
- Middle Management
- Interpersonal Skills
- Technology
- Distribution
- Quality programs
- Corporate manufacturing initiatives
- Engineering software and R&D

Took the following project actions to help Nokia continue to be a world class technology leader.

Project 1

Delivered a 2-day course on Continuous Improvement strategies to our Hong Kong Manufacturing HQ for Semiconductors products. Course focused on statistical process control [SPC] and problem solving methods delivered to 14 lead engineers (Black Belt Engineers).

Actions Prepare engineers to teach their staff how to reduce product development cycles while improving the production reliability yield in semiconductor manufacturing.

Result Reliability yield is projected to increase from 93% to 99.999 (five-9s reliable).

Project 2

Member of project team of 5 who redesigned an ATSO program (Applied Technologies Software Organization) for Nokia's use in training 1,800 Personal Communications software engineers.

Actions Nokia needed the newly adapted course material (8 sessions and 43 modules) developed in a reduced timeline of 4 weeks from the original 12 week schedule. I modified Instructor and Participant Guides as well as redesigned the PowerPoint Presentation.

Result Personally created 3 of 8 sessions with 18 individual modules and 750 unique slides.

Project 3

Create new training for Global Distribution Center with 40 technicians shipping 2MM units a month.

Actions Identified 15 areas of training need and developed training roadmap for 13 OJT solutions of which I implemented 5. Found 2 existing Nokia University courses which saved 16 weeks of development time and found vendor to deliver courses.

Result The structured training program brought the department into ISO 9000 compliance.

Project 4

Client needed Electro Static Discharge Training for 250 pick & pack distribution employees.

Actions Modified an existing 8-hour course into a 2 hour module (saving 1,500 productivity hours) and met with Quality and Production Line Managers to ensure their commitment.

Result Turned the 2 hour module into an *e*-learning solution delivered on CD-Rom and Internet link.

Project 5

Nokia relocated a major portion of manufacturing from the US to Maztalan Mexico.

Actions Personally travelled to Mexico and worked with the plant G.M. to set up and use web based OJT library database as a key resource to train 800 manufacturing operators.

Result Maztalan trained plant staff now produce 3.6 million units to US production standards.

—— ***Continued on page 2*** ——

Nokia Projects Continued...

Project 6

Phase 1 Training on a new European product packaging methodology (Paceline system).
Actions Created 8 hour course with classroom activity, assembly line training and 30 minute video delivered to 250 line employees.
Result Production rates increased by 25% from 1200 units to 1500 units.

Phase 2 Client needed course time reduced.
Actions Redesigned course from 8 to 4 hours, implemented a monitored OJT program as follow-up and trained 6 distribution personal to deliver the course without my further involvement.
Result Course reduction saves 3,200 man hours of lost productivity.

Project 7

Delivered Unix based computer engineering tool training on Metaphase.
Actions Developed working knowledge of this new Nokia system and trained 200 engineers.
Result By learning the system the original Metaphase trainer could go to Europe and ensure rollout was not delayed overseas.

Project 8

Reduce part time instructors, high turnover and instructor no-shows.
Actions Restructured all recruitment, training and evaluation steps. Implemented a behavioral interview process. Developed Instructor guidelines with performance metrics and audit controls.
Result Reduced PT Instructors from 65 to 17, eliminated no-shows and increased retention rate to 90% (the other 10% received promotions to higher performance positions).

Project 9

Launch Corporate Learning Maps.
Actions In order to launch this corporate initiative, I trained 25 learning map coaches and supervised training sessions of 150 people.
Result The Trainers I trained executed worldwide rollout to 100,000 Nokians.

Project 10

New Employee Orientation to communicate corporate Policies, Benefits, History and Future.
Actions Delivered New Hire Orientations to audiences in excess of 100 new staff on more than four dozen occasions.
Result Improved Nokia's ability to process 5,000 new-hires.

11/92-12/95 **Cellular Operator**, *Cellular Subscriber Group*
Overview.............. Performed board repairs on digital products. Served as team leader for one year. Participated on problem solving committees to improve quality. Revamped manufacturing line to increase production.

Training Coordinator, *Digital Cellular Factory*
Overview.............. Maintained training records, coordinated monthly training schedule, designed training database and created training library.

MILITARY
1983-1991 U.S. MARINES Assignments
- Aviation Structural Mechanic
- Corrosion Control Supervisor
- Contamination Analyst
- QA Inspector

EDUCATION Pursuing B.S. Business Management Boston College, GPA 3.91

Cont'd Training
- Nokia University
- Langevin Learning Services
- Marketing Your Training
- Marine Corps Instructor School
- Training the Trainer 101
- Training Needs Analysis
- Advanced Instructional Design
- Instructional Design
- Technical Writing

Patricia Tkaczyk 8 Fairmont Dr, New York, NY 10001 • 212-455-5670 pattka@msn.com

OBJECTIVE To continue corporate training and personnel development work in a Training/Development role.

STRENGTHS

- Training
- Assessment
- Team Collaboration
- Job Readiness Evaluation
- Creative Thinking
- Program Development
- Diligence
- Leadership

EXPERIENCE

10/02 - present
Mandate

Instructional Designer **CITIBANK -** Customer Security Operations - Credit Card Services

Re-engineer a 4-week-long **New Hire Training Program** delivered by 6 trainers to 240 credit fraud analysts and recovery specialists annually.

Impact Execute training initiatives to meet corporate expectations as follows.

Staffing Goal My training improves staff performance and helps reduce a 50% turnover rate among fraud specialists who are overwhelmed from job expectations (each handles 160 calls/day yet earns only $8-10/hr).

Technical Goal The training I deliver covers 3 computer applications used to identify fraud, verify identity, release blocked accounts and properly escalate problems.

Corporate Goal Help CitiBank recover 66% of all fraud or $200MM in revenues. Each analyst therefore solves $1,2500,000 in fraud a year.

Action 1......Research Held ***Focus Groups*** with new hires and senior fraud analysts to determine training gaps. Divided existing training manual into five modules. Began fraud analyst shadowing to master their operational processes.

Action 2......Design Created a new Info-Mapping Template to navigate the system and wrote a Content-Decision Process with Decisioning Tables on Verification.

Action 3......Implement Ensured training complied with Legal, National Quality Assurance and Business approval standards. Conducted Train the Trainer sessions.

Action 4......Evaluation Analyzed fraud analyst score-cards to determine effectiveness. Conducted 60-day retention evaluations to validate training effectiveness.

Result Greatly reduced fraud specialist turn-over rate.

2000-10/02
Mandate

Training Developer & Facilitator **JOB CORPS CENTER FOR N.Y.C.**

Designed, developed and implemented the Job Corps' first fully implemented Personal Growth Program. My program creates the personal identity component that is critical to building a foundation to complement the professional identity of the trainee.

Challenge Audience demographics are 100% non college educated, 90% without a high school degree, over 40% indicate substance abuse and nearly 50% express open hostility to authority.

Tactics Developed 6 ***Career Preparation Program*** seminars (the first completely developed level-2 program for the Job Corps in the US (out of 250 sites)). Assess trainee needs with pre-tests to identify who should participate. Conduct daily training programs that stimulate trainees' personal growth. Conduct post-tests to determine if my objectives were met.

Seminars Developed

- Anger Management
- Conflict Resolution
- Diversity
- Sexuality
- Parenting
- Substance Abuse

Impact My approach stimulated trainees by treating them as subjects not objects using professional courtesy. I taught them to understand their human dignity, potential to society and that their special attributes make them uniquely empowered to contribute in the work-force.

Actions Developed qualitative evaluation to assess trainee progress and increase retention rates. Conducted material research and analysis to create curriculum lesson plans.

Results Delivered 800+ hours of training- 100 classes at 8 hours per class attended by 1,000 trainees.

EDUCATION

GRADUATE M. Ed. **Instructional Leadership,** University of Massachusetts 7/02
UNDERGRAD B.A. **Psychology,** University of Massachusetts Amherst 5/99
CERTIFIED New York Bilingual Teacher

CHAPTER 26

CORPORATE REAL ESTATE CAREER

The Corporate Real Estate Category Has

1 Client Example

3 Job Titles

9 Years of Work History

NAME	JOB TITLES COVERED
1.FREDERICK KIRKPATRICK	................................V.P. Capitol Markets
	....Vice President
	...................................Property Manager

FREDERICK KIRKPATRICK

636 Eisington Ln., Richmond, VA 23219 804-744-7821

STRENGTHS

- Direct Marketing
- Financial Analysis
- Client Consulting
- Underwriting
- Due Diligence
- Asset Management
- Marketing/Sales
- Multi-Market Exposure
- Loan/Lease Origination
- Real Estate Sales & Acquisition
- Relationship Management
- Information Systems PRO-JECT/Excel

SUMMARY

Professional For 10+ years I've negotiated agreements for commercial properties or executed national marketing programs and RFP processes to qualify investors able to buy high value investment property. Expertise includes researching economic indices, real estate indices, real estate studies, and development trends as they relate to the property markets.

Personal Skilled at managing client relations, appraising sophisticated investments to determine risk-adjusted returns on assets and executing the actions to make deals happen.

EXPERIENCE

1996 - Present **Vice President - Capital Markets** **JOHN B. LEVY CO.** • *Real Estate Investment Banking*

Overview Since '96, I've generated $2.3M in fees from debt and equity placement, direct investment, and property sales of investment-grade institutional real estate (capital structures to $15M and individual assets to $30M).

ACTIONS

Reporting Report to investment firms, pension funds, insurance companies, banks, and institutional advisors. Summarize market feasibility studies, income and expense projections.

Originating Solicit commercial real estate owners to arrange first mortgage financing.

Negotiating Negotiate applications, commitments, contracts and perform contract administration.

Budgeting Qualify proformas to attain profit projections (ROI, P&L and cash flow).

Due Diligence Use Argus and Project to analyze capitalization and discounted cash flow and determine net present value.

SUCCESS ①

Sold a $29M building that was 75% vacant at sale - one of the 10 largest sales in Chicago, '98

Nominated as Deal of the Year out of 200 Levy deals.

Challenge A global capital market meltdown in 1998 pushed equity providers out of the market and threatened the deal. To close I, 1. Qualified the best buyer with a stable equity finance partner out of 7 pre-qualified bidders 2. Negotiated $1M per week nonrefundable earnest deposit thus locking in commitment

Result Winning bid exceeded client goals by $5M. Deal earned $350K for Levy.

Result My capital gains tax deferral strategy saved the client $10M, accomplished by acquiring 4 California and Virginia properties worth $30M, which earned Levy another $400K.

SUCCESS ②

Created First ever use of mass marketing at Levy used to sell a $25M mortgage note.

Challenge Levy never mass-marketed a first mortgage security, I took two steps to succeed.

1. Identified 2,500 potential buyers from a key trade publication
2. Wrote solicitation letter, created preliminary due diligence package and set bid guidelines

Result Winner exceeded expectations by $4M and closed in two weeks.

1996 - 1997 **Vice President** **RS CONSTRUCTION CO.**

Overview Restructured a small business that was $50K in the red by implementing a business plan to reorganize the company's operating systems, staffing, sales and marketing efforts. *Results* — Increased sales 50% in first year, tripled sales to $3M overall and increased per contract value by 300%.

SUCCESS ③

Created an automated project management system that helped RS win their first $1M+ contracts

Challenge Differentiating RS from the competition to grow build-out business of brand name retail accounts like GAP, Pottery Barn and Sunglass Hut.

Result Grew retail business from 5% to 30%. Pottery Barn and Gap became the largest 2 accounts in RSC's 20-year history, both 10X larger than any previous project.

SUCCESS ④

Transitioned Company to a General Contractor and tripled project management consulting fees

Challenge In order to capitalize on existing staff expertise, I created a set of consulting services.

Result Grew project management work by 500%.

1986 - 1995 **JONES LANG LASALLE**
Vice President 1988 - 1995
Property Manager 1986 - 1988

Overview Selected by the CEO as the redevelopment specialist for difficult internal and third party management projects. Delivered products and services in New York, Houston, LA, San Francisco, Tampa, and DC offices. Managed several million square feet of industrial real estate in New York, Virginia and Tennessee. Managed building operations, budgets, monthly reporting to ownership, AR/AP, vendors, and building engineers. Financial advisor to owner in redeveloping Michael Jordan's restaurant. Managed construction budgets, construction draws, client reporting and arranged for financing.

SUCCESS ① *Corporate saves* 1) Protected an exclusive relationship from terminating (our largest client)
2) Worked out a retention deal that netted $500K in management fees and another $500K from future deals with this client.

Strategy In '91, I inherited 2 properties where each anchor tenant was bankrupt and had a 50% occupancy in a down market. One property had a tax lien of $600K and a $5M loan in default the other property anchor was a shared office building with 60 sub-leases which had to be protected.

Results Achieved 90% occupancy in both buildings thus protecting the relation with our key client who is worth $300K-$500K in fee income a year. Stabilized the asset, renegotiated the debt, paid back taxes and won future business from client.

SUCCESS ② **Executed the first direct marketing campaign to sell a $7M industrial property**
Personally replaced CN Commercial after the exclusive ran out. Prepared investment sale package sent to 1,000 prospective buyers and tailored an automated contact management system for the first time that is now the corporate database platform.

Results Sold 2 properties in '94 during a "real estate depression" which saved $200K in broker fees.

EDUCATION BA Finance, Cornell University 1986

CHAPTER 27
INTERNATIONAL BUSINESS & FOREIGN CAREERS

The Int'l Business & Foreign Category Has

3 Client Examples

16 Job Titles

40 Years of Work History

NAME	JOB TITLES COVERED
1. MARISSA VON DER	.Manager /Liason Intl. Used Car Divsion
	..................Intern Sales & Export/Import
	................................Intern Direct Export
	................................Marketing Assistant
	................................Marketing Research
2. CHRISTINE CHEN	....Assistant GM
	..................................Executive Assistant
	..................................Marketing Assistant
	....Sales Manager
3. KIMBERLY FISHER*	..................................Business Strategist
	.....................Principal Consultant/Owner
	..........................Director of Marketplace
	........................Senior Account Executive
	.........Director of Business Development
	.................................Director of Finance
	.....................................Manager Finance

* Find the "before resume" in chapter 35

Marissa Von Der

Gerber 37, 61592

Date of Birth	22.10.1974
Place of Birth	Maastricht Netherlands
Citizenship	Dutch

EDUCATION

1993-1997 — **B.S., Business Management,** Paris, France
Thesis: Daewoo and their mission statement

1995-1996 — **School of Business, International Management,** Brussels, Belgium

1998-1999 — **Université des Sciences Humaines (IIEF),** French Language, Strasbourg, France

1999-2000 — **Université Paris Dauphine, Paris, France,** Faculté des Sciences Economiques et de Gestion
DESS **Post Graduate International Management Program - Cross Cultural Management**
Thesis: Influence of Domestic Production on the Purchasing Decision

LANGUAGES
- Dutch & German - Native
- English - Fluent
- French - Excellent

STRENGTHS
- Analytical
- Maintain High Expectations
- Leadership
- Objective oriented
- Team player
- Good organizer
- Culturally Adaptive
- Independent Worker
- Problem solver

EXPERIENCE

5/00-present — **BMW AG,** ***Manager/Liaison - International Used Car Division,*** Munich, Germany

Overview — One of only 5 staff in this division, who as a team support 23 **Market Profit Centers** (**MPC**) worldwide and 7 General Importers. We create and implement products, marketing strategies and corporate programs to help BMW compete aggressively and elevate their brand image.

My focus — Oversee the BMW ***Used Car Warranty Program*** and write the "***European Perspective***", a senior management report on Used Car sales statistics. I also support the Netherlands and Belgium **Market Profit Centers** as well as "the rest of the world-markets" namely, US, Australia, Japan and South-Africa as a project manager in pursuit of business goals.

The following projects outline specific areas of support and the value of my contribution.

Project — European Dealer Professionalization - Used Car Sales

Focus — This project represents the first full-force effort to raise our image in the resell car market.

Value — Created tools to help **Market Profit Centers** professionalize their used car selling tactics. This enhances BMW's identity and supports our premium brand image (for perspective, US and Germany generate $5.35 billion annually in used car sales).

Project — Growing Sales & Profit for Used Cars (retail & wholesale markets for Netherlands and Belgium)

Focus — Created a retail marketing plan for senior executives to determine profit potential in the used car field. Addressed market conditions, tracked strategies to gage the residual value of cars and audited the validity of reported buy-back residuals.

Value — The Strategic Plan presented to the Dutch Management Board, when fully implemented, is projected to earn $20 million in retail revenues and reduce operating expenses by over $1 million (as of 4Q02 $650,000 has been realized in optimization efficiencies).

Project — International Sales Report for Senior Management

Focus — Enhanced a report on used car sales that hadn't accounted for market or wholesale data from European franchises or financial data and performance indicators at corporate retail branches.

Value — Created the "***European Perspective***", a management summary with 3 parts: market overview, retail and wholesale sales results on 39 topics (many categories are new). The report separately reports on BMW's owned branches and franchised dealers. I benchmark all statistics for the MPCs to help them compare quarterly results and monitor residual values.

BMW Experience Cont'd ...

Project

Product Management: BMW European Warranty

Focus — Quantitative and qualitative development of a strategically important marketing tool. Analyzed annual warranty sales figures. Conducted market research on competitive programs with Mercedes Benz & Audi. Evaluated new EU laws/legislation on warranty standards. Prepared and led negotiations with insurance companies to expand warranty coverage.

Value — The Warranty is a significant marketing strategy since 33% of all used cars are bought with a warranty. This is also a critical factor for consumers when considering brand value during the purchasing decision.

Project

Market Support for IT and E-Commerce Strategies

Focus — Implemented and optimized the Used Car IT strategy

Value — Visited dealerships with the objective of finding out their general needs from headquarter's to support and define IT products that help with their business or operational jobs.

Focus — Implementing the Used Car E-Business strategy

Value — Currently working on an overall E-business strategy. From my side, I've worked with my MPCs to customize the Used Car strategy within the overall corporate strategy to the county's needs.

9/99-5/00 — **Sunrise Telecom** **Intern - Sales & Export/Import** Frankfurt, Germany

Overview — Supported two key initiatives; the Request for Quote (RFQ) business development role and the direct sales function. In support of RFQ's, I worked the Project Manager to create offer strategies that would ensure that we sold our $500,000 telecommunication switches internationally.

Focus — Helped close large bids - a complex process of quoting, specifying and order fulfillment.

Value — Upon winning a bid, I managed the process between order, fabrication and order fulfillment for subsidiaries in Germany, Austria, Switzerland and Belgium.

Intern - Direct Export. Managed the export chain for key customers in the Middle-East and Asia.

2/98-9/99 — **Flora 2000** **Marketing Assistant** Munich, Germany

Overview — Work with Flora's large client base to fulfill their orders for plants and flowers. On a typical day, I negotiated over 20 orders.

9/96- 2/97 — **Orion Marketing** **Marketing Research** Brussels, Belgium

Overview — Conducted multi-staged research for a broad range of industries and client types.

COMPUTER — MS Office: Word, Excel, Powerpoint, Lotus Notes, DCAG planning/reporting programs (GFG, Mapis).

References available on request.

CHRISTINE CHEN

633 Tahoe Ln, Los Angeles, CA 90212 • chen@hotmail.com • 310-323-5798

OBJECTIVE — Sales, marketing or international business development.

EDUCATION
2001 MBA Strategic Management/Marketing UCLA
1998 BS Management Engineering, Beijing University of Astronautics & Aeronautics

1999-2000 **Assistant G.M.** **China.com, Beijing Office (HQ in Los Angeles)**

Overview............ A network of online/offline marketplace resources to help buyers source vendors in Asia. VC partners included Goldman Sachs, Lehman Brothers, CitiGroup, SoftBank, IDG and Motorola. Clients included AIG, AON, Dunn & Bradstreet and First Union. Canon, Mitsubishi, and Stanley.

Focus International e-commerce site that helps buyers purchase from China safely and assists with Chinese export rules and regulations efficiently.

My role Find suppliers in the Beijing area who want to promote product to foreign buyers. Create sales plan and supervise sales team to achieve goals. Coordinate technology and marketing departments to meet deadlines.
Promote Software: Trade Pioneer, an online trading tool with the following:
1) Data base design 4) Product online show
2) Public sample room 5) International trading consultant services
3) Banner ads/domain names 6) Web hosting/design7) Online trading hall

Results Led sales team to close 150 of 400 opportunities over 6 months (closure rate of 40%) which netted $200K in first year income.

1997-1999 **Executive Assistant** **Arbed Damwand, Beijing Office**

Overview.......... A leading European steel company that operates sales, trading and distribution networks, as a subsidiary of Luxembourg based Arbed, a leading international steel maker.

Focus We contacted Chinese raw material suppliers and manufactures to supply material for Arbed's global business needs.

My role Took daily requests from Europe for products and put them out for bid to 150 Chinese manufactures and import/export companies, then negotiated product price, international contracts, delivery time, and shipping issues.

Products Metal and Non-Metal products, Ferro-Alloy, Ore, Silicon Metal, and Zinc

Results Helped elevate Beijing office to #1 trading revenue rank relative to 3 other global branches.

1995 -1997 **Marketing Assistant/CSR** **Fleishman Hillard, Beijing Office**

Overview............ A multinational conglomerate with marketing, distribution and services in Healthcare, Technology, Logistics and Consumer Goods markets.

Focus Drove sales, marketing promotions and worked with distributors to launch Hillard's 'Fasimile' infant milk powder, to 400 Beijing retailers.

My Role Product manager during consumer product launch into the Beijing market.

Results Market share grew to 5%, revenues from $6000 to $30,000 month and brand recognition from #6 to #2 among foreign competitors.

1990-1995 **Sales Manager** **Weifang Food & Beverage, Co., Beijing Office**

Overview........... A joint venture company between China and Japan to sell a mineral water and other soft drinks.

Focus Rollout the new Japanese product into the Beijing market.

My Role After translating the advertisements from English to Chinese, I was promoted into a sales role and began selling the product to Beijing Hotels.

Results Hotel revenues grew 1000%. I signed-up Beijing's best hotel.

KIMBERLY FISHER

777 Dixie Way #3B, Toronto, ON, L6T 5P6, 905.727.5616; kim@AOL.COM

Industry Knowledge	(10 years) Retail	(9 years)	Distribution
	(2 years) Government Procurement	(2 years)	Telecommunication
	(7 year) e-Commerce	(11 years)	Semiconductor Industry

4/00 - present **NORTEL** ***Business Strategist*** - Nortel Global Services (NGS), Toronto, ON

Overview Hired to uncover consulting opportunities from relationships I initiated in Toronto which resulted in closing engagements with academic institutions, utility companies, health care organizations and non-profits.

Challenge Educating 45 traditional telecom sales reps from 5 branches on the complexities of prospecting for opportunities in the arena of consulting engagements.

Result Closed the most business in the South West region FY00, leading to relocating to Montreal in order to replicate the same success.

1996 - 6/99 **MORNINGSTAR** ***Principal Consultant/Owner*** Sydney, Australia

Overview As a specialist of Tradex's technological architecture, I contracted with organizations who needed a Business Consultant/Project Manager to ensure that implementations met their business needs.

Project First-ever implementation of Tradex as an e-Commerce marketplace between the Australian Federal Government and 1,500 Australian Chamber of Commerce members.

Challenge 1. Build an acceptable business model for chamber members who were unaware of e-Commerce advantages.
2. Give the federal government better tracking controls of purchases from their suppliers

Result Won ***"Best Business to Business e-Commerce Solution"***, Gartner Group's 1997 International Product of the Year award.

Project ***British Telecom*** – Retained by senior BT executives to conduct a feasibility study for the "Web-World" initiative, BT's first attempt to use an internet marketplace to build add-on revenues from their existing customer base.

Challenge Identifying market segments and distributors who offered the best profitability margins.

Result The proof of concept justified BT's continued investment in the e-Commerce trading arena.

1993 - 1996 **TRADEX** ***Director of the Tradex Marketplace*** - Europe
Sr. Account Executive - International Broker Sales

Overview One of the world's first extranets designed to eliminate time/price/availability problems inherent to international trade. Initially Tradex was used by 85 corporate customers as a market clearing center for the IT wholesale distribution business they conducted in 35 countries.

-Tradex experience continued on page 2-

As a Director of the Tradex Marketplace: Promoted Tradex globally by planning and managing our exhibit efforts at international trade shows i.e. CeBit, Comdex, and MacWorld.

Challenge Growing the Trading Exchange - recruited new buyers and sellers to grow our revenues from associated commissions by their use of the Tradex Exchage.

Result Tradex's global market place grew to 800 customers and 200 vendors selling 5,000 IT products. Eventually, Tradex Marketplace became a stand alone application costing $100,000 that I sold to Fortune 1000 corporations to enable them to create trading exchanges.
• The long-term effect led to Tradex being acquired by Ariba in 1999 for $1.9 billion •

Overview ***As Sr. AE Int'l Sales***: acted as an international sales broker of US technology products to European and Asian clients (4-German, 3-Swiss, 3-Austrian and 1 each for Japan, France, Italy and Holland).

Challenge Managing an International Network of Clients and Vendors - closed 50-100 deals a month worth $1MM-$10MM in business volume by purchasing product through 400+ manufacturers, VARs and distributors.

Result Sales increased 60%.

1982 - 1993 **SOLID STATE TECHNOLOGY,** Vienna, Austria

Director Business Development & Purchasing	1990 - 1993
Director - Business Development	1985 - 1990
Director - Finance	1984 - 1985
Manager - Finance	1982 - 1984

Overview Three years as financial manager of the second largest distributor of semiconductor components in Austria led to handling the role of Manager of Business Development tasked with opening distribution opportunities to exploit exclusive contracts with Apple Computers and 8 other hardware OEMs.

Challenge Leading change in the organization - Transitioned the company from selling commodity priced electronic components priced $0.10-$15 each into a high margin distributor of computer systems costing $2,000-$4,000.

Challenge Developing New Markets - Leveraged exclusive distribution contracts to market Apple Computers, Sony monitors, UMAX scanners, Asante ethernet cards, Roland digital plotters and Micronet hard drives.

Actions Identified new markets for while also creating need from scratch by replacing outdated technology.
New markets penetrated
- Textile Manufacturing
- Industrial Graphics
- Masonry

Result Grew revenues 300% ($10M to $30M) in 5 years and distribution expanded into Asia, US and Europe.

LANGUAGE Fluent in German and English.

EDUCATION Business Degree (MBA equivalent), Austrian Business School, Vienna, Austria 1985

• REFERENCES AVAILABLE ON REQUEST •

CHAPTER 28

CAREER TRANSITIONS

The Career Transitions Category Has

3 Client Examples

13 Job Titles

35 Years of Work History

NAME	JOB TITLES COVERED
1. SAMUEL WHITFORD	...............Senior Equity Research Analyst
	...............Senior Member Technical Staff
	............................Senior Product Planner
	........................Senior Electrical Engineer
	..........................Electrical Engineer I &II
2. JACK HUEY*	.........................Vice President/Controller
	....Vice President
	...........................Assistant Vice President
	........................Commercial Loan Officer
3. DOUGLAS ATKINSON	....Legal Assistant
	....Sales Manager
	..........................Assistant Store Manager
	....Sales Associate

* Find the “before resume” in chapter 35

SAMUEL WHITFORD

178 Meadow Ln., Cincinnati, OH 45240 • 513-704-1998 • swhit@hotmail.com

OBJECTIVE To continue a successful career as a research associate or analyst at a top-tier financial firm.

EXPERIENCE

6/03 - 2/04 **SCHAFFERS INVESTMENT RESEARCH - *Sr. Equity Research Analyst*** **CINCINNATI, OH**

Covered 80 companies, sectors included:
- Technology (Electronics & Semiconductors)
- Transportation (Passenger Air/Ground Freight)
- Business Services

Overview One of four Sr. Analysts in an equity research department created 1Q03. **Our goal:** capture 25% of $433 million the SEC ordered Wall Street investment banks to spend on independent research (part of a record $1.4 billion fine and mandate that there be strict separation of research analysis from investment banking divisions).

Target Capture Morgan Stanley as the precedent investment bank client for Schaffers before pursuing others. Our team wrote analyst reports on the universe of equities Morgan Stanley historically covered.

Actions

Analyzed public companies by	• Industry economics • Strategic position • EBITDA • Revenue/Earnings growth • Management team • Discounted cash flow valuation
Determined Buy/Sell/Hold	Used Schaffer's proprietary business valuation and DCF models, competitive factors, world events and insider trading patterns.
Wrote equity research reports	Summarized fundamentals, industry outlooks, key business drivers, future risks and stock price valuation (averaged 1-2 new reports written daily and reviewed four from Jr. Analysts).
Team Management	Mentored, reviewed and led two Jr. Analysts in India.

Results

Production • Rated #1 on productivity based on carrying a -0- report backlog.
Innovation • Created the report methodology used as Schaffer's equity research model.
Quality • Achieved a superior grade by the senior editing staff on 99.5% of reports written.

2/01- 10/02 **TELLABS, INC. - *Senior Member of Technical Staff*** **BOLINGBROOK, IL**

Overview Led a team of 6 engineers to create a new optical switch interface for add/drop capabilities that large telecos bought, ie. Verizon and Sprint, to compete in metro markets throughout the US.

Actions Designed circuits — Used FPGAs and wrote VHDL code for CPLDs. Managed hardware design cycle Schematics, PCB layout, parts procurement, simulations, prototype, validation testing, and product release.

Results

Budget My team completed the design two months ahead of schedule.
Costing Redesigned product with new technology to help customers save 50% on capital expenditures.
Corporate Helped Tellabs capture a growing $2 billion/year market.

5/95- 2/01 **VERIZON, INC.** **NEW YORK, NY**
- ***Senior Product Planner*** 2000-2001
- ***Senior Electrical Engineer*** 1998-2000
- ***Electrical Engineer I & II*** 1995-1998

Overview Developed wireless products from concept to launch and mentored junior engineers.

Actions Managed development time, costing, and staffing needs as well as wrote code for a 16 bit CPU with a 32 bit Link Layer Controller. Spearheaded a joint design-effort between several engineering groups and a technical contractor.

Results

Launch Developed 2-way radio base station for Europe, Asia, Americas (generates $7MM /yr.)

EDUCATION

Graduate 6/03 **WHARTON UNIVERSITY OF PENNSYLVANIA** **MBA PROGRAM**
MBA, concentration in: Finance, Strategy & Entrepreneurship

Project • Wharton Consulting Team: helped write a business plan for ESO (Executive Services Onsite) used by the CEO of the company to raise money in a second round of financing.

UnderGrad 12/94 **UNIVERSITY OF PENNSYLVANIA**, BS., Electrical Engineering with Honors

JACK R. HUEY

632 Canterbury Way, Gainsville, FL 32611 352-619-7521

OBJECTIVE

To continue a successful career as a senior financial officer in a position that capitalizes on my analytical, research, project development and negotiation skills.

STRENGTHS

- Investment/Financial Analysis
- Market Studies
- Staff Management
- Research & Planning
- Portfolio Analysis
- Industry Research
- Due Diligence
- Risk Analysis
- Client Consulting
- General Ledger (GL)
- Change Management
- Budgets/Forecasting

SUMMARY

Expert in corporate research, negotiations, client relations and valuation of complex loan considerations. Consulting support to institutional owners of investment-grade projects includes sophisticated appraisal techniques to identify calculated risk opportunities and project ROI profit potential. Emphasis is on consistent preparation and execution of executive responsibilities as well as maintaining accountability at all levels.

EXPERIENCE

4/96 - Present **HUEY ENTERTAINMENT CO.** **VICE PRESIDENT/CONTROLLER**

Overview

Manage a family owned business with sales of $4,000,000 and 20-45 employees. Book festivals, negotiate contracts, raise funds for nonprofit organizations and prepare annual P/L projections. Schedule 65 events between Georgia, Illinois and Florida, manage equipment transport logistics, as well as setup/maintenance.

Results

- Saved $100,000+ by restructuring 3 existing contracts.
- Negotiated 3-year contracts to add 6 new events in past year worth approximately $375,000.
- Secured bank financing to buy $1,180,000 in new equipment.

12/95 - 4/95 **FIFTH THIRD BANK** **VICE PRESIDENT-** ***Commercial Lending***

Overview

Structured large value deals across a broad base of business that led to a $20 million portfolio consisting of 40 commercial customers in construction, manufacturing and service sectors. Composed project narratives, letters of understanding and market feasibility studies that included industry analysis, income projections and associated expenses.

Developed macro/micro-economic evaluations that applied direct capitalization and discounted cash flow analysis to determine net present values. Coordinated strategic alliances merging the expertise of architectural, construction and engineering companies.

Results

- Generated $3,500,000 in new depository/lending relationships via business development efforts.

2/90- 12/95 **MERCANTILE BANK**

VICE PRESIDENT- ***Commercial Lending*** [4/95-12/95]
ASST. VICE PRESIDENT-***Commercial Lending*** [3/93-4/95]
COMMERCIAL LOAN OFFICER [2/90-3/93]

Overview

Managed $30 million commercial loan portfolio. Met with customers to evaluate current loan services and discuss their specific business operational needs. Prepared and presented credit/loan presentations to loan committee.

Results

- By developing client confidence, I was able to network existing business to generate new depository/lending relationships worth $4,000,000 annually.

Deals

- Real Estate Development: 29 single family homes — $2,350,000 LOC
- Manufacturer of Residential Products — $2,000,000 LOC & equipment loan
- Consumer Product Manufacturer — $1,200,000 LOC & $300k equipment loan
- Industrial Manufacturer: Custom Machinery — $350,000 start-up loan
- Contractor: Sewer/Utility Projects — 750,000 LOC & $800,000 personal loan

EDUCATION

MBA, Management/Entrepreneurship *with Honors* (3.85/4.0) Univ of Florida, Gainsville, FL 5/96
B.A., Finance/Economics Dean's List (4.3/5.0), Univ. Central Florida, Orlando, FL 5/89

DOUGLAS ATKINSON

974 W. Camino St., Houston, TX 77002 • 713-232-5619 douga@yahoo.com

OBJECTIVE To pursue a law career that combines tactical, management and strategic planning skills.

SUMMARY Legal expertise encompasses administration and project management to achieve the firm's objectives. The combination of an MBA, law degree, and management skills demonstrates my ability to contribute immediately to any type of corporate structure.

STRENGTHS

- Training
- Research
- Client Relations
- Negotiations
- Time Management
- Staff Management
- Tenacity
- Writing

1/01 - present **MAYER, BROWN, POWER &MAW LLP.**, Houston, TX
• *Legal Assistant*

Overview............... A high pressure, tight-deadline, worker's compensation and personal injury law practice. Much work touches on investigating claims to determine case merit, writing motions (summary judgment and routine), presenting to the Industrial Commission, and interviewing as well as corresponding with clients. Researched Lexis/Nexus and Westlaw to provide litigation support for 50 cases.

Co-Author Wrote the chapter "Worker's Compensation" for the book "Causes of Action", CACLE (California Institute for Continuing Legal Education), 2003

7/94 - 1/00 **MUSICIANS FRIEND.**, Medford, OR
• *Sales Manager* • *Assistant Store Manager* • *Sales Associate*

Overview............... Managed 25-40 staff and a business operation that grew from $6.9 million to $10 million within a year.

Corporate Challenge Given the mandate to increase revenues 30% YTD.

Actions

Selling — Developed creative selling techniques and trained the sales force on how to execute the strategies to increase revenues.

Merchandising — Tracked consumer buying behavior to determine optimal product selection.

P & L — Analyzed sales results of entire product line and individual SKUs to refine merchandise selection and to choose '*best seller*' potential.

Results Of 30 US properties, I led one of only four that met the YTD revenue goal while also increasing profit by 14%.

Duties

- Represented company at conventions
- Managed payroll
- Trained new employees
- Hired and trained sales force
- Tracked competitor's strategies and products
- Built quality customer relations
- Helped develop advertising & marketing strategies
- Tracked revenue and profit results to meet budgets

Created

Program ***Started A Major Accounts Program*** - captured nearly 75% market share in a key sector, the religious marketplace of 400 area churches.
Benefit Captured 5 deals over $100,000 (the largest contracts for this 25 year old property)
Impact Before the program we sold to 150 churches which generated $25,000/month, a year later we had 300 clients generating $60,000/month.

Created

Program ***New Pay Structure*** - Changed the compensation plan for sales staff from percentage of gross profit to percentage of gross sales.
Benefit Increased items sold per ticket from 2.3 to 6+
Increased profitability by 10%
Impact This program was so successful it was rolled-out nationally to 300 stores.

EDUCATION

2001	J.D.	***University Oregon Law School***	Eugene, OR
1998	M.B.A., Management	***University Oregon Law School***	Eugene, OR
1994	B.A. - Political Science	***Southern Oregon University***	Ashland, OR

LICENSURE Member of Texas Bar, sworn on 5/9/02

CHAPTER 29

E-COMMERCE CAREERS

The eCommerce Category Has

4 Client Examples

16 Job Titles

50 Years of Work History

NAME	JOB TITLES COVERED
1. KAREN BLATTY	......................................Account Director
	..............................Career Services Intern
	..................Commencement Coordinator
	..........................Administrative Assistant
	......................Assistant Program Director
2. CAROL LASHINSKY*	..........................E-Commerce Consultant
	.............Community Service Coordinator
	...................................Team Lead & CSR
3. ADAM FONG	....................Team Lead/System Engineer
	....................Cumputer & Network Intern
	......................Production Control Analyst
	....Machinist
4. ANGELA SHAH	Marketing Manager Interactive Network
	.....................Strategic Marketing Analyst
	.....................Financial System Specialist
	....Senior Auditor

* Find the "before resume" in chapter 35

KAREN BLATTY
k_blat@yahoo.com

320 Ingram St., Chicago, IL 60614
847-505-3793 • Cell 847-225-5845

SUMMARY

Highly motivated, goal-oriented professional who contributes in a team environment to impact revenues and support the launch of new products and services. Perform duties with high-energy and at a high standard of integrity. Experienced at cultivating relationships with key accounts, over achieving corporate objectives and helping customers understand our value propositions at the executive level.

STRENGTHS

- Communication
- Event Management
- Customer Service
- Detail Oriented
- Time management
- Public Presentations
- Teamwork
- Integrity

EXPERIENCE

8/00- 12/03 **CAREERBUILDER.COM** — Atlanta & Chicago
Account Director

Overview Hired by the #1 ranked job site in the US - as noted by the Student Monitor. Promote and sell a partnership model where we delivered co-branded career management and recruiting solutions to colleges, graduate schools, universities and alumni organizations.

Action • Promoted online career center management solutions (i.e., tracking on-campus interviews, job postings, internship programs) and convinced academic institutions to adopt our technology solutions.

Action • Managed 150 accounts in 5 states including 3 of the largest academic consortiums:
1. The MBA Consortium of 20 Tier-1 programs (i.e. Notre Dame, Rice and Vanderbilt).
2. The Hire Big 10 Plus (i.e. Penn State, Univ. of Chicago and The Ohio State Univ.).
3. The Iowa Private College Consortium of 21 institutions.

Action • Scheduled and conducted 10-12 monthly presentations and demos by phone and in person at school sites (over 100+ to date).

Challenge • Building and sustaining client relationships by training and servicing clients on software use.

Challenge • Winning budget approval from administrative boards and by presenting Careerbuilder.com software at regional conferences. The key was demonstrating the functional ease of our new technology, as well as efficacy, relative to improving upon their legacy systems.

Challenge • Creating marketing and training materials for the account management team and assisting them with projects from start-up to final rollout.

Impact • I ensure 150 schools with 500,000 students can flawlessly manage 40,000 annual interviews by 5,000 on-campus corporations needing to recruit new hires.

Results
- Acquired 44 new institutional clients.
- Generated the highest revenues in the company from virtual career e-fairs.
- Captured the single largest institutional account in the company, ITT Educational Systems Inc., a group of 70 schools across the US.
- Nurtured University of Wisconsin to the single largest account with total student enrollment.

8/99 – 4/00 **UNIVERSITY OF WISCONSIN**, The Career Center, Madison, WI
Career Services Intern

Overview Handled data management for the Career Center's on-line recruiting system (FORUM). Analyzed and responded to student inquiries on use of FORUM. Counseled and advised students on job search strategies, resume writing, and internships. Organized and presented career exploration programs to students. Hired and supervised 7 students for the Recruiting Assistance Program.

10/95-4/00 **UNIVERSITY OF WISCONSIN WHITEWATER**, Student Services Office, Whitewater, WI

Commencement Coordinator 7/98 – 4/00
Administrative Assistant 10/95 – 7/98
Assistant Program Director (Reading Assistance Program) 11/97 – 6/98

Overview

As Commencement Coordinator, I organized, troubleshot, managed and recommended logistical changes to enhance event flow.

As Admin Asst., managed daily office operations, supervised 9 work study students. Solicited and edited submissions then produced campus wide biweekly newsletter. Revised the Student Handbook.

As Asst. Program Dir., supervised 15 college students. Trained students on how to interact and read to young children prior to participating in the program. Maintained all records of students' visits to site.

EDUCATION

Graduate	4/00	MA, Higher Education Administration, University of Wisconsin	Madison, WI
Undergraduate	6/93	BA, Elementary Education, University of Wisconsin, Whitewater	Whitewater, WI

AFFILIATIONS

- Midwest Association of Colleges and Employers
- Midwest Cooperative Education and Internship Association
- Midwest Association of Student Employer Administrators

COMPUTER SKILLS PowerPoint, Excel, Word, Goldmine, QuarkXpress, Anzio/Telnet

References available on request.

CAROL LASHINSKY —— **115 Piper Lane, Seattle, WA 98112 • 206. 889.8432 (cell) • clash@yahoo.com**

EXPERIENCE

2/02 – Present **E-Commerce Consultant** **SEATTLE BMW**
[The largest luxury car dealership in Seattle]

Overview ...... Negotiate sales and finance contracts for luxury car buyers through the internet. Provide editorial assistance on a monthly e-newsletter to attract a wider buying audience. Contact prospective customers via email, assess needs, arrange appointments, present offerings, negotiate price, secure financing and finalize sales.

PROJECT **CREATE AN E-COMMERCE DEPARTMENT** – Hired 2 months after Seattle BMW started the e-Department. My role was to work with the e-Commerce Manager and the Sales Operation Manager to create the ***first-ever*** selling methodology via the internet.

ACTIONS —
Built a Process Map for referrals from inception, initial contact, follow-up and final close. Designed dozens of response templates with customized features to create a 'warm-touch' appeal to the prospective customers.

RESULTS Referrals grew by 15 new leads a day which boosted e-Commerce sales 266% since 4/02 (from 30 to 80 cars a month, representing an additional $2,000,000 a month in Internet driven sales).

PROJECT **ENHANCE USE OF THE INTERNET AS A SALES TOOL** – Analyzed a half-dozen competitors each month to determine Seattle BMW's strengths and weaknesses relative to their prices and product offerings.

ACTIONS —
Highlighted Seattle BMW's exceptional service offering (i.e., pickup/delivery, free loaner cars), and increased our speed of delivering pricing information and customized contact via email.

RESULTS My recommendations, implemented by management, better captured client interest, won dealer visits, and improved market share/sales performance especially targeting internet shoppers, young buyers and value conscious consumers.

My Impact Enhancements to Seattle BMW's internet selling strategy, in combination with the in-house sales force, now captures $2,000,000 in additional revenues each month.

11/02- 2/03 **Temporary Assignments** **PC & ASSOCIATES**

Overview ...... In the span of 3 months, I was assigned to 7 corporations and assisted top management of Seattle-area companies and nonprofit associations by preparing project documentation and customer correspondence.

Smr. '02 **Community Service Coordinator** **LERNER SUMMER CAMP**

Overview ...... Piloted a teen-initiative that issued press releases for local and regional newspapers to promote the activities achieved by camp participants. Coordinated community service schedules, weekly trips and nightly activities.

1997-2000 **Team Lead & Customer Service Agent** **FERRIS & WILLS COMPANY**

Overview ...... Lead CSR for a team of 6 representatives. Supported Fortune 500 companies in the financial services market sector. Handled mission critical recovery operations and repairs. All trouble issues were escalated to my desk.

TECHNICAL MS Work, Excel, Access, PowerPoint, Illustrator and Photoshop

EDUCATION 5/02 B.S., Business Administration — Washington State University
Concentration: Marketing — Specialization: Data Management

Internship Sp. 02 *Jerrod Walters & Associates*
Marketing/PR/graphic design team creating a campaign to promote Washington State University. Market analysis, campaign strategy, budget projections and media plans.

Internship Smr. '01 *Armor Communications* **"The Truth"** Anti-Smoking Campaign.
Conducted focus groups, researched tobacco industry trends to decrease teen tobacco uses.

School Job '99-'00 *Washington State Alumni Relations*
Helped plan, budget and raise funds (over $5,000) for Alumni programs and events.

ADAM FONG

4710 W. Montrose Ave #3, Chicago, IL, 60657 • 817-822-7621

OBJECTIVE A network or technology role as a team lead or member using my technical and management experience.

TECHNOLOGY
- Win 9X, NT 4.0, 2000
- TCP/IP and related protocols
- Ethernet LAN
- MS Office 97/ 2000
- MS Exchange 5.5
- Internet Information Server
- Outlook Web Access

EXPERIENCE

2000- 2002 **E SAVY MARKETING Team Lead / System Engineer Network Operations Center (NOC)**

Overview E Savy Marketing™ is the 3rd largest US ORM (online relationship marketing) company. Their opt-in marketing strategy supports the largest companies in America wanting to use email marketing to acquire and retain customers.

Clients include Fortune 500 **• AON • HP-Compaq • American Express • Dell • AT&T • W.W. Grainger • Nine West • 3Com**

Role 1 Used Compaq's Insight to monitor and manage 130+ servers in an enterprise production network used by 180 staff in 3 national sites.

Role 2 Maintain networks to meet our corporate contract agreements with over 250 customers.

Role 3 Support sales and marketing efforts to grow E Savy's ability to increase volume, grow revenues and meet customer expectations on-time.

Role 4 Help E Savy leverage the email channel so that they could charge a premium price on our sendouts. Managed the customer lifecycle and improve performance efforts on a very tight delivery schedule.

Role 5 Personally provided technical support to network clients on a 24/7 basis (100% on call).

Role 6 Led a 4-person NOC Team to upgrade, rebuild and customize servers that we tailored for a team of 18 software developers (i.e. making non-Microsoft programs compatible with MS Exchange and ensuring dozens of Java script and HTML custom coded programs supported E Savy's emails).

Actions

Scheduled Team workload on rotating shifts.
Assisted Administration & Developers to build new databases.
Interviewed Prospective candidates as well as trained, managed, and directed new team members.
Created ***1st-ever*** NOC tech manual with
- Proactive troubleshooting procedures
- Scheduled maintenance calendar
- Installation and configuration procedures
- Escalation procedures

Result Managed a network e-mail delivery system that produced 1.8+ million emails a day.
Result My upgrades improved actual delivery rate from 90% to 99.5% (thereby earning an additional $250K annually by actually delivering more mail).
Result 100% server uptime (increased from 65%, which was the first time in company history.
Result Built a new software development server farm completely from scrap systems that were earmarked for disposal by a sister company. The savings were over $70,000.

1999 - 2000 **PC COMPUTER, Computer & Network Intern / Contractor**

Overview Maintained stand-alone or networked equipment. Repaired and maintained computer equipment at several service locations. Installed and tested newly installed architecture.

1995- 1999 **DIRECT MAIL INFORMATION SERVICE, Production Control Analyst**

Overview Liaison to clients, sales force and production staff. Coordinated direct mail projects from concept to final product. Produced in-depth analyses and presentations to implement projects cost efficiently.

EDUCATION Allied Computer Training 1999 -2000
Northern Illinois University, Math and Computer Science

CERTIFICATION Microsoft Certified System Engineer (MCSE) + Internet (MCP + I) A + Certification

MILITARY U .S. Army HONORABLY DISCHARGED

ANGELA SHAH

163 Janice St., Atlanta, GA 30303 404-775-2212 Email: amshaw@aol.com

OBJECTIVE To continue a successful career in interactive online media sales and marketing.

SUMMARY Expertise in broadcasting, publishing and interactive business development. Skills focus on vendor relations and networking multifunctional teams to build media revenues. Project development expertise includes formulating strategic plans, building business cohesion and managing communication channels. An intuitive problem solver with effective personnel management skills who can meet new business challenges, bring products to market and incorporate joint venture synergy.

STRENGTHS

- Consumer Trending
- Statistical Analysis
- Ad Operations
- Industry Research
- Marketing/Advertising
- Business Development
- Relationship Management
- Product Testing & Promotions
- Corporate Strategic Planning

EXPERIENCE
1989 - present

TURNER BROADCASTING

Marketing Manager, **Turner Interactive Network**	11/96 - Present
Strategic Marketing Analyst	5/95 - 11/96
Financial Systems Specialist	1/93 - 5/95
Senior Auditor	4/89 - 12/92

Promoted to integrate Turner Company's initial response to a competitive threat and to protect advertising revenues (40% of top line income) from erosion by internet advertising. Capitalized on existing brand equity and audience share of traditional media (newspaper, tv, radio, cable) to build a daily media habit of online consumer traffic. ***-Focus-*** Manage 5 staff, a $2,000,000 budget and operational steps to implement systems and set brand strategies for Turner Interactive's 30 internet products (launched 1 site a month).

Actions

1. Created brand identity and delivered advertisers to the Turner Interactive Network
2. Built audience share for Turner's 30 internet online products
3. Built tie-ins (chat, fan clubs), contests, Microsites, Online Coupons and Push email
4. Created affinity sponsorship targeting news, sports, weather, banners, classified, community

Advertising ✓ Created: -Media Kits -Sales Research -Presentations -Proposals
Sales Support ✓ Operations: Manage ad traffic systems and ensure campaigns execute according to plan.
Promotion ✓ Developed co-promotion plans with AOL to promote product launches
P.R. ✓ Hired Hill & Knowlton to execute PR plans & leverage cross-promotional opportunities

Delivered 30 internet sites: Newspaper, TV, City, 4 Entertainment and 2 niche (Black Reader, Braves)

PROJECT **LAUNCHED TURNER.COM** 3/96

FOCUS Combined traditional marketing with new internet strategies to launch webzine. Key executive challenge was shifting journalist, editors, marketing and sales professionals (department of 500 employees) to compete in a multimedia environment.

RESULTS Achieved a Top-40 site ranking based on 10,000,000 monthly page requests and 20% of our existing advertisers began to integrate their traditional and internet advertising.

PROJECT **LAUNCHED DIGITAL CITY INC.** 6/96

FOCUS Managed a complex partnership between AOL as distributor and Turner as branded content provider. Created marketing plans, promotional materials and selected niche products.

RESULTS Grew a 3 city start-up to 32 markets. Negotiated autonomy agreement allowing Turner to manage 4 key markets while providing branded content to the other 28 cities. AOL pays for the salaries of 16 Turner on-line producers (**saving** Turner **$500,000/yr in salaries**)

PROJECT **LAUNCHED VIRTUAL COMMUNITIES** 9/96

FOCUS Created mass customizing processes to launch sites for 30 Atlanta suburbs. Story feeds are distributed and updated every 15 minutes with only 3 employees.

RESULTS Turner is the only media company that is geo-targeting consumers at the micro level.

...Turner Interactive Experience Cont'd...

Team Manager — MARTT team- Measurement, Analysis, Registration, Targeting and Transaction. Prioritize, administrate and communicate with Corporate Technology and all Turner Broadcasting business units.

Project Manager — The ***Consumer Directory***. Analyze the competition, communicate AOL, DCI and Switchboard strategies, identify and select tele-sales vendors. Analysis helped close Bell South anchor tenant.

Training Manager — ***Project Management Methodology****-PMM*. Train Individuals and departments (Technology, Editorial, and Sales & Marketing) to adopt PMM strategies.

Vendor/Partner Manager — Manage contracted services, ensure compliance to industry standards, distribute research and network with multiple entities including: _

Examples:

I/PRO	- Site Traffic Auditor Vendor
Netgravity	- Ad Server Vendor
Internet Ad Bureau	- Partnerships to set internet standards for advertising
Jupiter, Forrester	- Syndicated reporters of market trends and forecasts
Media Metrix	- Syndicated reports of monthly online rankings
Cox Interactive	- Sales Rep. Firm

Strategic Marketing Analyst 5/95 - 11/96

Summary Prepared consolidated strategic and operating plans; in-house consultant to operating departments during planning stages. Conducted marketing and financial analysis for development projects like Atlanta Journal-Constitution, New Home Search, GenX, Center Stage & LEAP.

Financial Systems Specialist 1/93 - 5/95

Summary Prepared monthly operating plans and financial statements for senior management. Established the first Turner-wide finance seminar. Managed cross-functional teams to implement G/L, A/P & F/A systems during heavy acquisition period.

Senior Auditor 4/89 - 12/92

Summary Planned, executed, and reported the results of financial and operational audits.

RECOGNITION 1996 Hispanic Achiever Award 1994 Employee Service Award

6/87 - 4/89 ***Auditor***, SANDERS, KRAMER & CO. Ltd.
Performed audit, tax and consulting engagements; recruited clients.

LANGUAGE Fluent in Spanish

EDUCATION Masters of Management, G.S.B., University of Chicago 1998

B.S. in Accountancy, Georgetown University 1987

CERTIFICATION Certified Public Accountant 1990

References available on request.

CHAPTER 30

SOCIAL SERVICE CAREERS

The Social Service Category Has

2 Client Examples

10 Job Titles

34 Years of Work History

NAME	JOB TITLES COVERED
1. TONY BROWN	..............................Social Service Worker
	....Care Taker
	................................Program Supervisor
	..........................Senior Probation Officer
	..............Community Corrections Officer
2. KATRINA FOX	................................Program Coordinator
	...........................Graduate Social Worker
	....Consultant
	....Teacher
	..................................Research Assistant

TONY BROWN

179 Young St., Baton Rouge, LA 70802 TB2@aol.com 318-654-3212

SUMMARY

I've developed a fundamental organizational skills and the ability to use diplomacy, maintain sensitivity to human rights and knowledge of local/state policies to meet mission goals and objectives. *Personal:* I build unified staff management programs by setting specific goal criteria, articulating targeted objectives and encouraging staff input and participation until our goals are reached.

STRENGTHS

- Verbal/Written Reporting
- Public Relations
- Improving Program Quality
- Organization
- Planning & Execution
- Leadership
- Budget Management
- Coordination

SOCIAL SERVICE EXPERIENCE

10/00 - 5/01 **Social Service Worker** **LOUISIANA DEPT. OF SOCIAL SERVICES**, Baton Rouge, LA

Assigned to Austin Children's Center. Planned, developed and implemented social services at a site which was created to serve up to 100 at risk children. The key was revitalizing the center by networking with churches, families, municipal and institutional organizations to build awareness of our support programs.

Challenge Prior to my hire, this site had lost its Head Start Certification (county & state) and had been operating without a Director for 18 months.

Actions *Initiated or reestablished programs and operations.* To win recertification with Head Start, I helped accomplish the following.

1. Conduct community needs assessment.
2. Reviewed and updated all children records to ensure compliance.
3. Administer, score and evaluate developmental assessments.
4. Created a directory of Austin's community resources.
5. Created partnership with dental and medical clinics for services.
6. Created library for parents (job search, legal support, parenting classes).
7. Created a parent committee that was a requirement from Head Start.
8. Secured speakers who held open forum discussions with parents.
9. Organized a parental volunteer group to provide support at the center.
10. Developed partnerships with agencies to support disabled children.

Result Created a valid partnership between the community, various service providers and non-profits as well as municipal departments that allowed the Children Center to actively meet their core mission.

1997 - 2000 **Care Taker** Took care of a terminally ill father.

1995 - 1997 **Program Supervisor** **FAMILY & CHILDREN'S SERVICES**, Baton Rouge, LA

Supervised 2 United Way funded programs and managed a staff of 8 (5 social workers, a child care worker and 2 program aides).

Program 1 *Family Connections* **-** A program helping families and 122 clients with the mandate to strengthen the relationship between school administrators, teachers, parents and at-risk students at 4 elementary schools.

Program 2 *Project Empowerment* **-** A state/county funded intense intervention program supporting 31 families and 114 children who had a history of neglect and truancy.

Program 3 *F.A.C.T.* - Folded programs 1 and 2 into FACT [Families And Communities Together], to aggregate and deliver unique benefits from each program into one optimal set of benefits for the combined 73 families and 226 clients.

Results

1. 95% of the families enrolled did not open new cases with County Child Protection Services.
2. 80% of children improved academic performance as measured by the California Achievement Test and teachers reported that 73% of the children's behavior improved.
3. 86% of parents became more involved with their children's education.

Project Founded and secured funding for the ***Summer Recreation Program:*** 2-six week sessions which served a total of 80 children.

1980 - 1994 **HENRICO COUNTY COMMUNITY CORRECTIONS** Richmond, VA
Senior Probation Officer 1987-1994
Managed 30 clients, 14-18 year old boys and girls, defined as high risk, repeat and violent offenders. The challenge was writing opinions that determined whether a child would stand trial as an adult or as a juvenile.

Challenge Wrote 50 page reports used by both prosecutors and defense attorneys during trial. These reports substantiated recommendation for or against treating offenders as adults or as juveniles.

Project Created then managed the ***College Internship Program***
The program handled 16 interns a year and partnered with Augsburg College, Metropolitan State U., Florida A&M, Moorhead State U. and U. of Minnesota.

1984-1987 **COMMUNITY CORRECTION OFFICER**
Member on the **Intensive Probation Team** of 4 officers who rolled-out JIPS (Juvenile Intensive Probation Supervision) pilot program.

Program JIPS was a national program using electronic bracelets for the first time in Virginia to provide 24/7 monitoring of the 25 highest risk juveniles in the County.

Result The National Association of Counties presented us with the "County Achievement Award" in recognition of distinguished contributions to better County Government.

EDUCATION Pursued M.A., Counselling Psychology, West Virginia Univ., Morgantown, WV
B.A., Sociology and Psychology, University of Virginia, Charlottesville, VA

MILITARY Police Supervisor U.S. Army Fort Campbell, KY

References available on request

KATRINA E. FOX

• Licensed Clinical Social Worker •

2662 Freemont Ave, Houston, TX 77030 713-259-6142

OBJECTIVE A career in corporate employee relations.

SUMMARY

Professional Management strengths focus on training and developing at both individual and corporate levels. Expertise and strategic planning centers on meeting program goals, conserving resources and maintaining quality standards.

Personal A self-starter who creates effective relationships, maintains discipline and communicates mission direction. Leadership skills enable me to effectively solve problems, identify opportunities for improvement and positively impact the overall organization.

STRENGTHS

- Verbal Communications
- Client Relations
- Office Management
- Interpersonal Skills
- Directional Planning
- Problem Solving
- Team Leadership
- Conflict Resolution
- Resource Coordination
- Group Training
- Leadership
- Coordination

EXPERIENCE

7/97 - Present ADVOCATE CLINICAL CARE, INC., Houston, TX

Program Coordinator

Overview Created the company's first Juvenile Sex Offender Program (JSOP) while also handling duties in the Emotional/Behavioral Disorder program. Created the only social service specialized program in Texas targeting Sexually Aggressive Child & Youth [SACY].

On 4/99, I began focusing solely on preparing the JSOP for national rollout to our 25 regional offices. The program is critical since it impacts 20-40% of our client population who are diagnosed as sexually aggressive and need individual plans to be implemented by public school teachers and foster families.

PROJECT *CREATED THE JUVENILE SEX OFFENDER PROGRAM*
Wrote proposal to initiate program which was approved by the Director of New Business Development. In partnership with the Clinical Director from corporate headquarters, I am developing program structure, training tools and execution phases for national rollout.

Result Delivered staff training in Houston, Indianapolis, and Columbia offices: Taught how to treat juvenile sex offenders. Program is projected to earn $2,400,000 annually.

Case Manager 7/97 - 9/98

Overview Attended court hearings, case reviews and case staffings for children placed in specialized foster homes. Co-facilitated a psycho-educational group for foster parents with sexually aggressive children. Advocated in Houston Public Schools on behalf of children with SACY plans.

6/96 - 7/97 ***Graduate Social Worker*** SANDRA CROWNES YOUTHWORK, INC., NY, NY

Overview Taught crisis intervention skills and provided intense individual and family counseling to families at risk of the removal of their children. Co-facilitated a parenting skills group, anger management group, and a therapeutic children's group using play therapy.

9/96 - 6/97 ***Consultant*** PSYCHOLOGICAL INSTITUTE & SERVICES, NY, NY

Overview Provided individual, group, and family therapy. Facilitated parenting groups, play therapy groups, self-esteem, and anger management groups. Provided psychological assessments and diagnoses, used the DSM IV for each client. Presented in case conferences and participated in clinical training.

6/95 - 5/96 ***Teacher*** INTERNATIONAL SCHOOL OF EXCELLENCE, NY, NY

Overview Directed a recreational and instructional swim program, including teaching and hiring staff. Head teacher in aftercare program. Coordinated structured activities in the areas of art, drama, and sports.

RESEARCH ***Research Assistant*** NEW YORK UNIVERSITY, New York, NY 12/92 -5/93

Project ***The Effect of Maternal Depression on Child Development***
Developed strategies to recruit families for research and critiqued therapy sessions.

Results First Article published by the Journal of Experimental Psychology 1992
Second Article published by the Journal of Developmental Psychopathology 1993

ACTIVITIES

- Reading/Math Tutor. New York Public School System
- Safeplace Volunteer. Washington, DC Public School System
- Compeer. Cornell University, Ithaca, NY

MEMBERSHIP

- National Association of Social Workers
- Certifications and Specialized Trainings

TRAINING

- Juvenile Sex Offender Treatment Nexus Training Facility, Onarga, IL
- Sexually Aggressive Children and Youth (SACY) Training, IL DCFS, Chicago, IL
- Sex Offender Evaluation and Treatment Training Program, Sinclair Seminars, Cleveland, OH

EDUCATION

5/96 M.S.W. **CORNELL UNIVERSITY**, Ithaca, NY
Thesis: *Integrating Play Techniques Into A Model That Promotes The Quality Of Attachment Within Neglecting Families.*

9/94 - 4/96 CATHOLIC CHARITIES, New York,, NY

Tutor [11/95 - 4/96]

Overview Provided instruction in the areas of math, reading, and science for school children in the foster care system. Consulted with public school teachers. Provided organizational and study skills as well as motivational techniques.

Intern [9/94 - 8/95]

Overview Assisted in placing children into foster homes. Conducted home studies with prospective foster parents to assess the potential of quality care. Co-facilitated a foster parent support group. Assisted in developing individualized goals and plans for the futures of children in foster care.

5/93 B.A. Psychology, **NEW YORK UNIVERSITY**, New York, NY

References available on request

CHAPTER 31

BUSINESS ANALYST CAREERS

The Business Analyst Category Has

3 Client Examples

17 Job Titles

46 Years of Work History

NAME	JOB TITLES COVERED
1. PETER MCCABE	......................................Business Analyst
	..............................Operations Consultant
2. GREG BASCOM*	....Network Planning & Engineer Design
	........................Acting Network Manager
	.........................Senior Network Engineer
	...........................Senior Project Engineer
	Senior Network Communication Analyst
	......Manager-Network Services Retail IT
	Assistant Network Infrastructure Manager
	....Technician
3. JANICE ASAYESH	........................Business Systems Analyst
	SAP Business Warehouse Administrator
	Oracle Database Administrator/Programmer
	....................Consultant/Project Manager
	................................Programmer Analyst
	....................................Software Engineer
	....Research Fellow

* Find the "before resume" in chapter 35

PETER MCCABE 2 W. Division St., Battle Creek, MI 49014 - pmccabe@aol.com

OBJECTIVE To continue a successful corporate career where I enhance efficiency and impact corporate I.S. goals.

SUMMARY Experience in information technologies, project management, operational planning, and execution. I support business units by integrating complex information systems, delivering technology solutions and implementing system architecture. Operational decisions are executed in a manner to ensure system integration fosters a cohesive technology environment.

STRENGTHS

Functional
- Cost Benefit Analysis
- Systems Analysis
- Data Audits
- Client Services

Professional
- Interpersonal Skills
- Resource Management
- Training
- Problem Solving

EXPERIENCE

2/98 - Present *Business Analyst* **KELLOGS FOODS, INC.**

Part of a 7 person IT team that runs the corporate demand forecasting system that drives logistical planning for **25 plants and $14 billion** of food production impacting 50,000 products across 150 categories.

Duties
- Conduct training sessions to teach demand planners and category logistics managers.
- SQL query the database to generate client reports that track demand forecasting, shipment chains and sourcing issues.
- Setup testing protocols to eliminate supply chain disjunction.

Project *Schedule Optimization*

Focus As project leader, I determined key triggers to launch SAM, Quest & Rocket applications (these three applications integrate plant shipments with customer demand forecasts). I then directed IT scheduling to implement the triggers and the IT repository team to validate data results.

Result Achieved seamless integration of the three applications and reduced schedule run time by 55% (or 4-6 hours per night).

Project *Explosion Tuning Refinements - Product Sourcing Validation*

Focus Edited the matrix filtering module in the SAM application to tune a data explosion consisting of a 70 million row matrix. The matrix integrates product sourcing data with customer demand forecasts.

Result Reduced the tuning time commitment from 7 to 4 hours per night which saves $375,000 in annual CPU usage costs.

Project *ERP Implementation of a SAM (Sourcing Assignment Matrix) application*

Focus Helped transition the supply chain forecasting and product inventory sourcing system from an outside vendor while simultaneously integrating two legacy systems from recently acquired subsidiaries: Kashi and Morningstar Foods.

Result Program success is projected to save **$50,000,000** annually by eliminating mismanaged inventory, over production and inefficient demand forecast.

1993-2/98 *Operations Consultant* **S. M. R., INC.**

Developed marketing strategies and made daily operational decisions in a 4 restaurant corporation. Analyzed the G.L., cash flow statements, P/L statements and generated business reports. Computerized accounts and maintained accounting system for a $4 million company

TECHNICAL Languages, Applications, Environments: COBOL, Endevor, MS Office, MVS/JCL SQL, Visual Basic

EDUCATION

2000 MBA, Emphasis in Marketing HARVARD UNIVERSITY

5/97 B.S., Biomedical Engineering-Molecular Physiology UNIVERSITY OF MASSACHUSETTS

GREG BASCOM 654 Newcastle Dr., Minneapolis, MN 55402 • 612-772-0101 • gbascom@comcast.net

EXPERIENCE

12/99 - present **SENIOR ENGINEER CONSULTANT ACCENTURE**

Overview Enterprise network architect with systems experience in Financial, Manufacturing, Healthcare, Construction and Retail industries. Effectively use network technologies by aligning solutions to business objectives. Work with technical staff, executives and end-users to hit revenue/cost targets.

Role 1 **Network Planning & Engineer Designer**, **GE HEALTHCARE**

Challenge **MIGRATING AT&T WAN TO MCI FRAME RELAY** for 135 American and European sites (MCI's Top-5 largest WAN migration).
Action – Determined rollout and 'turn-up strategies' at 135 global sites. Coordinated migration with 180 stakeholders (35 IT managers, 100 site supervisors and 10 Operational Managers).

Result Produced a 99% operationally available network that saves GE $1 million a year.

Challenge **Turn a batch-mode EDI infrastructure into 24/7 real-time environment** for GE's hospital, product manufacturing and distributor partners i.e., Johnson & Johnson.
Action – Completely documented and mapped the EDI process to streamline future client connectivity to the Gentran EDI Systems.

Result Eliminated $300,000 in annual operational cost from legacy system.

Challenge **Integrate GE's IT systems after** a $5.4 billion purchase of Allegiance Healthcare made the combined $21 billion company the largest US healthcare products and services provider.
Action – Scaled Alligence's remote management and backup redundancy service capability to fit the GE network framework and allow it to grow intelligently.

Result Saved $250,000 through consolidation and integration strategies.

Role 2 **Acting Network Manager**, **OUTSOURCING CO.**, Account Receivables company

Challenge Replaced a Network Manager when 2 major customers, US Oncology and Southern Gas were scheduled to connect to OC's DataStage - implementation deadline was 2 weeks away.
Action – Created a new pre-stage process to prepare routers for rapid deployment to client.

Result Reduced time needed to add customers by 40%, my implementation strategy became the model for OC.

Role 3 **Senior Network Engineer, MERK CO.,** Pharmaceutical Research Lab & Manufacturer

Challenge **Vulnerability tested Gauntlet firewall to identify how hackers** were breaching security and then recommended best practices to secure access for 2,000 US and European staff.
Action – Added VPN and Client remote access technologies and deployed Solaris Variant Checkpoint using SolarWinds Tools.

Result Eliminated all security breaches as confirmed by the log and ISP monthly vulnerability scan.

Role 4 **Senior Project Engineer, POINTBASE INC.,** Sellers of Java Imbedded Technology

Challenge Expand Pointbase's web presence amongst the development community and support their e-Commerce business initiative.
Actions – Designed the network infrastructure requirements to maintain and implement 1. Internet and SQL Server, 2. Linux Server Hardware/Software, 3. Signio Account Manager, 4. Nokia Firewall, 5. ISP, and 6. Verisign Certificates.

Result PointBase increased on-line purchasing volume 1000%, from 200 to 2000 files a day.

Accenture Assignment
Role 5 **Senior Network Communications Analyst - AVEDA,** Corporate HQ

Challenge Became acting Network Manager for Aveda to maintain continuity and network performance when their Sr. Manager of Network Services departed.

Actions – Supported performance of Siebel and PeopleSoft. Created standards to backup network elements, i.e., RAS Server and the warehouse management system (WMS) on Linux.

Results Created ***First-Evers*** for Aveda as follows

1. Documented the enterprise network, topology, operational elements & carrier records.
2. Executed first Ethernet LAN between Ontario and Minneapolis, MN Center.
3. Configured and deployed Ipswitch network monitoring and alarm software.

8/89 - 11/98 **SHOPRITE** **Manager - Network Services Retail IT** S. Africa, International H.Q.
Assistant Network Infrastructure Manager

Overview................ Handpicked by Board of Directors to deploy the first corporate NETWORK WAN and LAN, originally scaled for 125 retail stores in S. Africa, it now accommodates 450 stores in 5 countries (Shoprite Holdings is the continent's largest retailer, *Africa's Walmart*, and earns $18 billion with average growth over 25% a year).

My Roles – Manage Enterprise Network (digital E1/E2 Trunk backbone and frame relay switching centers). Member of the Enterprise Architectural Committee. Integrated 5 Regional PBX's to a HQ Siemens 9000 series PBX using E&M trunk Signaling and TDM Technologies. Collaborated with GM's, technology vendors, the national teleco and multiple project installation teams.

Phase 1
WAN $9MM budget • Sole rollout manager directing 5-teams of 3 network engineers each from Philips Communications to deploy their CASE DCX Network Processor. Scope of deployment: • 375 NCR POS Processors • 575 TTY Terminals • 375 X.25 EFT Managers

Phase 2
LAN $3MM budget • Adopt ethernet technology corporate-wide (stores, offices, HQ). Replaced Network Processors with Cisco Routers and an NCR mainframe with Client/Server technology.

Phase 3
Optimize $1.2MM budget. Add scalability and control to the network by replacing trunk routers with a Lucent CBX 500 Frame Relay backbone infrastructure. Used Carrier Class Cascade Switches spanning 6 regions while maintaining business continuity and operational service levels

Results

1. Initiated debit/credit transaction capability.
2. Intelligently added 300% more stores in 5 new countries to the WAN.
3. Introduced JAVA technology for Advanced Retail Management -ARM software

1/80 - 8/89 **SEPA, The National Telecommunication Co.** ***Technician*** Cape Town, S. Africa

Overview................ Provisioned and supported Data Communications and Digital Telematics Services. Supervised 30 Data Engineers. Installed, tested and commissioned Carrier Class Marconi Digital Switching Hierarchies in 35 Telco Central Offices. Subject Matter Expert, COURSEWARE & WAVE TECHNOLOGY (CCNA & CCDA)

COLLEGE **National Telecommunication Diploma**, (NTD – Telecommunications & Digital Electronics).

CERTIFICATION **CCSE 2000:** Checkpoint 2000 Certified Security Engineer, (VPN-1/FW-1 Encryption and Policy Server).
I-NET+: CompTIA Certification, (Maintenance of Internet, Intranet and Extranet Infrastructure)
CCNA: Cisco Certified Network Associate. **CCDA:** Cisco Certified Design Associate.

JANICE ASAYESH —— 439 Talleyhoe Ln., Round Rock, TX 78682 • 512-679-2162

EXPERIENCE

9/99-1/04 **DELL**
- ***Business Systems Analyst***
- ***SAP BW (Business Warehouse) Administrator***
- ***Oracle Database Administrator/Programer***

Overview Business Systems Analyst for the Enterprise Reporting Group prior to becoming Project Leader of teams with 5-15 Business Analysts for Dell's Supply Chain Data Warehouse Group.

Role 1 ***Executive Forecasting*** - Created enterprise business reports for CEO, President, CIO, Executive VP, Server Division and SVP, Supply Chain. – ***My Impact*** – Provided the data to predict global market demand, forecast sales, account for finished goods and work-in-progress on $42.4 billion of corporate business.

Actions

Report Mgt.	• Realigned delivery process to enhance Supply Chain reports and enable business users 50% faster access. Provided weekly, detailed progress status reports to management.
Collaboration	• Established strong relationships with business users to determine requirements.
Training	• Developed and taught courses for the user community.
Technical	• SAP BW, Oracle, PL/SQL, MS Project/Office/Access, R/3, RdB, Data Modeling

Project 1 OFF-SHORING ENTERPRISE REPORTING TO "DIGITAL INDIA". Integrated business and cultural systems, mentored staff and supported each action throughout the transition.

Result Saved over $1,000,000 year and freed 6 Dell analysts to contribute to other projects.

Project 2 LAUNCH **SAP** BUSINESS INFORMATION WAREHOUSE **(BW)**. Part of the 5-person Central Team that planned and launched this $4MM project.

Result Created the model used to implement SAP BW for (1) Sales & Distribution (2) Europe/ Middle East/Africa Supply Chain and (3) Corporate-wide Logistics.

Role 2 Supported **Enterprise Server Group**, a $14 billion division with 27% global market share that represented a quarter of Dells $55 billion revenue stream.

Project 3 CORPORATE ACCOUNTS PROGRAM, co-led 20 developers and business analysts in five countries (Singapore, UK, Spain, Germany and the US) to build a business database and web-site that profiled Dell's Top 100 accounts.

Result Launched the first *International Major Accounts Management System* used by 350 business analysts across the globe to plan and execute their business building tactics.

12/97-7/99 **VERASCEND** ***Consultant/Project Manager*** - **Alliant Energy** Flemington, NJ

Overview Assigned to Duane Arnold Nuclear power plant where I provided systems support to the site nuclear engineers.

Actions

Project Mgt.	Translated business requirements into software solutions after gathering requirements, prototyping interfaces and data modeling (using PowerDesigner).
Training	Trained users as well as mentored and provided leadership for student interns.
Leadership	Conceived project plans and timelines as project leader.
Technical	Wrote Oracle 8.0 PL/SQL stored procedures. Set up tables, relationships and triggers. Used PowerBuilder 6.5.

Project 4 NUCLEAR MATERIAL TRACKING. Liaised with users to gather requirements and database 27 years of stored radioactive uranium inventory.

Project 5 CUSTOMIZING **MS** ACCESS. Led team of 8 EDS analysts to work with 125 nuclear engineers during a complex upgrade where my team helped each engineer convert their custom Visual Basic Access modifications to the upgrade version.

1/97-9/97 **BANK OF CANADA** ***Programmer Analyst*** Montreal, Canada

Overview Programmed in Visual C++ environment for relational database procedures. Developed user manuals for the database used globally. Interacted with users to tailor databases for their needs.

Project 6 **CREATED THE FIRST FOREIGN EXCHANGE TRADING DATABASE.** Administered a DB2/NT database and transitioned the "foreign exchange trading' data from a legacy environment to client-server platform.

6/96-12/96 **THALES** ***Software Engineer*** Addlestone, UK

UK's 2nd Largest Defense Co ***Anti Submarine Warfare***

Overview Programmed antisubmarine tracking devices that are placed on battleships. Created software using PowerPC Assembler and ADA.

5/95-8/95 **ARTIFICIAL INTELLIGENCE LAB** ***Research Fellow*** University of Oxford

Researching machine vision.

Overview Developed an algorithm in C and Unix to investigate how computers and robots could recognize random shapes. Authored scientific article on procedure and findings. Used C++ and Geomview to improve robot GUI being developed for disabled children.

PUBLICATION Palloi, D., Renner, F., Asayesh,J.. and Tanner, .1K. (1996). Empirically derived estimates of the complexity of labeling line drawings of polyhedral scenes. *Intelligence Weekly* 107, 37-76.

EDUCATION

2001	MBA (with Distinction)	University of Oxford
1996	B.Sc. (Honors)	Computer Science & Mathematics, University of Oxford

References available on request.

CHAPTER 32

ARCHITECTURAL & INTERIOR DESIGN CAREERS

The Architectural & Interior Design Category Has

3 Client Examples

5 Job Titles

39 Years of Work History

NAME	JOB TITLES COVERED
1. ANDY BARTLETT	....Principal
2.KATIE BENNETT*	............Jr. Architect & AutoCAD Drafter
4.CARRIE STEELE	......................Director Of Interior Design
	....Designer
	....Designer/Sales

* Find the “before resume” in chapter 35

ANDY K. BARTLETT

161 N. Deerpath Dr., Milwaukee, WI 53215 414.773.2190
abartlett@yahoo.com

ARCHITECTURAL SUMMARY

As business builder, architect and project manager, I've led 550 building projects from concept design to final walk-through and signoff. In each assignment, I control cost and quality from design, bid and implementation. As lead architect, I assemble and direct teams of specialists and act as liaison between clients, consultants and contractors to meet schedule and budget goals.

1985-present
PRINCIPAL
A.K Bartlett Architects

CATEGORY	VOLUMES	BUDGETS	COSTS	REVENUES
Residential	125,000 s.f.	$10.2 million	$9.5 million	$675,000
Commercial	185,000 s.f.	$10.8 million	$9.7 million	$585,000
Office Interiors	275,000 s.f.	$15.8 million	$14.5 million	$865,000
Educational	2,000,000 s.f.	$42.6 million	$40.2 million	$2,400,000
Totals (Summary)	2,585,000 s.f.	$79.4 million	$73.9 million	$4.6 million

COMMERCIAL DESIGN PROJECTS	Total 20 unique projects Size 3,000-30,000 sqft

EXAMPLES Renovate office/retail space, design restaurants and building facade restoration.

Michigan Ave. Renovated a 50,000 s.f. office that received the Silver Medal for "Excellence in Masonry Design". ***Facts*** Fast-track design and construction schedule included new brick, stone and window facade exterior work and design of all new tenant space.

C&D Commodities Chicago Board of Trade firm. ***Facts*** - Required in-depth design process of corporate office expansion on a time sensitive nature of the daily office schedule, while tenant occupied the construction space during the remodeling.

Master Planning Same-site thoroughbred horse farm and Ferrari auto restoration facility. ***Facts*** - Combined the family's dual passion for race horses and classic horsepower designed into their country farm setting.

EDUCATIONAL DESIGN PROJECTS	Total 500 unique projects Size 1,000-50,000 sqft

EXAMPLES

Downers Grove 16 year relationship covering 845,000 sqft and $14MM in budgets to develop 2 campuses. ***Hot Issues*** - Early 20th century masonry, decorative stone and terra cotta restoration, building additions and interior remodeling.

Villa Park 17 year relationship as primary architect on 500K sqft and $14.1MM in budgets across 7 different campuses. ***Hot Issues*** - Building additions, interior remodeling, environmental and fire/life safety.

LaGrange 20 year relationship in a special education school district funded by 12 communities. ***Hot Issues*** -Diplomatically building consensus between 12 school superintendents while collaborating with the primary project owner.

RESIDENTIAL DESIGN PROJECTS	Total 20 unique projects Size 100,000 total sqft

EXAMPLES Large and small-scale custom single family homes spanning price range from moderate to high-end.

North Shore 7,500 s.f. new Glencoe home overlooking Lake Michigan. ***Qualities*** - Open, spacious interiors and Green Design incorporating passive solar elements allow the house to be healthy, smart and long-lasting.

Vacation Home Multi-level 6,500 sqft home in a Lake Geneva hillside overlooking a private lake. ***Qualities*** - Expansive interior spaces with full-height glass windows and large wood decks control view of natural rolling terrain.

Mogul's Home Expanded a summer home and added a guest house which became the personal getaway for this owner. ***Qualities*** - The home, with pool/tennis court, is nestled in a wooded site near Lake Geneva.

AWARDS • Silver Medal For "Excellence In Masonry Design." • "Governor's Award For Barrier-Free Design."

LICENSURE • WI Registered, Lic. • EPA/IDPH Environmental Engineer, Lic.

EDUCATION • BA, Architecture, University of Wisconsin Milwaukee

KATIE BENNETT

281 Lomita Tr., Las Vegas, NV 89101 · 702-562-1597 · ben61@comcast.net

OBJECTIVE Jr. Architect and CAD drafter interested in the functional layout of a building to better suit user needs while maximizing use of space and maintaining the integrity of the edifice.

SKILLS Proficient in AutoCAD 14 & 2002.

ARCHITECTURAL EXPERIENCE

10/02-5/03 **TATE SNYDER KIMSEY** Las Vegas, NV
Jr. Architect & AutoCAD drafter

Worked on CADing construction documents and defining ADA compliance. Distributed multiple sets of drawings to 12 consultant firms.
Tracked plans during each construction phase; demolition, actual construction, bid documents, permit documents, addendum and Architectural supplemental instruction.

Project 12/02 -5/03 TRESPA NORTH AMERICA- INTERIOR RENOVATION
Supported project from preliminary phases through bid, permit and construction.
Duties Surveyed existing condition of the building interior from lower level through 13th floor. Executed the ADA upgrade of the fitting rooms.

ARCHITECTURE INTERNSHIP

Smrs. '00 & '01 **MIAMI CITY HALL, DEPT. OF BUILDINGS** - Intergovernmental Services.
Expedited nearly half of the construction documents submitted for permit for the Miami International Airport expansion.

EDUCATION 2002 **Bachelor, ARCHITECTURE** Graduated with Honors
UNIVERSITY OF MIAMI SCHOOL OF ARCHITECTURE Major GPA: 3.45
Honors: Deans List, 2001 & 2002, excellence in academic achievement.

ARCHITECTURAL PROJECTS

PROJECT #1 **HOTEL HIGH-RISE** Prof: Nicholas Patricios who had worked with Mies Van der Rohe.

Description

Studied vertical and horizontal circulation of the building's public and private sectors. Analyzed Miami city code for a South Beach site. The object was to leverage Miami and BOCA codes to build the most economically functional hotel.
Key Features:
All suites are ADA compliant. Multilevel garage, loading docks, laundry, bakery, restaurant, hotel locker rooms are handicapped accessible .
Structural Elements:
Every building segment, from the parking garage's lowest level through elevator machine rooms had to meet or exceed the minimum occupancy and fire-code requirements.

Result

Designed a very functional and user friendly hotel - economically. ***Pg. 1 of 2***

PROJECT #2 **3-LEVEL COMMUNITY CENTER** Prof. Roberto Behar
2414 SW 22nd Ave, Miami, FL Partner at Dover, Kohl & Partners

Description

Studied how materials work together aesthetically with emphasis on concrete structures.
Level 1: Public space with restaurant/lounge area for entertainment.
Level 2: Semi-public/private space with auditorium/theater.
Level 3: Private space with meeting rooms.
Key Architectural Features:
Ground floor layout has a series of doors on its East facade that is separated by structural concrete members to create a continuous traffic flow and allow the sidewalk to be used for extra seating in the summer, without obstructing pedestrian traffic.
Structural Elements:
To keep the building as light and simple in design as possible, I used post-tension concrete slabs @ 14" deep which minimized the number of columns in the building.

Result

Created a three story community center using the concept of the lightness of a modern parking garage.

PROJECT #3 **MUSEUM** -5,000 TO 50,000 SQ. FT. Prof. Allan Shulman
Sr. Partner of Shulman & Sexto

Description

In-depth study of materials, art, functionality, the language of a building, as well as movement throughout spaces. Study began by researching multiple world-class museums created by renown architects (I studied ideas contained in Mies Van Der Rohe's Barcelona Pavilion).
Key Features:
Created the understanding of function and aesthetics combined with movement. Each function was determined by the materials used to house each space; i.e., opaque spaces are private, translucent spaces are semiprivate, and transparent spaces are public.
Structural Elements:
When viewing the building each component is placed properly with respect to all other components (this includes the negatives, columns, and glazing structure). By using grid analysis, a 30 x 30 ft. horizontal grid, and a 2'6" modular system I confined the layout and explored an unlimited number of circulation options.

Result

The building is a 3-D piece of "ART".

•
•
•

References and portfolio available upon request.

CARRIE STEELE

600 West Ivy Rd, #13
Houston, TX 77230
713-638-2190

Objective

To continue a successful interior design career with a design firm or developer who focuses on the hospitality industry and needs a disciplined professional with management experience and creative vision.

Summary

Over 13 years as a designer, I've met challenges and created imaginative solutions for a spectrum of private, commercial and healthcare assignments. Project responsibilities encompass budget forecasting, interior design, purchasing and project management. I have developed a strong work ethic and personal commitment to achieving excellence whether I work independently, as a team player, or as project leader.

Strengths

• Creative Design	• Purchasing	• Research
• Project Management	• Leadership	• Budget Forecasting
• Client Relations	• Space Planning	• AutoCAD

Experience

10/90- present

ASPEN DESIGN GROUP, Houston, TX
Director of Interior Design / Senior Designer

Overview

Hired as the first in-house Designer of the Aspen Group - the largest developer of high-end elderly care facilities in Houston. By replacing outside design firms, Aspen eliminated associated design fees and increased control over all project phases.

Single-handedly led dramatic changes to redirect the image of Aspen's elderly care interiors to that of a luxury hotel with upscale, comfortable living environments and special amenities such as formal dining rooms, ice cream shops, libraries, chapels and beauty salons.

Hired and trained an assistant designer and support staff. Scheduled, assigned and supervised projects to assure successful completion.

Actions

- Prepare preliminary budgets for project financing.
- Review preliminary drawings, survey existing conditions, coordinate with architects, builders and contractors.
- Developed design concepts for each assignment based on the unique requirement of the local market.
- Specify all interior finishes, select furnishings, space planning and develop installation and electrical plans.
- Develop bid specifications, evaluate proposals, negotiate pricing and purchase all interior products.
- Custom design original, upscale case goods, millwork and patterned hospitality carpets to distinguish Alden from the competition.
- Handle all project management elements. Schedule and oversee subcontractors to assure quality installation.
- Represent Alden at H.U.D. inspections to assure fund allocation.

Healthcare Projects

Managed all phases of 9 new construction and 3 total renovation projects, creating 750,000 sq. ft. of senior living space with a combined construction value of $58 million– $11 million for furnishings, fixtures, carpeting and wall coverings.

Results

- Aspen's upscale image increased bed rates and ensured maximum occupancy.
- Our suppliers now use my designs in their marketing literature.

Corporate Project

Designed striking and beautifully functional working environments for Aspen's corporate HQ and their 3 divisional headquarters, an aggregate of 36,000 sq. ft. housing 115 staff.

9/89 - 10/90

POMERANTZ & CO., Philadelphia, PA
Designer

O*verview*

Pomerantz & Co. is a dealer of Steelcase office furniture and also represents many other manufacturers. As a staff designer, I worked both independently and on a team to create functional and inventive work environments for a variety of corporate, medical and bank projects.

Actions

- Marketed design services and wrote contracts.
- Space planned, created furniture layouts, installation & electrical plans.
- Specified furniture using AutoCAD and specifier programs.
- Developed color scheme, interior finishes and fabrics, selected artwork and accessories.
- Prepared presentation boards for client approval including layouts, furnishing proposal and interior finish selections.

Project Summary

Bank One Corporate HQ
A $250,000 project which showcased my AutoCad skills. Key project elements included interviewing client to determine needs, space planning, specifying furniture, and creating installation drawings with associated electrical layout.

11/87 - 9/89

MICHAEL'S DESIGNS, Washington, DC
Designer

Overview

A residential, model home and healthcare design firm in partnership with a retail operation. Originally hired to run the retail end where I dramatically increased sales and simultaneously developed residential and builder clientele. Within 3 months, I hired a retail store manager so I could focus on a heavy project load.

Actions

- Marketed design services and contract administration.
- Interviewed clients to determine their needs, inventoried and evaluated existing furnishings, coordinated with architects, builders and contractors.
- Drew floor and space plans, created furniture layouts.
- Advised clients on purchase of furnishings, floor/wall coverings and window treatments.
- Site visits ensured design intent and quality of contractors work.
- Supervised ordering and billing processes.

Result

- As designer, I increased sales 50%.

2/87 - 11/87

GALLERIA BATH & KITCHEN SHOWPLACE, Tampa, FL
Designer /Sales

Overview

Galleria Bath & Kitchen is a showroom and distributor of Kohler products.

Actions

- Developed designs and layouts for contemporary kitchens and bathrooms.
- Advised architects, builders, and home owners on product selection.
- Designed showroom displays.

Education

1986

Bachelor Arts, **Interior Design**, BOWLING GREEN STATE UNIVERSITY
- ASID Student Design Competition - Best of School

Training

1989 Atlanta Technical College, Computer Aided Design
1989 Pomerantz & Co. Basic Training Seminars
1992/1993 National Symposium, Health Care Design

CHAPTER 33

CHOPPY CAREER

The Choppy Career Category Has

1 Client Example

5 Job Titles

9 Years of Work History

NAME	JOB TITLES COVERED
1. JOSH HAUSMAN*	.................................Operations Manager
	.................................Account Exec\utive
	....Staff Recruiter
	....Branch Manager
	...................................Assistant Manager

* Find the "before resume" in chapter 35

Josh Hausman —— 851 Martinez Dr., San Deigo, CA 92161 • 760-313-7215 • haus11@aol.com

SUMMARY

Able to assimilate information, analyze problems and develop viable solutions. An imaginative, open-minded, original-thinker with strong analytical skills and ability to "see the whole picture" in detail and scope. Successful at training and developing team members and associates to their full potential.

GENERAL MANAGEMENT EXPERIENCE

1/03-8/04 **Operations Manager** **UNITED VAN LINES** San Diego, CA

Managed local marketing, direct and retail sales, inventory, transportation and warehouse operations in a safe and efficient manner. Provided outstanding customer service. Trained and motivated staff of 6 (drivers, loaders, CSRs, and warehousemen) to meet corporate expectations. Maintained communication with customers, vendors, staff and management. Developed and implemented warehouse inspection and inventory plans.

Results

- Recognized *Nationally :* Part of the Most Outstanding Region Of The Year FY03 (of 26 US regions).
- Developed management plan: Reduce delinquency tenant AR of 15-20% to below company goal of 10%.

ACCOUNT EXECUTIVE EXPERIENCE

1/02-10/02 **Account Executive** **LITIGATION SOLUTIONS INC.** Dallas, TX

Business-to-business sales and relationship-building for legal document management business. Generated new revenues by helping law firms and corporate legal departments apply current technology.

Results

- Negotiated a $500K deal that resulted in landing the 2nd largest bankruptcy project in company history.
- Ranked #1 sales representative in dollar volume on team of 6 reps.

6/01-10/01 **Staff Recruiter** **SRP** Dallas, TX

Developed relationships and leads, lists of employers and applicants. Coordinated and scheduled interviews, prepared candidates for interviews, and obtained candidate and employer feedback from interviews.

BRANCH GM EXPERIENCE

8/95-1/01 **Branch Manager** **HERTZ RENT-A-CAR** Dallas, TX

Led sales, marketing, business development, operations, customer relations, P&L and cost containment. Managed a $4M inventory of 200+ vehicles. Supervised 6 staff (3 management trainees). Developed marketing events and called-on large accounts to generate new business. Continuously trained employees to elevate them to management positions. Handled staffing, customer service, A/R and training at the branch level.

Results

- Recognized *Nationally* — Corporate President's Award for fleet growth FY00 (only the Top 10% of branches across the US receive this award).
- Recognized *Regionally* — Top Corporate Performer Award for increased corporate account revenues.
- New training program — Raised customer service score 18%.
- Negotiated agreements — Captured 4 of 5 local dealerships to grow branch fleet 51% in FY99.

Fiscal Growth
- In a controlled territory.

1999	$1.6MM Sales	$260K in profit
2000	$1.7MM Sales	$275K in profit
2001	$1.77MM Sales	$296K in profit

Project Created a territory inside/outside sales plan with marketing events targeting 100 insurance agents, body shops, dealerships, and service center accounts.

Impact Increased operating profits by 69%.

8/95-1/98 **Assistant Manager** Managed scheduling, daily operations and a $2MM inventory.

Results

- Received 2 "Boat" awards — For inside sales for FY97 and FY98.
- Received *Regional* award — Grew business by 15% the 3Q97.
- Received *Regional* award — Increased fleet by 13% and operating profits by 63% for FY98.

EDUCATION 1993 B.S., Advertising Communications, UNIVERSITY OF DALLAS, Dallas, TX

CHAPTER 34

CSR, COLLECTIONS & AR CAREERS

The CSR, Collections & AR Category Has

2 Client Examples

7 Job Titles

19 Years of Work History

NAME	JOB TITLES COVERED
1. MICHELLE JURKOVIC*	............Customer Service Representative ....Graduate Assistant ....Translator, Tour Guide, Journalist
2. CHRISTPHER SCHWARTZ	.........................Manager Collections/AR ....Supervisor Collections/AR ....Associate Asset Manager ....Accounts Recievable Specialist

* Find the "before resume" in chapter 35

MICHELLE JURKOVIC ——— 36 Bayside Dr., Torrence, CA 90503 • 310-776-2152 • mic88@aol.corn

OBJECTIVE To become a credit analyst.

EXPERIENCE

11/01-present **TOYOTA FINANCIAL SERVICES, Customer Service Representative**
After proving my value for 3 months, TFS spent $10,000 to buy my temp contract and hire me full time.

My Role Manage a portfolio of 5,600 commercial accounts (worth $60M). My challenge is to present financing options to customers in financial difficulty and create payment strategies that minimize the negative impact on their credit history. I am expected to make 500 outbound calls and handle 100 inbound calls a week.

Actions I've trained 3 new hires and implemented an organizational system of managing commercial accounts that is currently being modeled throughout the branch.

Result Reduced severely overdue accounts by 80% (these are TFS's most troubled accounts) this also represents the fastest resolution of these type of accounts in our branch.
Result I am the only temp hired during the last 6 months (hired during a hiring freeze).
Result My team won the Presidential Award in 2001 of 144 competing branches in the US.
Result Received multiple letters of appreciation from customers.
Result Generated $85,000 in collected fees, representing the highest percentage in the department.

Project Specialist: ***Lump Sum Payment Program*** for branch's 20,000 accounts.
My Value In addition to daily duties, I process ~ $500,000 in Lump Sum Payments a month and resolve customer confusion on their options on how the funds can be applied to their car loan balance.

8/00-5/01 **UNIVERSITY OF SOUTHERN CALIFORNIA, Graduate Assistant**
Research for 3 professor's. Analysis included creating computer models of data using Excel, SPSS, regression analysis and other tools.

9/99-7/00 **PUNA, Member of Presidential Council** (Poland at the United Nations).
My roles • Organized conferences • Handled Media Relations • Planning travel itineraries

9/97-9/99 **INTERNATIONAL CENTER, Translator, Tour Guide, Journalist** Warsaw, Poland
• Led and translated for groups of international professionals on company visits. I explained the challenges and changes facing East-European companies.
• Authored 8 articles for the Sentinel, a newsletter sent to 50 nations.

COMPUTER MS Word, Excel and PowerPoint, SPSS, PhotoShop

LANGUAGES English, Polish, Hungarian, French, Russian, German, Arabic, functional Spanish

EDUCATION

2001 **MA Political Science** University of Southern California, Los Angeles, CA
Competed with 40 students and won one of the two full-ride scholarships to an American university. Enrolled in 17 classes in the spring semester - accomplished 4.81 on a 5 scale GPA.

2000 **MA Economics** Warsaw University of Economic Sciences & Public Administration
Awards - One of two students awarded the *Pro Universitate*, the highest academic award for the school's 700 students. Received 6 national scholarships.
Student Council President: Trained and managed 40 students.

1998 **BA., Economics** Warsaw University of Economic Sciences & Public Administration

CHRIS SCHWARTZ ——————— 111 127th St., Atlanta, GA 30346 404-791-6344 chris _s@sbcglobal.net

Summary– developed a credit collections and AR management career that achieves goals. My management positions involve heavy client contact and interaction with attorneys. I'm result oriented expert at negotiating deals, managing customer relations and team building.

ACCOUNTS RECEIVABLE COLLECTION MANAGEMENT

2/00-4/02 **RANDSTAD** Staffing Agency — ***Manager Collection/Accounts Receivable*** 2/01-4/02 — Atlanta, GA
Supervisor Collection/Accounts Receivable 2/00-2/01

Overview................ Managed department with 10-12 Collections and AR staff for a $240MM company with $23.5MM in outstanding receivables that averaged $1MM in daily postings on a volume of 5,000-10,000 invoices per month.

Duties
- Client accounts reconciliation, process Bankruptcy filings, research cases of fraud.
- Analyzed credit reports of current and new clients.
- Helped develop policies & procedures for the Finance & Customer Service departments.

Challenge Replaced the corporate Billing Manager and became Randstad's first Manager of Collection/AR at a critical point where key accounts (SBC, AT&T, SW Bell and Lucent) disputed 6,000+ AR tickets amounting to $23MM outstanding.

Issues resolved
- 20% of our orders were unsigned or lost.
- 50% of the tickets were incorrectly billed (30 different negotiated rates).
- 30% of the tickets were signed by authorizing managers who had been replaced, at the client site which led to widespread confusion by new mangers.

Response 1 Built management cohesion between our corporate HQ and branch managers who were placing 1,300 temps with 200 clients where the disputes originated.

Response 2 Created a dotted-line of authority between the branch managers and my department to hold them accountable for negotiating reconciliation with their client contacts.

Response 3 Pushed for a 48 hour response time by branch managers for my department's request for documentation and invoice verification.

Results Reduced delinquency by $10MM within three months.

11/92-5/99 **AT&T CAPITAL** — ***Associate Asset Manager*** 6/97-5/99 — Livingston, NJ
Accounts Receivable Specialist 11/92-6/97

Overview................ Managed a $350MM portfolio of leased office, computer and copier equipment. Processed fee invoices, bill of sales documentation, buy-outs and returns. Supervised and trained new collectors.

Duties
- Resolved problem accounts by negotiating with customers.
- Analyzed financial statements using Dun & Bradstreet business reports, TRW credit reports, Financial Statements and Tax Filings.
- Processed repossessions and negotiated settlements (experienced in bankruptcy filings).
- Recommended write-offs or referred accounts to legal department and collection agencies.

Challenge Revamp AT&T Capital's End-of-Lease Remarketing program to boost Fair Market Value profits.

Issues resolved
- Reduced reliance on remarketing vendors to sell equipment at end-of-lease.
- Coached CSR's to push customers to buy at book value.
- Drive remarketer's to capture current market value rather than a quick sale.

Results Grew remarketing profits from 33% of fair market value to 75% which adds $4MM.

TRAINING Business Management, Seaton Hall University, South Orange, NJ

CHAPTER 35

RESUMES BEFORE SCULPTING

I offer these "before" resumes to give you the ability to directly compare with the "after" effect of sculpting an Red Hot Resume. The best way to find the "after" resume that I created is to look for the example with the asterisk (*) on the the listing of the resumes that accompany each new chapter.

For the sake of comparison, I tried to replicate the original exactly as it was given to me. Don't be surprised at the styles you will see on the next few pages, they are an honest representation of resumes that are typically sent out onto the employment market.

RACHEL WILLIAMS

RESUME BEFORE SCULPTING

OBJECTIVE:
To pursue a career opportunity with a company that will maximize my leadership skills and abilities while learning on the job.

BUSINESS EXPERIENCE:

UBS -Paine Webber - Hinsdale, IL
Dec. 1997 to Feb. 2002
Position: Office Manager/Executive Assistant

- Created and managed a database to control the inventory
- Complete Data Entry Responsibilities
- Highly educated in all aspect of Internet usage
- Produced monthly invoices for Registered Representatives using QuickBooks
- Serviced Customers for Executives
- Responsible for originating detailed spreadsheets
- Processed various Insurance and Variable Annuity applications
- Managed office records
- Screened phone calls for Executives
- Greeted Clients

Advanced Technology Consultants. — Oak Brook, IL
Jan. 97 to Dec. 97
Position: Office Administrator

- Responsible for order entry and customer relations
- Report monthly, quarterly and annual reports to regional office, an average of $200,000 a month
- Process orders for sales representatives using MS Excel & Word
- Collect customer data to facilitate billing
- Process various types of contract agreements

Direct Packaging Corp., Inc - Westmont, IL
Dec. 95 to Jan. 97
Position: Administrative Assistant

- Worked with Microsoft Windows 95
- Performed Data Entry on orders shipped and pick-ups
- Assisted with billing for 3 different branches

EDUCATIONAL DATA:

- New Horizon Computer Learning Center, Chicago, Illinois, Related Courses: Microsoft Certified
- Triton College, River Grove, Illinois, Related Courses: Continuing Education
- Oak Park River Forst, Oak Park, Illinois, Related Courses: 4 years of Computer Lab.
  Earned Diploma June 1989

SKILLS:

- Experience with Microsoft, Windows, Excel, Word, Power Point, Front Page, QuickBooks, Outlook, and Outlook Express
- Fluent Bilingual/in Spanish

RESUME BEFORE SCULPTING

TIMOTHY KRAMER
6740 Saddlebrook Ln. (314) 223-7410
St. Louis, MO 63129 (314) 543-1796 Office

Executive Summary

GENERAL MANAGEMENT EXECUTIVE with over 25 years operating experience in executive level positions. Proven track record in motivating and building a strong organizational climate through personal involvement and a proactive leadership style. Ability to streamline operations to achieve cost and profit goals. In addition to a European assignment, a 20 year history of direct international business experiences.

Professional Background

SEMCO PLASTICS COMPANY Inc. - St. Louis, Missouri 1998-2001

Chairman, President and CEO

Built a $400 million Manufacturing and Service Company producing highly engineered, highly complex plastic molded parts and value added services by acquiring 5 companies over a 13-month period. Company consisted of 16 manufacturing facilities in 4 countries with over 4,000 employees.

- Integrated 5 acquisitions into a new homogeneous business culture.
- Hired a completely new executive management team.
- Closed and consolidated 2 manufacturing plants to generate $4.2 million in annual savings.
- Implemented a major cost reduction initiative in 2001 yielding $9.5 million in annual savings.

STRATEGIC ACQUISITION ACTIVITY - St. Louis, Missouri 1997-1998

Successfully provided acquisition-consulting services to a New England based equity investment firm interested in consolidating a number of companies in the Precision Machining Industry.

- Provided due diligence and value analysis on 57 companies in the USA.
- Negotiated transactions with 12 companies.
- Agreed to acquire 3 companies that are now part of a very successful venture.

CALVERT WIRE & CABLE. — Brook Park, Ohio 1994-1997

President and CEO — Calvert Wire & Cable (1995-1997)

Responsible for a newly acquired group of companies producing bare and insulated copper conductor wire and wiring harnesses. Sales for 1996 were $575 million. The combined company had 29 manufacturing plants located in the U.S. and Mexico with over 6,000 employees.

- Doubled the size of the company in 15 months through acquisitions.
- Closed and consolidated 10 manufacturing plants in 13 months increasing EBITDA margins by 4.5%.
- Reduced inventories by 20% in 1996 thereby increasing cash flow by $13.5 million.
- Increased sales in 1994 by 22%.
- Accelerated the product design development process from 185 days to 70 days.

LARSEN'S MANUFACTURING — Ft. Lauderdale, FL 1987-1994

President — Larsen's Manufacturing — Ft. Lauderdale, FL (1993-94)

Responsible for the worldwide operations of six operating units with manufacturing and service centers located in the U.K., Italy, Brazil, Mexico, Australia, and the U.S. Annual sales were approximately $150 million.

- Expanded sales and distribution by $5 million in the Pacific Rim.
- Accelerated R & D to meet the current and future demands in Asia and the Eastern block.

EDUCATION Business Administration, University of Miami

JOSHUA SMITH
421 Roberts Rd., San Francisco, CA
94105 Home (415) 328-7979

RESUME BEFORE SCULPTING

OBJECTIVE — Position as a project manager in a technical environment.

QUALIFICATIONS — Successful project manager of a wide variety of projects during all project phases, from concept through development, selling, and roll-out.

EXPERIENCE
BECHTEL , San Francisco, CA
Senior Engineer, Project Engineer, and Engineer 1976 – 2003
Plan and coordinate efforts between technical specialists; maintain client contact; develop and manage proposals. Developed creative and effective solutions for new management needs of clients and internal organization. Examples of projects and assignments:
Most recently assigned as Lead Mechanical Engineer supervising engineers in the mechanical design of power plants: 1. Selective Catalytic NOx Reduction (SCR) projects to add SCR reactors to 12 operating Units at three Stations for one client. 2. All mechanical engineering work in the Engineer/Procure/Construct scope of work for a 1000 MWE, 2 unit, 2x2x1 combined cycle plant. The project, located in a desert, has extensive water treatment systems including a zero liquid discharge system.
Conceived, guided development and sold a creative interactive 3D CAD system for facilities management. This was also one of the first network applications placed at a client site by our company.
Developed and implemented a 5-year, $50,000,000 program to define the design basis for 12 operating nuclear power plants.
Developed root cause analysis of power plant operational problems and recommended solutions.
Provided technical direction and overall coordination for a portion of the piping design, analysis, and fabrication-erection specifications for a 839 MWe nuclear power plant.

Supervisor, Information Management Section (1992 - 1994)
Computer Services Division
Supervisor of the Information Management Section, chartered with helping project and administrative staffs to more effectively use the company computer resources, to develop innovative solutions, and provide a dedicated staff (18 maximum actual persons) for client projects requiring information management expertise. Coordinated with technical staff, administrative staff, and management. Examples of projects: 1. Conceived the idea and managed installation of a Wide Area Network TCP/IP & Novell link with a major client. 2. In 1994 convinced the company of the need for an Internet connection with email and other TCP/IP applications, and managed the implementation. The SMTP and X400 electronic mail portion of the project was highlighted in Information Week and Network World. 3. Participated in data base migration strategies. 4. Developed partnering strategic plan for major client and Bechtel on a unique Wide Area Network.

Project Engineer and Engineer (1976- 1981)
Control and Instrumentation Division
Directed five engineers and two technicians in the design and equipment specifications for all control and instrumentation systems within the company's scope of work for a 985 MWe nuclear power plant.
• Designed systems and wrote equipment specifications for variety of functions, such as service water, radiation monitoring, and emergency core cooling systems interface.
• Served as point-of-contact to the client and to company project management, for control and instrumentation design work.

GENERAL ELECTRIC COMPANY BETTIS ATOMIC POWER LABORATORY 1973 - 1976

Experimental Engineer, Thermal and Hydraulic Programs (1975 - 1976)
Assigned to hydraulic and thermal test facility, doing original research for reactor cores for the U.S. Navy Trident Submarine.

Engineer, Power Plant Engineering - Electrical (1973 - 1975)
Lead engineer of design work to upgrade complete instrumentation systems (neutron monitoring and primary plant controls and instrumentation) for a land based submarine-prototype nuclear power plant. Appointed project leader with overall project responsibility when project lead engineer developed a long-term illness.

EDUCATION — BSEE, University of California Berkeley, Berkeley, CA - 1973
BA, Monmouth College, Monmouth, Illinois (physics major) - 1973

REGISTRATION — Registered Professional Engineer in Arizona, Illinois, California, North Carolina and Pennsylvania

MEMBERSHIP — Eta Kappa Nu - Electrical Engineering Honorary Fraternity

AARON SCHULER

RESUME BEFORE SCULPTING

PROFESSIONAL OBJECTIVE - An executive-level position in financial sales and management.

SUMMARY OF QUALIFICATIONS

• Highly successful manager and investment counselor with over fifteen years experience at the executive level in sales and operations management roles.
• Special expertise in recruiting, building and leading top producing sales teams.
• Superb rapport builder; nurtures model relationships with top tier institutional investment decision-makers and affluent private investors through customer service focus.
• Astute analyst, expert in identifying and recommending solutions for clients' investment goals and risk tolerance level.
• M.B.A. in Finance from the University of Chicago.

PROFESSIONAL EXPERIENCE

1994 to Present CENTRAL BANK VICE PRESIDENT, Houston

Regional manager of Midwest and Southwest markets. Directs Private Advisory Services business with an asset book value of $700 million.

Initiates and grows accounts by addressing multiple issues important to each client, such as global asset management, risk management and estate planning.

• Highly valued as counselor by some of the wealthiest U.S. families. Assists in managing large assets within the global investment arena.

1993 to 1994 COMPASS BANK, VICE PRESIDENT, Houston

Developed, grew and maintained 15 top tier institutional investment accounts. Provided investment portfolio managers with sound basis for decisions on government, agency, mortgage, corporate, asset-backed and structured securities, plus off balance sheet derivatives. Specialist in structured note transactions.

• Brought in over $1 million in sales credits from loyal accounts.

1991 to 1993

HARRIS NESBITT CORP. SENIOR VICE PRESIDENT, Houston

Managed mortgage trading desk and marketing of mortgage backed securities to institutional market. Directed all aspects of trading including positioning, hedging and profitability.

• Doubled revenues in one year.
• Initiated security research activities.

1980 to 1990

ATLANTIC TRUST MANAGING DIRECTOR, Austin 1985-1990

Directed global markets sales activities in two regions. Developed and maintained client relationships focused on cash and non-cash derivative transactions. Marketed government, agency, mortgage, corporate, money market and asset-backed securities to institutional clients. Worked closely with money managers, insurance companies, banks and thrifts. Recruited, trained and led a small, sophisticated sales team with extremely high productivity per representative.

• Established more than 30 new business relationships in last two years.
• Built volume to over $125 billion.

VICE PRESIDENT, Dallas 1982-1985

• Initiated, expanded and managed Southwest global market activities that grew to over $50 billion annually.
• Personally developed and serviced a large, very profitable institutional client base.

ASSISTANT VICE PRESIDENT, Austin 1980-1982

Managed distribution of short-term products to corporations.

EDUCATIONAL BACKGROUND

UNIVERSITY OF BOSTON, Boston, Massachusetts

MASTER OF BUSINESS ADMINISTRATION, Finance, 1977

UNIVERSITY OF HOUSTON, Houston, Texas

BACHELOR OF BUSINESS ADMINISTRATION, Finance, 1974

RESUME BEFORE SCULPTING

Jeff Reynolds
2798 Fredrick Blvd.
Chicago, Illinois 60617
(773) 222-7766

Objective
My constant goal is to be a positive force and an impact performer. I strive to be proactive and productive, using my talents and experience for the benefit of the organization. My drive, extensive service background, managerial, organizational and computer knowledge allow me to coordinate multiple tasks efficiently and successfully.

Education
Bachelor of Arts - College of Letters, Arts and Sciences
Social Sciences / Emphasis in Communication
UNIVERSITY OF SOUTHERN CALIFORNIA

Activities Experience: USC Northwest Alumni Association; USC Trojan Band Alumni Club
Experience
Development Associate — **The New York Community Trust** -
October 2000 —Present
- Manage administration, recruitment, budgeting, correspondence and event coordination for two major group funds with over $500,000 in assets
- Act as point person on major award programs and company events
- Execute client requests for account maintenance and research

Executive Assistant/Administrative Assistant - **The Human Relations Foundation of NY** -
August 1998 — October 2000
- Managed database and archives while helping coordinate programs and events
- Handled scheduling, appointments and mailings

Customer Service Rep. - **Hewlett Packard** -
December 1998 June 1998
- Acted as a client liaison on shareholder accounts

Customer Service/Data Entry - **Office of the Special Deputy** -
November 1996 - October 1997
- Managed data entry and quality control responsibilities on various projects

Quality Control - **Peterson Consulting Limited Partnership** -
March 1996-September 1996
- Supervised the inputting and analyses of sensitive database documents

Customer Service/Correspondence - **Harris Bank** -
June 1995 - January 1996
- Monitored inbound phone calls and acted as a customer liaison

Consultant/Public Relations - **MacHelp** -
June 1993 - August 1996
- Conceived marketing strategy, promotions and advertising, as a client liaison

Personal: I enjoy reading, writing, cinema, and athletics.

SCOTT WOODMAN, M.D.
823 Jenkisson Avenue Lake Bluff, IL 60044

RESUME BEFORE SCULPTING

OBJECTIVE: Medical Consulting

SUMMARY OF QUALIFICATIONS

- 31 years of health care experience
- progressive executive responsibilities
- relates well with everyone at all levels
- excellence in leadership
- innovator
- recently retired from the US Navy as Director of Community Health

RECENT EXECUTIVE ACCOMPLISHMENTS

- Conceptualized and built 80,000 square feet of new clinical spaces ($18 million)
- Responsible for a health care staff of 350 providing 400,000 patient visits yearly
- National expert in student health annually providing 90,000 new students health care, health promotion and wellness care
- Provides Occupational Health and Industrial Hygiene services to 100,000 employees.
- Champion of advanced technology: designed and implemented Navy Marines first use of SMART CARD technology to provide easy recording and follow-up of immunizations, medical history and medical examinations, more than 150,000 are currently in use. Fluent in most computer uses.
- Transformed a bloated health care system that saw 60,000 patients a year into a smaller, better-trained system with updated equipment that now provides more than 400,000 visits per year.
- Brought from Washington specifically to develop staff, build the buildings, equip the facilities to manage all aspects of a diverse and complex organization that grew from 30,000 new Navy students to 90,000 new students annually.
- Developed systems to quickly assess the health of America's youth, provide full immunizations, full lab oratory screening, physical training, and medical examinations. Proven ability to manage the sophisticated and complex processes that provide superior medical services to the diverse population that makes up the United States Navy, many of whom come from under served communities.
- Developed tobacco cessation program for 50.000 new students yearly. 60% of tobacco users quit.
- Established a Health Promotion Council, bringing diverse community segments together to sponsor healthy community and healthy families wellness initiatives
- Designed and built a 10,000 sq. ft wellness center via a partnership with other corporate divisions and the public sector

LEADERSHIP AND MANAGEMENT STYLE

- Trained by W. Edward Demming and uses total quality management principles of leadership to build teams, gather staff ideas, and empower staff to carry out mission, vision and the strategic plan.
- Reports and collaborates regularly with a board of 2 that directs the course of the Naval Hospital.
- Formulates plans that enable the hospital to meet its vision and mission, a consensus builder.
- Listening to others' ideas and considering all sides of a project is a hallmark.
- Installed teamwork as the way of doing business.

INNOVATION

- Established the concept of "Total Health" for new patients whereby in a two week period these patients have all recommended screening, all immunizations, all wellness and health promotion lectures completed, and all medical conditions diagnosed and treatment begun

RESUME BEFORE SCULPTING

Kenneth Ballard
132 West Grainger St.
Austin, Tx 78757
512-732-7892
Kballard@aol.com

EXPERIENCE:

Burnett Assoc. August 96-Present
Austin, TX

Managing Consultant
Responsibilities include designing, installing, configuring and maintaining Microsoft and NetWare LANs and WANs. Managing multiple clients and various projects at the same time was essential in this position. While managing many of these projects, I was responsible for helping the client maintain and develop budgets and staff. Environments range in size from 250-5000 users and up to 250 servers. Installed network software and hardware, resolved network-related problems, and worked with communication products. Major projects include upgrading 35 offices from Novell 3.x-4.x to 5.0 and NT 4.0 to Windows 2000 Professional. Migrated users, organized data and structure, upgraded infrastructure switched networks, and centralized the backup. Environment consisted of NetWare 5.0, Citrix, Windows 95/98/NT, Microsoft Office and Outlook. I've setup and maintained IIS servers and have kept them patched with the latest Microsoft service packs and hotfixes. SQL installation, configuration and tuning using SQL 7 and 2000. Building many NT Servers I've installed most if not all Microsoft BackOffice Products. Configured them to the specs required for there operation with any organization.

PC Services 1992-August 1996
Austin, TX

Senior Network Specialist
Responsible for hardware and software maintenance on PCs and networks, on site as well as in house. Also, quoted, designed and implemented network installations. Implements new technologies in order to increase workplace efficiency. Resolves multi-vendor hardware and software incompatibilities.

TECHNICAL SKILLS:
Networks: Novell 2.x-5.0, NT 3.x-4.x, W2K, Terminal Server, Citrix
Operating System: Windows 2000, NT 4.0, Win 9X, MAC
Other: Cisco, Intel and 3Com switches and routers, VPN, ISDN, Frame Relay, DSL, SMS, ManageWise, LanDesk Management, Exchange, Groupwise, Lotus Notes, Arcserve and Veritas

EDUCATION:

MCSE
Compaq Server Configuration
Cisco Router Training
Citrix Winframe Certified Administrator

University of Texas, Austin, Texas
Major: Business Administration

Devry Institute of Technology
Major: Telecommunications

LAW EMPLOYMENT AND EXPERIENCE

Senior associate at Huer & Associates law firm, Minneapolis, September 1993 to present. Practice concentrated in medical malpractice and product liability.

Senior associate at Seiben, Grose, Von Holtman & Carey Ltd. law firm, Minneapolis, September 1987 to August 1993. Practice concentrated in medical malpractice and product liability.

Associate at Gallagher law firm August 1979 to August 1987. Practice divided between defense work for Farmers Insurance and plaintiff's medical malpractice, product liability, auto accidents, worker's compensation, and premises liability.

Summer legal clerkship at Jim Sanders law firm, Deluth, 1978.

LEGAL SKILLS

Approximately fifty tort law trials, numerous expert depositions, maintaining good client relations, legal research, legal argument, negotiating, thorough preparation of cases, and case load organization.

EDUCATION

University of Minnesota College of Law, Minneapolis, September 1976 to May 1979. Law School Admission Test: 672 out of 700. Grades: B average.

St. Mary's University, Minneapolis, September 1972 to May 1976. Bachelor of Science in Political Science, minor in English. Graduated Cum Laude.

PERSONAL DATA

Married. Two Children. Date of Birth: June 20, 1954
799 Pinkerton Avenue, Minneapolis, MN. 55438 (952)321-7891

Christopher Thomas
336 Westmoorland Ave.
Seattle, WA 98109, 206-766-3223

RESUME BEFORE SCULPTING

Career Accomplishments
Provided claims technical oversight for the largest exposure Lawyers & Accountants claims at Employer's Re with aggregate reserves in excess of $100MM. Professional liability claims department consisted of 9 Claims Coordinators and 30 Claims Technicians.
Participated in the development and implementation of a company wide Claim Cost Management System that measures claims overpayment and identifies training opportunities focused on reducing claim overpayment and improving claim-handling performance.
Identified a dispositive motion issue overlooked by counsel which resulted in a $2MM savings on a large exposure Professional Liability Claim.
Member of Claims Team that implemented training and other programs which contributed to a 3% reduction in claims overpayment in the Lawyers E&O book which resulted in LAE savings of $155,000 over a 3 month period.
Reviewed and identified causes of all pending TIG Specialty Bad faith claims and recommended changes in procedure to enhance file resolution.

Experience
1999 to Present Pemco Insurance Company Seattle, WA
Asst. Secretary / Corporate Claims Analyst
Member of Claims Team with technical / supervisory responsibility for oversight of the company's highest exposure claims with an emphasis on Professional Liability, Extra Contractual Liability and Director's and Officers Liability litigation. Reviewed current policy forms and drafted new language for Lawyers and Accountants policies and applications.

1985 to 1999 Unicare. Bolingbrook, Illinois

1993 to 1999 Asst. Vice President I/Technical Claims Manager
Member of Home Office Claims Team with technical / supervisory responsibility for oversight of large claims in the Chicago and Sacramento claim offices with an emphasis on Professional Liability and Extra Contractual Liability Claims. Conducted quality control audits on an annual basis and drafted audit reports. Prepared quarterly reports and made presentations to the CEO on the company's highest exposure cases. Acted as liaison to the Actuarial and Reinsurance departments.

1991 to 1993 Litigation Specialist
Directly responsible for small pending of large exposure Professional Liability and Extra Contractual Liability claims. National Coordinator for failed financial institution litigation.

1988 to 1991 Claims Unit Supervisor
Directed and supervised professional claims staff in the investigation and adjustment of Accountants Professional Liability claims. Responsibilities included the hiring and training of new claims technicians, completing performance appraisals, management of clerical staff and quarterly presentations to the AICPA Professional Liability Insurance Plan Committee.
1985 to 1988 Senior Claims Representative

State Farm Insurance. Seattle,WA
1984 to 1985 Claim Representative
Responsibilities included receipt of initial claim notices from insureds, verification of coverage, established reserves, conducted field investigations, analyzed medical reports, attended pretrial conferences and negotiated settlements.

PROFESSIONAL/ EDUCATIONAL
2000 Panel Speaker on Lawyers Malpractice issues, American Bar Association Meeting, Petersburg, FL
1997 Panel Speaker on Professional Liability Topics; Defense Research Institute Convention, Boston, MA
1991 Recipient of Cannon Financial Services Chairman's Award
1983 Admitted to Practice Law in Washington
1982 Seattle University Law School, Seattle, WA.
1978 Seattle Pacific University, Seattle, WA, B.A. with Honor

CHRISTY ADAMS

RESUME BEFORE SCULPTING

19255 S. Western Ave.
Brooklyn, NY 11238
(718) 729-8561

EXPERIENCE

SPY Entertainment
Production Manager October 97 - Present
Managed the pre-production, filming, and post-production for popular music videos aired on BET, MTV and VH1.

-Preliminary budget negotiations using excel spreadsheet program
-Film crew negotiations regarding pay rates and scheduling
-Vendor management regarding pricing and budget restraints
-Budget actualization using excel spreadsheet program

Global Advertising
Senior Account Coordinator January 95- October 97
Managed **The Kellogg Company (Wheat Bran, Complete Wheat Bran, Oat Bran, and Brand Buds)** print advertisement schedule targeted to Consumer and Professional users.

-Preliminary budget negotiations using excel
-Assist in concept development
-Vendor management regarding pricing and budget restraints
-Print schedule management for magazines and conventions
-Budget actualization

Managed the successful launch of the Kelloggs' Nutrition University Web site **http://www.kelloggsnu.com**

Robert A.Becker
Executive Assistant June 94 - January 95
Assist account executives with research and new business proposals for pharmaceutical advertisement. Client contact regarding scheduling of meeting deadlines.

-Presentation preparation
-Scheduling
-Account tracking

EDUCATION
Liberal Arts Degree - Columbia College 1990

SKILLS
Windows: Microsoft Word, Excel Power point, Microsoft Project Lotus, Word Perfect, Harvard Graphics, Scheduler, Movie Magic. Typing 65wpm

References provided upon request

Suzanne Katz (708) 332-1864
729 Eastern Ave., Chicago, IL 60623

RESUME BEFORE SCULPTING

PROFESSIONAL EXPERIENCE
Public Information Officer; June 1999 to December 2000
City of Chicago, 121 N. LaSalle, Chicago, IL 60602
Coordinate, supervise and direct public information activities for the Mayor's Office of Workforce Development (MOWD); coordinate and direct the research development and preparation of written and oral responses to inquiries from the media, public, agencies and community groups; manage day-to-day operations of the Marketing and Communications Unit; supervise professional and support staff responsible for public relations and marketing activities for the department - staff engaged in writing and developing press releases, in-house newsletter, pamphlets, brochures and other marketing materials; act as an official spokesperson for the department; supervise coordination of meetings, seminars and forums where information about MOWD services is shared with the public and interested organizations; and, write speeches and correspondence for the Commissioner.

Acting Deputy Director of Communications; February 1998 to June 1999
Chicago Park District, 425 E. McFetridge, Chicago, IL 60605
Manage day-to-day operations of the Communications Department and all Park District public relations activities; plan, coordinate and implement promotional strategies; assume full responsibility for the department in the absence of the Director; act as spokesperson in the absence of the Director, General Superintendent or Board President; supervise professional and support staff to generate positive publicity and provide information about Park District; target information to the appropriate source for publicity and promotional purposes; manage and monitor day-to-day activities, including attendance, scheduling staff assignments and work-flow; plan special events designed to enhance the public image of the Park District; help establish strategies, standards and policies related to the release of information; coordinate news conferences and interviews; implement public relations strategies by working with the media and other opinion-makers to increase the knowledge and use of Park District facilities and programs; write speeches, press releases, public service announcements, brochures and other promotional materials; and lend creative support and expertise to staff in marketing and other departments.

Communications Specialist; March 1996 to February 1998
Chicago Park District, 425 E. McFetridge, Chicago, IL 60605
Develop, plan and coordinate the collection, presentation and dissemination of information for in-house and public sources; use the media, published material, press conferences, special events and other creative vehicles to promote Chicago Park District programs and facilities; establish and maintain media contacts; develop and pitch story ideas to the media; write press releases and articles for in-house newsletter; advise park staff on how to improve communications internally and externally with communities and the media; and, write speeches for the General Superintendent, executive correspondence and copy for program brochures.

Media Relations Specialist; June 1990 to March 1996
St. Francis Medial Center, 1653W Congress Parkway, Chicago IL 60612
Coordinate and assist with media training program for Medical Center staff, develop story ideas and pitch them to the media; develop and write press releases; handle day-to-day media relations responsibilities, including answering telephone inquiries, providing background information on the Medical Center, arranging interviews between staff and media, and greeting/escorting reporters, crews and photographers; coordinate press conferences; brief supervisor on all media activity; monitor press coverage daily; oversee distribution and track ensuing coverage; provide follow-up reports to manager; help maintain mailing lists; track the section's media activity quarterly, especially as it relates to print vs broadcast and local vs national coverage; and, articles for the institution's publications.

Employee Communications Specialist; May 1986 to June 1990
Spiegel, Inc., 3500 Lacy Rd., Downers Grove, IL 60515
Work with employees at all organizational levels to gather data needed for special projects; co-edit employee newsletter, and supervise production and distribution of the newsletter; write articles for internal publications; write memos, speeches and correspondence for CEO and vice president of human resources; assist in planning and coordinating meetings and special events; assist in developing video concepts and supervising production for in-house use, e.g. employee orientation and United Way campaign videos; and, handle all requests for information about the company.

Education — Roosevelt University, Chicago, IL; B.A. degree in journalism (January 1986)
U.S. Army — O5H - Electronic Warfare Signal Intelligence Morse Code Intercept Operator; Sargeant

RESUME BEFORE SCULPTING

Andy Chamberlain
(708) 332-1864
5378 Hampton Ct, Cleveland, OH 44115
216-879-3658

1991-Present The Euclid Chemical Company. Cleveland, OH
Production Superintendent: Para Cresol, IPN, MNPC-DNPC

- Responsible for complete operations management for processing and distribution of Para Cresol, MNPC-DNPC , IPN Chemical products with superior quality at the lowest practical cost.
- Supervised, trained, scheduled all hourly production staff, field supervisors, contractual craftsmen in complete production operations (100 direct reports).
- Provided company training in emergency response, industrial hygiene, chemical, site safety and environmental assessment and inspection.
- Responsible for material purchasing activities, shipping/receiving activities, maintaining accurate production reports of in-process inventories, production goals, measure performance, direct labor costs, contractual bids, inspection of laboratory sample data/testing for correct plant operations adhering to quality control program (SPC), Juran.
- Negotiated 5 trades and P.A.C.E. union operators contracts, successfully saving company substantial salary costs.
- Directed and scheduled complete turn around from shut down to start up of maintenance for production equipment.
- Coordinated safety program consistently reducing work injuries of company by 50%
- Optimize efficiency: maximize production throughput (increased line productivity 18%) highest production rate in 5 years.

Union Stewart:

- Negotiated company/union contract disputes on behalf of union employees.

Chemical Operator

- Operational duties of the process include: sulfanation of toluene, operation of fusion pots, acid springing of crude and distillation of crude cresol through fractionation. (Efficient in refining process techniques; temperatures; vacuums; pressures; condensers; heat exchangers; cooling towers; reactors).
- Supervised and trained all new employees on production line.
- Interpreted laboratory data to ensure appropriate adjustment of the chemical process in compliance with O.S.H.A. regulations.
- Performed and expanded quality control of in-process and final product.
- Demonstrated a proven ability in startup and shut down of all phases of process.

C& P Development LLC, Cleveland,OH
1987-1992 Project Superintendent

- Responsible for project jobsite management, supervision of field operations with proven record for profitable, timely completion of projects with safety/quality standards.
- Exceptional record for project cost control, scheduling systems, cash flow management and negotiation/ administration of contracts, productivity analysis in all aspects of construction project.
- Arranging inspections of construction projects by regulatory officials to comply with building, electrical and related codes.
- Recruited and Interviewed potential subcontractors, scheduled labor, materials and equipment.

1984-1987 Quality-Safety Project Manager: Concrete

- Responsible for quality control testing and technical safety compliance of projects pertaining to OSHA, DOT, EPA, Air and Water, Unified Building Codes, Uniform Fire Codes.
- Chief investigator in charge of supervising project crews, contract employees and performing inspections or concrete/soil tests as required by contractual documents
- Developed company wide safety compliance training and education program of project crews while insuring profitability.
- Responsible for identification and auditing of safety programming in order to analyze control of hazards and ensure compliance with relevant safety regulations to minimize recurrence.

1982-1984 Project Estimator

- Responsible for planning, preparation of cost estimate services on all types of large residential-commercial projects/contracts with proven accuracy and profitability.
- Proven record of accurately and profitably estimating projects, cost control systems, project scheduling methods and techniques of residential and commercial projects while adhering to project deadlines.
- Extensive blueprint reading abilities as well as structural and mechanical design layout abilities.

Certificates-Special Training

US DOT, Hazardous Material HM 126f
29 CFR 191 0.120 HAZWOPER Emergency Response (40 Hours)
290FR-1 91 0-146 Confined Space — Rescue/Entry
29 CFR 1910-1 46 Rescue/Entry Supervisor Certification
Emergency Response Contingency Trainer
High Performance Work Team Trainer (HPW-T)
Lockout-Tag out Trainer
CONFINED Space Trainer
HAZMAT Certified
OSHA Safety Management Handeling Training (Hazardous Chemicals)
Hazardous Communication Training
Material Safety Correspondence training (U.S. Federal EPA Reporting & Regulatory Protocols)
EPA Regulatory Information training
First Aid and CPR trained — Status: Current through 2005
Fire Safety
Personal Protective Equipment
Computer literate:
MS Windows2000 MS Project
MS Office MS Excel
Lotus Timberline Estimator

Education:
University of Phoenix: Bachelor of Arts Operations/Production Management
John Carroll College: Business Management
Cleveland State University: Construction Management-Superintendent Distance Learning

Rachel Caruso
1152 Sundown Ln.
Nashville, TN 37212 (615) 663-2189

RESUME BEFORE SCULPTING

Objective Seeking an opportunity to apply my training and experience in a career related position with potential for further professional growth development.

Mar. 2000-Present
***Special Events Supervisor/Staffing Manager,* SANDRA'S CATERING**
- Consult, supervise and coordinate corporate and private events.
- Hire and train service staff
- Payroll

Mar. 2000-Present
***Owner*, CATERING CUISINE & EVENT PLANNING**
- Catering sales, event planning and decorating
- Purchasing, inventory and delivery.
- Food preparation and cooking.

1999-2000
***Customer Service/Event Planning,* NASHVILLE PARTY RENTALS**
- Handled corporate and private equipment rental orders.
- Ensured all necessary equipment was ordered for all events.
- Advised customers and suggested best equipment for events.
- Created monthly table design for display in showroom.

Mar. 1998-1999
***Sales & Event Planning/Executive Account Manager*, SANDRA'S CATERING**
- Specializing in off-premise catering.
- Improved and monitored customer satisfaction and quality control.
- Prepared proposals and follow-ups to meet sales goals.
- Worked with staff and equipment rental coordinator on large events.
- Handled inactive account files.
- Closed on incoming leads from CSR referrals.

Mar. 1996-1998
***Outside Sales Representative/Accounts Payable,* MCBROOM CO.-** Miller Beer Distributor
- Conducted outside sales calls to perspective accounts and existing accounts as well as presale of non-alcoholic products to chain accounts.
- Merchandising and promotions for Miller Beer.
- Maintaining accounts payable , freight, wage garnishments, expenses for sales staff tracked sales for chain accounts and data entry.
- Created Point of Sale for Sales Department.

1993-1996
***Sales Representative*, PORTILLO'S CATERING**
- Specialized in off premise catering.
- Conducted inside/outside sales presentations to perspective customers.
- Scheduled and coordinated special events for corporate and private affairs.

JANET SCHULTZ
555 Martinez Dr. San Jose, CA

RESUME BEFORE SCULPTING

PROFILE Results-driven professional with progressive retail industry experience and proven vendor relations, sales analysis, and forecasting abilities. Possess the initiative to excel in challenging environments. Skilled at building cooperative relationships with vendors and staff across organizational channels. Able to develop creative strategies to increase profitability and operational efficiency.

EXPERIENCE **ULTA**, San Jose, CA
2000 to Present **Assistant Buyer**

Scope of responsibility includes marketing, merchandise selection, promotional programs, vendor and store relations for Prestige Cosmetic, Fashion Hair Accessory, Hosiery, Sunglass and Cosmetic Bag categories; combined annual sales total $35M

- Compile and analyze advertising results. Review performance of featured items and provide marketing strategy recommendations.
- Manage co-op collection and provide vendor with proof for bill back.
- Select merchandise for planogram; develop forecasts for new items, write opening orders, and negotiate return authorization for discontinued products.
- Design corporate promotional programs to drive sales for the Prestige Cosmetic Department, including Winter Rescue and Murad's Results You Can 'C'.
  - Negotiate with vendors to secure visual collateral, gift with purchase or sampling programs.
  - Develop directives and selling scripts for stores to execute promotions or product launches.
- Prepare reports and analyses for VP of Merchandising and SVP of Merchandising and Marketing.

<u>Selected Achievements:</u>

- Created programs to improve customer service that received recognition from ULTA President and were rolled out corporate wide. Personally recognized by President as a "passionate entrepreneur".
  - Programs included a Consultation Kit and Hip On Hygiene, a hygiene standard program.
  - Created a training module and traveled throughout the country to educate Beauty Advisors.
- Increased sales by creating a formalized ordering process for stores to improve tester accessibility.

1999 to 2001 **Replenishment Analyst**

Purchased and maintained in-stock position for over 5,000 line items in Popular Cosmetic, Professional Haircare and Salon Supply categories. Determined stock levels for 80 stores.

- Analyzed sales histories and trends to develop forecasts for advertised items and buyers.
- Researched and analyzed history of salon supply movement and established replenishment standards that reduced inventory by $150K.

1998 to 1999 **LANCÔME**
Executive Account Coordinator - ***Lord & Taylor***

Directed five business managers and 18 sales associates in five Massachusetts locations. Educated staff on products and strategies to increase productivity and sales. Hired, trained and evaluated staff

- Prepared and evaluated monthly competitive, daily business and class analysis reports.
- Selected to coordinate promotions for Saks Fifth Avenue, Neiman Marcus, Bloomingdales and Nordstroms; hired assistants and managed budgets.
- Generated a 10% increase in sales. Only coordinator in the region to meet and exceed sales goals.

1995 to 1998 **Promotional Assistant**

Contracted to coordinate diverse promotions in major department stores across New England.

1996 to 1998 **Assistant Visual Manager** - Bloomingdales

Organized promotions and collaborated with vendors and managers to develop selling strategies.

- Worked with vendors, public relations and advertising to develop presentation goals and plan large scale functions for Harpers Bazaar, Tahari and other industry leaders.
- Increased sales for all product lines through high impact presentations and creative marketing.

EDUCATION **MISSION COLLEGE**, San Jose, CA, Associate of Science Degree
SANTA CLARA UNIVERSITY, Santa Clara, CA, Computer and Marketing Courses

RESUME BEFORE SCULPTING

ZOE YOUNG
1633 Madison St. #16B
Chicago, IL 60622
(312) 469-3212

Objective: To obtain a position as a sales representative with a market leading pharmaceutical company.

Experience: ***Wyeth-Ayerst*** Chicago, IL
Pharmaceutical Sales Representative 6/99 — Present

- Present and sell portfolio of Wyeth-Ayerst products including Altace, Effexor XR, Premarin, Protonix, and Sonata to primary care physicians and specialty physicians.
- Acquire product knowledge through extensive sales training and utilize approved sales aids and clinical research studies.
- Provide physicians with updated formulary status for individual managed care organizations.
- Identify potential business opportunities and establish relationships with key physicians, detailing with appropriate frequency.
- Coordinate efforts with counterparts to allocate field sales time and maximize use of data and resources to develop an optimal targeting strategy to increase market share.
- Maintain accurate computer records of physician sales calls and key business information.
- Adhere to Wyeth-Ayerst and PDMA regulations regarding sample inventory.

Gap Chicago & Oak Brook, IL
Store Manager 7/95—11/98

- Instrumental in generating and establishing business in downtown location.
- Attained a 79% increase over previous year's sales in May 1997, earning Regional Medallion.
- Achieved Best Year-to-Date statistics in 1997 for district.
- Consistently exceeded district, region, and company in % sales and % transactions.
- Assigned to a task force that collaborated to revise the store manager's training manual.
- Led conference calls and assisted district manager with additional responsibilities.
- Trained store managers as well as district managers new to the company.
- Supervised and coordinated schedule for staff of up to 40 employees.
- Evaluated performance of part-time and full-time employees.
- Conducted physical inventory in 7000+ square feet store.

Limited Too Springfield, IL 1/92 — 7/95
Co-manager

- Contributed to opening stores in four locations.
- Recognized for individual top sales performance in company.
- Created visual presentation of merchandise.
- Ensured accuracy of paperwork, register transactions, and efficient use of payroll.

Education:
University of Illinois Champaign, IL
B.S. in Human Resources and Family Studies 1992
Concentration: Marketing of Textiles and Apparel

References: Available upon request.

RESUME BEFORE SCULPTING

Vanessa Rodriguez
1710 West Trailsend Rd.
Albequerque, NM 87131
505-629-1735
vrode@yahoo corn

Education
University of New Mexico, Albuquerque, NM
BA English 1996

New Mexico State University, Carlsbad, NM
Teaching Credential 1997

Work Experience
Albuquerque High School
10th and 11th grade English teacher 1997-present

Del Norte High School
9th and 12th grade English and Independent Study 1997

Eldorado High School
11th grade English 1996

Power Score
SAT instructor 1997-present

Score Learning Center
Tutor 1999-2000

Other
Research Assistant, library research, courthouse research, data entry
- Law Office Assistant, filing, mail, copying, depo. Summaries
- Packing shed weighmaster, bills of lading, delivery organization, data entry
- Temp, ad. Agency receptionist
- Insurance Office assistant

Activities
Race for the Cure
Aids research bracelet sales
Soccer team

EDWARD WALSH

RESUME BEFORE SCULPTING

7521 Battle Creek Rd
Detroit, MI
Home 313-963-4665

TRANSPORTATION INDUSTRY EXECUTIVE

Expertise in Sales/Marketing Leadership and Logistics Management

Seven years experience in the Transportation Industry. Combines expert qualifications in sales/marketing, business development and key account management with equally strong operating unit and P&L management qualifications. Delivered strong financial and operational gains in highly competitive markets.

PROFESSIONAL EXPERIENCE:

Walsh Teaming Company, Detroit, MI 1996-2003

Turnaround of 1.5 million dollar transportation business. Challenged to identify new markets and develop a client base within those markets. Established a firm niche market presence and captured key commercial accounts. Increased profits 300% in 3 years through entering new markets with higher profit margins. Delivered significant and sustainable financial gains through efforts in cost reduction, productivity improvement, service improvement and staff consolidation. Successfully recruited operational employees that were highly successful in the marketplace.

- Developed very high sales numbers in previously unexplored markets, bringing in new sales equal to 20% of gross revenues per year.
- Troubleshot and turned around poorly performing operations.
- Developed relationship with lenders to provide equipment financing and operational line of credit to manage turnaround and buyout. Successfully paid equipment and buyout debt in short period of time.
- Successfully negotiated union contracts with three labor unions.

Law Offices of Micheal Sandburg, Detroit, MI 1994-1996

Researched and drafted litigation-related briefs and memoranda of law concerning corporate contract law, real estate and banking law issues. Drafted pleadings, discovery motions, and motions for summary judgment. Conducted and responded to all forms of discovery, prepared cases for trial, drafted trial motions, briefs and prepared witnesses for trial. Edited and drafted loan and loan workout agreements with corporate counsel for Lakeside Bank. Reviewed, edited and drafted commercial lease agreements.

EDUCATION:

Executive Programs, Eastern Michigan University, The Transportation Center, 2003
Juris Doctor Degree, University of Michigan Law School, 1996
B.S. Degree, Business Administration, Eastern Michigan University, 1991, Dean's List Continuing Professional Education—60+ hours of Sales/Marketing, Negotiating and Leadership Training.

PROFESSIONAL AFFILIATIONS:

Board of Directors, Detroit Regional Trucking Association
American Subcontractors Association
Specialized Carriers and Riggers Association
Michigan Special Olympics

RESUME BEFORE SCULPTING

NICHOLAS ROTH
323 Kensington Ave.
Sherman Oaks, CA 91403
818-332-1797

OCCUPATIONAL OBJECTIVE: An executive level position in an established film or television production company.

EMPLOYMENT RESPONSIBILITY & ACCOMPLISHMENTS:

April 15, 1997-Present
Telepicture Productions Inc.
OPERATIONS MANAGER

- Payroll
- Human Resources
- Benefits Administration
- Benefits Research & Implementation: Health, 401(k), Dental, Flexible Spending Acct.
- Company insurance: Errors & Admissions, General Liability, Worker's Comp etc.
- Overhead budgeting and expenditures
- Corporate event organization & planning
- Company policy planning and implementation.
- Oversaw company move to new location: Space selection, rehab & move.
- Assisted legal team in defense of Towers in lawsuit with former landlords.
- Office Management

October 15, 1996-April 15, 1997
Telepicture Productions Inc.
OFFICE MANAGER
Supervision of Administrative Assistants
Oversaw the maintenance of the physical space
Computer/software maintenance, troubleshooting and administration
Tracked employee attendance
Maintained office supplies
Organized and data entered American Express receipts
Maintained AVID schedules
Distributed completed programs to local television reviewers

April 15, 1996-Oct. 15, 1996
Telepicture Productions Inc.
EXECUTIVE ASSISTANT TO PRESIDENT

- Executed all duties common to executive assistantship.

May 1, 1994-Present
Archdiocese of Boston
ASSISTANT SUPERVISOR MAIL CENTER

- Assists in all aspects of Mail Center operations, including the oversight of staff during Supervisor's absence.
- Responsible for the processing, qualification and tracking of all time critical items.
- Maintenance of computer databases, supply inventories, and postage accounts.
- Assists the Supervisor when investigating or selecting vendors.

June 1993 - May 1, '94
Archdiocese of Boston
MAIL CENTER ASSOCIATE

- Prioritize and complete incoming copy requests, utilizing the Xerox 1090 and 5090 repo-graphic machines.

RESUME BEFORE SCULPTING

Mobile +020-7672-4730
Email: flevin@aol.com
Fax: +020-7672-4893
FRANCES LEVINSTEIN

PROFESSIONAL EXPERIENCE:
1979 — President: Somar 1994
Present North American Division

Accomplishments
1979. 1 founded Somar Agencies in a BUYING AGENCY with expertise in men's North America (primarily USA) retail markets.

1980-mid 1990s: grew the agency to 20 employees.
client list includes:
- SEARS one of the worlds largest retailers.
- NORDSTORM — the leading customer service retailer.
- REITMANS — Canada's largest women's specialty retailer.

1994: Merged Somar with a similar operation whose expertise is in the European market. Today, cover N. America and Europe.
1996: I established office in Cairo. Egypt.
2000-1: Researched Jordan and clients began to visit Jordan.

Responsibilities
My main responsibility is to cultivate relationships with key accounts (current customers and future prospects) and to convince customers that Nomar can
deliver quality product, on time, on spec and on budget. This helps to ensure
that we land the account and provides us with ongoing business.
Some examples of how I do this:
- Presented high level corporate overview to President of Sears
- Presented product and sales strategy to 250 Sears Senior Managers and Buyers.
  Other operational responsibilities include:
- Select and screen vendors to validate creditworthiness, feasibility, pricing.
- Outsource customer orders, enabling them to 'forget about' all logistics and quality issues. We get the product to the customer on time.

1978 - 1979 Export Manager: Castro Fashions
Manufacturer of men's, ladies and kids clothes
Accomplishments
Increased sales by 33% in one year

Responsibilities
I was responsible for all customer contact with customers
1977 - 1978 Export Manager: Jeans Fashions:
Manufacturer of ladies clothing increased sales by 75%

1971 - 1976 Salesman for Ontario Region: Carden Fashion Group Toronto. Canada

Laura Stark
print & web design

RESUME BEFORE SCULPTING

Summary of Qualifications

Self-motivated, independent worker & team player
Responsible, dependable & hardworking
Creative & knowledgeable

Professional Experience

1999-2001: Timberland Corporate Headquarters,Stratham, NH, Internet Communication Specialist

2/99- 10/99: Timberland Corporate Headquarters, Stratham, NH, Graphic Designer

1998- 1999: Creative Marketers Inc., Chicago, IL, Graphic Designer

Freelance & Volunteer Experience

Chicago Utilities Association, Chicago, IL: Website (design and programming)

Sporting Goods Coalition, Stratham, NH: Logo design

Spring Life Baptist Church, Stratham, NH: Postcards, flyers, website maintenance

Computer Experience

QuarkXpress , Photoshop, Illustrator, Dreamweaver, Flash, Microsoft Suite
Macintosh and IBM PC platforms

Education

1995-1998: Triton College, Chicago, IL Associate Applied Arts Degree
Member of Phi Theta Kappa Honor Society

788 Westington St., Stratham, NH 03885
Ph. 603.224.9743 I EMAIL lstark@yahoo.com

KIMBERLY FISHER

RESUME BEFORE SCULPTING

Business Strategist
777 Dixie Way #3B, Toronto, ON, L6T 5P6
Tel: 905-727-5616

BACKGROUND AND CURRENT POSITION

Kimberly Fisher is a Business Strategist for Nortel . She has 19 years of European, North American and Australian Information Technology and Consulting experience. She is One of the founding employees of Tradex Technologies: subject of (Dec '99) E-Commerce acquisition by Ariba Corp. (1 .9bn). Demonstrated expertise in applying Electronic Commerce technologies to improve business performance and business strategies for major national and international corporations. She offers multifaceted perspective with excellent understanding of today's business conditions and alliances to customize and integrate state-of-the-art technologies, against client expectations and competitive influences.

PROFESSIONAL HIGH LIGHTS

Consulting 1988-2003

Retained by British Telecom as an advisor for the value added extensions to its existing client base via the newly introduced "BT WebWorld" initiative.

Retained for a project funded by the Australian Federal Government, as an international expert in electronic commerce trading systems with focus on the business implementation of a new, innovative internet-based paradigm for electronic commerce. This pilot was conducted by the Australian Chamber of Manufacturers; involving 1,800 Australian firms Advisor to Microsoft (Australia) and Digital Corporation (Australia) for the implementation of net-based trading services on behalf of the Department of Agriculture and the Australia and New Zealand Banking Corporation (ANZ Bank), Australia's third largest Bank.

Business Development

Developing and promoting an Electronic Commerce based marketplace - nationally and international

Sales and Distribution of Electronic Components, Semiconductor Industry, third party OEM Hardware and Software

Financials

CFO ($3O mill Corporation in Austria) from 1982 - 1988

EDUCATION

Austrian Business School 1982 to 1985, Vienna, Austria, Business Degree (MBA equivalent)
Additional Training Courses in business communications, sales, electronics and marketing

LANGUAGE

Fluent in German

JACK HUEY
632 Canterberry Way
Gainesville, FL 32611
352-619-7521

RESUME BEFORE SCULPTING

Work Experience:
Apri1 1996 - Present
Huey Entertainment
<u>Vice President-</u>

- Managed and operated small family amusement business with gross sales of over $4.0 Million, over 30 rides and 20+ employees.
- Booked equipment for events, negotiated contracts, worked closely with festival committees, raised funds for non-for-profit organizations, handled all accounting issues, assisted in securing bank financing for new equipment purchases including preparing annual profit/loss projections, responsible for managing 10-15 pieces of ride equipment, 18 employees and 2 managers on a daily basis during festival season May - October. Managing responsibilities included transporting of equipment from location to location, set-up/maintenance/dismantling of equipment, training and meetings on ride/general public safety, ensuring that equipment is being operated in safe as well as profit producing manner.

December 1995 - April 1995
Fifth Third Bank
<u>**Vice President- Commercial Lending**</u>

- Managed existing $20 Million portfolio consisting of over 40 commercial depository customers.
- Generated over $3.5 Million in new depository and lending relationships through business development efforts.

February 1990 - December (April 95 - December 95)
Mercantile Bank
<u>**Vice President- Commercial Lending**</u>

- Managed $30 Million commercial loan portfolio
- Met with customers to evaluate current loan services and discuss issues relating to their particular business operation.
- Successfully generated new depository and lending relationships totaling over $4.0 Million annually through aggressive calling program combined with networking of existing client base.
- Prepared and presented credit/loan presentations to loan committee.
- Responded to loan requests
- Prepared and reviewed loan documentation
- Responsible for keeping credit and collateral files in order

(March 93 - April 95)
<u>**Assistant Vice President- Commercial Loans**</u>
(February 90 - March 93)
<u>**Commercial Loan Officer**</u>

Education:
University of Florida, Gainesville, FL
Graduate School of Business (May 96)
Concentration: Management/Entrepreneurship
Graduated with Honors (3 .85/4.0)
University of Central Florida, Orlando, FL

Carol Lashinsky

RESUME BEFORE SCULPTING

115 Piper Lane, Seattle, WA 98122
clash @yahoo.com (206) 889-8432

EMPLOYMENT EXPERIENCE:

SEATTLE BMW , Seattle, Washington **(Feb. 2002 - Current)**
E-Commerce Consultant

- Assisted in the creation and structuring of the E-commerce department
- Negotiated sales and finance contracts for clients buying luxury cars
- Spearheaded the re-design of Seattle BMW's customer newsletter, implementing changes to increase the marketing of products to our target demographic base
- Exceeded personal sales quota nine out of the last twelve months at the largest luxury car dealership in
- Conducted monthly competitor sales analysis to determine Seattle BMW 's relative strengths and weaknesses

PC and Associates, Seattle, WA **(Nov. 2002 - Feb. 2002)**
Administrative Assistant

- Assisted top management of Seattle-area companies by preparing project documentation and customer correspondence
- Edited monthly newsletter, interacted with clients and submitted proposals to upper management detailing how to maximize client satisfaction

Lerner Camp, Seattle, WA **(Summer 2002)**
Public Relations and Community Service Coordinator

- Piloted an initiative that issued press releases for local and regional newspapers to expound upon the progress and activities achieved by camp participants

Washington State University Alumni Relations, Pullman, WA **(1999-2000)**

- Raised over $5,000 of funds for various Washington State University programs and initiatives and assisted in the planning and budgeting of Alumni events

Ferris & Wills Company, Seattle, WA **(1994-2000)**

- Team lead customer service agent partially responsible for mission critical recovery operations and repairs

INTERNSHIP EXPERIENCE:

Jerrod Walters and Associates, Seattle, WA **(Spring 2002)**

- Elite advertising program focused on marketing, public relations and graphic design
- Worked on an inter-disciplinary team responsible for creating and promoting a campaign that included market analysis, campaign strategy, tactical response results, budget projections and media scheduling plans

Armor Communications, Seattle, WA **(Summer 2001)**

- Worked on "The Truth" Campaign; conducted focus groups while researching the tobacco industry and teenage user trends to develop solutions to teenage tobacco abuse
- Presented ongoing research and ideas during weekly meetings with clients and department management

SKILLS:

Proficient in Microsoft Work, Excel, Access, PowerPoint, Illustrator and Photoshop
Strong oral and written communication skills

EDUCATION:

- Washington State University, School of Business Administration

RESUME BEFORE SCULPTING

654 Newcastle Drive
Minneapolis, MN 55402

Greg Bascom

Tel: 612-772-0101
Cell: 612-524-6132

COLLEGE & INDUSTRY CERTIFICATION
National Telecommunication Diploma. (NTD-Telecommunications & Digital Electronics).
CCSA: Checkpoint Certified Security Administrator. (FW-I Installation. Configuration & Administration).
CCSE 2000: Checkpoint 2000 Certified Security Engineer. (VPN-1/FW-1 Encryption and Policy Server).
I-NET+: Comp TIA Certification. (Maintenance of Internet, Intranet and Extranet Infrastructure and Services).
CCNA: Cisco Certified Network Associate.
CCDA: Cisco Certified Design Associate.

PERFORMANCE & PROJECT SKILLS APPLICATION
1. **GE Healthcare** - Healthcare Product Manufacturer & Distributor, (Jan 2001- Present).
As the Senior Technical Consultant in the Network Planning and Engineering Design team, worked with internal IT groups, customers, Technology Suppliers and Service Providers, i.e. Anixter, Cisco, SBC, MCI and AT&T Local and Global Account Management teams. Technology expertise and leadership to business units was provided, offering technology solutions for many business technology initiatives. I played a significant role in deployment of all network technology projects initiatives.
• Strategic migration and upgrade implementation of current Wan Infrastructure from AT&T to MCI Frame Relay Services. This high visibility project produced High-Availability Network access to the Groups SAP Business Application Services to levels of more than 99% for 120 Sites in North and South America and 15 Sites in Europe.
• Consolidated and converted multiple BRI ISDN Circuits in the Data Center to 2 x SBC ISDN PRI Services, $25K/Year Cost Savings on the ISDN Account was realized. Additional cost reduction of 50% on the Telephone Bills were also achieved by deploying telephone sharing devices -120 x -4PMAS DataProbe Product.
• Improved substantially, the MCI and AT&I ordering Process of provisioning complex and non-complex Carrier Services. Increasing service times from approximately 55 Days to 30-35 Day's.
• Designed and implemented Private Network Communications Paths through complex internal network resources, facilitating business communications to current EDI partners reducing deployment complexities in connecting future partner Systems to the Groups EDI Gentran Application Systems.
• Reduced the ISDN Bill Payment verification processing, by consolidating multiple AT&T ISDN Long 'Distance Accounts into four identifiable Business Bill Groups. Payment Errors rates and amount conflicts was resolved and the process normalized after Five months. The long-term benefits and cost savings were immeasurable to this processing team and the GE Healthcare.

2. **OUTSOURCING CO..** - Account Receivables Management & Processing, (Oct 2000 - Dec 2000)
As the Senior Implementation Engineer acting as the temporary "Network Manager", interconnected two business customer sites systems to OC Application Servers within a demanding timeframe to my Client's Data Centre. The three business partner sites connected were located in Pittsburgh, Cannonsburg and Connecticut using Cisco 2600, accuracy and speed was imperative.
• Worked and teamed with Business Partner personnel, coordinated site delivery of network equipment.
• Developed, reviewed and applied Cisco IOS Network Address Translation and Access Control Lists matching the company's security requirements. Compiled detail Configuration Changes and updated Project documentation as a value-add to my client. I convened. Successfully the hand-over meeting with the VP IT, the Project Director and the Network Manager.

3. **MERK CO.** – Pharmaceutical Research Lab and Manufacturer (Aug 2000 - Sep 2000)
As the Senior Network Engineer, I evaluated the Client's Solaris/Gauntlet firewall environment, collaborating with the responsible Network Engineer and Firewall System Administrator. Identified and recorded, in detail any weakness in the current firewall environment and made several operational and system reconfiguration recommendations. This successful exercise led to $35, 000 funding, approval to implement the 2nd Set of recommendations to extend current connectivity capabilities, which included VPN and Client remote access Technologies deploying the Solaris variant Checkpoint. Using Solar Winds Tools and services from Gibson Research Corporation, produced and was responsible for the following:
• Performed perimeter penetration and services vulnerability tests on all operational interfaces including UUNET. Audited all Firewall Assets including Network Elements. Software and Cisco IOS Revision levels, Physical and System Level Accesses. Compiled full documentation set of the test results, trust relationships and physical assets. Reviewed and Analyzed the Gauntlet firewall, its policy and system configuration files and the Cisco 2600 IOS Services. Scheduled and convened a document presentation and recommendation review meeting, with senior managers and administrators.
• First Phase recommendation Implementation costs was negligible, latest IOS, Gauntlet FW, SunOS revision levels was installed, these costs was absorbed by current service and maintenance agreements. Updating Policy Configuration Files and Router Configuration was implemented, through in-house resources. ISP routing recommended changes, was implemented through existing service level agreements.

4. **POINTBASE INC.**, E-Commerce, (Jun 2000 -Jul 2000).
As the Senior Project Engineer, was responsible for developing and defining network infrastructure requirements necessary to successfully support the customer's E-Commerce initiative. This requirements document was incorporated into the final 'Statement of Work" proposal document for customer review and approval. The initiative would expand their business presence on the web amongst the embedded systems development community, increasing on-line purchasing volumes from 200 to 2000. Was responsible for and produced the following:
• Detailed and realistic costing for Internet and MS SQL Server, Linux Server Hardware and Software, Signio Account Manager, Nokia Firewall, ISP, Verisign Digital Certificates, Maintenance and Implementation costs.
• Developed and Documented the Firewall configuration. Account Manger, Application Servers and Router placement and deployment details. The customer was able to review and finalize project costs of $65,000 early and adjust their funding budgets accordingly for submission and approval.

5. **AVEDA** - Personal Care Products Manufacturer, (Mar 1999 - July 1999).
As the Senior Network Communications Analyst, was actively engaged and responsible for maintaining the integrity of the group's heterogonous network and providing Network Services continuity during a very challenging transitional phase. Network Performance and stability issues were also a great concern to senior management, particularly the critical Siebel and PeopleSoft Business Application Services. I was also tasked to support the Norand (RF) Application and systems at the following Manufacturing and Distribution Sites. Melrose Park 15th Ave. George St. AC Foods, Chatsworth and Nordhoff. Responsible for and successfully achieved the following:

• Compiled and produced comprehensive documentation and diagramming sets for the Enterprise Network. These included but not limited to Network Topology, Network Operational Elements, Telecommunication and Carrier Circuit records, Password control and change management of all network and infrastructure elements. I performed weekly configuration backup of Routers Switches, Hubs, Shiva RAS Server and two Warehouse Management Application Linux (variant) Servers (WMS).
• One of the priorities identified by Senior Management was to accurately identify and report Enterprise wide network system outages and non-responding Mid-Range Platform Application Servers at Melrose Park, to respective support personnel via the paging system. Configured and deployed lpswitch "What Up Gold v4" software package and the network monitoring and alarm system were operational within 3 weeks. This critical process improved substantially, network and system support levels and problem resolution responses.

SHOPRITE - Corporate Retail IT Division, (Aug 1989 - Nov 1998).
As proactive Manager Network Services was responsible for Managing the Enterprise Network, including the Digital El/E2 Trunk Backbone and Frame Relay Switching Centers. I was accountable for the Network performance and operational status, reporting Director- IT Systems.
• Key member of the Groups' Enterprise Architectural Committee, provided Technology and Infrastructure leadership input into the development, growth and funding of the Groups Network Resources, supporting over 250 Retail Stores and thirty-five franchise operating sites.
• Integrated five Regional Office PBX's to Corporate Office Siemens 9000 series PBX using E&M Trunk Signaling and TDM Technologies. Achieving a combined cost reduction and saving of 35% on the substantial Monthly Telephone Budget.
• Migrated amid transformed the Pure Cisco Router Backbone to arm IP Frame Relay Network Switching Network (Carrier Class using Carrier Class Cascade Switches, spanning six major cities over a period of four months while maintaining business continuity and operational service levels. Business and IP Capabilities was extended, allowing Debit Card Purchases, offering more purchasing options to the approximately 120, 000 Customers initially, grew to 200,000 the first year.
• As Senior Network Infrastructure Specialist (Assistant Manager Position), was given the key role by Senior Management board to design and implement the Groups IP Network Infrastructure from the ground up in the most economical manner within a projected 24-month timeframe to centralize and meet their Data Processing and Retail Operations needs.
• Received spending approval for the Multi Million Rand initiative, connecting 120 Retail Stores country wide within 18 Months. Made possible through an aggressive deployment and implementation schedule and very close collaboration with General and Regional Managers, the retail stores, preferred technology vendors and suppliers, SEPA the Carrier Service Provider and an excellent project implementation and installation team of about 15 members.
• Retail Stores were online sending daily sales Figures to the Groups' Data Center in Cape Town, a company milestone. With the IP Cisco and DCX Statistical Multiplexer network infrastructure in full production mode, it paved the way for retail innovation. Shoprite was the First retailer to implement 'Electronic Funds Transfer" services at "Pont of Sale" terminals, facilitating customer use country wide of MasterCard/VISA Credit Cards.

SEPA — National Telecommunications Company, (Jan 1978 - Aug 1989).
As Senior Telecommunication Technician, specializing in Data Communications & Digital Telematics Services.
• Provisioned and supported Telematic Services, including ISDN, X25 and Digital 64K Circuits.
• Daily Operational Supervision of approximately 30 Data Engineering staff.
• Installation, Testing and Commissioning of Carrier Class Marconi Digital Switching El/E3 Hierarchies
Exchange Areas (Central Office Facility) in the Western Cape. SA.

RESUME BEFORE SCULPTING

Katie Bennett
7765 S. Lomita Tr.
Las Vegas, NV 89109
Home: 702-562-1597

- **PERSONAL STATEMENT**

Diligent multitask talented Jr. Architect and CAD drafter highly interested in becoming proficient in the management of a project throughout the construction phases. I want to know that the building is being erected correctly. I am highly interested in the functional layout of a building to better suit the user, along with maximizing the use of space without destroying the integrity of the edifice.

- **HIGHLIGHTS OF QUALIFICATIONS**

-Proficient in AutoCAD 14 & 2002. Familiar with Excell and Lotus.
-Ability to read construction documents as well as help develop construction documents. Have greater understanding and interest in commercial buildings.
-Ability to use plotters, printers, and any other PC peripherals.

- **PROFESSIONAL ACCOMPLISHMENTS**

- Trestpa North America Interior Renovation Team member from December of 2002 through May of 2003. I have conducted on site ceiling and floor layout existing condition surveys of the buildings interior from the Lower Level through floor 13. ADA upgrade to fitting room design and restore areas. Worked on project from preliminary phases through bid and permit phases, to the start of construction phase.

- **EMPLOYMENT HISTORY**

Tate, Snyder, & Kimsey, Las Vegas, NV (Jr. Architect/AutoCAD drafter:2002-2003). The experience I obtained from working at McClier ranges from simply Cadding up construction documents and defining the ADA compliance to the distribution of multiple sets of drawings to 12 consultant firms. This distribution was both hardcopy and on-line. Along with distribution came tracking of the plans in their separate phases of construction, i.e. demolition, actual construction, BID documents versus Permit documents, addendums, and Architectural Supplemental Instructions, all of which needed to be logged into the system for record keeping purposes and distributed to the correct consultant. Department of Buildings, Miami City Hall--Completed two consecutive internship programs in Intergovernmental Services. Summer 2000 and 2001.

- **EDUCATION**

B.A., Architecture - (2002), Graduated with Honors.
University of Miami School of Architecture, Miami, FL
GPA: 3.05, Major GPA: 3.45

- **HONORS AND AWARDS**

Deans List-Spring Semester 200 1, for excellence in academic achievement.
Deans List-Spring Semester 2002, for excellence in academic achievement.

Josh Hausman RESUME BEFORE SCULPTING

851 Martinez Dr., San Diego, CA 92161
#760-313-7215, E-mail: Jhaus3 @aol.com

SUMMARY OF QUALIFICATIONS

- Highly motivated and versatile regarding designated projects and responsibilities.
- Ability to assimilate information, analyze problems, and develop viable solutions.
- Open-minded, original thinker with strong analytical skills and ability to "see the whole picture" in detail and scope.
- Ability/success in training and developing other professionals.

EMPLOYMENT HISTORY

Operations Manager **UNITED VAN LINES, San Diego, CA** **January 2003 to August 2004**
Managed local marketing, direct sales, retail sales and inventory to increase revenue; managed transportation and warehouse operations in a safe and efficient manner. Provided outstanding customer service. Trained and motivated staff of six to perform to their fullest potential. Maintain professional communication with customers, vendors, staff, and all levels of management.
Accomplishments:

- Recognized Nationally as part of the most outstanding region of the year for 2003.
- Developed and implemented warehouse inspection and inventory plans.
- Developed delinquency tenant management plan that reduced 3-month average to below company goal of 10%.

Account Executive **LITIGATIONS SOLUTIONS, Dallas, TX** **January 2002 to October 2002**
Business-to-business sales utilizing long-term relationship-building skills for legal document management. Generated new business working with paralegals and associates to assist law firms and corporate legal departments in overcoming the challenges associated with information access, control and dissemination of document management/reprographics by leveraging the latest technology to create efficient document management solutions.
Accomplishments:

- Negotiated an agreement that resulted in landing the second largest bankruptcy project in company history.

Recruiter **SRP, Dallas, TX** **June 2001 to November 2001**
Obtained leads by developing relationships and forwarding necessary information, developed perspective lists of employers, applicants or other resources as needed, coordinated and scheduled interviews, prepared candidates for interviews, and obtained candidate and employer feedback from interviews.

Branch Rental Manager **HERTZ RENT-A-CAR, Dallas, TX** **August 1995 to January 2001**
Oversaw sales, marketing, new business development, and all operations of the largest rental car company in North America, with full responsibilities for sales, customer relations, P&L, and cost containment strategies. Managed a $4 MM inventory of 200+ vehicles. Supervised a staff of six employees, including three management trainees. Developed inside/outside sales plan, marketing events, developed leads, and called on larger accounts to develop and build relationships and generate new business.
Accomplishments:

- Recognized Nationally with a Corporate President's Award for 34% fleet growth for the 2000 fiscal year.
- Recognized Regionally with Top Corporate Performer Awards for increased revenues in the corporate accounts segment of business for 1999 fiscal year.
- Developed comprehensive training program for employees that raised customer service index score by 18%.
- Through extensive fleet management and cost/expense analysis, increased branch operating profits by 69%.
- Negotiated agreements with 4 out of 5 local dealerships that enabled branch to achieve 51% fleet growth for 1999 • Refined reservation/phone skills and developed/implemented a detailed sales plan for inside/outside sales and marketing events for a territory of over 100 insurance agents, body shops, dealerships, service centers and corporate accounts resulting in an increase of operating profits fleet growth.

Assistant Manager **January 1996 to November 1998** Dallas, TX (11/97 to 11/98) Austin, TX (1/96 to 11/97)
Management Trainee **August 1995 to November 1996** Dallas, TX (1/96 to 11/96) Corpus Christi, TX (8/95- 1/96)
Managed scheduling and daily operations and controlled a $2MM inventory of fleet.
Responsibilities included staffing, customer service, A/R, and training/development of employees at the branch level.
Accomplishments:

- Received "Boat" award for inside sales for fiscal years 1997 and 1998.
- Recipient of a Regional growth award for the 3rd quarter of the 1997 fiscal year for increasing business by 15%.
- Recipient of Regional growth award, 1998 fiscal year for increasing the fleet by 13% and operating profits by 63%.
- Negotiated agreement with a local dealer to take over their loaner fleet, which led to fleet growth of 13% and operating profit of 63% for 1996.

EDUCATION **UNIVERSITY OF DALLAS, Dallas, TX. 1993**, B.S., Advertising Communications

Michelle Jurkovic
36 Bayside Drive, Torrance, CA 90503
310-776-2152

RESUME BEFORE SCULPTING

Objective: To meet today's business challenges with effective, original solutions.

Personal: Energetic self-starter with excellent organizational, analytical and communication skills.

Education:

1998	Bachelor's Degree in Economics	Warsaw University
2000	Master's Degree in Economics	Warsaw University
2001	Master's Degree in Political Science	University of Southern California

*Received PRO UNIVERSITATE, the highest honor, given to the top two graduating students at Warsaw Univ. for academic and social achievements.

Related Experience:

November 2001 Toyota Financial Customer Service Representative

I am currently handling over 5,300 commercial retail accounts in my portfolio. My responsibilities include working with customers who are having financial difficulties by presenting them with the various financing options still available to them with the minimum negative impact on their credit history. My goal is to become a credit analyst within the next year. Because of our dedication and deep passion for business spirit I am proud to be part of a team that won the Presidential Award for 2001.

August 1996- August 2000 Self-employed Financial- and Stock Analyst

I first became acquainted with the stock exchange in the summer of 1996. I started investing in telecommunication and oil shares and within two years I had over ten times the assets I had originally invested. I received special training in the brokerage market and I have a very good understanding of the mechanisms of financial markets.

August 2000-May 2001 USC Graduate Assistant

My duties included extensive research and information analysis for my professors' published works. Analysis included creating computer models of data using Excel, SPSS, regression analysis and other tools. My good work ethic, attention to detail and excellence are noted in my many letters of recommendation from these professors.

September 1999-July 2000 Poland at UN Member of Presidential Council

Due to my status and hard work I had the privilege of serving on the Presidential Council of the national Polish United Nations Association. My duties included organizing conferences, planning travel itineraries, providing financial analysis, and handling the media relationship. In the summer of 2000 I met UN Secretary-General Kofi Annan and was also selected to be a team-leader in a mission to Vienna to discuss his Agenda for 2001.

October 1996-June 2000 Warsaw University President, Student Leader

I trained, managed and supervised about 40 people. I rose to the position of President in several student organizations while attending university. The two largest organizations I belonged to were Student Council and Model United Nations Student Association, both of which I presided over as President. I was responsible for the annual budget and financial forecast for the organizations. I also was a spokesperson for the Body and participated in countless meetings with the Director and the University Council.

September 1997-June 2000 International Center Translator, Tour Guide, Journalist

I led groups of international professionals on many company visits, translating tours and explaining to them the challenges and changes East-European companies had to face after 1989-1990. I was also asked to attend academic conferences and make special reports for the Sentinel, a newsletter sent to over 50 participating nations worldwide. In addition to authoring many academic articles, I interviewed various international students.

Related Profile:

Computer programs: Proficient in Microsoft Word, Excel and PowerPoint, SPSS, Adobe PhotoShop, Email, FTP and web browser software
Languages: English, Hungarian, French, Spanish, Russian, German, Arabic, accompanied by extensive international experience

About The Author

Robert Wm. Meier is a career coach, executive mentor and job market specialist. Between 1991 and 2005 he built his consulting practice in Chicago to where it became the largest career coaching business in the city. In the Summer of 2005 he, his wife Marisa and his two children, Arielle and Colten moved to Tampa Bay, Florida where he now conducts his executive coaching practice.

Mr. Meier has written nearly 4,000 resumes, has written "The World's Greatest Resumes" (published by Ten Speed Press). It was chosen by the LA times and Joyce Lain Kennedy as one of the top ten career books of 2005 (the only resume book).

He is passionate about the importance of the resume to a profesional's career success and is available to answer your questions at mhunt-svp@jobmarketexpert.com, www.jobmarketexpert.com or purchase a "Job In The Box Career Kit" on Amazon for his complete suite of career tools.

www.ingramcontent.com/pod-product-compliance
Lightning Source LLC
Chambersburg PA
CBHW082058210326
41521CB00032B/2465
* 9 7 8 0 9 7 4 4 4 8 3 1 2 *